PREVIOUS BOOKS BY PHILIPPE LEGRAIN

Open World: The Truth about Globalisation (2002)

'Excellent' – *The Economist*
'We have waited a long time. But at last a good book on globalisation
has appeared ... wonderfully lucid and intelligent' – Martin Wolf,
Financial Times

Immigrants: Your Country Needs Them (2007)
Shortlisted for the *Financial Times* Business Book of the Year award

'Invaluable ... A superb combination of direct reportage with detailed
analysis of the evidence' – Martin Wolf, *Financial Times*
'Energetic and right-minded ... Sense as good as this needs cherish-
ing' – *Guardian*
'The single best non-technical defence of a liberal immigration
policy' – Tyler Cowen, *Marginal Revolution*

Aftershock: Reshaping the World Economy after the Crisis (2010)

'Legrain has a gift for combining big numbers that offer a sense of the
scale while zeroing in on what all this means for people ... a particularly
good survey of what made up the unpleasant cocktail which the world
has yet to digest' – *The Economist*

***European Spring: Why Our Economies and Politics are in a Mess – and
How to Put Them Right*** (2014)
Among the *Financial Times*' Best Books of 2014

'Philippe Legrain provides an original and insightful analysis of what
has gone wrong with Europe's economies and politics and a timely
warning that the crisis ultimately threatens our open societies. Better
still, he provides a blueprint for a brighter future and how to achieve
it' – George Soros

Them and Us

How Immigrants
and Locals Can
Thrive Together

PHILIPPE LEGRAIN

ONEWORLD

A Oneworld Book

First published in Great Britain, the Republic of Ireland and North America
by Oneworld Publications, 2020

ISBN 978-1-78607-790-5
eISBN 978-178607-791-2

Typeset by Jayvee, Trivandrum, India
Printed and bound in Great Britain by Clays Ltd, Elcograf S.p.A.

Oneworld Publications
10 Bloomsbury Street, London, WC1B 3SR, England

Stay up to date with the latest books,
special offers, and exclusive content from
Oneworld with our newsletter

Sign up on our website
oneworld-publications.com

MIX
Paper from
responsible sources
FSC® C018072

In memory of Peter Doyle and Mike Moore

To Marion, Martyn, my parents and all those who have been there for me in good times and bad

CONTENTS

ACKNOWLEDGEMENTS

Writing a book is an intensely individual endeavour, and yet *Them and Us* would not have been possible without the help and support of many other people. I'd like to thank my agent Jonny Geller at Curtis Brown and his team, including Viola Hayden, Ciara Finan and Catherine Cho, for all their help. Many thanks also to everyone at Oneworld who helped to publish *Them and Us*, notably Alex Christofi for commissioning and editing it, Cecilia Stein for taking it through to publication, editorial director Sam Carter for agreeing to publish it in 2020 with only a slight delay due to the coronavirus crisis, Laura McFarlane for overseeing its production, Anne Bihan for handling foreign rights, Juliana Pars for editorial assistance and Kate Bland for publicising it. Thanks too to Ian Greensill for his copy editing. Many people kindly provided their time and insights as part of the research, only some of whom are quoted in the book. The research of Giovanni Peri and Michael Clemens has been particularly inspiring, and Howard Duncan at Metropolis has always been very supportive.

Many people have helped me throughout my career, only some of whom I can mention here. Nick Barr was my tutor when I studied economics at LSE, and he has continued to support me now that I am affiliated to LSE's European Institute as a visiting senior fellow, something of which I am immensely proud.

George Soros and Heather Grabbe helped me set up Open Political Economy Network (OPEN), an international think tank on migration and other openness issues, while Matt Browne made possible OPEN's partnership with Hamdi Ulukaya's Tent Foundation. Hosuk Lee-Makiyama co-founded OPEN with me and is an invaluable business partner. A big thank you to Andrew Kaldor, Travers McLeod and everyone at the Centre for Policy Development with whom we published fantastic research on refugee entrepreneurship. Thanks too to Will Somerville at Unbound Philanthropy and Eileen McGowan for their support.

Many people have contributed to OPEN's success, notably its fellows and the members of the Advisory Board: Erik Berglof, Bill Emmott, Kate Hampton, Ratna Omidvar and Danny Sriskandarajah. Three have sadly passed away: Peter Sutherland, Jean-Pierre Lehmann and Mike Moore, who was my boss at the WTO and a friend and mentor after that. This book is dedicated to his memory; his wife Yvonne is in my thoughts.

I started my writing career at *The Economist*, where I still have many friends. I now write for a variety of international publications, notably through Project Syndicate – thank you Ken Murphy – and *Foreign Policy*, with thanks to Sasha Polakow-Suransky and Cameron Abadi. Thank you too to Jonadav Apelblat at *The Brussels Times*. Many other journalists have supported my work, including Martin Wolf and Martin Sandbu at the *Financial Times*, Jonathan Freedland at the *Guardian*, Danny Finkelstein and David Aaronovitch at *The Times*, Tom Clark at *Prospect*, Jeremy Cliffe at the *New Statesman*, Kenan Malik and Bill Keegan at the *Observer*, Christian May at *City AM*, Angela Wilkes at *The International Economy*, Iain Martin and Andrew Neil. Thank you too to everyone at the BBC, Sky, LBC, Al Jazeera, Joanna Bostock at ORF and other TV and radio stations that have invited me as a guest commentator.

Thanks too to everyone at Oracle Partnership, an exciting start-up that uses artificial intelligence to enhance thinking about the future, notably Peter Kingsley and Thierry Malleret.

Many people have invited me to come and speak on a wide variety of topics. A big thank you to Sandra Nolan at Connect Speakers Bureau and to Steve Bagshaw and Rachel Baker at Leading Authorities International for their help in making this possible.

Last but not least, thank you to my friends and family who are always there for me. This book is also dedicated to the memory of Peter Doyle, who is sadly no longer with us. You will always be in my heart.

PART ONE
FEAR AND LOATHING

INTRODUCTION
The Populist Peril

I t was a scorching hot August weekend in the border city of El Paso, Texas. Saturday morning shoppers congregated in the air-conditioned cool of the Cielo Vista Mall. Among them were many Mexicans who had crossed over to the United States to shop at Walmart, along with locals stocking up at the crowded hypermarket.

One happy young couple who had recently celebrated their first wedding anniversary were out shopping for school supplies. Jordan Anchondo had just dropped off her five-year-old daughter, Skylin, at cheerleading camp and was at Walmart with her husband, André, and their two-month-old son, Paul.

Suddenly shots shattered the peace. A gunman was firing into the crowd of shoppers. Many ran. Some cowered. Others tried to hide. André leapt in front of Jordan to protect her, while she shielded their baby. The shooter mercilessly gunned them both down. Baby Paul was grazed by a bullet and suffered broken bones, but survived thanks to his parents' bravery.

Seemingly senseless mass shootings are all too common in the US, a fractious country with easy access to semi-automatic weapons. But the deaths of Jordan, André and twenty other innocent victims in El Paso were not random. Their alleged assassin, a twenty-one-year-old white suprema-cist called Patrick Crusius, deliberately targeted Latinos. Jordan was not Latina; her husband, a car mechanic and entrepreneur, was the locally born son of a Mexican immigrant.

'This attack is a response to the Hispanic invasion of Texas,' stated a message posted just beforehand on 8chan, an online message board favoured by far-right immigrant-haters. Put aside the fact that El Paso was actually founded by the Spanish and that Texas was part of Mexico until 1836. The mass murder in El Paso was an act of terrorism – an act of unlawful violence and intimidation against civilians in the pursuit of political aims. Although President Donald Trump subsequently sought to distance himself from the racist hate that motivated it, the terrorist's manifesto echoes Trump's repeated mischaracterisation of the peaceful attempts of people to cross the US-Mexican border, often to seek asylum, as an 'invasion'.[1]

Words matter. When Trump visited El Paso after the attack, purportedly to console its grieving residents, he was met with protests. (He also had his picture taken – grinning, thumbs up – with baby Paul and his relatives.)[2] In his 2019 State of the Union address seven months earlier, President Trump had slandered the peaceful, Latino-majority city. He had falsely claimed that El Paso was 'one of our nation's most dangerous cities' until the erection of a border wall to separate it from its neighbouring Mexican city, Ciudad Juárez.[3] Soon after, he compounded the insult when, at a rally on the city's outskirts, he accused unauthorised migrants of 'murders, murders, murders, killings, murders', while the crowd bayed, 'Build the wall!'

Yet it was actually a white supremacist, from a town more than 1,000 kilometres away, who massacred innocent people in that diverse city – a successful union, like Jordan and André were, of races and cultures.

Polarised

Saturday 3 August 2019, the date of the El Paso terror attack, happens to be when I started writing this book. That tragedy is an extreme symptom of a debate that is tearing Western societies apart. Are immigrants and people with a foreign background a threat and a burden – or do they in fact have a lot to contribute? Are divisions between 'Them' and 'Us' set in stone – or can people of different ethnic, racial and cultural backgrounds live together and mix peacefully and productively? In short, diversity: merit or menace? Those are the big questions this book addresses.

The El Paso attack is part of a global rise in far-right, anti-immigrant terrorism. In 2011 Anders Breivik, a white supremacist, assassinated seventy-seven people, mostly young social democrat activists, in Norway.

In 2018 an Italian man in the town of Macerata shot six people whom he thought were African; the previous year he had stood as a candidate for Matteo Salvini's far-right Lega Nord, now known as Lega. In 2019 an Australian gunman massacred fifty-one people in a mosque in Christchurch, New Zealand. And in February 2020 a neo-Nazi who expressed hatred for non-Germans shot nine immigrants dead in the German town of Hanau.[4]

Individual politicians who stood up for immigrants have also been murdered. Days before the UK's referendum on European Union (EU) membership in 2016, British MP Jo Cox was murdered in the street by a neo-Nazi who shouted 'Put Britain first!' In 2019 Walter Lübcke, a German politician who supported his country's welcoming of refugees, was also killed; the mayors of Cologne and Altena have been stabbed for similar reasons but fortunately survived.[5]

Overall, far-right terrorists murdered 109 people in the US between 11 September 2001 and September 2019 – slightly more than Islamist jihadi ones did[6] – and caused 70 percent of terrorism deaths between 2009 and 2018.[7] Police in the UK say the fastest-growing terrorist threat is from the far right, which was associated with seven of the twenty-two plots to cause mass casualties between March 2017 and September 2019.[8] Globally, there were thirty-eight fatal far-right terrorist attacks in 2018, up from nine in 2013.[9] In the West, there were more than twice as many far-right terrorist attacks in 2018 than Islamist ones.[10]

While violence remains rare, the international debate about immigration is also increasingly inflamed. In the final days of the Brexit referendum campaign, leading Leave campaigner Nigel Farage stood before a poster depicting a huge line of non-white refugees and warned that Europe was at 'breaking point'. Viktor Orbán, Hungary's nationalist prime minister, claims Muslim migrants threaten Europe's Christian identity and are 'the Trojan horse of terrorism'. Scott Morrison, Australia's prime minister, has suggested that seriously ill asylum seekers detained offshore and admitted into the country for medical treatment could be 'paedophiles, rapists and murderers'.[11] Trump himself was categorical about Mexican immigrants at the launch of his first presidential campaign in 2015. 'They're bringing drugs. They're bringing crime. They're rapists,' he railed, pledging to build a border wall to keep them out.

Immigration is perhaps the most controversial issue in the West today. Our (relatively) open and liberal societies are under attack by people who blame outsiders in general and immigrants in particular for everything they think is wrong with their lives and society as a whole. Immigrants stand accused of stealing jobs, depressing wages, straining public services, sponging off welfare, pushing up house prices, increasing congestion, threatening our identity, security and way of life – and even eating the Queen's swans.[12]

In the US, the fact that Trump said outrageous things about Mexicans and Muslims and still became president has broken taboos and made it easier for others to express more extreme anti-immigrant views. In many other countries, slandering immigrants is deemed much more acceptable than explicit racial prejudice. Politicians dehumanise them. Tabloid headlines vilify them. Radio shock jocks and Fox News TV pundits incite violence and blare out abuse.[13] Facebook groups foment extremist views. No wonder hate crimes have soared in many countries.[14] Violent words sometimes beget violent actions.

More broadly, anti-immigrant feeling is a rallying cry for President Trump and far-right populist nationalists in Europe whose rise poses an even greater threat to our societies. In the 2019 European Parliament elections, Matteo Salvini's Lega came first in Italy, as did Marine Le Pen's Rassemblement National in France. In Germany, the Alternative für Deutschland (AfD) is the largest opposition party in parliament. The Swiss People's Party is the country's largest. In November 2019 the Sweden Democrats, who have neo-Nazi roots, topped the polls for the first time,[15] while the Forum for Democracy was the second most popular party in the Netherlands. Austria's Freedom Party was in government in 2018–19.

This trend is not universal. A new anti-immigrant party failed to win any seats in Canada's 2019 election. Ireland lacks a significant far-right party. In Australia Pauline Hanson's One Nation party has faded. Portugal's National Renovator Party has no seats and hardly any votes.

There is no room for complacency. Until recently, the far right had failed to make inroads in Spain either, perhaps because memories of General Franco's fascist dictatorship were still fresh, as well as because many Spaniards had relatives who had emigrated. But in the November

2019 elections the anti-immigrant Vox party came third, its far-right views having been legitimised by centre-right parties that had sought to capitalise on opposition to Catalan separatism by becoming more nationalistic.

Far-right populist nationalists blame corrupt liberal elites (their enemies) for betraying 'real people' (their supporters) by bringing in unwelcome foreigners. They exploit fears that white locals are being replaced by non-white outsiders.[16] As well as threatening immigrants and people from an immigrant background, they also often have a reactionary social agenda. Through their typically close ties to Russia's Vladimir Putin, they are a menace to Europe's security. They want to undermine, take over, leave or destroy the EU. And as Hungary's example shows – which Orbán has turned into a corrupt, authoritarian state where the press is muzzled, the judiciary is politicised, helping refugees is criminalised and he can now indefinitely rule by decree – populist nationalists ultimately threaten liberal democracy itself.[17]

Even out of government, far-right populists can wield huge political influence. Witness how then prime minister David Cameron called the Brexit referendum to stave off the perceived threat from Farage. While the collapse of Farage's successive political outfits has left Britain without a viable far-right party, Prime Minister Boris Johnson is often opportunistically Trump-like. Having long insisted Europeans were welcome to stay in Britain after Brexit, during the 2019 election campaign he said they should no longer be able to 'treat the country as their own'.[18]

The coronavirus crisis has provided new ammunition to immigrant-haters. Foreigners can be portrayed as vectors of disease. Mass unemployment seemingly undermines the need for immigrant workers. For instance, many argue that jobless Britons can pick crops instead, while in April 2020 President Trump suspended many visa applications 'to protect jobs'.[19] And even liberal governments have temporarily closed borders on public-health grounds, providing greater legitimacy to those who view shutting borders as the solution to every ill.

In short, the fevered debate about immigration is no longer just about whether admitting newcomers is a good thing. It is the frontline of a much bigger culture war about whether we want to live in an open, liberal and progressive society, or a closed, illiberal and reactionary one.

Fightback

The good news is that while nativism is on the rise, it has now sparked a backlash.

When I first started making the case for immigration in 2006, BBC TV and radio producers used to apologise for the need to have anti-immigrant speakers on the programme for the sake of 'balance'. A decade later pro-immigrant voices could scarcely be heard.

During the EU referendum campaign, Brexiteers suggested that the UK was about to be overrun not just by refugees but also by immigrants from Turkey, falsely claiming that it was about to join the EU and that all eighty million (brown-skinned, Muslim) Turks would then be free to move to Britain. Meanwhile, the Remain camp didn't even try to make a positive case for immigration, let alone for the wonderful right to free movement across all EU member countries that EU citizens enjoy.

Then, in 2018, the Windrush scandal and growing concerns over the post-Brexit fate of the 3.5 million EU citizens in the UK finally provoked a pushback. In 2012 Theresa May, then home secretary, had introduced a 'hostile environment' policy. This sought to make life so unpleasant for people presumed not to have a right to live in the UK that they would leave, and more broadly sought to 'deport first and hear appeals later'.[20] The predictable upshot was that people who couldn't prove their immigration status were wrongly accused of being in the country illegally; some were even deported. Many were migrants from the 'Windrush generation', who were invited to come and work in Britain from the Caribbean after the Second World War at a time when citizens of the British Empire and the Commonwealth had the right to move freely to the UK, as Chapter 3 discusses.

When the scandal broke in 2018, the ensuing uproar forced anti-immigrant campaigners on to the back foot, led to the resignation of Home Secretary Amber Rudd and persuaded her successor to water down the policy introduced by Theresa May, who had since become prime minister.

More broadly, the Windrush scandal was a warning of the potential fate of EU citizens who could not establish their right to stay in the UK after Brexit. And while Britons fretted about their family, friends and colleagues who were EU citizens, businesses started to worry about being able to recruit and retain much-needed EU workers.

In the US, President Trump's outrageousness has polarised the debate and energised pro-immigrant voices. When a neo-Nazi killed a counter-protester at a 'Unite the Right' rally in Charlottesville, Virginia, in 2017, Trump said there were 'very fine people on both sides' of the white supremacist gathering. In 2019 he told four non-white Democratic members of Congress (three of whom were born in the US) to 'go back'.[21] Having promised during his election campaign to ban Muslims from entering the US, he suspended entry from seven Muslim countries soon after taking office.[22] And on the US-Mexican border, small children claiming asylum have been separated from their parents and locked up in cages, among other inhumane policies.

Trump's behaviour has provoked a popular, legal and political backlash. Protesters have taken to the streets. Judges have ruled against the worst excesses of his policies. And Democrats have rallied to defend immigrants' rights. Whereas immigration reform was not a priority for Trump's predecessor as president, Barack Obama – whose administration removed or returned more than five million people[23] – candidates for the 2020 Democratic presidential nomination competed to sound more enthusiastically pro-immigration than each other.

In France, the run-up to the 2017 presidential election saw conservative hopefuls increasingly echo the anti-immigrant rhetoric of Marine Le Pen, the leader of what was then the Front National. Former president Nicolas Sarkozy said, 'the only community that matters is the French community... We will no longer settle for integration that does not work, we will require assimilation.'[24] François Fillon, the eventual conservative candidate, argued that immigration should be 'reduced to a strict minimum'.[25]

But Emmanuel Macron, a social liberal political newcomer, ultimately beat Le Pen to the presidency in 2017 by attacking the far-right leader's vision of a 'fractured, closed France' and declaring that he was 'for an open society' and 'a progressive world', although his policies in office have not always lived up to that positive rhetoric.[26]

The coronavirus crisis has also highlighted the contribution that immigrants make. When he emerged from hospital after almost dying from coronavirus, Boris Johnson paid heartfelt tribute to his nurses 'Jenny from New Zealand' and 'Luis from Portugal', two of the thousands of immigrants who serve in the UK's National Health Service (NHS).[27]

The lockdowns imposed in many countries to limit viral transmission have likewise underscored the essential functions performed by key workers – often immigrants previously dismissed as 'unskilled' – such as caring for the elderly, providing public transport and picking, packing, stacking and delivering food. Many of the researchers rushing to try to develop a vaccine are foreign. And Zoom, the video conferencing app that has substituted for face-to-face meetings, was founded by a Chinese-born American entrepreneur, Eric Yuan.

Britain, America and France show how the fightback against nativism can begin. Countries where the debate about immigration is generally much more positive, such as Canada and Ireland, also provide lessons for others. But although this fightback is welcome, anti-immigrant voices still pose a huge threat. The stakes could not be higher: everything that liberals and progressives hold dear is in danger.

Them and Us?

That's why *Them and Us* is desperately needed. While the immigration debate tends to be framed as Them (bad immigrants) versus Us (good locals), this book's core argument is that They are neither a burden nor a threat; on the contrary, We all can thrive together.

When I speak about immigration to a variety of audiences around the world, the top question I'm asked is, 'What do we need to do to combat anti-immigrant views?' We need to dispel misperceptions, combat prejudice and better explain how immigrants' dynamism and diversity can benefit society. But that is not enough. We also need to address the many problems that are wrongly blamed on immigrants, reassure sceptics that diverse societies have a place for everyone and foster a broader sense of Us. Read on to find out how.

Immigration is often talked about in the abstract: it does this or that, is good or bad. Yet in very real terms, immigration is about people – all sorts of different people who are moving for all sorts of reasons: to study, work or retire; to be with the one(s) they love; to learn a new language, discover a new country and explore a new culture; out of fear for their lives and in search of freedom and security. *Them and Us* brings the issues to life by presenting some of their stories and reporting from around the world on how different countries are addressing various aspects of this fraught debate. While immigration consists of millions of different individual decisions, it cannot be properly understood without taking a broader perspective, as this book does.

How do immigrants benefit our societies today? We'll find out how Jan Koum, a poor refugee to the US from Ukraine, ended up co-founding a $19 billion company that makes the app more than 2 billion people use to communicate each day: WhatsApp. We'll discover how a revolutionary education technology start-up that provides online lessons to schools and homes and enables disadvantaged students to catch up with their peers relies on foreign talent. We'll talk to Yusra Uzair, a Pakistani-born Canadian student at the London School of Economics and Political Science (LSE), one of the increasing number of international students who are paying top dollar for a foreign degree.

Are there too many immigrants or too few? We'll hear from people who think there are too many – and travel to Japan, the greyest society on earth, to find out whether robots rather than immigrants could care for the elderly. We'll also visit a dying village in eastern Germany revitalised by young Syrian refugees. And 'EU Supergirl' Madeleina Kay explains why she has campaigned so passionately against young Britons like her losing their EU free-movement rights after Brexit.

While many of the objections to immigration are ostensibly economic, others are cultural and indeed racial. How does the history of immigration shape today's debates about identity and integration? We'll discover the mosque on Brick Lane, in London's East End, that was previously a synagogue and originally a church. We'll retrace the steps of Donald Trump's German grandfather and Nigel Farage's German great-great-grandfather. And we'll tell the story of Sam King who came to Britain from Jamaica on the *Empire Windrush* ship in 1948 and went on to become a postman, politician and community organiser.

What to do about the thorniest aspects of immigration – irregular (or 'illegal') immigrants and illiberal ones? We'll hear from Reza Adib, an Afghan journalist who sought asylum in Greece, about how badly Europeans treat people who need their help. We'll talk to Gabriela, who came to Britain from then-communist Poland as a student, overstayed her visa, worked without papers and became a legal resident again when Poland joined the EU. We'll hear about José Antonio Vargas, a prize-winning journalist and founder of Define American, who came to the US from the Philippines as a child – without papers, he later found out. And we'll look at jihadi terrorists who grew up in the West and went on to murder their fellow citizens in Paris, Manchester and elsewhere.

Immigrants: Your Country Needs Them

This is my second book on immigration. Some of you may have read my first, *Immigrants: Your Country Needs Them*, which was published in 2007.[28] If so, thank you; I'm hugely grateful to all of you who have read my four previous tomes. If not, thank you for taking a chance with this book; I hope you find it stimulating and useful.

Why, though, do I need to write another book on immigration? For a start, the political context has changed so much since 2007. The financial bubble has burst, the coronavirus pandemic has struck, nationalists are on the march and liberals are on the back foot.

A silver lining of the increased controversy about immigration is that it has stimulated plenty of new academic research, providing better insights into its impacts. While *Them and Us* is aimed at a much wider audience, it draws on this deep well of knowledge and scholarship.

My own understanding of the many facets of the debate has also improved with all my experience and work in this field since 2007. As well as speaking and writing about immigration and diversity issues, I have set up an international think tank, Open Political Economy Network (OPEN), that focuses on migration and other openness issues.[29] We've done some groundbreaking work, notably on the economic contribution of refugees.

Them and Us is much more than an update of *Immigrants: Your Country Needs Them*. It covers new and different topics such as refugees, climate change and overcrowding fears. It responds to the arguments of recent anti-immigrant polemics such as Paul Collier's *Exodus*, David Goodhart's *The Road to Somewhere* and Douglas Murray's *The Strange Death of Europe* and examines the arguments in Eric Kaufmann's *Whiteshift*. And it explains not just why immigration is generally a good thing, but also how we might better persuade moderate sceptics of this. So if you read and enjoyed *Immigrants*, there are plenty of good reasons to dive into *Them and Us* too.

Family flight

'Grab your bags. We need to go now. The Russians are coming.' It was 20 September 1944 and the Red Army was approaching Tallinn. My grandfather had long feared the worst for his family. When the Soviet Union had previously occupied Estonia in 1940–41, Joseph Stalin's brutal regime had deported more than 10,000 people to Siberian labour camps; most never came home. Since then my grandparents had always kept their suitcases packed, ready to go. With the Russians returning, they fled Tallinn together with my three-year-old uncle on one of the last convoys of ships that left the Estonian capital. There was a Red Cross ship and two unmarked ones. Soviet bombers sank the Red Cross boat by targeting its cross. My grandparents, who had tried and failed to get on the Red Cross ship thinking it would be safer, survived.

It was a lucky escape. My mother was born in August 1945 in a refugee camp for Estonians in the US-occupied part of Germany. Europe was in turmoil, recently defeated Nazi Germany especially so. At least my mother and her family were safe. The worry, though, was getting stuck there. The Geneva Convention on refugees did not exist yet; it was signed only in 1949. Everyone in the camp was desperately applying for some kind of visa that would enable them to move to a new home. My grandfather had a PhD in aeronautical engineering, which ought to have made him a good catch. But foreigners couldn't just slot into good jobs.

Eventually in 1948 my grandfather obtained the necessary sponsorship to secure a visa to move to the US. His first job was in a factory making wooden floors; as it turned out, he had experience working with wood from the German occupation of Estonia in 1941–44 when the Nazis forced him to do manual labour. He was delighted to have his first job in America. It was certainly much better than picking peaches in the boiling sun. And it was the first step towards rebuilding his life and building a new one for his young children in America.

My father's family history is tumultuous too. His mother was born in Constantinople, then the capital of the Ottoman Empire, now the Turkish city of Istanbul. The collapse of that empire and the rise of Turkish nationalism after the First World War made life more difficult for Greeks like her family, who moved to Athens, Vienna and then Tabriz, in the Azeri part of Iran. There she met my paternal grandfather, who was a French consular official there. They moved to Paris, where my father was born. My parents then met in New York, before moving to the UK in 1972.

Why am I telling you all this? My life has been much more settled than theirs. I was fortunate enough to have been born in London in 1973, so the worst political disruption I've suffered is the rolling power cuts of the Three Day Week in 1974 and the Winter of Discontent in 1978–79 when rubbish went uncollected and the dead unburied.

While I've worked abroad on a few occasions, London is my home. I have an international background and at the same time I feel very rooted here. Contrary to then prime minister Theresa May's nasty claim that 'citizens of the world' are 'citizens of nowhere', I feel connected to many other places in the world while also feeling a very strong sense of belonging to my home city. Perhaps more so than May; unlike her, I was actually born in London.

At the same time, I empathise with those who have been forced from their homes, or who have moved in search of a better life for themselves and their family. They aren't doing something unnatural or threatening; they are just like the rest of us. They want to be free, safe and better off – and for them, circumstances dictate that this involves moving. Indeed, their aspirations are very similar to those of people who migrate from small towns around a country to work in big cities – except a border happens to lie in the way.

People who are fortunate enough to have been born in a relatively rich, safe and free country such as Britain and don't have a recent family history of immigration may find it hard to conceive that they too might need to move at some point. But Brexit is changing that. For the first time, many Remainers are considering whether they might want or need to migrate. Some British Jews with German roots are even applying for German passports. And with the loss of their EU free-movement rights, young Britons in particular suddenly have some sense of what it is like to be someone from a less fortunate country who may struggle to move elsewhere. Unsurprisingly, they don't like it.

The case for openness

The case for allowing people to move is simply put. Openness to newcomers is morally right, economically beneficial and culturally enriching.

Migration is natural – something that human beings have always done. And it is also necessary for human and economic development. People often need to move to take – and create – opportunities, to trade goods and ply services, and to congregate in diverse cities where they spread new ideas and spark off each other.

Most people who move do so within countries' borders, not across them. Indeed, internal migrants within China alone outnumber international migrants worldwide. As Chinese people have migrated from toiling in the fields to more productive jobs in urban factories and office facilities, they have made themselves and their country much richer. Up to a third of China's enormous economic growth since the late 1970s is due to this great migration.[30]

When migration is national, it is typically considered normal and beneficial. Yet when it happens to cut across an often arbitrary national border, this natural and necessary process suddenly seems sinister to many people. It becomes 'immigration', movement into a country, something that is done to us by outsiders. That narrowly negative national perspective obscures the bigger picture: that people flows are not just normal and beneficial, they are a global phenomenon.

The world is a desperately unequal place. The biggest determinant of someone's life chances is not their talent or hard work but where they were born. But migration can change that. Allowing an African to move to America is life-changing, as Bozi Kiekie tells us in Chapter 6. And as the local children he teaches can testify, it's good for the countries that receive immigrants too.

The rest of the book is structured as follows. The next chapter considers why immigration is often so unpopular. Part Two sets out the history of migration, the current picture and plausible future flows. Since immigration is set to continue, we need to make the best of it. Part Three highlights the global benefits of migration, examines eight economic dividends to the societies that welcome newcomers as well as to their countries of origin and dispels fears about migration's potential economic downsides. Part Four sketches the cultural benefits of migration and considers some of its challenges: irregularity, identity, illiberalism and 'integration'. Part Five concludes by outlining how to win over moderate sceptics and looking forward to possible futures, both bright and bleak.

A brief note on terminology. I will use the terms 'migrants' and 'immigrants' interchangeably to mean people who live outside the country of their birth; sometimes I also refer to them as 'newcomers'. Academics tend to call people born in the country in which they live 'natives'; I think that term is misleading and use 'locals' instead. They call the children of immigrants 'second-generation immigrants'; I don't. When I need a broad term to encompass people who, like me, have parents or grandparents who were immigrants, I use 'people with an immigrant background'. But while we may have an immigrant background, we are locals too.

WHY IS IMMIGRATION SO UNPOPULAR?

'We're British,' exclaims Mike, a retired lorry driver in the small town of Boston in Lincolnshire. 'We're top of the league for wanting them [immigrants] out. Some of the Polish people are nice, but there are too many… [Immigration's] gone too far anyway, I doubt much will change [when Britain leaves the EU]. We should've listened to Enoch Powell. Good old Enoch,' he chuckles.[1] His wife looks at him sternly; Powell was a Conservative politician who in 1968 foresaw 'rivers of blood' as a result of immigration from non-white Commonwealth countries.

Boston has long been a place that people leave. Perhaps its biggest claim to fame is that migrants from there gave its name to the now much bigger American city in Massachusetts. When immigrants moved to British cities in post-war decades, they steered clear of the sleepy farming town. But that all changed when Poland and seven other east European countries joined the EU in 2004 and Britain threw open its doors to their workers. Suddenly, people flocked to Boston.

In the local fields east European migrants in fluorescent orange boiler suits now pick the healthy kale and humble spuds that end up in supermarket trolleys. Picking vegetables involves long days of hard, poorly paid work. Growers had previously relied on workers bussed in for the day during the brief harvest period, and before that on seasonal Irish migrants, explains Paul Gleeson, a former Labour councillor who produced a study of the impact of migration on the local community. But since the east Europeans' arrival, local vegetable production has soared and harvesting takes place most of the year. The vegetables they pick are now processed and packaged – cleaned, sorted, wrapped and barcoded – locally too, as are some shipped in from elsewhere in Europe. The factory workers tend to be migrants, the supervisors and managers British.

Boston has boomed. Yet like Mike, many locals don't welcome the newcomers. 'I have nothing to do with them,' says a market trader in the town square. 'If you want to see the difference in this town, take a walk along West Street. They have got nearly all the shops along there now. People are bothered by immigration because of the size of the town. It's ridiculous how many shops and supermarkets they have.'[2]

East European immigrants now account for a higher share of the population in Boston than anywhere else in Britain – nearly one-ninth according to the 2011 census, and possibly twice that in 2018–19 according to the less accurate Annual Population Survey.[3] The market trader's feeling that They are an invading army depriving locals of resources helps explain why Boston recorded the highest Leave vote in the country in the EU referendum: 75.6 percent. And while in Britain as a whole immigration is now less of a bugbear than it was before the referendum, people in Boston are still just as bothered by it.

'Immigrants have fundamentally altered the character of the town,' says Jonathan Noble, a local Conservative councillor. 'They've put pressure on local hospitals, schools and housing. And they've depressed wages in the agricultural economy.'

If you walk down West Street, you'll see shops called Baltic Food and European Market; so much so that some locals now dub it 'East Street'. Yet the bustling businesses show that east Europeans are spending their wages locally, revitalising the town centre. Many stores used to be boarded up, Gleeson explains. (Noble also acknowledges immigrants' entrepreneurial contribution.)

Gleeson's report debunked local misperceptions about the newcomers. For all the grumbling about boozy east European young men causing a ruckus, police recorded more public-order offences by local people. Contrary to fears that immigrants were a welfare burden, hardly any claimed unemployment benefits.

Yet Noble emphasises the pressure on local services. 'Because of all the extra immigrants, local people are waiting longer to see a doctor. At one secondary school 40 percent of the children are foreign nationals. Some learn English quickly; others don't.'

'There has been pressure on public services,' Gleeson acknowledges. 'But immigrants aren't to blame. The pressure is due to austerity and a failure of the authorities to adjust quickly enough to a rise in the local population. And all the newcomers aren't being counted properly, so local services aren't receiving adequate funding from central government.'

'That's a fair point,' Noble concedes. 'We haven't had our fair share of government funding. It's incumbent on government to be more generous. But it's not much help to a local person struggling to see their GP [primary doctor].' True – but it's no reason to blame newcomers for government failure.

The cost of housing is another issue. 'Even though wages in Boston are low, we have the highest rents in Lincolnshire,' Noble exclaims. Yet as he later points out, some east Europeans live in mobile homes on farmers' land, so do not compete with locals for housing. Others live in crowded, shared accommodation, so occupy much less space than retirees who have moved to Boston from elsewhere in Britain. Insofar as newcomers do drive up local demand for housing, the real issue is that planning restrictions, local nimbyism ('not in my back yard') and the cost of building on a flood plain have all prevented the construction of enough new homes to accommodate Boston's rising population.

Perhaps the biggest gripe is that the migrants have harmed locals' job prospects. Marius Wlodarczyk, a factory worker from Poland, says he can feel the tension with local people. 'They don't like us much. They keep saying that we're taking their jobs and they're blaming us,' he said. 'There are some very angry people out there,' says Robin Hunter-Clarke, formerly a local UK Independence Party activist. 'It's mainly about jobs. There's too many people in the low-skilled labour market.'[4]

Undeniably, workers in Britain have had a torrid time since the financial crisis. Allowing for inflation, median wages were still lower in 2019 than their 2008 peak.[5] Moreover, pay in Boston is well below the national average. So it is perhaps understandable that locals attribute their crimped pay packets to the influx of east Europeans.

But while Boston was already poor before the east Europeans' arrival, wages there have not fallen further behind the rest of the country since then. In 2004 local median wages were 69.3 percent of the national average; in 2016 they were 69.1 percent. That local experience in the area of Britain that has received the biggest influx of east Europeans chimes with the national evidence that immigrants typically do not depress British people's wages significantly. On the contrary, they tend to boost Britons' earnings and living standards.

It might seem common sense that having more immigrants entails fewer jobs for locals. But as Gleeson observes, 'There's more work in Boston than there's ever been.' Remember that locals didn't pick vegetables even before the east Europeans arrived. Farming and food processing have also grown massively in the past fifteen years. That has created other jobs too. Taxi companies are busier driving vegetable pickers to and from work. The local Asda supermarket hired more people when it became a superstore. Immigrant-owned businesses employ locals too.

For sure, some individual locals may have lost out from migration. But in general, they haven't. The local unemployment rate was less than 5 percent in 2019. Ziedonis Barbaks, a representative of the local Lithuanian community who first arrived in the UK in 2006, dismisses suggestions that east Europeans are stealing locals' jobs. 'Even someone who does not speak good English can find a job so I think these local people can find one if they want one,' he says. Even when unemployment soared as a result of the coronavirus crisis, hardly any Britons were willing to pick crops.[6]

The crux of the matter is that east European migrants are willing to do dirty, difficult and dull low-paid jobs that locals spurn because they have different options. What young Bostonians consider drudgery appeals to young Bulgarians because it pays more than even a good job back home. The seasonality of agricultural work is a big negative for locals who want year-round employment; for Latvians who want to spend part of the year back home, it is a plus. Migrants are also willing to make do with less living space; economising on rent enables them to save up a nest egg to buy a house or start a business back home, or get a step up in Britain. After a year picking cauliflower, Miroslav, a Romanian migrant, had saved enough to become a taxi driver. A former typographer, he aims to open a business in Boston. 'I have the opportunity to use my head, to start a business and put it back in Britain,' he said.[7]

Nobody denies that many people in Boston face real problems. But scapegoating migrants is neither fair to them nor helpful to locals.

Myths and misconceptions

Boston's example illustrates a bigger point. If newcomers' impact on the economy and society is generally positive, why are public perceptions of immigration often so negative?

One issue is that measuring public opinion on immigration is tricky; similar surveys by reputable pollsters yield very different results. For example, while Ipsos typically finds that only a minority of people in rich countries think immigration is 'good for the economy' of their country,[8] sizeable majorities in most countries agree that 'immigrants today make our country stronger because of their work and talents,' according to the Pew Research Center.[9] The differences are glaring. Within a few months, the former found that only 31 percent of Swedes had a positive view of immigrants' economic impact, the latter that 62 percent did. They can't both be right; they may both be wrong.

Nor can one necessarily read too much into election or referendum results. Many people don't vote, including some who think things are broadly fine and others who believe voting won't improve their plight. And those who do vote do so for all sorts of reasons. Not everyone who voted Leave was against immigration from the EU, while some who voted Remain wanted limits on EU migration but nonetheless favoured EU membership for other reasons.

Interestingly, Ipsos surveys suggest that people in two of the countries that have experienced the biggest backlashes against immigration in recent years – the UK and the US – actually had a much more positive view of immigration in 2016, the year of the EU referendum and President Trump's election, than they did five years earlier.[10]

With the important caveat that perceptions are hard to measure accurately, all surveys find that many people in rich countries – a sizeable minority and in some cases even a majority – have negative perceptions of migration and would like less of it.

Some assert that evidence of immigrants' positive economic impact fails to reflect voters' lived experience, and that people's first-hand perceptions are surely more accurate than dry statistics and aloof academic analysis. Yet a subjective interpretation of an anecdote – an unemployed local builder sees a Polish one working and blames the immigrant for his lack of a job – is scarcely conclusive.[11]

Indeed, negative perceptions of immigration are often not based on personal experience. It is telling that while few people in Britain think immigration is negative for them personally, many believe it is detrimental to the country as a whole.[12] In both the UK and the US, attitudes towards migration are often much more negative in areas where there are few or no migrants than in big cities where there are many. Mediated misperceptions are even less credible than first-hand ones.

If one accepts that evidence – albeit inevitably imperfect and incomplete – is more accurate than perceptions, what explains the misperceptions? Unduly negative perceptions about immigration may be due to ignorance, misinformation, misinterpretation or prejudice. They are exacerbated by the fear-mongering, xenophobic rhetoric and outright lies of unscrupulous politicians, anti-immigrant campaigners and media propagandists; in the six years leading up to the EU referendum, for instance, the Daily Express ran 179 anti-immigration cover stories and the Daily Mail 122.[13] And they are validated by governments which often find it convenient to blame migrants for their own failings.

Public ignorance about immigration is glaring. Many critics argue – sometimes disingenuously – that they have no problem with immigration per se but only with the scale of it ('the numbers'). According to Ipsos, 48 percent of people in the twenty-five countries they surveyed thought there were too many immigrants in their country.[14] Most rich countries clustered around that average, although the proportion was as high as two-thirds in Italy and as low as a third in Canada.

Yet in almost every country people greatly overestimate the immigrant share of the population – and opponents of immigration especially so. In rich countries, people tend to think there are roughly twice as many immigrants as there actually are. Germans thought immigrants were 30 percent of the population and Americans 29 percent, when migrants were in fact around half that. Britons thought nearly one in four residents were immigrants when at the time just over one in eight were.

People with less education, those in 'low-skilled' occupations that employ lots of immigrants and those on the political right overestimate the immigrant share in the US and Europe most.[15] In addition, voters overestimate the proportion of immigrants who are Muslim (see Chapter 18) and underestimate the share of Christians. They underestimate immigrants' education levels and overestimate their dependence on welfare. Almost one in four French respondents, nearly one in five Swedes and about one in seven Americans think the average immigrant gets twice as much government aid as locals do. In no country is this true.

Before the EU referendum, Ipsos found that people thought EU migrants made up 15 percent of the UK population (which would be around 10.5 million people).[16] In fact, they accounted for only 5 percent (around 3.5 million people). Those intending to vote Leave reckoned 20 percent of the population were EU migrants, compared with 10 percent among those planning to vote Remain. On average, respondents thought one in four migrants were from the EU. This would suggest – assuming they had done the arithmetic – that they thought 60 percent of the UK population were immigrants!

This ignorance is reinforced by the misinformation of politicians and pundits who routinely assert that countries are experiencing 'mass immigration'. Yet in some countries, the rate of new arrivals is low. In 2018 the foreign-born population of France rose by a mere 39,000 – a drop in the ocean in a country of 65 million.[17] That same year, when far-right leader Matteo Salvini warned darkly of the threat to Italy of an invasion of immigrants from Africa, a mere 23,000 desperate asylum seekers and migrants arrived by sea to a country of sixty million people.[18]

Looking longer term, it is true that the foreign-born share of the UK population has doubled in twenty-five years, from 7 percent in 1993 to 14 percent in 2018.[19] In 1993 net migration – arrivals minus departures – was negative; in the year to June 2016, just before the EU referendum, it reached 311,000.[20] But relative to the UK population at the time of 65 million, that net migration rate was 0.48 percent, and by mid-2019 net inflows had fallen to 212,000, or 0.32 percent.

At its peak, the UK's net migration rate was less than half the 1 percent rate in Australia, a country which Britons tend to think tightly limits immigration.[21] Is the arrival in Britain of less than one additional migrant a year per two hundred existing residents 'mass immigration'? It is equivalent to fewer than three hundred extra newcomers in a Premiership football crowd of sixty thousand people. Britons are hardly being 'swamped'.

As well as ignorance and misinformation, there are misinterpretations. Some may be genuine mistakes. When wages fall, as they did after the financial crisis, it may seem logical that an increase in the labour supply is to blame, especially since immigrants tend to be more visible than the true causes of declining pay. The fallacy that there is a fixed number of jobs to go around – so that each job taken by a migrant entails one less for a local – also seems like common sense to many people. Yet whether they were born locally or abroad, people don't just take jobs, they also create them – both when they spend their wages and in complementary lines of work, as Chapter 11 explains.

Where misinterpretations are due to failures of government policy, ministers and officials have no incentive to correct them. If people don't know that migrants typically pay more in taxes than they take out in benefits and services, as Chapter 13 details, they may blame immigrants for putting a strain on local services. Yet as Boston's example shows, the real problem is often the failure of public services to respond quickly to changing needs. Nobody blames migrants for shortages at local supermarkets – because there aren't normally any.

Often, complaints against immigrants are symptoms of broader concerns. People who feel threatened by change over which they have no control may lash out at one of its most visible (and vulnerable) manifestations. Many white working-class men feel they have lost status both locally – with the decline of manufacturing jobs, the entry of women into the labour market and moves to reduce discrimination against women, ethnic minorities and other groups – and globally with the rise of China and other countries. Elderly people who are nostalgic for an idealised past – their youth – may express their social conservatism through opposition to immigration. Strikingly, the Leave vote was strongly correlated not just with opposition to immigration, but with dislike of social liberalism and support for the death penalty.[22] In such cases, voters' real objection may not be to immigrants in particular, but rather to modern liberal societies in general. Since stopping immigration would not turn the clock back to the bygone age that such voters romanticise, or tackle the socio-economic problems that they worry about, it would scarcely address their discontents.

Conversely, increased immigration can be acceptable if other factors change. The proportions of Britons and Americans who thought there were too many immigrants in the country have declined since 2011 even as actual numbers have risen, perhaps because the economic situation has improved.[23] This contradicts the claim by Eric Kaufmann in *Whiteshift* that opposition to immigration is primarily due to white people's fear of being replaced by non-whites, although it is clearly a factor.[24]

Some assert that it isn't necessarily racist – or xenophobic – to oppose immigration. That may be true, but in many cases negative perceptions of immigration are due to prejudice. People with an emotional dislike of foreigners tend to come up with pseudo-rational arguments to justify their xenophobia. Thus when immigrants are working, they are taking our jobs; when they are unemployed, they are scrounging off the state. When they are rich, they are driving prices up; when they are poor, they are driving wages down. Sometimes the two are combined to ludicrous effect: one politician with whom I was debating accused immigrants of living ten to a room in unacceptably cramped conditions and in the next breath blamed them for rising house prices. Immigrants can't win: they are damned if they do and damned if they don't.

While the weight of evidence suggests the impact of immigration is mostly positive, ignorance, misinformation, misinterpretation and prejudice all create negative misperceptions that need to be addressed. Indeed, people have always been on the move, as the next chapter explains, and who We are now has often been shaped by those who were once considered Them.

PART TWO
PEOPLE ON THE MOVE

2

A VERY BRIEF HISTORY OF MIGRATION

In the shadow of the skyscrapers of the City, London's financial centre, lies the district of Spitalfields, on the edge of the capital's East End. Wander down Brick Lane on a Sunday afternoon and you'll witness a cosmopolitan crowd of Londoners and tourists speaking a smattering of different languages. They've come to browse the market stalls, eye the street art and eat in one of the street's many curry houses.

At first glance, it may be hard to distinguish the diverse locals from the many different foreigners; neither the colour of their skin nor even the language they are speaking are reliable giveaways. Perhaps the most accurate tell is whether they look like they know where they are going. Welcome to super-diverse modern London. That diversity would make most Bostonians blanch, yet more than nine in ten Londoners say people from different backgrounds get along with one another in their local area.[1]

While Londoners are very diverse – four in ten people in inner London were born abroad,[2] in as many as two hundred different countries, and many more come from around Britain – Brick Lane has a distinctly Bangladeshi British feel. The 'Indian' restaurants that line the lane are actually run by people of Bangladeshi background. Alongside staples of British Indian cuisine such as chicken tikka masala – sometimes described as Britain's national dish – they serve up the likes of hilsa fish curry, a Bangladeshi favourite.

Walk past Eastern Eye Balti House, Al-Halal Fried Chicken and Zam Zam gift shop and on the corner with Fournier Street you reach the Brick Lane mosque. At this point, xenophobic nationalists who claim to love their country but actually wish it was completely different may start spluttering about this alien intrusion in London's traditional East End, and mutter that 'indigenous Britons' have been driven out of the capital as Muslims such as Mayor Sadiq Khan take over. As if to confirm their point, adjacent to the splendour of the Georgian building stands a huge stainless-steel minaret.

Except that the minaret is in fact the Minaret Like Sculpture, a stunning piece of street art designed by David Gallagher, a British architect who is not Muslim. Made with cutting-edge metalwork techniques, it shines beautifully at night. Like Brick Lane itself, it is a delightfully modern remix of different cultures, old and new.

Spitalfields has long been an area where immigrants congregate. What is now the Brick Lane Mosque was built in 1743 as L'Église de l'Hôpital (the Hospital Church) by the local community of Huguenots, Protestants who had fled religious persecution in Catholic France. Go round the corner on to Fournier Street, look up and you'll see the church's original sundial dated 1743.

As the Huguenots spread out and new immigrants moved in, the church's use changed. After an interlude as a Methodist chapel, the building became the Spitalfields Great Synagogue in 1891. In the late nineteenth and early twentieth centuries, some 140,000 Jews who fled pogroms in Tsarist Russia and Eastern Europe settled in Britain, many of them in the East End. Spitalfields became known as 'Little Jerusalem'.

Like Muslims today, the Jewish newcomers were widely reviled. Indeed, Britain's first immigration restrictions, through the Aliens Act of 1905, were introduced to curtail their entry. Yet Jewish immigrants went on to establish quintessentially British businesses such as Marks & Spencer, Moss Bros and Burtons, and their descendants are fully accepted as British by all except a small minority of anti-Semites.

Over time, the Jews also moved on, many of them to North London, and in 1970 the synagogue followed them to Golders Green – although you can still buy delicious Jewish bagels at the famous Beigel Shop on Brick Lane. As Bangladeshi immigrants moved in, they bought the building, which reopened as a mosque in 1976.

Thus Brick Lane Mosque is a building built and repurposed by successive waves of immigrants, each of whom have made Spitalfields their home before spreading out across the country as they settled in.

A good way to get a sense of the changing nature of the area is to visit

19 Princelet Street, one road up from Fournier Street.[3] This wonderful, informal immigration museum records the many uses over the years of what was once a Huguenot house and how different people lived, worked, played and prayed there. But because it is so desperately underfunded, it opens only sporadically. The same is true of a bigger effort, the Migration Museum, in south London.[4] The UK seems to have a deliberate amnesia about its long history of immigration.[5]

Migrants made Us

Humans have always been on the move. We all originate from Africa, science suggests. Our ancestors have since spread out and settled on every continent. Even the remotest tribes in the depths of the Amazon rainforest, who would appear to have been there since time immemorial, actually came from somewhere else. There is no such thing as a truly indigenous Briton, native American or aboriginal Australian. We were all migrants at some point in our family tree.

Not only are there are no native Britons, successive migrants made the country what it is today. Cheddar Man – the oldest complete human skeleton found in Britain, of a man who died more than nine thousand years ago – was, it seems, a dark-skinned hunter-gatherer.[6] Archaeological finds suggest that farming was introduced some six thousand years ago by immigrants from what is now France.[7] English is written in an alphabet that derives from the Phoenicians, whose merchants spread it from their native Lebanon across the Mediterranean, and which was brought to Britain by the Romans. While the languages of Roman Britain were Latin as well as Celtic tongues, the English language is a mishmash that comes from Germanic dialects, Viking Norse and Norman French – all of which are Indo-European languages with their origins in India. While Roman Britain was already Christian by the fourth century, the pagan Anglo-Saxons who subsequently settled there were converted to Christianity, a Middle Eastern religion, by foreign missionaries. Our numbering system, which displaced Roman numerals, was introduced to Europe by Arabic speakers from North Africa, who in turn had derived it from India.

Monarchs are said to embody the nation, yet they too are of foreign origin. From the Battle of Hastings in 1066 to 1154, kings of England were Norman French, who in turn were Vikings who had settled in Normandy and taken on Frankish airs. They were followed by the Angevin French house of Plantagenet until 1485. Since 1714 British monarchs – including Queen Elizabeth II – have been of German origin, first from the House of Hanover and then that of Saxe-Coburg and Gotha (whose name was changed to Windsor during the First World War). Britain – and England – are mongrel nations.

Few societies fully recognise their mixed heritage. On the plus side, this shows how elastic our sense of Us can be; over time, the alien has become local. On the downside, this historical forgetfulness fosters dangerous illusions: misguided nostalgia for an idealised past when everyone was settled and similar, together with misconceptions that today is different and that recent immigrants will never fit in. Past dividing lines may have been different, but most of the issues in today's immigration debate are age-old.

That's one reason why immigration museums matter so much – and why their neglect or absence can tell you a lot about how a society sees itself. Germany – a country where nearly one in four have a foreign-born parent – does not yet have an immigration museum.[8] Sydney – a city where nearly half the population were born overseas and almost all the rest are descended from people who moved to Australia in the past two centuries – no longer has one; the New South Wales Migration Heritage Centre closed in 2012 for lack of funding. Fortunately, Melbourne has a magnificent museum housed in the beautifully restored Old Customs House, where newcomers used to be processed.

France is perhaps the European country that has received the most immigrants over the past two hundred years, yet its National Museum of the History of Immigration was officially inaugurated only in 2014. Housed in a palace in Paris that had previously hosted the country's colonial museum, it shares the building with an aquarium for tropical fish. Yet it belatedly does a splendid job of conveying how France has always been a country of immigration.

In the US, where more than one in four have a foreign-born parent, the most evocative experience is visiting Ellis Island in New York Harbour, the world's most famous immigration-processing centre, which I depicted at length in chapter two of *Immigrants: Your Country Needs Them*. More than twelve million newcomers to the US were vetted there between 1892 and 1954.

Less known is the Castle Garden Emigrant Landing Depot, the US's first immigration station, where more than eight million people arrived in America between 1855 and 1890. Now known as Castle Clinton, the massive sandstone fort lies in Battery Park by the southern tip of Manhattan Island.

On 19 October 1885 a penniless and sickly sixteen-year-old Bavarian trainee barber, who had fled Germany to escape compulsory military service, landed at Castle Garden. US immigration records list his name as 'Friedr. Trumpf', occupation – 'none'.[9] Why would America want a draft-dodging good-for-nothing like him? Fortunately for Friedrich, the US then had an 'open-door' immigration policy, so even seeming undesirables such as him were admitted. Migrants didn't require a passport, let alone a visa; there were no illegal immigrants or failed asylum seekers in those days.

Frederick Trump, as he later became, went on to make a fortune operating restaurants and brothels in mining towns in the Wild West during the gold rush. He returned to Germany with his family in 1904 a wealthy man. But despite petitioning the government to stay, he was ordered to leave the country the next year for having emigrated to evade military service. Stripped of his German citizenship, Donald Trump's German grandfather ultimately returned to the US, not because he loved America but because he was forced out of his homeland.

Like many other German Americans, Frederick Trump sought to hide his German origins when the First World War provoked a wave of anti-German feeling. His son Fred, who was conceived in Bavaria in 1904, later denied his German heritage altogether, claiming his father was Swedish – a lie repeated by Fred's son Donald in his 1987 book, *Trump: The Art of the Deal*.[10]

Out of Europe

Friedrich Trumpf was one of around sixty million mostly poor Europeans who moved freely to the Americas in the century after 1820. German migrants like him were the Mexicans of their time: the largest category of immigrants to the US whose language, culture and, yes, 'complexion' were often seen as inferior and threatening by the established Anglophone majority.[11]

Before 1820 the 'New World' had relied primarily on forced migrants for labour – African slaves in the Americas and British convicts in Australia, as well as poor European indentured servants. But the transport of slaves on British ships was banned in 1807 and slavery became illegal in the British Empire in 1833.

Primarily Indian and Chinese indentured labourers – workers in debt bondage to their employers – often replaced slaves, until Britain finally abolished the practice in 1916. Most went home again, but some stayed, as the presence of long-standing Indian and Chinese communities in the Caribbean and many other former British colonies attests. While the slave trade to the US collapsed in the 1850s, it did not end until the Confederate South lost the Civil War in 1865. Brazil did not abolish slavery until 1888.

With the decline of forced migration, the age of free movement took off. In the 1820s only one in five migrants crossing the Atlantic were free; by the 1840s, four in five were.[12] The New World had plenty of land and natural resources, but few people. It was crying out for both workers – farmers, miners, railwaymen and increasingly factory workers too – and settlers.

Meanwhile, Europe was in economic and political turmoil. As the Industrial Revolution gathered pace, peasants were leaving the land for factory work in towns and cities. Monarchs and the aristocratic classes were being challenged by the burgeoning bourgeois classes and restless working classes. No wonder Europe's many young, poor people were often tempted to move to the Americas, where wages were appealingly high.

Doing so was easier than ever. First postal services and newspapers, then the telegraph and telephones brought news of opportunities in distant places. Railways and steamships made getting there faster and cheaper, while money sent home by earlier migrants helped foot the bill. And governments mostly welcomed the newcomers. While arrivals at Ellis Island were vetted to weed out those 'liable to become a public charge', only one in fifty was denied entry.

The exodus from Europe was unprecedented. First Britons, then Irish and Germans moved. Soon they were joined by Scandinavians and others from north-western Europe. Later, Italians, Poles and other southern and eastern Europeans crossed the Atlantic too.

At the peak of this mass migration in the first decade of the twentieth century, nearly 9 million Europeans moved to the US, nearly 2.5 million to Argentina and Brazil, more than 1.5 million to Australia and New Zealand and over 1 million to Canada.[13] In 1907 alone 1.3 million Europeans moved to the US. Since the US population was only 76 million in 1900, the rate of new arrivals was far greater than today. By 1910 one in seven people in the US was foreign-born – a slightly higher proportion than today.[14]

Overall, some ten million Britons moved to North America, Australia and New Zealand in the century after 1820.[15] That compares with a UK population of 38 million in 1901.[16] Starting with the catastrophic Great Famine in the 1840s, nearly half the population of Ireland also emigrated. So did well over a third of Italy's population.[17] Much smaller numbers of Chinese and Japanese people also moved to the Americas.

People were also on the move within Europe. Irish people migrated to British cities. Italians moved to France and Germany. East Europeans went west to Germany.

Meanwhile, millions of Russians migrated to colonise Central Asia. Nearly twenty million Chinese migrants settled across South East Asia. And nearly thirty million people moved from India to other British colonies such as Malaysia, Ceylon (now Sri Lanka) and Burma (now Myanmar).[18]

Much movement was temporary. More than half of those who migrated subsequently went home again[19] – as Friedrich Trumpf tried to do. Others criss-crossed the Atlantic for seasonal work: Italian peasants to pick the harvest in Argentina during the European winter, Irish navvies to build American railways before returning home.

Closed off

At the beginning of the twentieth century an open world seemed normal and enduring. It had existed for nearly a century and self-reliant people's right to move where they pleased was considered a natural right – although the US had restricted the entry of Chinese labourers in the 1880s. As Britain's foreign secretary, Earl Granville, had put it in 1872, 'by the existing law of Great Britain all foreigners have the unrestricted right of entrance and residence in this country.'[20] Fine words. But governments soon had other ideas.

The collapse of the era of free migration began with the First World War. While people flows bounced back immediately afterwards, the US and other governments soon began imposing immigration restrictions. Amid mass unemployment, the Great Depression of the 1930s then stifled migration. In that decade, fewer than 750,000 newcomers were allowed to stay in the US. Migration to Latin America dried up too. Only after the Second World War would people flows resume.

3

POST-1945 MIGRATION

On 21 June 1948 a former German cruise boat, the *Empire Windrush*, steamed up the Thames Estuary and docked at Tilbury, just east of London. On board were some five hundred Caribbean passengers who had made the crossing from Kingston, Jamaica. They had been lured by an advertisement offering cheap passage to those who wanted to work in Britain. Among them was twenty-two-year-old Sam King.[1]

King had served as an engineer in the Royal Air Force (RAF) during the Second World War. While he had returned to Jamaica when he was demobilised the previous year, he had failed to settle back in. So his family had sold three cows to buy his passage on the *Windrush*.

As subjects of the British Empire, Jamaicans had the right to travel freely to Britain and live there. Even so, as the ship approached land, many were anxious that the authorities would turn them back. So King persuaded two former RAF radio operators to play dominoes outside the ship's radio room to listen in on incoming transmissions.

They were right to be apprehensive: it turns out that the then Labour prime minister, Clement Attlee, had considered preventing the migrants embarking or even diverting the ship to East Africa. But fortunately he discarded those options and the domino players instead heard Colonial Secretary Arthur Creech Jones state that 'these people have British passports and they must be allowed to land.' Jones is said to have reassured his cabinet colleagues that the Jamaicans 'would not last one winter in England anyway', so there was 'nothing to worry about'.[2]

Post-war Britain was desperately short of labour to help it rebuild, but many viewed the black newcomers with alarm. Around half were eventually accommodated in the air-raid shelter under Clapham Common. Since the nearest labour exchange happened to be in Brixton, the area became one of London's first West Indian enclaves.

King rejoined the RAF and later settled in the south London borough of Southwark where he became a postman. When a resentful white worker yelled: 'Send 'em back!' King replied: 'I'm all in favour of sending them back, as long as you start with the *Mayflower*.'[3]

In addition to a thirty-four-year career with the Royal Mail, King became a community organiser. He co-founded the precursor to the Notting Hill Carnival, a Caribbean street party that is now Europe's biggest. He helped start the first British newspaper specifically for black people, the *West Indian Gazette*. He became the first black mayor of Southwark in 1983. And he helped set up the Windrush Foundation to preserve the memories of those who travelled with him on that historic journey and to campaign on behalf of West Indian immigrants. To cap it all, he received an official honour, being awarded the Most Excellent Order of the British Empire (MBE).

King, who died in 2016 aged ninety, was a lifelong socialist, but confessed to reading the conservative *Daily Telegraph* for its coverage of his beloved cricket. He certainly had a good innings.

Into Europe

Sam King and his fellow passengers on the *Windrush* were part of a new pattern of migration that emerged after the Second World War. In the immediate aftermath, millions of refugees – including my grandparents and mother, and Jews whom Hitler had sought to exterminate – were displaced from war-torn European countries. Soon after, Europe shifted from being a continent of emigration to one of immigration. Together with North America and Australasia, it began receiving migrants from the rest of the world: Asia, Africa, Latin America and the Caribbean.

In many respects, post-war immigration to Europe closely resembled emigration from it before the First World War. It was primarily driven by the demand for labour in high-wage economies attracting willing young workers from lower-wage countries. The wartime experience of people such as Sam King had created greater awareness of the opportunities in Europe, as did radio and then television. Travel continued to get cheaper and faster too.

But unlike in the age of free movement, governments in the post-war period were often far from welcoming. On the contrary, people flows were often increasingly restricted and controlled over time. While the post-war era is often dubbed an age of 'managed' migration, this gives governments far too much credit. Most long-term settlement was unplanned and often unwanted.

While economics determined migrants' direction of travel, history – notably colonialism – often decided their ultimate destination: Indians moved to Britain, Indonesians to the Netherlands, Algerians to France. Geography mattered too: many Portuguese moved to France and Turks to West Germany. Once immigrant communities became established in a country, they tended to grow since the presence of relatives made it easier for family members to move and less daunting for compatriots to join them.

Migration to richer parts of northern and western Europe took off in the 1950s and 1960s as economies boomed. Newcomers came from both far-flung former colonies and poorer European countries – Irish to Britain, Italians to France and Germany, Finns to Sweden – and then from Turkey and North Africa. The newcomers drove buses, cleaned streets and worked in factories.

In some countries, notably Germany, many immigrants came as 'guest workers' for a few years and then left again. But when economies turned sour in the 1970s and unemployment rose, especially after the oil crisis of 1973, European governments sought to stop migration and indeed encourage existing immigrants to leave. Many guest workers then became permanent settlers instead. As the Swiss writer Max Frisch remarked: 'We imported workers and got men [people, actually] instead.'

Migration to Europe slowed to a trickle, mostly foreign family members. Some refugees were also admitted, notably from the wars in Vietnam and Afghanistan, the revolution in Iran and the Pinochet dictatorship in Chile. The newly rich, oil-producing Gulf states became the main importers of migrant labour from poor countries.

The sequence in Britain was slightly different. Citizens of the Commonwealth – former British colonies that had gained their independence – continued to enjoy the right to settle freely in the UK in the 1950s. A Conservative home secretary at the time even declared that this was an 'unalienable right'. People from the Caribbean were soon joined by Indians and then Pakistanis. Among the newcomers were the Pakistani parents of former Conservative chancellor Sajid Javid, who arrived in Yorkshire in 1961; the former UK finance minister's father landed with a pound in his pocket and became a bus driver.[4]

But in 1962 such economic migration was restricted and in 1972 entry was limited to those holding a work permit, with Commonwealth citizens losing their privileged access to the UK labour market. In the meantime the Pakistani parents of Sadiq Khan, the Labour Mayor of London, moved to the UK, and his father also became a bus driver.[5]

Among the final arrivals in 1972–73, before the door slammed shut, were South Asian refugees expelled from Uganda by Idi Amin's brutal dictatorship. They included Rumi Verjee, now a Liberal Democrat lord, who made his fortune by franchising Domino's Pizza in the UK.

Across Europe

Migration to Western Europe took off again in the 1990s after the fall of the Berlin Wall, the end of communism in Eastern Europe and the collapse of the Soviet Union. Many moved from east to west – including ethnic Germans from the former Soviet Union and nearly a million refugees from the wars in the former Yugoslavia. Among them were the Bosnian parents of Zlatan Ibrahimović, the star Swedish striker.

Meanwhile, poorer countries on Europe's periphery that had previously been countries of emigration – Greece, Italy, Spain, Portugal and Ireland – became countries of immigration too. Foreigners flocked to Ireland's tiger economy and Spain's booming one – at least until the financial crisis knocked them back in 2008. One of the few foreigners who moved to Ireland before that period was the father of former Irish prime minister Leo Varadkar, an Indian doctor who met his Irish wife while working in a British hospital in the 1960s and moved to Dublin in 1973.[6]

The biggest shift in the pattern of European migration came with the entry of Poland and seven other eastern European countries into the EU in 2004, followed by Romania and Bulgaria in 2007 and Croatia in 2013. Since the creation of the EU's single market in 1993, EU citizens have been free to live and work in any EU country. While governments were allowed to restrict the right to work – but not the right of entry – of citizens from new member states for up to seven years after their admission, Britain, Ireland and Sweden chose not to do so in 2004. This led to a sharp rise in east European migration to Britain and Ireland.

At the turn of the century, there were only 56,000 Polish-born people in the UK.[7] By 2004 their numbers had risen to 94,000. By the EU referendum in June 2016, there were 883,000 and Poles had overtaken Indians as the largest immigrant community in Britain.[8] But since the Brexit vote, that trend has reversed. By 2019 their numbers had fallen to 827,000.[9] By then there were nearly 1.9 million east Europeans in the UK, accounting for just over half of the 3.6 million EU migrants and a fifth of the total foreign-born population of 9.4 million. Many serve in bars, restaurants and hotels, pick and process food in places such as Boston, are builders and plumbers and increasingly work in highly skilled occupations too.

EU migration to the UK has been substantial, but not exceptional. More than twice as many Poles (1.9 million) have moved to Germany, where they have overtaken Turks as the top category of immigrant. Germany has also received more immigrants from the EU than the UK, both in absolute numbers – 6 million as of 2018 – and as a share of population (7.2 percent). Meanwhile, Romanians, who speak a Latin language, have moved primarily to Italy, where they are the largest category of migrant, and Spain, where they are the second-biggest. By 2018 there were 21.8 million people born in one EU country living in another.[10]

EU free movement was not one-way traffic. British pensioners increasingly retired in sunny Spain. Others moved to France. There are twice as many Brits in Spain as Spaniards in Britain, and nearly as many Britons in France as French people in the UK. Among those retired in France is the chair of Vote Leave and former Conservative chancellor Nigel Lawson who hates the EU so much he wants to live there. And in a historic turnaround since the Brexit vote, more people are now moving from the UK to Ireland than in the other direction.[11]

Since 2010 the UK government has been obsessed with reducing net migration, which then prime minister David Cameron had pledged to cut to 'tens of thousands' a year. First as home secretary under Cameron from 2010 to 2016, then as prime minister until July 2019, Theresa May made this her overriding priority. Since the government could control neither emigration nor EU immigration, it focused on cutting non-EU immigration.

Visa rules for international students were tightened. Outrageously, British people who weren't rich enough were denied the opportunity to obtain a visa for their foreign spouse. The visa system for skilled workers was made more expensive, restrictive and burdensome. Meanwhile, the 'hostile environment' policy sought to drive out unwanted migrants. Even so, net migration topped 300,000 in the twelve months before the EU referendum. The victorious Leave campaign's 'take back control' slogan was particularly appealing to those who wished to limit EU migration.

Elsewhere in the EU, EU migrants have typically been much less controversial, with the notable exception of Romani ('gypsies'). The small number of workers 'posted' to another EU country, and employed on the wages and conditions in their home country, have been another bugbear.[12] Although far-right politicians, notably Geert Wilders in the Netherlands, have tried to make an issue of east European immigrants, he soon reverted to bashing Muslims instead.[13] Popular concerns about migration have tended to focus on poor, non-white non-Europeans, notably refugees.

Refugees

When the drowned body of three-year-old Alan Kurdi washed up on a Turkish beach near the holiday resort of Bodrum on 2 September 2015, the images of the toddler prompted a wave of sympathy for people fleeing the barbarism that the regime of Bashar al-Assad has inflicted on innocent Syrians.[14] Two days later, Chancellor Angela Merkel decided to open Germany's borders to the many Syrian refugees who had traipsed across Europe to safety and were now trapped in hostile Hungary.

Europe's crisis over refugees in 2015–16 captivated media attention, dominated European politics, boosted populist nationalists and contributed to fears of uncontrolled migration that helped Leave win the EU referendum. The number of people claiming asylum in the EU more than doubled to 1.3 million in 2015 and 1.2 million in 2016, before halving again in 2017–19.[15] Germany alone is now home to more than one million refugees, half of them from Syria.[16]

Germany's welcoming of refugees is admirable. But the perception that Europe is overrun with refugees while the rest of the world doesn't accept their fair share is false. Total arrivals from 2014 to 2018 amounted to less than 1 percent of the EU population. Five in six refugees and asylum seekers are in developing countries.[17] Turkey alone hosts more refugees (3.6 million) than all of Europe (3 million). Tiny Lebanon has nearly as many as Germany.[18]

For all the fears in Britain – epitomised by Farage's Breaking Point poster – of seemingly barbarian hordes swamping the country, the number of asylum seekers was barely higher in 2015 and 2016 (just under 40,000) than in 2014 (32,000).[19] Sweden, with less than a sixth of the population, received four times more asylum applicants in 2015 than the UK. Chapter 16 highlights how shabbily asylum seekers in the UK and the rest of Europe are often treated.

New Americans

One of the most emotionally charged images of current migration is a fragile boat overladen with Syrian refugees seeking to reach Europe. It echoes an earlier tragedy: the plight of the Vietnamese 'boat people' who fled their country after the victory of the communist North and the defeat of the US-backed South in the Vietnam War in 1975. Like today's refugees, they were typically seen as an undesirable burden and often turned away.

Eventually, many Vietnamese refugees were allowed to move to the US, Canada and Australia. Among them was David Tran, who had been a major in the South Vietnamese army. He finally arrived in the US in 1980 and settled in Los Angeles. But he couldn't find a job – or a hot sauce to his liking. So he started making his own by hand in a bucket, bottled it and drove it to customers in a van. He named his company Huy Fong Foods after the Taiwanese ship on which he fled Vietnam.[20]

Their main product is Sriracha sauce, the bottle of spicy red sauce with an emblematic rooster that you see in Vietnamese restaurants. What began as a tiny local venture in LA's Chinatown has become a global exporter with hundreds of employees and tens of millions of dollars in sales.

Vietnamese refugees are now widely seen as valued Americans. Even though most arrived speaking little or no English, with scarcely any assets or relevant job skills, they are now more likely to be employed and have higher household incomes than people born in the US.[21] But more recent refugees from Somalia still have a more negative image.

More than 50,000 Somali Americans now live in Minnesota, many in the neighbourhood of Cedar-Riverside. Often known as 'Little Mogadishu', after the Somali capital, signs for halal meat and African imports proliferate in both Somali and English and most women wear a hijab (headscarf).[22]

Among them is Ilhan Omar, who was born in Mogadishu in 1982, two years after David Tran arrived in the US. At the age of seven, she fled the civil war in Somalia with her family and spent four years in the huge Dadaab refugee camp in Kenya. In 1992 she arrived in New York and three years later her family obtained asylum.

In 2018, aged thirty-six, she was elected to the US House of Representatives, the first Somali-American, the first naturalised citizen from Africa and one of the first two Muslim women to serve in Congress. Indeed, Congress had to change its rules to allow her to wear her hijab on the floor. Omar claims she started wearing a headscarf after 9/11 as an expression of cultural identity rather than religious piety. 'I wear a hijab. I'm a feminist. Deal with it,' she says.[23] Omar is one of the four female Democrats in Congress whom President Trump told to 'go back' to their home countries.

Post-war immigration to Europe has come in two big waves – pre-1973 and post-1989 – primarily from neighbouring countries and former colonies. In contrast, permanent migration to the US remained low until around 1970, when the foreign-born share of the population had fallen to less than 5 percent. Although until 1965 many Mexicans were allowed to come to the US as seasonal agricultural workers, they tended not to stay. That year the national quotas that had discriminated against non-European migrants were also scrapped, and preference instead given to the relatives of US citizens and residents.

Since then the influx of permanent immigrants has more than trebled, averaging a bit over one million people a year since 2000.[24] And whereas previously immigration to the US was mostly from Europe, it is now primarily from the Americas, Asia and Africa. Newcomers to the US no longer look like Friedrich Trumpf; they are people like Victorina Morales (whom we shall meet in Chapter 16), David Tran and Ilhan Omar.

Reforms in 1990 increased the number of immigrants admitted on the basis of their skills rather than their family connections or refugee status. A diversity lottery was created that offers 55,000 permanent-residence permits ('green cards') to applicants from countries that don't send many migrants to the US. At the same time, irregular immigration, mostly from

Mexico, soared, with the estimated number of undocumented residents peaking at 12.2 million in 2007.[25]

But after the financial crisis in 2008–09, the pattern of immigration changed again. Many Mexicans went home, including two million of the seven million undocumented ones. By 2017 there were an estimated 10.5 million irregular migrants, of whom 1.9 million and rising were Central American.[26] Even once the US economy recovered, more Mexicans continued to leave the US than move there.

While there is still substantial immigration from Latin America and the Caribbean – notably from the Dominican Republic, Cuba, Central America, Venezuela and Colombia – more than half of newcomers now come from Asia, notably from India and China.[27] Migration from Africa has been growing fastest, albeit from a low base.[28]

Since 2017 President Trump has cut the legal pathways to enter the US through a blizzard of regulatory and policy changes, rather than new legislation. Among many things, he has made it much harder for Central Americans to claim asylum at the US-Mexican border. Refugee numbers have been slashed from 110,000 in the final full year of the Obama administration to a cap of 18,000 in the fiscal year ending September 2020.[29] With his mantra of 'Hire American', Trump has also made it much harder for highly skilled workers to obtain temporary work visas. America's doors are closing again.

More diverse Anglosphere

Canada, Australia and New Zealand have also sought immigrants from an ever-wider geographic pool since the Second World War. Unlike the US, as they have shifted away from seeking British or European settlers, they have selected newcomers primarily based on their skills and education rather than their family connections.

Canada has continually encouraged immigration in the post-war period. Initially, only Europeans were admitted but after 1976 so too were non-Europeans. Among them was Ahmed Hussen, who arrived in Toronto in 1992 aged sixteen as a refugee from Somalia and went on to become minister of immigration, refugees and citizenship from 2017 to 2019.[30]

Economic migrants are selected through a skills-based points system that does not discriminate by nationality. Since 2001 the selection criteria have shifted away from a narrow focus on specific occupations to broader attributes, such as education, language and the possession of flexible and transferable skills. Justin Trudeau's Liberal government has announced that immigration will rise to 350,000 a year in 2021 – equivalent to nearly 1 percent of the existing population.[31] The refugee quota for 2020 was set at 53,200 – nearly three times the US's cap in a country with a ninth of the population. Indeed, when President Trump announced a ban on entry to the US from seven Muslim-majority countries, Trudeau tweeted that 'Canadians will welcome you, regardless of your faith.'

After narrowly escaping Japanese invasion during the Second World War, Australia sought to attract large numbers of settlers under the slogan 'Populate or Perish'. More than a million British migrants were attracted between 1945 and 1972 through the Assisted Passage Migration Scheme; since they were charged only ten pounds for their passage, they became known as 'Ten Pound Poms'. Among the beneficiaries were future Labour prime minister Julia Gillard, who was born in Wales, and future Liberal prime minister Tony Abbott, who was born in London.

While the net was soon widened to other Europeans, notably Italians and Greeks, the 'White Australia' policy was only fully repealed in 1973. Since then, newcomers, who are selected through an elaborate points system, have increasingly come from Asia. At the same time, Australians and New Zealanders are allowed to move freely between their countries. While political rhetoric about immigration is often caustic, net overseas migration more than doubled in the twenty years to 2019.[32]

The big picture, then, is that across the 'West' – shorthand for Europe, North America and Australasia – immigration has increased substantially in recent decades. While many migrants in Europe come from other European countries, newcomers to all three continents increasingly come from Asia, Africa and the Americas. Western societies are ever more diverse.

4

THE CURRENT PICTURE

Whenever I visit New Zealand on a speaking tour, I need a work visa. By some measures, that makes me a temporary migrant. Yet my shortest stay in the country was only two days. Does that really make me an immigrant? What if I stayed for a few weeks as a consultant assisting local businesses? Or was seconded to a local organisation for several months? Where does one draw the line?

While the coronavirus pandemic has brought most of the world to a halt, mobility will resume once it passes. Until recently, more people were on the move than ever before – and no doubt many will soon be moving again. Most move temporarily, often for only a few months. But official statistics count as migrants only those who stay longer than a year. By that definition, nearly 272 million people were estimated to be living outside the country of their birth in mid-2019 – 56 percent more than in 2000.[1] Yet since the world population has also risen considerably since 2000, the migrant share has increased much less – from 2.8 percent to 3.5 percent.[2] Fewer than one in twenty-eight people worldwide is an immigrant. For sure, official figures may miss some migrants, notably undocumented ones. But the discrepancies don't alter the big picture. Globally, immigrants are a tiny minority.

That is only part of the picture, though. While people of all kinds move in all directions for all sorts of reasons, the global pattern of migration is highly uneven. In large part, people from poorer countries move to rich countries that have low birth rates, where they account for a rising share of the population and an even greater proportion of the population increase.[3] Alongside this economic dimension is an ethnic one: the newcomers tend to be culturally different, and are often racially different too. One crude way of putting it is this. In the colonial era, the West put its stamp on the rest of the world. Now the Rest are making their mark on the West.

Nearly two-thirds of the world's migrants – 176 million – were in rich countries in 2019. Some 30 million of those were in the oil-rich Gulf states, notably Saudi Arabia (13.1 million) and the United Arab Emirates (8.6 million). Two million were in Israel. More than 9 million were in high-income Asia, notably Hong Kong, Singapore and Japan. And some 130 million migrants – nearly half of the global total – were in high-income Europe, North America, Australia and New Zealand.

The US is home to far more immigrants than any other country: it had 50.6 million in 2019 according to UN estimates and 45.4 million in 2018 according to the US Census Bureau.[4] Canada had 8 million. But together high-income Europe has a far bigger foreign-born population than the US: 63 million. Germany (13.1 million) was in second place globally, while the UK (9.6 million), France (8.3 million) and Italy (6.3 million) were also in the top ten countries with the most migrants in 2019. Australia was home to 7.5 million immigrants.

The only country in the top ten that isn't rich is Russia, which had 11.6 million in 2019, but that figure hasn't increased over the past thirty years. Most of that number are due to borders moving, not people; they are mostly people who moved within the Soviet Union before its collapse in 1991. For similar reasons, there were 10.5 million Russians living abroad.

While nearly two-thirds of migrants are in rich countries, nearly three-quarters originated in developing regions. Of those, 112 million were from Asia, 40 million from Latin America and the Caribbean and a similar number from Africa in 2019.[5] There were 17.5 million Indians living abroad, 11.8 million Mexicans, 10.7 million Chinese and 8.2 million Syrians, mostly recent refugees. Britain ranked thirteenth globally with 4.3 million citizens living abroad, more than any other rich country, and almost as many as Poland's 4.4 million.[6]

Granted, many people move from one developing country to another. For decades the busiest global migration route was from Mexico to the US, but since 2010 this has been dwarfed by the exodus of Syrian refugees to Turkey.[7] Just over half of African migration is to another African country, notably relatively prosperous South Africa. Some people from rich countries also move to poorer ones, often former colonies. There were some 186,000 Portuguese-born people in Brazil in 2019 and more than 130,000 UK-born people in South Africa.

But in poorer countries, immigrants account for a small and stable share of the population of less than 2 percent. In rich ones, they are a much larger and rising share of the population – up from 9.3 percent in 2000 to 14 percent in 2019.[8] Most of the increase in international migration since 2000 has been from poorer countries to rich ones, and to a lesser extent within Europe. While people also increasingly move between rich countries – think American bankers in London and European tech entrepreneurs in Silicon Valley – their numbers remain small as a share of the global total.

Globally, almost as many migrants are women as men.[9] Three-quarters are of working age.[10] And while most migrants move to work or study, three in eight migrants in the rich countries of the Organisation for Economic Co-operation and Development (OECD) are the spouses, children or relatives of migrants (who also often work once they arrive).[11]

In proportion

When I first visited the Gulf region, I gamely tried out the few words of Arabic that I knew on taxi drivers and hotel staff, such as *shukraan* (thank you). But I would get bemused responses, or none at all – and not just because of my terrible accent. Most people working in the Gulf aren't from there.

In Dubai, Abu Dhabi and the other members of the United Arab Emirates eight in nine residents were born abroad. Tiny tax havens such as Liechtenstein and Monaco also have a majority of foreign residents. Some poorer small countries also have lots of immigrants: more than a quarter of the population of Lebanon was born abroad, notably many Palestinian and Syrian refugees.

In countries such as the US and the UK where the backlash against immigration has been particularly severe, many people believe that immigration is exceptionally high. But in fact both are around the rich-country average: around one in seven residents were born abroad in each case.[12]

Some Brexiteers look to Singapore as a model for post-Brexit Britain. What most don't know is that nearly four in ten people in Singapore are immigrants.[13] Those who think the UK ought to be as tough in restricting immigration as they perceive Australia to be may be shocked to find out that nearly three in ten residents there are foreign-born, with New Zealand close behind at one in four.[14] And if Americans look north, they will find a thriving economy and successful multicultural society – Canada – where more than one in five is foreign-born. Americans often think their country's immigration experience is unique; it isn't.

Nor is immigration to the UK particularly high by European standards. Three in ten Swiss residents were born abroad. Immigrants are a higher share of the population in Germany (one in six), not to mention Ireland (more than one in six), Austria and Sweden (nearly one in five).[15] But the immigrant share of the population is somewhat lower in Spain (13.3 percent), Netherlands (more than one in eight), France, Denmark and Greece (less than one in eight), Italy (one in ten) and Portugal (less than one in eleven).

While one of the first things that strikes a Western visitor to Japan is its remarkable ethnic homogeneity, even Japan is starting to open up. Nearly 2.7 million foreigners now live there – 2.1 percent of the population.[16] In Tokyo one in twenty-five residents is foreign. That is not a patch on a global city like London or New York, but it is change all the same. The number of foreign workers in Japan has doubled in the past five years.[17]

As a share of population, emigration is highest in tiny island states, reaching 70 percent in the Caribbean country of St Kitts and Nevis. It is around a third in both Bosnia and Syria, largely due to refugee flows. One in five Portuguese also live abroad.[18] But such high emigration rates are rare: excluding micro-states, only twenty countries have emigration rates that exceed 20 percent.

Immigrants account for a rising proportion of the population of rich countries – and a much greater share of the population increase. People in rich countries are having ever fewer babies, typically fewer than the 2.1 needed to ensure a stable population. So, in the absence of migration, the population will eventually fall unless Westerners start having many more children. And if migration continues at current rates, the share of the population who were born abroad will continue to rise.

The UN estimates that women in high-income countries will have an average of only 1.67 babies over their lifetime.[19] The figures are fractionally higher in the UK, the US and Australia, but still well below 2.1. In southern Europe – Italy, Spain, Portugal and Greece – the figure is as low as 1.3. In Korea, women average scarcely more than a baby each.[20]

The upshot is that net migration now accounts for a hefty proportion of population change in advanced economies. In 2017 it accounted for nearly half of the population increase in the US, for nearly two-thirds in the UK and Australia and for four-fifths in Canada.[21] In Germany, the population would be falling were it not for migration. In Italy, the population would be falling nearly twice as fast were it not for new arrivals and in Japan more than twice as fast.[22]

Different origins

While immigrant numbers have increased and their share of the population has risen, their ethnic composition has also shifted dramatically. In North America, Australia and New Zealand, newcomers have become much less European and much more global in recent decades. While non-European migration has continued to rise in Europe too, migration from other European countries has risen even faster in the UK and many EU countries since the EU began expanding eastwards in 2004.

Overall, more than a third of migrants in rich OECD countries in 2015–16 were born in Europe, more than a quarter in Asia, a similar proportion in Latin America and the Caribbean, only a tenth in Africa and the small remainder in North America or Oceania.[23]

In the US, half of the foreign-born population in 2017 were from Latin America and the Caribbean, a bit more than three in ten from Asia, just over one in ten from Europe and one in twenty from Africa.[24] Whereas in 1970 the top three countries of origin were Italy, Germany and Canada, by 2017 they were Mexico, India and China.

In Canada, Britain was the immigrants' top country of origin as recently as 2006,[25] but by 2016 India, China and the Philippines had overtaken it.[26] Britain was still the top country of origin in Australia in 2018, but China and India were the biggest source of new migrants.[27] The picture was similar in New Zealand.[28]

In contrast, Europeans have accounted for a rising share of Britain's immigrant population. In 2018 a bit more than four in ten were from Europe, primarily EU countries, up from a third in 2013.[29] Slightly more than three in ten were from Asia, three in twenty from Africa and one in twenty from Latin America and the Caribbean. The final one in twenty were from North America and Australasia. The most common countries of origin overall were India, Poland and Pakistan. Among newcomers in 2017, China, Romania and India were the top three.[30]

While the pattern of immigration varies widely across Europe, the leading countries of origin are typically nearby countries or former colonies. Germany is the top country of origin in Switzerland and Austria. Albania is second to Romania in Italy. Britain is first in Ireland. France is second to Morocco in Belgium. Morocco is also top in Spain. Poland is top in Denmark and Norway, as well as in Britain and Germany. There are a few exceptions. Because of the large influx of refugees to Sweden in recent years, people born in Syria now outnumber those from Finland.[31]

In France the top countries of origin are its former colonies of Algeria and Morocco, followed by Portugal. In Portugal they are its former colonies Angola and Brazil. In the Netherlands, they are Turkey, its former colony Suriname and Morocco.

Back and forth

When I was economic adviser to the president of the European Commission, I worked in Brussels. When I wasn't travelling or busy, I used to come home to London on weekends. After three years, I moved back permanently.

People tend to think of migration as primarily a movement of permanent settlement: that people move from one country to another and then stay put. But most migration tends to be temporary, especially when people know they can move freely. Many people intend to move for only a while – to study, do a specific job, experience a different country or earn enough to buy a house or start a business back home. Others leave because migration doesn't live up to their expectations, or new opportunities open up elsewhere. It is easier to move repeatedly because travel is much cheaper than before, the internet increases awareness of alternative jobs and locations and, especially within the EU, there is a big choice of attractive places to go to. Many people move for a while and then go home; others move on somewhere else. Increasingly, those who can tend to move back and forth repeatedly – like international commuters.

Countries count arrivals better than departures, so the data is inexact. But in Europe as many as half of migrants may be gone again within five[32] to ten years.[33] In North America and Australasia perhaps a fifth are. People who remain longer than ten years tend to stay put.

At any time it's impossible to know whether a migrant is going to stay permanently or temporarily. Some people move with the intention to stay, then end up leaving. Since the Brexit vote, for instance, some Europeans who had planned to remain in the UK for the foreseeable future have upped sticks. Others move for a short while and end up staying. When my parents moved to the UK in 1972 they intended to stay only a few years, but they're still here now.

If one instead counts migrants who have the right to stay permanently, or can readily renew their visas, they accounted for only two-fifths of the 12.8 million new visa recipients in rich OECD countries in 2017.[34] More than a quarter of those are EU citizens exercising their right to move to another EU country. While they have the right to stay permanently, most don't. Likewise, others who gain the right to stay permanently – whether as the family members of existing citizens and residents, workers or refugees – often leave too.

Set against that, some international students end up staying for good after they graduate. Some asylum seekers gain permanent refugee status, or fail to do so but don't leave. All in all, though, probably less than a third of migrants are permanent.

Another way to gauge the churn of people coming and going is to compare inflows of immigrants with outflows of former immigrants. The UK has collected this data since 2012; between then and early 2019 immigration inflows averaged 616,000 a year while outflows of former immigrants averaged 211,000 a year. Assuming that pattern is sustained, one can estimate that roughly a third of earlier immigrants leave each year.[35]

Highly skilled migrants often move regularly. Their employer may post them to a different country. They may also be trying to get to their ultimate destination step by step. Since the US is particularly attractive and especially difficult to get into, some migrants from developing countries get there in stages. Some Hong Kong Chinese moved initially to Canada, some Indians to Britain and some Chinese to Australia. Nearly 15 percent of high-skilled migrants to the US arrived from a country other than their place of birth.[36]

Increasingly, then, the terms immigrant and migrant are misleading. It would be better to speak of people as mobile.

The big picture is that ever more people have been on the move globally in all directions, but that most have moved from poorer countries to rich ones, where they account for a rising share of the population. The Rest are making their mark on the West. What, though, may the future hold?

5

FUTURE FLOWS

Tomorrow's immigrants may be packing their bags as you read this. She may be a Guatemalan girl about to trek north to seek asylum on the US-Mexican border. He may be a Nigerian doctor who has been recruited by Britain's National Health Service. They may be a Venezuelan family planning to seek refuge from their country's economic collapse in neighbouring Colombia. He may be an Indian IT consultant boarding a business-class flight from Hyderabad to Houston. She may be a Chinese student setting off to university in Australia. They may be Pacific Islanders seeking a new home in New Zealand as rising sea levels engulf their homes. She may be a British businesswoman moving her operations to the EU to escape Brexit disruption. They may be Vietnamese teenagers squeezing into the back of a refrigerated lorry on their way to work in cannabis farms in the UK. Or one of myriad other possibilities. Who knows who else may soon be on the move?

The future is unpredictable and people flows particularly so. The 2008–09 financial crisis disrupted established migration patterns, sometimes temporarily – both Irish people and immigrants fled Ireland after the crisis but have flocked back since the economy recovered – and in other cases enduringly: more Mexicans continue to leave the US than move there. Nor did anyone foresee that Syria would sink into a civil war so brutal that more than a third of its citizens would seek refuge abroad. Nobody expected a coronavirus pandemic to bring the world to a standstill in 2020.

But with that important caveat, at least eight big factors are likely to shape future migration patterns: demography, economic disparities, geography, technology, conflict, climate change, politics and government policy.

Demography and economics

Start with demography. Migrants tend to be young, because young people have the least to lose and the most to gain from taking the gamble of trying to achieve a better life in a foreign land. Globally, the UN expects the number of young people aged 15–29 to rise from 1.8 billion to 1.9 billion between 2020 and 2030.[1] While there are set to be fewer young people in richer countries, there will be more in lower middle-income countries (up from 813 million to 868 million) and low-income countries (up from 218 million to 280 million). Almost all those additional young people will be in Africa (up from 363 million to 468 million).

Those young people are most likely to migrate to places with better prospects when they lack opportunities at home and are able to move. Contrary to what Western politicians often argue, fostering development in poorer countries, notably through trade and aid, is unlikely to discourage migration. In fact, emigration rates tend to rise as countries get richer, reaching a peak when countries achieve what the World Bank calls upper middle-income.[2] Beyond that, they tend to fall again. Put simply, the poorest can't afford to move, while most rich people don't want to.

Demography and economics shape the demand for migrants as well as their potential supply. Ageing societies with shrinking workforces require more immigrants to help care and pay for the elderly, as Chapter 12 discusses. Prosperous ones need foreigners to do jobs that locals spurn, as Chapter 11 explains. Countries such as South Korea and Japan are ageing particularly quickly. So too is China, where living standards are rising fast; on current trends, the 1.4 billion Chinese will on average be as rich in 2030 as the Portuguese are today.

Piece that together and the following possible future can be glimpsed. Many more people are likely to seek to emigrate from African countries such as Nigeria that are populous, young and poor (but not the poorest) – not to mention corrupt and often violent. Those fortunate enough to have family in the US or sufficiently high educational qualifications may move to America, but geography suggests that most Nigerian migrants will move to richer or safer African neighbours, or Europe. The same may be true of Egyptians. In North America there may be fewer migrants from Mexico (richer, stable young population) and more from Guatemala (poorer, younger). Because Africa will have many more young people with few skills and Latin America fewer, Europe is likely to experience more irregular migration than before and the US less.[3] By the 2040s the only countries that will still have high population growth are likely to be in sub-Saharan Africa and parts of the Middle East.[4]

Richer, ageing Asian societies – including China – are likely to attract more migrants, potentially from populous, poorer Asian countries such as Indonesia and the Philippines that will have more frustrated young people. The Gulf region may increasingly rely on workers from Pakistan, a populous, poor Muslim country with a booming young population.

Conversely, there are likely to be fewer migrants from Eastern Europe, because their societies are ageing and are now relatively rich. Indeed, countries such as Poland and Hungary are likely to increasingly attract migrants, politics permitting. While Orbán demonises immigrants, the Hungarian government is also increasingly trying to recruit foreign workers.

Robots, not migrants?

Technology aids migrants in all sorts of ways: to discover job opportunities abroad, to find safer routes for refugees to travel, to stay in touch with loved ones back home, to send money to them, and much more besides. Smartphones are powerful tools in everyone's hands.

But while demographic pressures and economic incentives are likely to increase both the demand for migrants and their supply, digital technologies may reduce both. If robots and computer systems powered by artificial intelligence (AI) increasingly take over human tasks, there may be less need for workers, local or foreign. And even if humans continue to be necessary for many tasks, foreigners may increasingly be able to perform them remotely, removing the need for them to migrate.

The digital revolution is transforming our world, but like previous waves of innovation it has not so far caused mass unemployment. On the contrary, until the coronavirus crisis, jobless rates in the UK, the US and Germany were at new lows. Yet many fear that this time may be different – that AI has the scope to quickly displace much human labour faster than society is able to adjust.

According to one widely quoted study, nearly half of American jobs are at high risk of automation by the mid-2030s.[5] But while it estimates that as many as 47 percent of jobs are at risk of being automated, this does not mean they actually will be, as one of its authors points out.[6] More comprehensive studies suggest that far fewer jobs are at risk. The OECD estimates that only 9 percent of jobs in twenty-one rich OECD countries are fully automatable.[7]

Whatever the correct figure, economies have previously adapted to huge technological changes that automated many tasks, such as the deployment of electricity and the popularisation of personal computers (PCs), without incurring job losses overall; new and better jobs were also created.

Jobs tend to consist of a number of tasks, some of which may be readily automatable, others not. Fully autonomous vehicles, for instance, may do away with the need for many human drivers – although aeroplanes that are capable of flying on autopilot still have human pilots.

But while in some cases AI will fully substitute for human labour, they will often complement each other. For instance, AI may make it easier and faster to collect and process data about a business's logistic operations, making managers more productive, not replacing them.

At the same time, AI will help create new products and services, and hence new jobs for those who provide them. The explosive growth of social media has created new jobs for digital marketers and content moderators. Some even earn a good living playing computer games as a spectator sport.

The higher productivity – and thus the increased incomes – that AI generates will also raise demand for services that are not readily automatable, such as nursing, personal trainers, creative professionals, consultants and other advisory functions, and much else besides. Personal care and business professionals are two of the categories of fastest employment growth.

In short, some jobs will disappear, others will change and new ones will appear. Overall, there is unlikely to be a net change in the total number of jobs in the economy.[8] Crucially, migrants often do jobs that are among the least susceptible to being fully automated, such as cleaning offices, caring for the elderly and corporate consultancy.

Remote workers?

Even if technology doesn't remove the need for human labour, it may reduce the need for people to move. In his excellent book *The Great Convergence*, Richard Baldwin argues that digital technologies will increasingly allow labour services to be provided remotely – as the coronavirus crisis has highlighted.[9]

International trade in services often requires people to move. Sometimes suppliers of services – such as IT workers, management consultants, construction teams, doctors and academics – do the moving. In other cases, consumers – such as tourists, patients and international students – do. Yet in some cases that might change.

Global online platforms such as Upwork already allow you to hire people on the other side of the world to perform all sorts of tasks remotely: edit a book, prepare a presentation, design a website and much else besides. The cover of my previous book, *European Spring*, was designed by someone in Indonesia whom I found online. Some of the skilled professionals on Upwork might seek to migrate if they couldn't boost their income by serving a global market through the platform.

Entire companies with a disparate workforce can also operate wholly online. Kwiziq, a friend's start-up that uses AI to help foreigners improve their French or Spanish, does not have an office; its team members in various countries collaborate online.[10] Founder Gruff Davies splits his time between London and Madrid. Co-founder Simon, who is from Sydney, lives in the French city of Montpellier. Content and language manager Shui is based in Paris (but grew up in Oxford). Web developers Bartek, Grzegorz and Jakub live in different parts of Poland. Moroccan-born social media guru Hajar also calls Poland home. British-born designer Eliot is based in Berlin. Marketing and grammar expert Laura lives in Guadeloupe, a French island in the Caribbean, but is from the US. Thanks to digital technologies, Kwiziq's team can work together without being in the same place. That said, most of them are still migrants. Moreover, 'being completely virtual we miss out on the organic, osmotic knowledge transfer and creativity that occurs from being in the same physical room,' Gruff explains. 'We try to get the whole team together once every year or so for a week of intense work and socialising, which is great but not enough.' He is also aiming to establish hubs where staff can meet and work.

More broadly, videoconferencing allows university professors to give lectures to students in distant places. In London, doctors who are often foreign-born now provide consultations online; in principle, the doctor need not be in the UK at all. Surgeons can operate on people remotely using robotic arms. Even the archetypal local service – a haircut – could eventually be provided from afar.

Immigrant-haters might celebrate: fewer foreigners around. But they should be careful what they wish for. Whereas immigrants work at prevailing local wages, remote workers would be paid in line with rates in their home countries. For instance, an engineer in the Philippines earns only $570 a month, less than a tenth of the $6,200 average in the US.[11] A schoolteacher takes home only $300, an even smaller fraction of the $4,100 average in the US. Importing the digital services of Filipino workers would doubtless be beneficial for them and generate hefty savings for companies and consumers in richer countries. Even though wages in the Philippines would doubtless rise if such trade took off, the economic disruption to workers in rich countries from such remote working would be far greater than that from immigration, which does not tend to depress local wages or jobs.

While technology may sometimes substitute for people moving, it is unlikely to do so completely even when it theoretically could. Videoconferencing has not eliminated business travel because face-to-face meetings are still often crucial. Even though many people could work remotely and sometimes do, people still tend to cluster together in offices and big cities, where they spark off each other and engage in office politics to try to get ahead. There is also much more to university than lectures, not least mixing with other students. While the coronavirus pandemic has accelerated the adoption of digital working, it has scarcely extinguished the desire for human contact.

Moreover, all sorts of services will continue to need to be delivered locally for the foreseeable future. Old people cannot be cared for from afar. Offices and hotel rooms have to be cleaned on the spot. Buildings have to be erected on site. Food and drink have to be served face to face.

Indeed, as the online world expands, people increasingly value direct personal contact too; while music streaming is booming, so too are concert tours. Technology is not going to eliminate the need for migration any time soon.

Forced out

The number of people forced out of their home continues to rise each year. An estimated 11 million people were newly displaced by conflict or persecution in 2019, according to UNHCR, the UN refugee agency. While most remained within their own country, 2.4 million became refugees and asylum seekers. In total, UNHCR counted a record-high 79.5 million forcibly displaced people worldwide at the end of 2019, of whom 30.2 million were refugees and asylum seekers.[12]

That figure is set to rise inexorably unless ongoing conflicts and crises are resolved. Now that the Assad regime has all but defeated the Syrian rebels and is seeking to rebuild cities destroyed during the long civil war, it is possible that some refugees will return home, however loathsome they may find the regime. If Nicolás Maduro's regime in Venezuela, whose epic mismanagement has brought an oil-rich state to the brink of bankruptcy, were to fall, many refugees would doubtless return home.

At the same time, new and existing conflicts could easily add to the numbers fleeing for their lives. War between the US or Saudi Arabia and Iran – a country of more than 80 million people – could displace many more people than even the Syrian conflict. Further aggression by Vladimir Putin's Russia – whose covert invasion of Ukraine has displaced more than 1.5 million people – could force out others living in Russia's neighbour-hood. Continuing gang violence and unrest in Guatemala, Honduras and El Salvador could send many more Central Americans fleeing to Mexico and the US. Those are but three examples of many that one could think of.

Relatively few refugees make it to rich countries; most remain in poor countries neighbouring their homeland. There are also established legal channels for processing their asylum claims. Even so, their arrival often causes huge political controversy. Yet many more people may soon be displaced by climate change.

Climate refugees

Climate change and other environmental issues are already forcing many people to move, or contributing to their decision to do so. Droughts, floods and natural disasters not only displace people directly, they can also destabilise societies, leading to conflict and further displacement. Most displaced people move within their country, but some move further afield.

Rising temperatures tend to trap people in the poorest countries in penury, while encouraging those in middle-income countries to move from rural areas to cities, and some then to emigrate.[13] Extreme weather conditions – both exceptionally high temperatures and freak frosts – have slashed crop yields in the Guatemalan highlands, one reason why emigration to Mexico and the US has spiked.[14] The Sahara Desert advances each year, displacing people – some of whom seek to move to Europe – and fomenting the conflicts in arid countries such as Mauritania and Niger. Droughts have become more common in Somalia, another dangerously unstable country. Unprecedented storms and hurricanes are striking Caribbean islands. Small, low-lying island states, such as Tonga and Samoa in the Pacific and the Maldives in the Indian Ocean, are particularly threatened by rising sea levels. It would be a cruel irony if Australians who refuse to admit desperate foreigners arriving by boat were forced to seek refuge from catastrophic bushfires by taking to boats themselves.

Given the huge uncertainty about almost every aspect of climate change – how much the planet will heat up and how fast, what the local impacts will be, how governments and people will seek to adapt, and much else – it is impossible to put a precise figure on the likely number of future climate refugees. Estimates range from fifty million people worldwide to as many as a billion. Much of low-lying Bangladesh – whose rapidly rising population already exceeds 165 million – is threatened by rising sea levels, more intense cyclones and more irregular monsoon patterns.

But whereas legal migration channels exist for those fleeing conflict and persecution, none exist for climate refugees. In the absence of such channels, they may remain stuck in neighbouring countries, claim political asylum or seek to migrate to rich countries without permission. Even if such legal channels were created, it may be hard to disentangle environmental factors from other issues that prompt people to move.[15] For example, drought increases the risk of conflict, which in turn may prompt people to seek refuge elsewhere.[16]

Governments are only just starting to grapple with the issue of climate migration. The Global Compact for Migration, a UN agreement endorsed by most governments in 2018, recognises the need to create pathways for predictable movements of people in response to climate change.[17] New Zealand became the first country to introduce such a scheme when in

2017 it introduced a climate refugee visa for Pacific Islanders likely to be displaced in the near future.

Furthermore, there has otherwise been little recognition of, or preparation for, the masses of people likely to be displaced by climate change. The non-binding Compact 'includes tangible commitments but no tangible implementation plan,' observes Rebekah Smith, a migration expert.[18] And countries such as the US, Australia, Austria, Switzerland, Poland and Hungary have refused to sign up altogether.

Politics and policy

The desire to migrate seems unlikely to abate, while the demand for migrants in ageing, rich societies looks set to continue, digital technologies notwithstanding. Wars and increasingly environmental change will be further drivers. But whether, where and how people move depends on government policies, which in turn will be shaped by politics.

The coronavirus pandemic has paused most people flows. Public-health concerns are likely to lead to ongoing travel restrictions until a vaccine or cure is developed, or until societies adapt to the presence of a novel contagious disease. But once the pandemic passes, much mobility will resume.

Where people can normally move freely – as they can between Britain and Ireland, between Australia and New Zealand, and across the EU – they can do so for any reason they like without needing to justify themselves to government officials or to bend their lives to satisfy tortuous conditions placed on their movement. Globally, the super-rich can likewise move around the world more or less freely by, in effect, buying local citizenship or residence permits. Those fortunate to have close family members in rich countries can often aspire to move to that particular country. But not always. When Theresa May was home secretary, the UK decided to ban British citizens who earned less than £18,600 from obtaining a visa for their non-EU spouse. That is a grotesque violation of one of the most basic human rights, not just of foreigners but of poorer British people: the right to live with the person they love most.

Where people can't move freely, they either require a visa to migrate, or must do so without permission. Many countries increasingly compete to attract highly skilled migrants, while making life much harder for less-skilled ones. In the absence of legal channels for less-skilled Afghans, Arabs, Africans and Asians to move to Europe to work, some pay to be smuggled into Europe while others claim asylum, justifiably or not, on arrival. Australia has a substantial refugee resettlement programme and also processes the asylum claims of those who fly into the country on a tourist visa, but locked up those who risked their lives trying to reach the country by boat in offshore detention camps with terrible conditions.

People are going to keep seeking a better life in safe, free, rich countries. It would be better for everyone if future migration was safe and legal, yet that requires a change of government policies. That in turn requires a shift in public opinion. A starting point is to highlight the huge economic benefits of migration.

PART THREE
ECONOMIC DIVIDENDS

6

THE LOTTERY OF LIFE

Bozi Kiekie was born in 1967 in a poor farming village in the war-torn Democratic Republic of the Congo (DRC), the world's poorest country. 'When I opened my eyes, I was crying in the hands of an aunt singing to me. My mother could not nurse me until that evening because she had returned with father to the manioc and plantain fields,' he says.[1]

As soon as he was able, he started helping his family scrape a living working the land. His father sold palm nuts to pay for his son's education, and when his mother died, he was sent to a faraway uncle. 'I had to struggle to finance my studies,' he says. 'I tilled vegetable gardens and traded fruits, bread, sugar, oil, cookies and fish.'

His hard work eventually paid off. He qualified as a teacher, taught in secondary school, gained a bachelor's degree and then got a job teaching English in a teacher-training college. By Congolese standards, he was well paid: he earned $150 (£115) a month in a country where the average was barely $30 (£23). But he was still desperately poor and his salary wasn't enough to provide for his wife and three children.

Then in 2009 he won the lottery – America's diversity visa lottery. This offers a 'green card' that provides the right to permanent residence in the US to 55,000 eligible applicants selected at random each year from the many people around the world who apply; more than 23 million did so in 2018.[2] Bozi managed to borrow money from friends and relatives and in 2010 bought a flight to the US, leaving his family behind.

In the US, his Congolese qualifications were of little use. But he soon found a job as a janitor at a slaughterhouse in Beardstown,

Illinois, a small town around 300 kilometres south-west of Chicago. 'The job wasn't at all something that I could enjoy, but it was my only choice,' he says. 'I had a family back home, and they depended on me.'[3]

Bozi's new job wasn't pleasant but it was hugely better paid than his teaching position in the DRC: he earned $12.30 an hour. Within a year he became a union steward, overseeing other immigrant workers. 'Because of my language skills I was in a good position to help other people, to translate for them, to fight grievances,' he explains.

Bozi – who speaks English and French as well as three African languages – studied at night for a master's degree in education. Four years later, having obtained a US degree, he was eventually able to get a more rewarding job teaching French and English as a foreign language to secondary-school students.

It had been tough. 'If you don't sacrifice, you can't get what you want,' he says. He also missed out on seeing his children grow up. 'I got phone calls every single day from my kids telling me that they're missing me and they need me.'

But Bozi thought the separation was worth it. 'I thought: I'll stop family life now, I'll sacrifice five or six years for a better life in the future,' he explains. 'My children will benefit, and this is the only gift I can give them. There's no comparison between life in the United States and life in our poor country.'

In 2016 Bozi became a US citizen and in September 2018 he was finally able to obtain visas for his family. They have all gained a better life – and they will also give back to America because they are determined to make the most of their opportunities there.

'This country has been built on immigration,' Bozi says. 'America needs people like me to come and contribute – and there are so many people in countries like mine who can contribute to the development of this country.'

It may seem odd to select who can move to the US on the basis of a lottery. Indeed, President Trump has called for the diversity lottery to be scrapped as part of a shift to a 'merit-based' immigration system (although his own grandfather would doubtless have been turned away had such a system been in place when he immigrated).

Yet life is a lottery. The single biggest determinant of your life chances is not how talented you are or how hard you work, it's where you happen to have been born.[4] Even a hard-working and talented person like Bozi, who is born in a poor African village and does his best to get ahead, is likely to lead a worse life than a lazy bozo born in America.

That is not just ethically wrong – most people think it is wrong for the accident of birth to determine the life chances of people within a society, and surely the same is true globally too. It is also economically wrong-headed, since people are not making the most of their potential.

Migration can change all that. Moving to a rich country doesn't just open up vastly better opportunities for people like Bozi and his family; they also contribute to the society that welcomes them. Migration tends to make immigrants themselves, the societies they move to, the societies they come from and the world as a whole much better off.

Much, much, much better off, in fact. Sober economists reckon that abolishing all immigration controls could more than double the size of the world economy,[5] which was worth $87 trillion in 2019.[6] Those potential gains dwarf those from any other public policy change. Even a small increase in migration from poor countries to rich ones could deliver many trillions of dollars in gains.

According to the McKinsey Global Institute, migrants who then made up 3.4 percent of the world's population contributed nearly 10 percent of global economic output in 2015. They added roughly $6.7 trillion (£5.2 trillion) to the global economy – some $3 trillion (£2.3 trillion) more than they would have produced in their origin countries.[7]

When people move from poor countries to richer ones that are better governed, have more machinery, computers and other capital equipment to work with and make use of superior technologies, they become much more productive and can earn much higher wages. This makes them, the country they move to and the world as a whole better off.

'The main reason Haitians suffer in poverty is not because they are *from* Haiti but because they are *in* Haiti [my italics],' observes Bryan Caplan, the author of *Open Borders*. 'If you were stuck in Haiti, you, too, would probably be destitute.'[8]

Even allowing for the higher cost of living in Illinois than in the DRC, Bozi was earning nearly ten times more than previously, doing a much more menial job. Similarly, Indian construction workers can earn four times more on building sites in the UAE than domestically.[9] People from the Pacific island of Tonga who win a visa lottery more than treble their incomes when they move to New Zealand.[10] Highly skilled workers with transferable skills, such as Indian computer programmers, can earn four times more in Houston than in Hyderabad.[11] The earnings multiple for footballers is vast: had Yaya Touré remained in Ivory Coast he would have earned a pittance yet he went on to make £240,000 a week at Manchester City, before moving to play in China for even bigger bucks.

The biggest gains go to migrants like Bozi and his family; their life chances are transformed. If people in rich countries care even a little about the wellbeing of people in poor countries, this is something they ought to celebrate too. While anti-immigrant voices argue that 'we' should look after 'our own kind' first, most people have some concern for fellow human beings less fortunate than them. They support government spending on overseas aid, which is 0.7 percent of gross domestic product (GDP) in the UK. They give money to international charities. They want to help people struck by tragedy such as Syrian refugees.

Granted, people's willingness to help others is limited if it costs them. But in the case of migration, opening up opportunities for others need not cost us anything.

Eight economic dividends

Better still, we can help people less fortunate than ourselves while making our own societies better off too. The key reason why immigration is so economically beneficial is precisely what makes it so politically controversial: newcomers are different to locals.

Some say it would be better if immigrants were 'more like us'. But if immigrants were identical to locals in every respect, they would bring nothing extra to the party except additional bodies. Everything that they did, locals could do just as well. Identikit immigrants might still be beneficial in some respects. Having a bigger local market and workforce would bring economies of scale, and enable the government to spread the fixed costs of items such as national defence over a larger number of taxpayers. But that's about it.

In practice, though, newcomers have diverse attributes, skills, perspectives and experiences that tend to complement ever-changing local resources, needs and circumstances. Those differences generate eight big economic dividends.

Newcomers may be more willing to do dirty, difficult and dull jobs that most locals spurn – such as pick fruit, prepare food, clean offices and look after children – making such essential services more affordable and freeing locals to do better-paid, higher skilled jobs that they prefer. Call this the drudgery dividend.

They may bring valuable skills that a country lacks, such as medical training or fluency in Mandarin, and enhance the productivity and wages of their local colleagues. That is the deftness dividend.

They may be international students who tend to pay higher tuition fees that subsidise local students, make more courses viable, help to attract better professors, create jobs for local academics and college staff and spend money in the local economy. That is the diploma dividend.

They may have diverse perspectives and experiences that help spark brilliant new ideas and technologies that boost productivity and improve our lives. They may also help provide a much wider variety of cultural experiences, such as a better choice of ethnic restaurants as well as novelties such as yoga, salsa classes, R&B music and much more. That is the diversity dividend.

As dynamic outsiders, they are more likely to start businesses that provide valuable products and services, create wealth, generate tax revenues and employ locals. They may also have contacts and know-how that open up new opportunities for international trade and investment. And having moved once, they are typically more willing to move again, helping the economy adapt more readily to change. That is the dynamism dividend.

They may simply be young and hard-working, a huge bonus for ageing societies with shrinking local workforces. Young migrant workers complement older, more experienced local ones, help pay for – and care for – the growing ranks of pensioners and support population numbers, thus spurring investment and growth. That is the demographic dividend.

Newcomers tend to pay more in taxes than they receive in public services and welfare benefits, subsidising locals and helping to service government debt. That is the debt dividend.

Last but not least, allowing people to move is also the best form of development aid. It transforms the life chances of migrants and their children, while the money they send home tends to be spent more effectively than official aid. And when they return home, as many do, they start businesses that invigorate local economies. That is the development dividend.

These eight dividends add up to a hefty contribution to local economies and societies. Subsequent chapters look at each in turn. Along the way, we will also address some of the myths and misconceptions about migrants' economic impact.

In many respects, migration is like another form of mutually beneficial international exchange: trade. Consider a British patient who seeks treatment from a foreign surgeon. If the Briton goes abroad to have the operation, this is classified as trade; if the surgeon comes to Britain to perform it, this is classified as migration – yet the operations are analogous. Likewise, consider a British company that outsources its back-office work to an Indian IT company. If the Indian computer programmers perform the work in Bangalore, it is called trade; if they come do the work in Birmingham, it is called migration.

So it is ironic that many people on the Right who are all in favour of free trade – such as British Conservatives and pre-Trump Republicans in the US – are hostile to immigration. If free trade makes both their country and foreigners better off, surely so too does the form of free trade that involves people moving? In this case, at least Trump is consistent: he is hostile to both free trade and migration. As am I: I'm in favour in both.

More broadly, most governments sign up to grand declarations opposing protectionism; the communiqués of the Group of Seven (G7) big rich countries and the Group of Twenty (G20) big advanced and emerging economies used to routinely do so until Trump objected. Yet they systematically engage in extreme protectionism on migration.

Although people who move from poor countries to rich ones can multiply their wages many times over, most are prevented from doing so: migration barriers generate effects equivalent to import tariffs of hundreds of percent on their labour.[12] There are huge mutual gains to be reaped from reducing those barriers.

Narrowly misleading

Anti-immigrant voices object that many economic studies find that the benefits of migration to the existing population are relatively small. However, such studies are misleadingly incomplete.

Many narrowly focus on migrants' impact on the labour market or public finances, ignoring newcomers' broader impact on the economy as a whole (which, in turn, also affects locals' wages and employment, as well as taxes and spending).

Even studies that take a broader view usually analyse the impact of immigration in an artificial world without economic growth, ignoring migrants' dynamic impact on investment and productivity growth, and hence on future living standards.

And even dynamic models generally define away migrants' contribution to innovation and enterprise because they assume that new technologies fall like manna from heaven, ignore the role of individual inventors and entrepreneurs, and fail to consider the creative boost of diverse people with different perspectives sparking off each other. Yet how can one explain technological progress if one ignores the role of Albert Einstein, Google co-founder Sergey Brin and Silicon Valley?

Fortunately, some economists are now trying to measure the gains from migration more broadly and realistically.[13] Florence Jaumotte and co-authors at the International Monetary Fund (IMF) found that by raising the diversity of skills and ideas in advanced economies, migration tends to boost local living standards significantly.[14] A one-percentage point rise in the share of migrants in the population tends to lift living standards (GDP per person) by 2 percent longer term. Both high-skilled and low-skilled migration are beneficial, and the gains are shared by rich and poor.[15] By that measure, people in both the UK and the US are nearly 30 percent richer thanks to migration. That's an enormous economic dividend.

7

DYNAMISM DIVIDEND

Do you use WhatsApp to send messages on your smartphone? We're in good company: more than 2 billion people around the world do too. We all have Jan Koum to thank for that – and also the US for allowing him to move there as a refugee from his native Ukraine, at the age of sixteen.

Jan Koum grew up poor. His family relied on food stamps to get by. His first job was as a cleaner in a grocery store. But he became interested in computer programming, went to university and then dropped out to start working at Yahoo, then the hottest thing in the internet world. There he met Brian Acton, an American computer programmer. By then the iPhone had just been launched and they spotted the opportunity to develop a messaging app. Together they ended up founding WhatsApp.

Almost immediately, WhatsApp was a huge success. It grew and grew and grew. Soon Mark Zuckerberg from Facebook came calling. He was so impressed with WhatsApp that Facebook ended up buying it for $19 billion (£14.6 billion). So the story behind the amazing app that so many of us use to send messages involves an immigrant who studies hard, gets a job in a diverse workplace, meets a local partner and together they start a business that changes the world.

Jan Koum is exceptional but not unique: nearly half of the start-ups in Silicon Valley were co-founded by migrants.[1] The most successful have grown into immensely valuable companies such as Google, Facebook, Intel, eBay, PayPal, Stripe, LinkedIn, YouTube, Nvidia, Uber, Slack, Zoom and Tesla Motors.

As of 2016, immigrants had also co-founded more than half of the US's eighty-seven unicorns, as start-ups valued at $1 billion (£770 million) or more are known.[2] One unicorn, valued at $13 billion (£10 billion), is Door-Dash, the country's fastest-growing meal-delivery app and a lifeline for millions of Americans during coronavirus lockdowns, which was founded by Tony Wu, who moved to the US from China as a child.[3] Across the entire US, nearly three in eight new businesses have at least one immigrant founder.[4]

Newcomers' children have an outsized impact too. Apple's Steve Jobs had a Syrian-born father. Fourteen of America's twenty-five most valuable tech companies were co-founded by migrants or their children.[5] Overall, immigrants co-founded 101 of the Fortune 500 most valuable listed companies in the US and their children 122, so an astonishing 45 percent in total.[6] Those firms had $6.1 trillion (£4.7 trillion) in revenues and employed 13.5 million people.

Of course, not all the companies that immigrants found end up that huge. But overall, immigrants were twice as likely to start a business in 2018 as people born in the US.[7] They comprise three in ten new entrepreneurs[8] and owned 28 percent of small businesses in 2015.[9] Those businesses employed eight million people in 2017 and had $1.3 trillion (£1 trillion) in sales.[10] It's not Donald Trump who makes America great, it's immigrant entrepreneurs.

Migrants tend to be much more enterprising than locals because they are a self-selected minority who have taken the risk of uprooting themselves, and tend to have a burning desire to get ahead. Like starting a new business, migrating is a risky enterprise and hard work is needed to make it pay off. Since migrants usually start off without contacts, capital or a conventional career, setting up a business is a natural way to get ahead. And because outsiders tend to see things differently, they may be more aware of opportunities and go out and grab them.

The businesses that immigrant entrepreneurs start deliver a big boost to the economy and society. They provide valuable products and services, create jobs and wealth, bolster both local economies and international trade, pay taxes and reduce welfare outlays – and they fuel economic growth, raising everyone's living standards. All of that adds up to an absolutely huge dynamism dividend.

Not just in Silicon Valley

'F¥€K. Your bank is overcharging you on your overseas money trans-
fers. New time you transfer money, TransferWise.' Such punchy ads have
helped make TransferWise, a fintech start-up that enables people to avoid
the rip-off bank charges on foreign currency transactions, famous.

The company is the brainchild of two Estonians, Taavet Hinrikus and
Kristo Käärmann, who came up with the idea while both working in London. Taavet had worked for Skype in Estonia, so was paid in euros. Kristo
was paid in pounds, but had a mortgage in euros back in Estonia. They
devised a simple scheme. Each month the pair checked that day's mid-
market rate to find a fair exchange rate. Kristo put pounds into Taavet's UK
bank account and Taavet topped up his friend's euro account with euros.
Both got the currency they needed and neither paid a penny in hidden
bank charges. That is how they how came up with the idea for Transfer-
Wise, a crowdsourced currency exchange service.

By 2019 it had six million customers worldwide and was helping them
to transfer £4 billion a month at a fraction of the previous cost. Unlike
many tech start-ups it is profitable, earning £10 million after tax in 2018.
And in 2019 it became Europe's most valuable fintech company, after a
funding round gave it a valuation of \$3.5 billion (£2.7 billion).[11] That makes
it one of the rare UK-based unicorns.

Taavet Hinrikus and Kristo Käärmann are exceptional but not unique.
Nine of the UK's fourteen unicorns have an immigrant co-founder, including food delivery app Deliveroo and mobile-only bank Monzo.[12] More
broadly, forty-nine of Britain's hundred fastest-growing companies have
at least one foreign-born founder. While high-growth small businesses
make up less than 1 percent of UK businesses they create 20 percent of
new jobs.

Nearly half of the immigrant founders of high-growth businesses in
Britain were born in the EU, Switzerland and Norway. But with Brexit,
the citizens of those countries will lose their right to move freely to the
UK. Many may then go elsewhere. 'My thinking was as simple as, "Where
in Europe can I go that has the biggest potential for me?"' explains Joshua
Wohle, the Dutch co-founder of SuperAwesome, a company that makes
the internet safer for children. 'At the time, this was London, because of
freedom of movement. Without that, London wouldn't have even been

part of my decision matrix and I would probably have ended up in Amsterdam, Paris, Berlin or Madrid.'[13]

Across the economy as a whole, migrants are much more likely to start a business than locals. Some 12.5 percent of migrants were starting a business or running a young firm in 2017, compared to 8.2 percent of UK-born lifelong residents.[14] Non-whites were nearly twice as likely – 14.5 percent – to be starting a business as whites: 7.9 percent.[15] Contrary to the belief that migrants tend to become entrepreneurs out of necessity – because they can't find a suitable job – almost all say they do so to seize opportunities that they spy.

Immigrants founded many longer-established UK companies too. The country's most valuable technology company, Arm Holdings, which designs the chips in most smartphones and was bought by Japan's Softbank in 2016 for £23.4 billion, was co-founded by Austrian-born Herman Hauser. EasyJet, Britain's biggest – and Europe's second-biggest – low-cost airline, was set up by a Greek entrepreneur, Stelios Haji-Ioannou.

Sukhpal Singh Ahluwalia arrived in the UK in 1972 at the age of thirteen as a refugee from Idi Amin's regime in Uganda. Along with his family, he spent his first year in Britain in a refugee camp.[16] He went on to found Euro Car Parts, which grew into the largest distributor of car parts in Europe, employing more than 12,000 people. He sold the company in 2011 for £225 million and is now an investor and philanthropist.[17]

Thus in Britain as well as America, immigrant entrepreneurs deliver a massive dynamism dividend.

Foreign-born entrepreneurs have made an outsized contribution to Australia too. The country's second-richest person, Harry Triguboff, is a property developer who arrived as a refugee from China, to which his parents had previously fled from Soviet Russia.[18] Malaysian-born property developer Maha Sinnathamby is another immigrant from humble beginnings who is now a billionaire.[19] Another migrant from Malaysia, David Teoh, founded TPG Telecom, a big internet service provider, and is now worth $1.6 billion (£1.2 billion).[20] Fourth-richest Australian Frank Lowy, a refugee from post-war Czechoslovakia, founded the Westfield shopping mall group, which he sold in 2018 for $16 billion (£12 billion).[21] Manny Stul, the 2016 EY World Entrepreneur of the Year, arrived in Australia from Poland as a child refugee, made his fortune from an innovative gift company and went on to build Moose toys into a global brand.[22] Like else-where, many immigrants in Australia have founded businesses that remain small; overall, they own a third of them across the country.[23]

Refugees are the most entrepreneurial migrants in Australia – and are nearly twice as likely to start a business as taxpayers in general.[24] Kinan Al Halabi arrived in Australia in 2016, after fleeing the civil war in Syria and spending a year as a refugee in Lebanon. He spoke English, had a uni-versity degree, had taught computer science in Syria and had experience working for Swedish telecoms company Ericsson. Yet his qualifications weren't recognised in Australia and obtaining an Australian degree would have taken three years, so the best job he could find was as an entry-level business analyst for Telstra, a mobile phone company. Undeterred, on Sundays he learned to become a driving instructor. That was what his Australian-born brother-in-law did and Kinan reasoned that 'because I was working for fifteen years in teaching, I feel that maybe I will be able to do that job – and that is what happened.' Thanks to a loan from Thrive Refugee Enterprise, a non-profit that seeks to assist refugee entrepreneurs, he was able to buy a car and start his own business.[25]

While he got his business off the ground, he spent a month as an Uber driver. 'The main reason for that work was learning English. Every client, I ask them to practise English, and I got very amazing feedback [ratings]!' As his business took off, he soon stopped driving for Uber. In his first year as a driving instructor he worked seven days a week; now he works six days, sometimes twelve hours a day. He feels more confident and comfort-able as an entrepreneur and is delighted to no longer be reliant on benefits.

'I don't like to take anything for nothing,' he says. 'I am always trying to improve my business. I use everything I learned in my studies, and I use my teaching skills. All these things make my business successful.' So suc-cessful, in fact, that he is already thinking of starting another one, since he can't readily expand his current one. 'All of my clients are very happy,' he says. 'But I can't do more than what I am doing now.'

Immigrants are disproportionately successful in Canada too. Shopify, a $40 billion (£31 billion) e-commerce company that provides a platform for many online stores, was co-founded by German-born entrepreneurs Tobias Lütke and Daniel Weinand with a Canadian partner. Blackberry, a smartphone company that now specialises in enterprise software, was co-founded by a Greek-born entrepreneur and a Canadian one. Magna International, the largest car parts manufacturer in North America, was founded by an Austrian-born immigrant, Frank Stronach. Rai Sahi, an immigrant from India who started off working as a labourer, founded the country's third-biggest trucking company and is now the biggest owner of golf clubs in Canada. Murad Al-Katib, a Turkish-born immigrant who grew up in rural Saskatchewan, was the 2017 winner of the EY World Entrepreneur of the Year award.[26] He founded AGT Food and Ingredients, an agribusiness with more than C$2 billion (£1.2 billion) in revenues across five continents.[27]

Immigrants are more likely to start businesses, big and small, than people born in Canada.[28] Moreover, the businesses they start tend to create more jobs and grow faster than those started by locals.[29] Immigrant-founded companies are also more likely to export and be innovative.[30]

Plus-sized

Immigrants are more likely to start a business in countries where it is easy to do so – such as the US and the UK – than in those where entrepreneurs are strangled in red tape. And even in Germany, which the World Bank ranked 125th in the world in 2019 in terms of the ease of starting a business, immigrant entrepreneurs are making their mark.[31] Remarkably, some 42 percent of newly registered businesses in Germany were founded by people with foreign passports in 2015.[32] Foreigners were more than six times as likely to start a business as Germans.

Zahir Dehnadi and Bahman Nedaei both arrived in Germany as child refugees from Iran. In 2009 they started Navabi, an online fashion retailer for plus-sized women. 'We talked to many industry experts and their view was a bit like, "You know, plus-size women don't really want fashion, they just want clothes,"' Dehnadi says. 'When we started, there was no research on this market and its potential,' he recalled. 'Because of this, we did our own and realised you need to take a different approach. You can't just do a tiny collection, half-heartedly,' Nedaei adds. By 2015 Navabi employed more than 150 people and exported to more than thirty countries, notably France and the UK.[33]

Starting a business is tricky in Italy too. Yet a survey in 2015 found that the most common surnames for founders of new firms there were

Hu, Chen and Singh, with Rossi, Italy's most common surname, a distant fourth.[34]

In Sweden young migrants are twice as likely to start a business as locals. One in five new businesses are started by immigrants and the businesses they founded employ around 250,000 people.[35]

Saeid Esmaeilzadeh was born in Iran and moved to Sweden as a refugee at the age of eight. When he was growing up in the suburbs of Stockholm in the 1980s, his parents were unemployed and he resolved that he would not suffer the same fate. He studied hard and at the age of twenty-eight became the youngest associate professor in Sweden. He then went on to discover the world's hardest glass and set up his own company, Serendipity, to commercialise it. Now a billionaire, he has since built up more than fifteen businesses to sell all sorts of groundbreaking inventions, including individually customised implants for damaged joints and environmentally friendly ways to treat wood pulp and textiles.

Many of the winners of EY's World Entrepreneur of the Year competition are also migrants. As well as those already mentioned, 2015 winner Mohed Altrad grew up as a nomadic Bedouin in Syria, was forbidden from attending school, taught himself to read, came to France on a scholarship and ended up building a billion-dollar construction empire in his adopted country.[36] Hamdi Ulukaya, the 2013 winner, arrived in the US from Turkey and started Chobani Greek yoghurt, a billion-dollar company, and then set up the Tent Foundation to help refugees.[37]

Globally, migrants are typically much more likely to start a business than locals.[38] Risk-taking and resilient people are more likely to move in the first place – and more determined to succeed after they do. Immigrants may also be frustrated by the opportunities open to them in the job market and so set up on their own. Their knowledge of two or more cultural and business contexts may also help them come up with creative new business ideas. They may identify new niche markets, serve existing customers differently, import or produce foreign products or come up with new combinations of ideas. One study found that those who study abroad came up with better business ideas than those who stay at home.[39]

Dietrich Mateschitz came up with the idea for Red Bull while travelling in Thailand in the 1980s. There he noted that truck drivers and construction workers drank Krating Daeng, a cheap energy drink, to stay awake. Rather than simply importing the product to his native Austria, he realised that there was huge potential in modifying it for a European market. By adapting the size, taste and brand, he created the first energy drink for the alternative clubbing scene – something new to both Thailand and Austria.[40]

Migrants also tend to make economies more dynamic and adaptable by moving to where the jobs are.[41] Having moved once, they are more willing to move again, helping companies and places adapt to change.[42] In the aftermath of Hurricane Katrina, for example, 100,000 migrants flocked to Louisiana for work.[43] Immigrants are also more likely to move to new clusters of innovative businesses within the US, helping them grow quickly.[44]

Start-up visas

The dynamism dividend from immigrant entrepreneurs is so huge that it is a compelling reason to be open to newcomers in general. Instead, many governments increasingly try to attract and select immigrant entrepreneurs by offering start-up visas. But these have a patchy record at best.

Their entry criteria tend to be unduly burdensome, while government officials are ill-equipped to assess the potential of would-be entrepreneurs. Australia's entrepreneur visa requires applicants to be nominated by a state government agency and have A$200,000 (£105,000) funding for an innovative business.[45] Britain's new start-up visa is better than most: applicants are vetted by venture capitalists and innovative universities such as Cambridge, not immigration officials.[46]

Even so, start-up visas fail to cater to most entrepreneurs. They tend to focus on high-growth businesses, excluding many other valuable ones. They miss out the many migrants who get their business idea and motivation to become entrepreneurs after arriving and experiencing the local business scene. And they ignore the crucial fact that entrepreneurs often arrive penniless with few qualifications yet go on to great things. A start-up visa scheme would not have admitted Jan Koum, who went on to found WhatsApp, Sukhpal Singh Ahluwalia, who went on to establish Euro Car Parts, or many other successful immigrant entrepreneurs.

Start-up visas have their place, though they are not a substitute for an open immigration policy. Next, we look at another category of migrant in hot demand: international students.

8

DIPLOMA DIVIDEND

Yusra Uzair was born in Pakistan, grew up in Canada, has worked in Mexico and Peru and studied for a master's degree in international migration and public policy in London. She chose to study in the UK partly for personal reasons; much of her mother's family is based in Britain. But her main motive was professional: the superb reputation of the LSE and all the benefits its location provides.

'LSE was the only university I considered applying to,' she said. 'It has an esteemed reputation and a very strong alumni network. The course was just what I wanted to study. Being based in London was also a big draw. And with such an international student body, LSE offers many opportunities for cultural exchange and broadening my network.'

When I myself decided to study economics and then international political economy in the early 1990s, one reason I chose to do so at LSE was because it was so international. Today it is even more cosmopolitan: seven in ten students are foreign. LSE is the UK university with the highest proportion of international students and it ranked second-highest globally in 2018.[1] Many of the staff are international too.

'At LSE we're proudly global in our outlook and a vital part of this comes from the students who travel from all over the world to study here – their perspectives, their ideas, their friendships and the diversity they bring to debates inside and outside the classroom,' explains director Minouche Shafik, who was born in Egypt and studied in the US as well as at LSE. 'Beyond LSE, our international students make an enormous contribution to the UK's social, cultural and economic life – and our alumni spread across more than 150 countries go on to serve as great ambassadors for the School and for the UK. It is obvious, then, that we should be actively encouraging top students from around the world to come here. Everybody wins: the students, our universities, the towns and cities which benefit from investment and the firms who want to employ talented graduates.'

When I interviewed her, Yusra was studying at the European Institute, to which I am affiliated as a senior visiting fellow. 'There are students from all across the EU,' she said. 'It's a huge learning benefit.' The tuition fees are substantial – £21,744 a year – but since the UK offers one-year master's courses whereas Canadian ones take two years, it is not much more expensive than a Canadian degree even allowing for the costs of London living.

By the time you read this, Yusra will be back on the job market.[2] 'I have lots of public sector experience, mostly recently working for the British Consulate General in Toronto. After I graduate, I'd like to work for an international organisation, perhaps UNHCR. Or maybe a think tank or a consultancy.'

Global boom

International education is booming. Students such as Yusra increasingly want a foreign degree. Universities are keen to attract them. And governments typically welcome them too. While the near-term outlook is clouded by the coronavirus pandemic, longer-term prospects for international education remain bright.

International students benefit from studying abroad in many ways. They gain a better education, signal their value to employers, profit from the reputation of their university, broaden their horizons and professional networks and have a better chance of securing rewarding work abroad after graduating.

The countries where international students study gain a hefty diploma dividend too. Foreigners typically pay higher tuition fees than locals, thereby subsidising them. They also spend money locally, creating jobs and supporting businesses. They enhance locals' study through their diverse perspectives and by enabling local universities to offer a wider range of courses, and attract better professors. They are a source of talent for local businesses after they graduate. And they create international networks that tend to boost trade and investment and enhance relations with their home country after they graduate.

More than four million students worldwide were on a foreign degree course in 2017 – twice as many as in 2000.[3] Most were in rich OECD countries. The US alone hosted nearly a million foreign students. The UK was a distant second, with 436,000. Third-placed Australia, with 381,000, was catching up fast. While international student numbers in the UK stagnated between 2013 and 2017, they rose by half in Australia – and by nearly as much in sixth-placed Canada.

Since English is now the global language of business, English-speaking countries have a competitive advantage in the international education market. As well as welcoming foreign students, universities increasingly open foreign campuses too. But other countries are increasingly trying to capitalise by also offering degrees in English. Germany and France each attract a quarter of a million foreign students, often from Africa in the latter case. Outside the OECD, Russia and China are increasingly popular.

Relative to the size of its population, Australia hosts more international students than any other country except for tiny Luxembourg. More than a fifth of the student population there was foreign in 2017.[4] New Zealand, with a fifth, and the UK, with slightly less than a fifth, were just behind. In the US, in contrast, only one in twenty students were foreign. But this proportion rose to 26 percent among PhD students and a whopping 65 percent among PhD students in natural sciences, mathematics and statistics.

More than half of international students are from Asia. China alone accounts for nearly 860,000, India for 300,000.[5] Thanks in part to the EU's Erasmus+ programme that helps Europeans study in other EU countries, Europe accounts for a fifth of the global total. That includes some 117,000 Germans, 85,000 French students, 70,000 Italians and 32,000 Britons. More than 16,000 UK students benefited from Erasmus in 2017; unless the UK government negotiates continued participation in the EU scheme British students will no longer be eligible for it from 2021.[6] Some 70,000 Americans, 46,000 Canadians and 13,000 Australians also studied abroad in 2017.

Countries try to attract international students through organisations such as the British Council and the Australian Agency for Education and

Training. Canada's international education strategy likewise seeks to lure more international students. With the US increasingly hostile to Chinese students, whom President Trump accuses of spying and political agitation, the numbers applying to UK universities have soared.[7]

International education is an increasingly large export industry. It is Australia's largest service export (surpassing tourism) and its third-largest export overall, behind iron ore and coal. Sydney University receives more than a fifth of its revenues from Chinese students alone.[8] Foreign students in Australia (including those at vocational-education and English-language colleges) spent more than A$35 billion (£18 billion) in 2018 on tourism, food, travel and housing – a 16 percent rise on the previous year.[9] That amounts to a diploma dividend of A$1,400 (£740) for every person in Australia. Almost a third of students are from China and further 15 percent from India. This huge expenditure supported more than 240,000 local jobs and many small businesses across the country.

International students are also a big bonus for Britain. They provided a net boost to the UK economy of £20.3 billion in 2015–16 through their tuition fees and other spending.[10] The net impact is a whopping £68,000 per EU student and £95,000 per non-EU one. That amounts to a diploma dividend of £310 for every person in Britain. Overall, education is Britain's fifth-largest service export sector. It is the UK's second-biggest export to China, after cars.

In the US, international college and university students contributed $41 billion – a diploma dividend of $125 (£96) per American – and supported more than 450,000 US jobs during the 2018–19 academic year.[11] Education is a far bigger export than soybeans, America's top agricultural export.[12]

Such figures underestimate the economic contribution of international students. They exclude the taxes students pay while working during or after their studies, the benefits to locals of a more diverse student population, the increased investment, business and trade that international graduates generate and the boost to a country's international reach from educating foreign talent. Worries about the near-term threat to the international education sector from the coronavirus pandemic underscore how valuable foreign students are.

Local students benefit too

Florent Sherifi is a recent British graduate of LSE's European Institute. 'LSE's international student body was one of the deciding factors when choosing to study there,' he said. 'It has greatly benefited me. Studying with, and being taught by, the brightest minds from Europe and internationally was an unrivalled experience. I now have friends, colleagues and networks in over fifteen countries as a result!'

The European Institute is particularly international: it had seventeen UK students, 186 from the EU, Norway and Switzerland and twenty-two other international students in 2019–20.[13] The staff include top academics from across Europe and further afield. 'The classes were very interactive, and this is where I greatly benefited from the different perspectives in the room,' said Florent. 'It really helped me to learn perspectives of students that had gone through different education systems to mine, with group work particularly interesting.' The only downside was that not all international students' English was up to scratch. His international LSE education has clearly been a big boost: he is now adviser to the director-general and chair of the Institute of Directors, a UK employers' organisation.

Florent's experience is representative. Most UK-based students say that studying with foreign students gives them a broader world view and helps them develop a global network.[14] Few think that foreigners' presence slows the class or undermines academic discussions, although it does require greater awareness of cultural sensitivities.

International students make more courses viable, increasing choice for locals, helping to attract and retain better professors and providing greater employment opportunities for local academics. LSE's European Institute would not be viable if it catered only to UK students.

Foreign students also tend to subsidise locals. At LSE, UK undergraduates paid £9,250 a year in 2019–20, while non-EU ones were charged more than twice as much.[15] PhD students from outside the EU were charged four times more than British ones. In the US, foreign students also tend to boost domestic enrolments and subsidise locals, especially at public universities where their fees are twice or three times higher than Americans'.[16] The University of Sydney charges international students more than five times more – A\$48,500 (£25,500) a year in 2020 – than it does locals for its highly rated degree course in advanced computing.[17]

Staying on to work

As students, foreign postgraduates bolster local research and innovation. In the UK they account for 45 percent of early-career researchers.[18] At US universities they are much more likely to serve as research assistants[19] and raise research outputs[20] and patenting.[21] Their larger international networks help share ideas and boost joint research projects.[22] Chinese PhD students, whom President Trump wants to keep out, have a particularly high scientific output.[23] In 2019 the US slashed visas for Chinese students of aviation, robotics and advanced manufacturing from five years to one.

Beyond university, the prospect of staying on to work after graduation is a key attraction for many international students – and their doing so is a big bonus to the local economy, as the next chapter on the deftness dividend explains. The US has been particularly fortunate: between 1960 and 2008 the most talented foreign students were likeliest to remain working there after graduation.[24]

Many governments are making it easier for international students to obtain work visas once they graduate. Canada grants foreign students work permits for up to three years after graduation. In Australia foreign graduates can apply for a work visa for two to four years.[25]

In the US, President Obama argued in 2014 that the government ought to 'staple a green card' to foreign science graduates' degrees.[26] But his reform proposals got nowhere. So foreign graduates instead have to compete for a small number of temporary-work visas each year. Many remain working in universities, where they are not subject to the temporary-worker visa cap.

US policy deters international students from coming. Both the quantity and the quality of international applicants to US universities fell in the 2000s after temporary-work visa numbers were cut.[27] UK policy has also been counterproductive. In 2012 Theresa May cut the time that foreign graduates could stay on to look for work from two years to four months. Her overriding objective was to slash net migration numbers and she wrongly believed that many international students overstayed their visas.

The damage to UK universities from her economically illiterate parochialism is finally being reversed by Prime Minister Boris Johnson, who is restoring the two-year visa option.

While that move is welcome, UK universities face an even bigger threat from Brexit. This will make it harder to recruit European academics, who will have to apply for work visas. It will deter EU students, who accounted for more than a quarter of international students in 2016–17 and who will have to apply for a visa and pay higher fees.[28] And it will deny UK universities EU research funding, of which Britain received €5.5 billion (£4.7 billion) between 2014 and 2019.[29]

International students who subsequently work elsewhere often continue to benefit the country in which they studied. In London 60 percent of international students and alumni of UK universities say that they are more likely to do business with the UK having studied there.[30]

Mark Bouzyk studied at University College London and Hertfordshire University before going on to co-found AKESOgen, a US genomics company that provides services supporting clinical trials, testing and research. It trades with the UK and has collaborated with Cytox, a UK-based company with offices in Oxford and Manchester, to verify a genetic test for assessing Alzheimer's disease risk from saliva samples.

The benefits from educating future foreign leaders may be particularly large. In 2019 sixty-two heads of state and government from fifty-five countries had been educated in the US, fifty-nine heads from fifty-three countries were educated in the UK and forty leaders from thirty-two countries were educated in France.[31] With luck, this can boost future relations. US president Bill Clinton remained fond of Britain after studying at Oxford as a Rhodes Scholar. That said, Hungarian prime minister Viktor Orbán, who also studied at Oxford thanks to a grant from billionaire philanthropist George Soros, has hardly shown much gratitude to either since. Nor are relations with Iran particularly cordial even though President Hassan Rouhani got his doctorate from Glasgow Caledonian University.

International students provide a hefty diploma dividend to local students, universities and taxpayers – and a pipeline of foreign talent for local businesses, as the next chapter explains.

9

DEFTNESS DIVIDEND

Priya Lakhani is a woman with a mission. As she paces the stage and delivers her presentation at a rapid-fire rate, the intensity of her drive to revolutionise education is palpable. The start-up that she founded, Century Tech, uses AI to deliver personalised learning plans and progress assessments for students around the world. Its groundbreaking technology assesses every aspect of how people learn and tailors its approach to help them overcome their challenges, providing a wealth of insights for teachers, parents and students themselves. Thanks to her company's technology, students perform much better. Indeed, it levels the playing field for disadvantaged students: thanks to Century's app they tend to do as well as their peers.[1]

Based in London, Century Tech provides a teaching and learning platform for students, schools, colleges and universities both locally and worldwide – including Syrian refugees in Lebanon. Such online platforms provide a lifeline for those who cannot attend courses in person, not least because of the coronavirus pandemic. As well as being fuelled by computing power, this award-winning start-up relies on the brainpower of its talented programmers, designers, salespeople and other staff – most of whom are foreign.

Rúben Canhoto joined Century Tech in January 2016, just as the start-up moved from the pilot stage to developing the actual app. 'I was working in a small tech company in Lisbon and I had been considering moving to London because of the wider range of interesting projects and companies there. Then a Portuguese guy at Century whom I had worked with previously got in touch and recommended me to Priya. It all went very quickly.

Priya interviewed me over the phone and within two months I had moved to London.'

Century was tiny at the time: just ten employees. Among the seven-strong tech team, two (including Rúben) were Portuguese, one was Polish, one was Ukrainian and two were British, while the chief technology officer was German.

'I was the first designer to join the company. My job was to design the platform and build the app's user interface. Priya hired me because I had a unique set of skills: I design, I code and I deliver things very quickly. I was really excited to join Century because it's great to be using cutting-edge technology to help disadvantaged children learn. It's really interesting and rewarding to work with a great team, do something useful and make a difference.'

Rúben has certainly made his mark. 'Students tell me they love the simplicity of the user experience,' he explains. 'They think it's simple, it's fun and it looks good. An autistic kid who was struggling to learn told me that thanks to our platform he was more confident and was interacting more with others. That made me so happy and proud.' By late 2019 Rúben had already been promoted twice and was head of design.

Foreign brains

Losing talent such as Rúben would be a big loss for Century and all the students it helps, as well as for the London and UK economies. In advanced economies where brainpower is at a premium, highly skilled migrants provide an outsized deftness dividend. They contribute their own talents to their employers, clients and society as a whole. With their different educations, experiences and backgrounds, their diverse skills tend to complement those of their colleagues and other locals, boosting each other's productivity; think of Indian doctors and Filipino nurses working with British colleagues in a UK hospital to save local people's lives. They help spark new ideas and technologies – providing a diversity dividend that the next chapter will discuss. And crucially, they congregate in big cities such as London, New York, Toronto and Sydney, as well as regional clusters such as Silicon Valley and Hollywood, that are both magnets for talent and magnifiers of it.

Foreign brains can make a huge contribution. More than half of the scientists working in Switzerland are immigrants.[2] The president of the

Royal Society, the top scientific academy in Britain, is Venkatraman Ramakrishnan, an Indian-born and US-educated biologist now at Cambridge University who won a Nobel Prize for determining the structure of the ribosome, a key part of every living cell. More than half of doctors in Australia were born outside the country.[3] In Britain 37 percent of hospital doctors working for the NHS are foreign-qualified.[4] Even a massive economy such as the US derives huge benefits from highly skilled migrants. More than a quarter of US residents with a PhD are foreign-born, as are 58 percent of those with a doctorate in computer science.[5]

Talent flows often go hand in hand with foreign investment. When then British prime minister Margaret Thatcher enticed Nissan to open the first Japanese car plant in Europe in Sunderland in 1986, Nissan insisted on bringing in Japanese managers; the factory also employed 8,000 locals in 2019.[6] The presence of talented foreigners can also help attract international capital. As tech workers move to Toronto, the Canadian city is attracting more venture capital flows too. Through their business networks, skilled migrants also tend to boost exports to their country of origin, as well as foreign investment there.[7] Their knowledge of foreign markets is particularly helpful for small exporting businesses, notably in Sweden.[8]

Moreover, migrants increasingly lead global businesses. Quintessentially American Coca-Cola has a British boss; its rival PepsiCo a Spanish one, who succeeded one from India. International Airlines Group, British Airways' parent company, is piloted by an Irish executive; easyJet by a Swedish one. Dara Khosrowshahi, who leads Uber, arrived in the US as a refugee from Iran. French carmaker Peugeot has a Portuguese chief executive. German sportswear firm Adidas is run by a Danish boss. Migrants from India are particularly successful: they lead Google, Microsoft, Adobe, IBM, WeWork and many other US technology companies, as well as Mastercard, a card payments firm.[9]

Prominent politicians

Migrants are succeeding even in that most parochial of professions: politics. With their different backgrounds and perspectives, they bring something extra to the mix. Austrian-born Arnold Schwarzenegger muscled his way to being governor of California. Madeleine Albright, a Jewish refugee from what was then Czechoslovakia, represented the US abroad as President

Clinton's secretary of state. Henry Kissinger, who fled Nazi Germany, performed the same role for President Richard Nixon. Elaine Chao, Trump's secretary of transportation, hails from Taiwan. Senator Mazie Hirono of Hawaii was born in Japan. In 2019 the US House of Representatives had thirteen naturalised foreign-born members.[10]

Canada's defence minister Harjit Sajjan, who fought for his country in Afghanistan, was born in India. Maryam Monsef, minister for women and rural economic development, is an Iranian-born refugee from Afghanistan. Ahmed Hussen, minister of families, was a refugee from Somalia. Small business minister Mary Ng was born in Hong Kong.

Australia has had two UK-born prime ministers recently: Julia Gillard and Tony Abbott. Twenty-two of their MPs were born overseas, including Malaysian-born Penny Wong, the country's first Asian-born cabinet minister.[11]

UK prime minister Boris Johnson was born in New York. While he was born British, many of the UK's other foreign-born MPs were not. They include Conservatives such as Indian-born business secretary Alok Sharma, Iraqi-born business minister Nadhim Zahawi and Polish-born Brexiteer MP Daniel Kawczynski. On the Labour side they include former minister Margaret Hodge, an Egyptian-born Jewish refugee, Bangladeshi-born Rushanara Ali and Pakistani-born Yasmin Qureshi, who previously headed the criminal legal session of the UN Mission in Kosovo. Before Brexit, Magid Magid, a refugee from Somalia, was a Green member of the European Parliament.

In France, Paris mayor Anne Hidalgo was born in Spain. Far-left presidential candidate Jean-Luc Mélenchon grew up in Morocco to parents of Spanish descent. Former prime minister Édouard Balladur was born in Turkey to Armenian parents; one of his successors, Manuel Valls, was born in Barcelona. Former education minister Najat Vallaud-Belkacem was born in Morocco, former culture minister Fleur Pellerin in South Korea. Norwegian-born magistrate Eva Joly was a Green MEP.

Cosmopolitan clusters

Skilled migrants don't just contribute to society through their individual efforts in business and politics. Talented people also tend to complement each other – think of the striking partnership of Raheem Sterling and

Sergio Agüero at Manchester City, or Fred Astaire and Ginger Rogers on the dance floor – and migrants and locals particularly so. But whereas a football team can have only eleven players on the pitch, highly skilled people's collective efforts are multiplied in global clusters of highly productive businesses that can employ ever more talent as they expand.

Take London's Tech City, where computer programmers code for fintech companies such as TransferWise. Because their efforts complement each other and their employers can serve a global market, an influx of foreign talent can create a virtuous circle, helping to attract additional investment, sparking extra start-ups and enabling the sector to expand, luring in yet more talent, both foreign and local. The deeper the talent pool, the more talented workers can specialise in what they excel at, the more combinations of talent are possible and the likelier better matches are. And as skilled workers both compete and collaborate, spread ideas and spark new ones, so productivity, pay and profits tend to prosper. Chapter 10 looks in more detail at how diverse workplaces stimulate innovation, generating a diversity dividend. Such virtuous circles are what make open cities and regions thrive.

In Silicon Valley, the home of Apple, Google, Facebook and so many other companies that epitomise America's technological prowess, six in ten highly skilled technology workers are foreign-born.[12] Apple's iconic iPhone was designed by a Brit, Jony Ive. Hugo Barra, who led Google's Android mobile phone operating system division and now runs Facebook's Oculus virtual reality division, is Brazilian. Ajay Bhatt, the chief technologist at chipmaker Intel and co-inventor of USB (Universal Serial Bus, a standard computer interface), was born in India. Since 2005 inventors of non-European origin account for more than two in five patents issued to Google, Intel and Oracle.[13] Not one of these talented foreigners has taken an American's job; on the contrary, Americans have flocked to good jobs in the Valley as it has grown and grown.

British banks no longer bestride the globe, but London prospers as a global financial hub by attracting international financial institutions, along with their cosmopolitan staff. Nearly 300,000 people in London work in financial services, four in ten of whom were born abroad. Without that influx of American investment bankers, German insurers, Indian securities traders and French fund managers, the City would not be as globally competitive and there would be fewer (and worse-paid) jobs for the six in ten financial workers who were born in the UK.[14]

Coco Chanel, Christian Dior and Yves St Laurent are no longer alive, yet Paris remains one of the world's leading capitals of fashion in large part thanks to foreign talent. The artistic director at Givenchy is British: Clare Waight Keller. Her counterpart at Dior is an Italian, Maria Grazia Chiuri, who succeeded a Belgian, Raf Simons. The creative director at St Laurent is Italian-Belgian designer Anthony Vaccarello. His counterpart at Maison Margiela is John Galliano, a Gibraltar-born Brit.[15] At Balenciaga, artistic director Demna Gvasalia is from Georgia (the country in the Caucasus, not the US state). French fashion is increasingly foreign.

Hollywood may seem essentially American, yet it has always thrived on outside talent. Think back to Alfred Hitchcock, Charlie Chaplin, Elizabeth Taylor and the many other British stars who once illuminated Tinseltown. Nowadays Hollywood is a global movie-making hub that attracts the world's best actors and directors to southern California.

Top-notch Hollywood directors come from countless different countries. They include Mexico (such as Guillermo del Toro, who directed *The Shape of Water*), South Africa (for instance, Neill Blomkamp of *District 9* fame), New Zealand (Peter Jackson, who did *The Lord of the Rings*) and Chile (Alejandro Amenábar, who directed *The Others*). *Sicario* was directed by French Canadian Denis Villeneuve. The many British directors in Hollywood include Steve McQueen (*12 Years a Slave*), Christopher Nolan (*Dunkirk*) and Ridley Scott (*Blade Runner*).

James Cameron, arguably Hollywood's most successful director – he directed both *Avatar*, the second-highest grossing film of all time, and *Titanic*, the third-highest – is Canadian.[16] *Avatar* starred Australian actor Sam Worthington, while Leonardo DiCaprio's co-star in *Titanic* was Kate Winslet, a Brit.

British actors are particularly successful in Hollywood. They have played quintessentially American superheroes Spider-Man (Tom Holland and Andrew Garfield), Batman (Christian Bale) and Superman (Henry Cavill). They have portrayed real-life American heroes: in *Selma*, David Oyelowo plays civil rights leader Martin Luther King. They have even played the US president (Daniel Day-Lewis in *Lincoln*). And they run rampant on TV too: watch Damian Lewis in *Homeland* and now *Billions* or Dominic West in

The Wire and *The Affair*, while the cast of *Game of Thrones* was overwhelmingly British.

It's not just British actors, though. In *Steve Jobs*, the Apple founder is played by German-Irish actor Michael Fassbender. In *Jackie*, Jackie Kennedy is portrayed by Israeli-born Natalie Portman and President John F. Kennedy by Caspar Phillipson from Denmark. So many Hollywood superstars are foreign: Ryan Gosling (Canadian), Alicia Vikander (Swedish), Penelope Cruz (Spanish), Cate Blanchett, Nicole Kidman and Margot Robbie (all Australian). Hollywood wouldn't be what it is without them.

Now that Hollywood is out to capture the lucrative Asian market, it is increasingly attracting Asian talent too. New faces are joining established stars such as Taiwanese director Ang Lee (*Brokeback Mountain*), Malaysian actor Michelle Yeoh (*Crazy Rich Asians*) and Hong Kong's Jackie Chan.

All these foreign stars enable Hollywood to produce more and better films. And it creates jobs for locals: American writers, directors, actors, camera operators, special-effects designers, make-up artists, publicists and so on.

Increasingly qualified

Both individually and collectively, highly skilled foreigners benefit the companies and clusters that attract them. And the more talented people are, the likelier they are to migrate – in part because it is often necessary for career development, but also because governments make it easier to do so. Worldwide, university graduates are four times more likely to migrate than those with less education.[17] Inventors who have obtained patents are nearly twice as likely to move as graduates in general.[18] More than three in ten Nobel Laureates in science – physics, chemistry, medicine and economics – worked abroad; half of 2019's prize winners did.[19]

Contrary to fears that rich countries are being overrun by foreigners with few formal skills (who also have plenty to contribute, as Chapter 11 on the drudgery dividend explains), highly skilled migrants outnumber low-skilled ones in OECD countries and account for an ever-increasing share of new arrivals. Overall, around a third of migrants in rich OECD countries in 2015–16 had a university education.[20] Moreover, half of new arrivals since the turn of the century have been to college. Newcomers are typically more likely to have gone to university than the population as a whole; across the OECD three in eight people of working age have some form of tertiary education.[21] Women are moving much more than before; highly skilled female migrants now outnumber male ones.

In the US just under a third of immigrants aged twenty-five and older in 2017 had a university degree, as did a similar proportion of US-born adults.[22] Even though the US mostly admits newcomers on the basis of family ties, nearly half of those who arrived between 2012 and 2017 had a degree.[23]

The proportion is even higher in Canada, which places a greater emphasis on selecting highly educated migrants. Nearly half of immigrants aged twenty-five to fifty-four in 2018 had a university degree, while a further quarter had a post-secondary certificate or diploma.[24] Among those who had arrived in the previous five years, 58 percent had a degree and 22 percent a diploma.

Australia selects significantly on the basis of skills too. In 2016 some 65 percent of migrants who had arrived in the previous ten years had a post-secondary qualification, three-quarters of whom had a university degree.[25]

The UK and Ireland are also increasingly attracting highly skilled migrants. In the UK, more than half of immigrants aged twenty-five to sixty-four had a university education in 2018, up from three-tenths in 2004.[26] In Ireland the proportion was even higher: 55.8 percent. But other major European countries are much less successful at attracting highly qualified immigrants. Less than a third of immigrants of that age in France had a tertiary education, as did only a quarter of those in Germany. In Italy the proportion was 14 percent, the lowest in the EU.

As recently as 2000, the top country of origin for highly skilled migrants globally was the UK.[27] But by 2015–16 Britain had been overtaken by India, the Philippines and China. While highly skilled migration from such emerging economies is rising faster than it is from rich countries, graduates such as Rúben are also increasingly on the move within the EU.

Highly skilled migrants come from all over the world but tend to end up in only a handful of countries. Nearly three-quarters are in rich OECD countries.[28] In 2010 half were in four English-speaking countries: first and foremost the US, followed by Canada, the UK and Australia. The US alone is home to nearly six in ten immigrant inventors[29] and more than half of Nobel scientists affiliated to foreign universities.[30]

Some brainy migrants move first to study and then stay on to work (as Chapter 8 on the diploma dividend discussed). Others are transferred from country to country within big global companies with international operations. Within the EU, many move freely. But for the most part, highly skilled migrants globally need to obtain a work visa.

For that, they often need a job offer, although those that are deemed exceptionally talented may be admitted without one.[31] Alternatively, they may need enough points to qualify. Canada and Australia both select immigrants in part on the basis of elaborate points systems that reward youth, education, English-language proficiency, work experience and other criteria. Prime Minister Boris Johnson has said he wanted to introduce an Australian-style system in the UK too; Gordon Brown introduced a points-based system between 2008 and 2010 but this was, in effect, scrapped by Theresa May during David Cameron's coalition government.

Global talent contest

While governments typically seek to limit low-skilled migration, both companies and countries increasingly compete for international talent. Global firms want to hire the right person in the right place at the right time, while smaller ones such as Century Tech seek out the special candidate with the specific skills they need. They might be looking for a digital marketer who speaks Korean and has experience from a cutting-edge start-up. Or a salesperson with a technology background who has contacts in both the US and Chinese markets. Even in a huge economy such as the US, the likelihood that the best person for the job is located on the spot is low. In a much smaller economy such as the UK, let alone Sweden or New Zealand, the probability is even lower. So openness to migration is crucial.

Governments tend to be keen to attract highly educated foreigners who can fill skills shortages in areas such as medicine, boost the competitiveness of local exporters, lure lucrative foreign investment and pay plenty of tax. Between 2005 and 2015, the proportion of governments with a policy to raise high-skilled migration doubled to 44 percent, while most of the rest (41 percent) sought to maintain existing levels.[32] But a handful have sought to reduce high-skilled migration in recent years, notably the US and the UK.

The US is often the destination of choice for talented migrants: it offers among the highest wages, many opportunities to get ahead and a pathway to citizenship for skilled migrants and their children. Yet gaining admission is difficult. A country of some 330 million people offers relatively few visas for foreign talent. That includes only 85,000 temporary visas a year for highly skilled workers, most of which go to Indians in computing.[33] A further 18,000 were awarded to Canadian and Mexican professionals in 2018 and 5,000 to Australians under similar special schemes.[34] In addition, 74,000 visas were awarded to intra-company transferees.[35] While many temporary migrants go on to seek permanent residency, only 124,000 'green cards' for skilled workers are awarded each year.[36] With so many bottlenecks, the wait for a visa – not to mention a green card – is typically long and rejection rates are high.

To make matters worse, President Trump has championed a 'hire American' policy, piled extra requirements onto the already bureaucratic application process for temporary-work visas,[37] made it harder for computer programmers to get them and in June 2020 used the coronavirus crisis as a pretext to tighten entry rules even further. Trump has also demonised Chinese migrants as a national security threat.[38]

That last move is particularly short-sighted since people of Chinese ethnicity contributed more than one in ten patents issued in the US in 2015.[39] Eric Schmidt, the former Google chief executive who now chairs the US's National Security Commission on Artificial Intelligence, has warned that excluding Chinese researchers and Chinese graduate students would harm innovation. 'A decoupling at the human level would hurt the United States,' he said.[40] One Chinese scientist, Weihong Tan, was hounded from the University of Florida in 2019 by federal restrictions on scientists with ties to China. Back in China, he switched from cancer research and created a faster coronavirus test.[41]

The UK has also been increasingly turning away foreign talent. Successive governments have made it harder for skilled migrants from outside the EU to enter the country. They have capped visa numbers, raised minimum salary requirements, restricted entry to a limited list of occupations deemed to be suffering skills shortages and made visa applications prohibitively costly, burdensome, time-consuming and unpleasant.

The increasing rigidity and restrictiveness of the rules for non-EU talent were offset by the open door for EU citizens that the UK had as a member of the EU – and those who came were often highly qualified. But while Boris Johnson has said he wants to boost skilled migration, EU migrants will be subjected to the same burdensome rules as those from outside the EU under the planned post-Brexit immigration system. Worse, many foreigners in the UK may decide to leave, as European doctors and academics are already doing.[42]

Rúben's starting salary at Century Tech was high enough that he would probably have been able to gain a UK visa had he not benefited from EU free-movement rights. But the visa process could have taken six months or more – an eternity in the fast-moving tech scene. Some of Century's attempted hires have fallen through for visa reasons. Indeed, once the annual cap for skilled worker visas is hit, even great hires such as Rúben would be turned away.[43]

Even before Britain left the EU, the Brexit vote had already made things more difficult. 'There's been a shift in the market,' Rúben explained. 'We are getting fewer applicants and it's harder to hire. And for me personally, the Brexit vote has created a lot of uncertainty. Depending on how things go, I may want to leave. That's a feeling I didn't have before.'

Canada capitalises

With the US and the UK taking a nativist turn, Canada has redoubled its efforts to attract highly qualified newcomers. Prime Minister Justin Trudeau champions liberalism and openness to immigration, and his government is determined to 'win in the global race for talent'.[44]

In its 2019–21 immigration plan, the Canadian government is planning to welcome a quarter of a million skilled workers in three years through its Express Entry system.[45] Its Global Talent Stream programme now allows companies to hire top international talent within two weeks, instead of the many months such processes usually take.[46]

Some successful applicants have been turned down for a US visa; others choose Canada over America, in part because it is so much more open and welcoming. When Kollol Das, an engineer from Bangalore, had to choose between job offers in New York and Toronto, he found it hard to decide until he discovered it might take more than a year to find out whether he would get a US visa. So he opted for the job in Canada and his visa was issued in five days.[47]

The long wait for permanent residence in the US is another repellent. Uma Kanekar, an Indian computing expert, moved to Canada after a decade in the US waiting for a 'green card'. When she realised that her daughter Disha, a university student who had lived in the US since she was six, might be sent back to India when she turned twenty-one and was no longer covered by her mother's temporary work visa, she had had enough. Canada gave the family permanent residence in eight months. 'It's so nice to be in a country where you feel you belong,' said Disha.[48]

As the US turns away talented tech workers, Toronto's appeal is growing. In 2017 it added more tech talent than the San Francisco Bay Area (which includes Silicon Valley), Seattle and Washington DC combined.[49] Meanwhile, venture capital investment in Toronto-based start-ups more than quadrupled between 2013 and 2018.[50] Among those flocking there are Canadians who had previously moved to Silicon Valley to work.

Australia too is fast-tracking visa decisions for temporary skilled workers.[51] But at the same time it has tightened visa requirements, while government rhetoric is much less welcoming than Canada's.

Counting the benefits

In an age where digital technology is transforming the world, science, technology, engineering and mathematics (STEM) workers are of critical importance. Businesses are crying out for them. Countries compete for them. Cities seek to attract clusters of them. And often, they come from abroad. But what is their impact on local workers? Might some lose out?

An hour's drive north-east of San Francisco lies the small town of Davis. It's home to the US Bicycling Hall of Fame and an outpost of the University of California where my friend Giovanni Peri works. Himself an immigrant from Italy – he was born in the Umbrian town of Perugia, where his retired parents produce their own olive oil – he is perhaps the world's leading expert on the economics of immigration. Giovanni has done excellent, groundbreaking research on pretty much every aspect of the subject. And he's a very nice man to boot.

Giovanni and his co-authors found that in American cities that received more foreign STEM workers between 1990 and 2010, both college-educated workers and those who hadn't been to college tended to see their wages grow considerably faster, without costing any local jobs.[52] Insofar as immigrants specialise in technical occupations that rely on readily transferable skills such as coding, Americans may specialise more in complementary roles that rely more on communication such as sales and marketing,[53] as well as in occupations where skills are less transferable such as law.[54] Research in Australia likewise finds that temporary skilled migrants have not displaced Australian workers or depressed their wages.[55]

Remarkably, Giovanni also found that inflows of foreign STEM workers explain between 30 percent and 50 percent of total productivity growth across the entire US between 1990 and 2010.[56] That is a huge deftness dividend – and it doesn't just accrue in America. An increased share of skilled migrants boosts economy-wide productivity across advanced OECD economies.[57]

At company level, other US studies find similarly positive results. Hiring skilled migrants tends to boost productivity, growth and profits.[58] It raises patenting by both migrants and locals.[59] And it increases product innovation and thus revenue growth.[60] More foreign hiring also tends to be accompanied by increased employment of locals.[61] Start-ups that win visas in America's skilled-visa lottery are more likely to expand.[62] Cuts to temporary-work-visa numbers in 2004 hit the highest-paid – and presumably highest-skilled – migrants most, didn't boost employment of locals[63] and drove US-based companies to move operations offshore instead.[64]

Selection issues

So skilled migrants are super – but how best to select them? Where people can normally move freely, as they can within the EU or between Australia and New Zealand, there is no need to do so. Those who choose to move are often highly skilled; EU citizens who have moved to the UK freely are twice as likely to have some form of higher education as people born in the UK.[65] But insofar as governments restrict who can come and select those who want to do so, should they rely on some form of points system, or let businesses decide?

Skills-based points systems sound rigorous, objective and fair. Hit the pass mark and you qualify; fall short and you don't. But in fact they are deeply flawed.

For a start, they are based on the false premise that only highly skilled migrants are beneficial. But as Chapter 11 explains, migrants who lack formal qualifications provide a sizeable drudgery dividend. They are often the key workers who have provided essential services to societies in coronavirus lockdowns. Unless countries also allow them in, sectors that rely on them, such as care homes for the elderly, will struggle. Alternatively, and perversely, highly skilled migrants will end up doing jobs for which they are hugely overqualified – which they may still be willing to do, not least to give their children better opportunities – while migrants who would be more suited to such jobs are turned away. Chat to an Uber driver in Sydney or Melbourne and you'll often find they are highly educated.

Regrettably, the UK's proposed points-based system announced in February 2020 would deny entry to the key workers – notably carers for the elderly (see Chapter 12) – for whom Prime Minister Boris Johnson and the rest of the country clapped every Thursday evening during the coronavirus lockdown.[66] It would also turn away ambitious, enterprising people who work hard to improve their lot. Take Sushil and Anjana Patel, who arrived in the UK in the 1960s from Uganda with few qualifications. Had they had to apply for a UK work visa under the proposed new rules, they would have been denied entry. Yet they went on to build a successful chain of newsagents, while their daughter Priti is now home secretary – and thus the architect of that new immigration system.[67]

Points systems are also arbitrary. Take Australia's skilled independent visa, which offers permanent residency to successful applicants.[68] You need a minimum of sixty-five points to be eligible, but sometimes much more than that depending on how many visas are remaining that year. You get twenty points for a doctorate from an Australian university or a foreign one of a 'recognised standard', fifteen for a bachelor's degree – bad luck if your qualifications aren't recognised. If you have a science, computing or engineering degree, you get a further ten.

As well as being educated, preferably in science, you need to have work experience, preferably in Australia. You get a maximum of twenty points after eight years of work in Australia, but only fifteen for experience abroad. So promising young talents – those who fuel tech start-ups that change the world – are discriminated against.

That is compounded by the age criterion. To get top marks, you need to be young, but not too young. You get a maximum thirty points if you are aged twenty-five to thirty-two. Why? When you turn forty, which can be traumatic enough for some as it is, your score drops to fifteen points. When you turn forty-five, that falls to zero – because we all know that people aged over forty-five have nothing to contribute, right? You also get up to twenty points for your English-language skills – if they are 'superior'.

Combine all that and you realise that a top-scoring candidate – the ideal migrant in the Australian government's eyes – needs to complete their computing doctorate before they turn twenty-five, immediately get a job in Australia for eight years and then apply for a visa before they turn thirty-three. Good luck with that, mate.

It's actually even more complicated than that, as visa applicants know all too well,[69] and the Australian government also caps how many visas are allocated to particular occupations. The ceiling for accountants in 2019–20 was 2,746, for management consultants 5,269 and for economists only 1,000.[70] When, say, more accountants apply, the points minimum goes up; accountants required ninety-five in June 2019.

In effect, government bureaucrats are, under the guise of an objective points system, trying to micro-manage the migration needs of the entire Australian economy, while also pursuing political objectives such as encouraging study in rural Australia (five points). And because, like all central planners, they don't have the requisite information to second-guess the ever-changing employment needs of all businesses across Australia while also satisfying political biases and constraints, the system becomes ever more complicated as new needs and problems arise. In addition to the five visas for which different points systems apply,[71] Australia has a further nineteen different work visas, including many based more directly on business needs, albeit within bureaucratic constraints.

Points-based systems may be effective at attracting high-skilled migrants,[72] but they don't select them well. Governments aren't any good at picking winners; they don't know how many people to admit or whom. Does anyone think that Britain would be better off if the Home Office decided who could – and couldn't – move to London from the rest of the country? Why would such a system be any better at regulating movement into a country?

The main alternative to a points system is one based on employers' needs. All rich countries offer at least some visas based on an eligible migrant receiving a suitable job offer from an appropriate employer. Work-permit systems have huge advantages. Businesses know best what employees they need, whether they are recruiting locally or from abroad. Although recruiters may have biases and make mistakes, they are better placed than bureaucrats to assess whether an individual applicant is qualified for a vacancy and have a strong incentive to get the decision right because they suffer the consequences otherwise. Migrants are also guaranteed a job as soon as they arrive. Governments don't meddle in businesses' domestic employment decisions – except with broad requirements not to discriminate inappropriately – so why would it be desirable for them to do so with foreign hires?

In practice, governments can rarely resist the urge to impose constraints and conditions on businesses' foreign hiring, with the current UK system for non-EU migrants mentioned earlier in the chapter particularly bad. A further issue is that migrants are typically tied to the employer that sponsored their visa, which reduces their bargaining power and job mobility.[73] So a second-best system, short of EU free movement, would be as flexible as possible, wouldn't discriminate arbitrarily and would allow migrants to change jobs once they arrive.

The UK's proposed points-based system falls between these two stools. To obtain a work visa, skilled migrants will need to speak sufficient English and have a job offer at an appropriate skill level from an approved UK sponsor. This will need to pay at least £25,600, or the 'going rate' in their sector, if this is higher. The salary threshold is lower – a minimum of £20,480 – for jobs in designated shortage areas (such as nursing) and applicants with a PhD, especially in a science or technology subject. Under the guise of creating a future-focused and fairer immigration system that seeks to attract the 'brightest and best' foreigners and treats EU and non-EU migrants equally, the UK is actually seeking to turn away ever more of the industrious and enterprising individuals who help power its economy and provide for the basic needs of its greying population.[74]

Globally, Sweden's labour migration system is by far the best. It allows companies based in Sweden that cannot find suitable local workers to hire people of all skill levels from anywhere in the world on two-year renewable visas, with no cap on entry numbers. It is an open, flexible and non-discriminatory system that provides many of the economic benefits of free movement, while reassuring voters that migrants are coming only to work. However, it isn't perfect. If incompetent employers fail to provide the required insurance paperwork for migrant workers, foreigners can lose their visa and their right to stay in Sweden.[75]

Which country is most attractive?

Many governments increasingly compete to lure international talent, as they do investment by foreign companies. So highly skilled workers often have a choice about where they could work. The flexibility, speed and generosity of a country's visa policies are important factors. But many other factors weigh in too: the attractiveness of local job opportunities and wages, the cost of living, the quality of life, tax rates, the quality of public services and migrants' eligibility to use them – and much else besides. Especially important is how welcome newcomers are made to feel, which depends not just on their personal interactions with locals but also on what they read in the newspapers, see on TV and observe on social media.

Clearly, people have different preferences. To some, London is a bustling global metropolis with superb job opportunities, amazing restaurants, fantastic cultural life and reasonably low taxes. To others, it is an overpriced and congested city with poor infrastructure and terrible weather that feels increasingly unwelcome to foreigners.

With that important proviso, the OECD has ranked countries according to their perceived attractiveness to highly educated workers.[76] In terms of raw appeal to highly skilled workers, the OECD ranks the US first, with Australia and New Zealand close behind. The UK is tenth.[77] But factoring in the restrictiveness of visa policies and practices changes the picture substantially. Overall, Australia comes first, followed by Sweden and Switzerland.[78] Because their visa policies for highly skilled workers are particularly rigid and restrictive, the US sinks to seventh place, while the UK falls out of the top ten – to sixteenth, behind Estonia. If you were to account for the perception that Brexit has created among many foreigners that the country is hostile to immigrants, its ranking would doubtless be even lower. Yet Britain is still more appealing than Italy and Greece, the OECD finds – at least among those who aren't sun worshippers.

Talent fuels advanced economies. Foreign science talent accounts for as much as half of productivity growth in the US in recent decades. The cost of not attracting and allowing the best-suited people from anywhere in the world to fill jobs is not just that companies have to settle for second-best or even much worse options. It's that economies are poorer and companies are less successful, hire fewer locals, offer lower wages, earn lower profits, pay less in taxes – and may ultimately relocate or be forced out of business. The lesson is clear: the US and the UK are shooting themselves in the foot, while Canada capitalises. Even more so, because diverse migrants also provide a diversity dividend, as the next chapter explains.

10

DIVERSITY DIVIDEND

As a long-suffering Arsenal fan, it pains me to recognise that Liverpool are the best football team in England, not to mention the winners of the European Champions League and Club World Cup in 2019. At the same time, anyone who appreciates the beautiful game cannot fail to admire how well Liverpool play as a team. Yet there is a striking difference between the great Liverpool teams of old and today's: its remarkable diversity.

Many people think that to work well as a team everyone needs to be similar. But Liverpool's near-watertight defence shows otherwise. Brazilian goalkeeper Alisson is protected by a diverse defence that consists variously of Dutch centre-back Virgil van Dijk (whose mother is from Suriname), German-born Cameroon international Joël Matip, Croatian centre back Dejan Lovren and England's Joe Gomez (whose father is Gambian). At left back is Scotland's Andy Robertson and on the right is England's Nathaniel Clyne (who is of Grenadian descent) or Trent Alexander-Arnold. Shielding the defence is Brazilian defensive midfielder Fabinho.

'Having different characters always helps; if you are all mainstream, all the same way, that is difficult,' says German manager Jürgen Klopp. 'Wherever good players are coming from, wherever they are raised, wherever the dream started, they are welcome … now it feels to me they are a proper bunch of players together, they really stick to each other … in a way which is exceptional.'[1]

Liverpool excel at counterattacking football, which requires players with pace who anticipate each other's moves. Again, one might think that players from similar backgrounds would gel best. Yet the Liverpool team suggests otherwise. The diverse defence pass seamlessly to the equally diverse midfield, wingers and strikers. Passing moves combine English players such as midfield dynamo Jordan Henderson and foreign ones such as Guinea's Naby Keïta, while the star strikers are an international trio of Brazil's Roberto Firmino, Egypt's Mohamed Salah and Senegal's Sadio Mané.

Take Liverpool's amazing 4–0 Champions League semi-final victory against Barcelona in 2019, in which they bounced back from losing the first leg 3–0. Dutch midfielder Georginio Wijnaldum, who is of Afro-Surinamese descent, scored two goals, the first from an Alexander-Arnold cross, the second from a cross by Kosovo-born Swiss winger Xherdan Shaqiri. Belgium's Divock Origi (who is of Kenyan descent) sealed the victory by converting a quick corner from Alexander-Arnold. That's diversity in action. Teams with a more diverse range of skills, in which different players complement each other, learn from each other and try out new ideas, tend to perform much better.

Immigrants often make an incredible individual contribution to both the companies they work for and the societies they live in. But they tend to have an even bigger impact as part of diverse teams. These involve people of different backgrounds, skills, perspectives and experiences – immigrants of all kinds and a variety of locals, women and men, people who went to different universities or none – learning from each other and sparking off each other.

This fundamentally important point is neglected by visa policies that focus solely on immigrants' individual characteristics. It is also omitted by most economic studies on the impact of immigration, which therefore greatly underestimate its benefits. Because whether it is football, scientific research or business, pretty much everything we do relies on teamwork – and diverse teams can provide a powerful diversity dividend.

3D innovation

Nobel Laureate Andre Geim had an inauspicious start to his physics career: he failed to get into a top university in Moscow. Twice. Even though he had graduated from secondary school with top marks, he assumed his first rejection by the Moscow Engineering Physics Institute was due to a lack of preparedness. When he was again turned down the following year, he did some investigating. It turned out that all the candidates in his exam room had Jewish or foreign-sounding names – and all had failed. Despite its professed egalitarianism, the Soviet Union discriminated against people from non-Russian ethnic groups.

Fortunately, Geim eventually graduated from the Moscow Institute of Physics and Technology. After the collapse of the Soviet Union and a spell as an academic in the Netherlands, he ended up at the University of Manchester. There the atmosphere was much more welcoming: 'Every staff member is an equal quantity,' he said. It was in this open and diverse environment that Geim went on to discover graphene, a revolutionary super-material that has all sorts of promising uses. That won him a Nobel Prize in 2010. Another discovery was gecko tape, an adhesive based on the lizard's climbing mechanism that is so strong that it enables human beings to latch on to buildings as if they were Spider-Man.

Where do the new ideas that improve our lives come from? Governments tend to emphasise the importance of investment in education and skills, as well as research and development. Popular narratives tend to centre on individual geniuses coming up with incredible insights in isolation – and those few are disproportionately immigrants. But in fact, most ideas come from creative collisions between people.

Take the discovery of DNA, the code of life. English physicist Francis Crick and American biologist James Watson concluded that it consisted of a three-dimensional double helix, based on the earlier discovery of DNA by a Swiss scientist, Friedrich Miescher, developed by Phoebus Levene, a Lithuanian-born American biochemist, and Erwin Chargaff, an Austro-Hungarian one.[2]

Or consider DeepMind, a London-based company doing groundbreaking practical research on artificial intelligence. Mustafa Suleyman, whose father was a Syrian-born taxi driver and mother an English nurse, met Demis Hassabis, whose father was Greek-Cypriot and mother Chinese Singaporean, when they were teenagers in north London. 'Demis and I had conversations about how to impact the world, and he'd argue that we need to build these grand simulations that one day will model all the complex dynamics of our financial systems and solve our toughest social problems,' Mustafa explains. 'I'd say we have to engage with the real world today.'[3] Demis went on to become a neuroscientist and met Shane

Legg, a Kiwi machine-learning researcher, at University College London. Combining their different talents and perspectives, they co-founded DeepMind, which was bought by Google for $500 million (£385 million) in 2014. In 2017 DeepMind's AlphaGo bested the world number one at the Japanese game of Go – not by copying successful human strategies, but by devising its own better ones.

Less than a third of recent patents and only a fifth of recent scientific papers were written by a single author – and even lone authors are stimulated by others.[4] 'Creativity comes from spontaneous meetings, from random discussions,' observed the late Apple founder, Steve Jobs. 'You run into someone, you ask what they're doing, you say, "Wow" and soon you're cooking up all sorts of ideas.'[5] For those interactions to be fruitful, people need to bring something extra to the party. The saying 'two heads are better than one' is true only if the two heads think differently. To generate lots of new ideas, you need to bring lots of people with different talents and viewpoints together. That tends to happen in dense, diverse cities with people of different disciplines sparking off each other – what I call the 3D model of innovation.

The stimulus for new ideas may be a questioning mind, a pressing demand for solutions to problems or the pressure of competition. Wherever the demand for innovation comes from, it tends to be supplied in cities, as Jane Jacobs, a great American urbanist, first pointed out in the 1960s.[6] More recently, Harvard economist Ed Glaeser documented in *Triumph of the City* how most innovation takes place in diverse, densely populated cities, where people are forever interacting with each other and experiencing new things. 'We are a social species and we learn by being around clever people,' he observes.[7] 'Cities have long sped this flow of ideas.'

Such diverse cities also act as a magnet for the innovative, entrepreneurial talents of what Richard Florida calls the 'creative class'. 'A great city has two hallmarks: tolerance for strangers and intolerance for mediocrity. These are precisely the qualities that appeal to members of the creative class – and they also happen to be qualities conducive to innovation, risk-taking and the formation of new businesses.'[8]

Denser cities tend to be more inventive.[9] Moreover, single-industry towns are much less creative than a metropolis where lots of different people jostle together. Breakthrough ideas generally occur when people from different disciplines interact and bring concepts from one field into a new, unfamiliar territory, as Frans Johansson documents in *The Medici Effect*.[10]

At an individual level, psychological research shows that people who have been thoroughly exposed to two or more cultures tend to consider a wider range of possibilities.[11] Simply by being aware that there are several ways of approaching a problem, someone from a multicultural background is more likely to view any situation from multiple perspectives. Indeed, someone who is different from most people around them is more prone to question traditions, rules and boundaries – and to search for answers where others may not think to.[12] People who are fluent in several languages also tend to be more creative. 'Languages codify concepts differently, and the ability to draw upon these varied perspectives during a creative process generates a wider range of associations,' Johansson notes.

What is true of diverse individuals is even more so of diverse groups that involve a variety of migrants and locals working together. A growing volume of research shows that groups with a diverse range of perspectives and experiences can solve problems better and faster than like-minded experts.[13] Whether it is devising a new marketing strategy, coming up with better policies to curb carbon emissions or trying to find ways to cut costs without harming product quality, solving problems in teams is what most work consists of. Adding scientists with diverse cultural backgrounds to a team of local researchers is not just about promoting equal opportunities; it boosts productivity too. The same is true of adding women to an all-male corporate board or a minister educated in a northern state school to a cabinet full of privately educated southerners.

The beauty of diversity is that innovation often comes about by serendipity. One day in 1904, at the World Fair in St Louis, the ice-cream vendor ran out of cups. Ernest Hami, a Syrian waffle vendor in the booth next door, rolled up some waffles to make cones – and the rest is history. Just as waffles and ice cream combine to create something new and better, so does a diverse range of people.[14]

1 + 1 = 3

Evidence of the diversity dividend adds up. Across economies and within individual organisations, diversity tends to boost patenting as well as productivity. For a start, migrant scientists tend to outperform locals, according to a six-country study.[15] Better still, they complement each other. A 1 percent increase in foreign-born graduates in the US raises patenting by a whopping 15 percent, partly because it stimulates higher patenting among locals too.[16] Indeed, a comprehensive study of over 1.5 million scientific papers written in the US between 1985 and 2008 found that those co-authored by people of different ethnic backgrounds tended to be published in higher-impact journals and cited more often. The authors concluded that 'diversity in inputs into papers leads to greater contributions to science.'[17]

More than three in four patents generated at top US universities in 2011 had at least one foreign-born inventor.[18] Migrants were especially important in cutting-edge fields such as semiconductors, digital communications and pharmaceuticals. Contrary to the popular perception that only Asian immigrants outperform, the patents were filed by inventors from eighty-eight different countries. Across the US, foreign nationals held slightly more than half of all patents filed by 2015.[19] Indeed, more than 30 percent of US innovation since 1976 can be credited to immigrants' direct and indirect contributions.[20] Take the 2019 Nobel Prize in economics. This was shared among three US-based economists, two of whom were born abroad. Esther Duflo from France and Abhijit Banerjee from India make a particularly great team: not only do they work together, they are also married.

Diversity also boosts performance in particular places. Between 1960 and 2010, US states that had a greater diversity of highly skilled migrants had higher living standards; a 10 percent increase in diversity raised GDP per person by about 6 percent.[21] In Canada too, provinces with more skilled migrants tend to have higher innovation rates.[22]

In Europe, diversity is beneficial economy-wide, in particular regions and in specific sectors. Although a 2003 paper by Alberto Alesina found that ethno-linguistic diversity hampered economic growth, his study compared apples and pears.[23] While long-standing divisions – such as the polarised relations between whites and the descendants of African slaves in the US or the antagonism between Dutch-speaking Flemish people and French-speaking Walloons in Belgium – may indeed be harmful, an influx of diverse newcomers may have a different impact. Indeed, Alesina's more recent research finds that 'diversity of skilled immigration has a positive impact on [richer countries'] income and productivity levels.'[24]

Across twelve European countries, an increase in the foreign-born share of the population, in migrants' skill level and in a region's diversity are all associated with increased patenting.[25] They likewise boost product and process innovation in British regions.[26] In twenty European countries highly skilled immigrants have high patenting rates and enable locals to be more innovative too.[27] German regions with a more culturally diverse workforce innovate more.[28] In the UK the diversity of inventor communities boosts patenting.[29] The diversity of migrants also increases innovation in Germany's tech sector.[30] Polish inventors increase patenting in Germany, both through their own efforts and by stimulating more patenting among Germans.[31] Having a more diverse workforce boosts the number and range of patents in Denmark,[32] and lifts companies' product and process innovation in the Netherlands.[33] In Germany it raises productivity both within the firm and locally,[34] while also boosting local wages and employment.[35] All this amounts to compelling evidence of the diversity dividend.

Business benefits of diversity

Organisations that tend to hire people from the same background are missing out on the many talents of our increasingly diverse societies. A diverse workforce can also be a crucial part of the appeal of working for a business, helping it attract and retain the people it needs. 'If you want to attract the best talent, you need to be reflective of the talent in that market,' says Eileen Taylor, Deutsche Bank's global head of diversity.[36]

Diverse perspectives can also help generate better solutions to problems. In Chapter 9 on the deftness dividend, we met Rúben, the Portuguese head of design at Century Tech, a London-based edtech company. He manages a team made up of a Lithuanian designer, a Dutch one and three Britons. Century also employs a Chinese-born data scientist who studied in Toronto, San Diego and London, both a Brazilian engineer and an Argentinian one who previously worked in Germany, a developer who is an Eritrean-born Swede, an account manager from Lebanon and a project manager from Ukraine, among others.

'It's great to work with a diverse team with people from different back-grounds,' Rúben remarks. 'Back in Portugal, all the developers I worked with had been to the same school and had the same teachers. They had the same approach, the same strengths and the same flaws. Here at Century we discuss issues better. We come up with more ideas. We learn new things. It makes work more interesting and leads to better end results.'

We've all been in meetings where everyone around the table thinks the same. It may feel comfortable and safe, and a decision may be reached quickly – but it's often the wrong one. Participants haven't considered all the options and thought things through. A different opinion would make all the difference.[37] That can have a critical impact: ethnically diverse juries consider more perspectives and make fewer inaccurate statements than homogeneous ones.[38] Likewise, diverse teams of stock market traders out-perform homogeneous ones.[39]

Team leaders who impose their own thinking and biases tend to overemphasise one or two ways of solving problems and discard other approaches. They also tend to neglect the risks, the implications for staff and customers, the implementation process and the evidence to justify and measure a solution. Yet studies find that trying to solve problems by applying a single dominant approach has only a 30 percent success rate, whereas applying five different ones can lift that to nearly 100 percent.[40]

Diversity doesn't just bring different perspectives to the table: it forces participants to challenge their own thinking. Adding diversity to a group makes people think that others might have different perspectives and that belief makes people change their behaviour even before they interact.[41] Visible racial diversity brings 'cognitive friction that enhances deliberation'.[42]

Imagine you're preparing a presentation. You're anticipating some disagreement and difficulty communicating because your collaborator is from a different culture. In all likelihood, you'll work harder on explaining your rationale and anticipating alternatives than you would have done otherwise. Diversity can thus promote hard work and creativity and encourage people to think differently even before they enter the room with colleagues.

Research by Scott Page shows that the diversity of the members of a team is as important as their ability in determining how they perform at solving problems.[43] In practical terms, what that means is that if an organisation is looking to recruit a new employee and most of its existing team are from a similar background, they would do better to hire someone very different even if on paper she seems less talented or qualified than someone similar to the existing staff. Of course, if she is as qualified, or better, the benefits will be even greater.

As well as making teams more creative and innovative, diversity can make them more adaptable. Exposure to other cultures tends to broaden people's horizons and make them more accustomed to difference. This mental flexibility helps both managers and employees think 'outside the box', be more open to change and adapt more readily to it. Businesses with a diverse workforce also have a wider variety of skills at their disposal, so they can adjust more quickly to changing circumstances.

That's a huge advantage at a time when new technologies are continually disrupting the business landscape, the global economy is going through momentous changes and people's tastes and expectations are forever changing.

A diverse team can also build a stronger connection to clients and suppliers, both locally and globally. Western societies are increasingly diverse in every respect, and people increasingly want products and services tailored to their particular tastes and needs. A diverse team helps achieve that because the diversity of society is reflected within an organisation.

Immigrants can also provide contacts and know-how on foreign markets around the world. They speak the language and understand the culture of the people firms want to do business with, and can open up new markets and generate new trading links and investment opportunities.

Nats Subramanian moved from India to New Zealand in 2004 to work in computing. He has since set up two travel companies that craft personalised holidays for guests, TakeMe2India and TakeMe2NewZealand. 'Our roots in India help us to sell the "real" India better to Kiwis,' he explains. 'Our successful integration here has given us an innate advantage in promoting New Zealand more effectively. And as immigrants we're sensitive to different cultures, as much as we are curious about them. That helps us in surprising our guests during our tours.'

In short, for individual businesses and organisations, the diversity dividend consists of a wider pool of talent, added creativity and innovation, greater adaptability and better access to new markets near and far.

The diversity dividend for businesses can be measured. Consultants at McKinsey found that companies in the US, the UK, Canada and Latin America that were in the top quartile for racial and ethnic diversity were 35 percent more likely to have above-average financial returns. They concluded that 'diversity is probably a competitive differentiator that shifts market share towards more diverse companies over time.'[44] An updated study across twelve countries found similar results.[45]

Companies in London whose management is diverse are more likely to introduce product innovations than those with homogeneous 'top teams'.[46] Across the UK such companies are also more likely to introduce process innovations.[47] The Boston Consulting Group found that companies with more diverse management teams are more innovative, resulting in 19 percent higher revenues.[48] Deloitte identified an 80 percent performance boost at three large Australian businesses when levels of diversity and inclusion were high. In the US, companies with an ethnically diverse workforce have increased sales revenue, more customers, a higher market share and greater profits.[49] More diverse US companies also tend to be faster growing.[50] Publicly traded US companies that meet nine diversity yardsticks – including on gender, LGBTQ and disabilities as well as race and ethnicity – announce an average of two extra products per year, whereas other major companies average only one. Companies with pro-diversity policies were also more resilient in terms of innovation during the 2008 financial crisis.[51] In short, diversity boosts the bottom line.

Making the most of diversity

The diversity dividend can be huge, but it's not automatic. It needs to be earned. To capitalise on it, organisations need to change their culture, encourage communication and manage cultural differences.

For a start, organisations need to truly value people's diversity. Those that view hiring a diverse workforce as a legal obligation, a box-ticking exercise or as window dressing for corporate social responsibility are missing the point. To make the most of diversity, you have to do more than just pay lip service to it: you have to genuinely believe that it is good for your business and change your culture accordingly. You need to go out and hire the best people for your team and then make them feel welcome. You need to value people's differences, not try to stifle them; treat them as an asset, not a cost; and make sure that everyone feels included as part of the team.

Communication is key. You have to encourage all team members to speak their minds, listen to what they have to say and be open to different points of view. Diverse teams need to share their perspectives, not keep them to themselves. Managers then have to follow through, make changes and invest in new ideas.

Organisations also have to help everyone fulfil their potential: make the best use of people's skills, invest in training and offer opportunities for promotion. To reap the diversity dividend, you have to bring people together, believe in them, value them and match words with actions.

As well as cultivating diversity, you need to manage it properly. Diversity is beneficial partly because it challenges people, but that creative discomfort can also lead to misunderstanding, mistrust, a lack of cooperation and even conflict. If it isn't properly managed, diversity can generate more heat than light. That's why managers need to communicate clearly and make sure everyone in their organisation shares its goals and values. They need to be aware of the potential for misunderstanding and conflict, and try to manage it.

Seemingly small things are sometimes really important. Pointing with one finger is considered rude in some cultures; Asians typically use their entire hand. In Western culture, eye contact means you're attentive and honest; in many other cultures, it seems disrespectful or rude.

As well as being culturally aware, you need to accept that evaluating different perspectives takes time. Be patient in allowing diverse teams to gel and build trust. People need to learn to appreciate each other's differences and the benefits of working together. There's no single right way to do this: teams build trust in different ways.

Making the most of the diversity dividend is also about society as a whole, as Chapter 19 on integration discusses.

So far we've shown that immigrant entrepreneurs, international students, foreign talent and diverse teams provide outsized economic dividends. But with the big exception of immigrant entrepreneurs, most of these people tend to be highly educated. What about the less-educated migrants we hear so much about?

11

DRUDGERY DIVIDEND

Mohammed arrived in Malta by accident. 'Three hundred of us got on a boat in Libya in 2011. We were heading for Italy, but the outboard motor failed so we stopped in Maltese waters,' he explains. 'The Maltese navy saved us from drowning.'[1]

Back in his native Ivory Coast, Mohammed – not his real name – was a taxi driver in the capital, Yamoussoukro. Like many Ivorians, he fled the country after it was wracked by two bloody civil wars in quick succession. When he landed in Malta, he was locked up in a detention centre – standard practice for unwanted arrivals, including asylum seekers, at the time. 'Getting out of detention is the biggest challenge,' he says. 'But if you make it, you are saved.'

Fortunately, a year later Mohammed was granted 'subsidiary protection' – a form of asylum with fewer rights than full refugee status – due to the ongoing turmoil in Ivory Coast. He moved to an open asylum centre. 'There I was able to move freely and I could work,' he explains. He worked first as a tiler then as an assistant storekeeper in a four-star hotel in Bugibba, a popular tourist resort on the northern coast of the island.

While the coronavirus pandemic has clouded the immediate outlook, tourism in Malta has been booming. This small Mediterranean island just south of Sicily is blessed with sunshine, seaside and scenery – and foreigners can't get enough of it. A country with less than half a million residents welcomed 2.6 million foreign tourists in 2018, a quarter of them from Britain. They spent €2.1 billion (£1.8 billion) – more than €4,200 (£3,600) per Maltese resident. But without migrant workers such as Mohammed to do the menial work that most Maltese no longer want to do, it wouldn't be possible to sustain Malta's tourism boom and the country would be much poorer.

Along with the tourism industry, the economy as a whole has been in fine fettle. It expanded around 7 percent a year between 2013 and 2018.[2] With businesses crying out for workers, pretty much every employable local who wanted a job could get one. The unemployment rate plunged to a mere 3.5 percent in 2019, with most of those being people between jobs. So Malta increasingly called on foreign workers too.

Malta has had the highest immigration rate in the EU each year since 2014.[3] In 2018 alone, some 17,000 additional migrants arrived, boosting the population by 3.6 percent – a net migration rate ten times Britain's.[4] It's equivalent to 2.4 million extra immigrants a year pitching up in the UK, or 20 million in the US.

Many of the newcomers are European, notably Italians seeking opportunities outside their own stagnant economy. A few are wealthy non-Europeans who can, in effect, buy an EU passport by investing one million euros in Malta and becoming citizens a year later. Increasingly the new arrivals have also included migrants and asylum seekers from Asia and Africa. They have been attracted by Malta's sizzling economy and helped to fuel it too. 'We cannot do without foreign workers,' exclaims Clyde Caruana, the head of Jobsplus, Malta's employment agency.[5]

With tourism booming and the population rising fast, property development has been on the up too. Cranes and construction sites sprouted up everywhere. There too, many of the workers are African.

Souleymane arrived in Europe from Togo in 2015 on a rescue boat that docked in Italy. After finally obtaining a two-year residence permit, he travelled to Malta on a ferry to try to find a job in the informal economy. The West African migrant now works on a construction site. It's hard work – eight hours a day, six days a week – for pay that seems low for Maltese workers: 500 euros a month.[6] But whereas his wages are only a third of the average salary in Malta,[7] they are more than five times what he could earn in Togo. Even allowing for the higher cost of living in Malta, Souleymane is much better off. No wonder he is willing to do difficult work that locals with higher aspirations and better-paid alternatives spurn.

While people who move from a poor country to a rich one may increase inequality within that country – because they start off at the bottom of the income scale – their moving reduces inequality globally because even if they are relatively poor in a rich country they are still better off than before.

Migrants such as Mohammed and Souleymane generate a drudgery dividend for the societies that welcome them. They are willing to do dull, dirty and difficult jobs that locals dislike. Undesirable as their tasks may be, such migrants provide a vital service: the economy would grind to a halt without cleaners or construction workers. Nor would we have food on our tables without foreign farm workers. Immigrants also complement local workers, who are able to do better-paid, higher-skilled jobs instead. And their hard work may reduce the cost of services such as childcare, food preparation, house cleaning and building work, making them more affordable to locals.

Unlike many Western politicians, then Prime Minister Joseph Muscat recognised less-skilled migrants' contribution to the Maltese economy. 'Like every country which becomes wealthy, we need to attract people who do certain kinds of work, and these people are themselves creating wealth,' he said. It's mutually advantageous. 'I've found happiness here,' Mohammed says. 'I was going to Italy but landing in Malta has been lucky for me. They saved my life and gave me work. I can only give thanks.'

While migrants improve their lot doing jobs at which locals turn up their noses, locals are able to do more appealing, better-paid jobs instead. For instance, while migrants such as Mohammed work in basic, support roles in the tourism sector, Maltese increasingly work in sales and service roles. Moreover, both migrant workers and Maltese ones have benefited from rising wages.[8] In short, migrants are making the Maltese more moneyed.

Drudgery isn't disappearing

Contrary to public perceptions, less than a third of migrants in rich OECD countries in 2015–16 had a low level of education, a proportion that has fallen considerably since the turn of the century.[9] While people in rich countries often view migrants doing low-paid, less-skilled jobs as a burden and a threat, the Maltese model highlights how they can in fact provide a sizeable drudgery dividend.

A common misconception is that migrants' economic contribution depends on their skill level, with highly skilled ones making a positive contribution and less-skilled ones having a negligible – or even negative – impact. But in fact migrants' labour-market contributions depend largely on whether their characteristics are different and complementary to those of the local workforce. That includes a greater willingness to do menial work. As the coronavirus crisis has highlighted, jobs such as stacking supermarket shelves, delivering parcels and cleaning hospitals may not be glamorous, but they are essential for society's wellbeing.

Another misconception is that in our increasingly high-tech economies, low-skilled jobs are disappearing. In fact, many of the occupations with the most long-term job growth are relatively low-skilled and low-paid. In the US, thirteen of the twenty occupations with the most projected job growth between 2018 and 2028 pay less than the median wage.[10] They include fast-food restaurant workers and their supervisors, as well as cooks, waiters and waitresses; janitors and cleaners; construction and freight labourers; and landscaping and groundskeeping workers. (Increased demand for less-skilled jobs associated with ageing is discussed in the next chapter on the demographic dividend.)

In Britain, three of the top ten occupations with the highest projected employment growth between 2014 and 2024 are relatively low-skilled.[11] While mostly associated with care for the aged, they also include teaching assistants. Nursery assistants are also in the top twenty. Across the EU, there is also projected to be a big rise in employment between 2016 and 2030 for some low-skilled jobs, notably labourers in the mining, construction, manufacturing and transport industries, as well as cleaners.[12]

Immigrants in the US are much likelier than locals to work in low-wage service occupations and jobs involving producing, transporting and materials, while locals are more likely to work in sales and office jobs and in management and professional jobs.[13] Immigrants are particularly prevalent in physically demanding manual labour such as farm work. Without foreign farm hands, food would go unpicked.[14] In Australia, more than half of those employed in poultry processing are immigrants.[15]

Perhaps the most pernicious misconception is that less-skilled migrants 'steal' the jobs and depress the wages of less-skilled local workers. That wasn't the case in Malta's booming economy, but might it be so elsewhere?

Stealing our jobs?

'They're taking our jobs. They're taking our manufacturing jobs. They're taking our money. They're killing us,' Donald Trump said in July 2015 about Mexican immigrants.[16] In 2009, Gordon Brown, then the UK's Labour prime minister, infamously called for 'British jobs for British workers', echoing an old slogan from the racist National Front.[17] A Conservative successor, Theresa May, claimed in 2016 that people 'out of work or on lower wages because of low-skilled immigration' found life unfair.[18]

It may seem obvious that every job filled by a migrant is one less for a local. But there isn't a fixed number of jobs to go around. When women entered the labour market in large numbers after the Second World War, many men thought that women would deprive them of jobs. But that didn't happen. Most women now work and so do most men.

People don't just take jobs; they also create them – when they spend their wages, which boosts demand for the people who produce and sell the goods and services that they consume, as well as in complementary lines of work. Migrant construction workers such as Souleymane create jobs for the locals who supervise them as well as for those who sell them building supplies – not to mention accountants and architects. Also, foreign child-minders enable local women to go back to work.[19]

Many countries have many more immigrants than they did in 2000, yet until the coronavirus crisis the unemployment rate was at historic lows in the US, the UK and Germany. Employment among the UK-born was at record highs. Elsewhere in Europe, unemployment had fallen sharply in recent years. It is hard to argue that migrants as a whole are depriving locals of jobs.

More specifically, newcomers' direct impact on local workers depends on whether their skills and attributes are complementary and how the labour market and the economy adjust to change. In effect, critics of immigration often hold the misguided belief that newcomers compete directly with existing workers and that the economy never adapts to their arrival.[20]

Imagine a town with a single factory that employs generic workers and is operating at full capacity. New identikit workers arrive. Since they compete directly with existing workers, wages will tend to be driven down. Assume that the factory does not expand and hey presto, a rise in the labour supply harms local workers. This simplistic example may sound ridiculous, yet it is akin to economic models that assume that migrants and locals are perfect substitutes, hold the capital stock fixed and thereby conclude that migrants drive down wages. Only by using such ludicrous assumptions does leading immigration sceptic George Borjas conclude that newcomers have depressed the wages of US-born high-school dropouts, a flawed finding that has been comprehensively debunked.[21]

Even if newcomers were perfect substitutes for existing workers and there were no vacancies in the economy, they would harm existing workers only temporarily. In countries with a flexible labour market such as Britain or America, wages would fall; in those with an inflexible one such as Italy, where wages and employment cannot readily adjust, unemployment would rise. But migrants' arrival would also create opportunities for profitable investment. Once business investment responded to the increased supply of workers and their higher demand for goods and services, the demand for labour would rise, and with it wages and employment.

In practice, it is unlikely that local workers are harmed even temporarily because migrants are not perfect substitutes for them. The newcomers, after all, are foreign: they speak the local language less well, have less knowledge of local norms and working practices, have fewer job contacts, may have different attributes (such as a willingness to work longer, more unsociable hours) and their foreign qualifications may be less valued by employers. Even migrants with similar education, skills and experience to local workers are at most imperfect substitutes for them and compete only indirectly with them in the labour market.

It is possible that some local workers may lose out from migration. An unreliable builder who does shoddy work may find himself out of work and need to up his game or retrain. But even if Polish builders are willing to work for lower wages than local ones, they don't necessarily deprive British brickies of work. If home repairs are cheaper, more people can afford house improvements, while reliable, established builders may be able to charge richer clients more (and employ Polish workers).

Often, immigrants take jobs that local workers can't or won't do, and thus do not compete with them at all. Even young Britons and Americans with few skills don't want to pick fruit or vegetables, while university students who might once have helped pick the harvest during their summer holidays now seek career-enhancing internships instead. Even during the

2008–09 crisis when unemployment spiked in the US, Americans didn't want to work on farms; indeed, seasonal migrant farmworkers created additional jobs for Americans by boosting farm output.[22] Likewise, even when unemployment soared in 2020 due to the coronavirus crisis, hardly any locals in Britain were willing to pick crops.[23]

Far from competing with local workers, immigrants typically complement their efforts, raising their productivity and thus lifting their wages. Foreign builders may use different techniques from which their local colleagues may learn (and vice versa). They may also work harder and spur their local colleagues to do so too. And a foreign childminder may allow a local doctor to return to work, where her productivity may be enhanced by hard-working foreign nurses and cleaners.

Longer term, the economy may adapt in other ways. The pattern of migration is likely to change the mix of goods and services produced and the technologies employed. An influx of less-skilled labour will tend to cause sectors that intensively employ such people to expand. Britain now has many car washes where immigrants do the cleaning by hand. Were those migrants not around, it is doubtful that locals would be doing the cleaning; Britons would probably make do with the mechanical cleaners at petrol stations that scratch your car and don't clean the interior. Some argue that Britain would be better off without such low-productivity jobs, but that is wrong-headed. Immigrants are earning more than in their home country by doing such jobs, thereby raising their productivity. The productivity and wages of British people who would never do such jobs is largely unaffected, but they benefit from cheaper, better car washes. Like other forms of international trade, migration enables countries to specialise in what they do best, making them better off.

Examining the evidence

Many Western workers have had a difficult time over the past decade. Allowing for inflation, median wages in the UK in 2019 were still below their pre-crisis peak in 2008.[24] In the US, wages for locals who lack a university degree have stagnated for much longer. After inflation, the wages of those with a high-school diploma fell by 8 percent between 1980 and 2014, while those with no diploma at all suffered a 14 percent fall in their real wages.[25]

This is terrible for the workers concerned and corrosive for society as a whole. It's a big reason for the rise of populist nationalism. It contributed to the Leave vote among working-class voters outside London and other big cities. And it helped foster the anger and despair that propelled President Trump into the White House. But does it have anything to do with low-skilled immigration?

The economic evidence suggests it doesn't. In the US, Giovanni Peri found that across the country immigrants didn't contribute to the decline in wages of local non-graduates between 1970 and 2014.[26] On the contrary, he found that locally immigration was associated with higher average wages.

In the UK, studies typically find that immigration boosts average wages and that any negative impact on the wages of the lowest-paid is negligible.[27] EU migrants had little or no impact on UK-born workers' pay.[28] In any case, low-paid workers have enjoyed significant pay increases in recent years thanks to the rises in the minimum wage.

Even where the influx of foreign workers has been huge, no negative impact can be discerned. At the turn of the century, hardly any self-employed construction workers in London were from Eastern Europe; by 2016 more than half were. Yet the earnings of self-employed builders born in the UK rose relative to the national average over that period.[29]

Furthermore, immigration doesn't reduce the training of local workers, the UK government's independent Migration Advisory Committee (MAC) has found.[30] Indeed, skilled migrants may have a positive impact on the training available to the UK-born workforce.

Nor do migrants deprive locals of work. 'There is little or no impact of immigration on the employment or unemployment of existing workers,' according to an exhaustive 2018 study of the impact of EU migration on the UK economy by the MAC.[31] Likewise the US National Academies of Sciences finds that 'the impact of immigration on the wages of natives overall is very small.'[32] Any negative effects are concentrated on those most similar to newcomers, such as Hispanic high-school dropouts who speak poor English.

Migrants may not harm locals overall, but might they harm low-skilled locals in particular locations? Many studies in many countries conclude not. But sophisticated critics argue that if migrants tend to move to locations where there is increased demand for labour, the fact that wages are unchanged is inconclusive; local wages may otherwise have risen. Moreover, when comparing employment in a locality before and after migrants' arrival, studies may jumble together the employment of locals who stayed put with those who moved from other parts of the country and miss out those who moved away.

Fortunately, a groundbreaking study by Giovanni Peri and Mette Foged that addresses both those objections confirms that low-skilled migrants don't harm low-skilled locals. They look at the impact of refugees on the Danish labour market between 1991 and 2008. Those refugees arrived for political reasons and the authorities dispersed them around the country without taking account of their skills or local economic conditions. And since Denmark has an integrated register of where particular people are employed, the academics can identify the impact on locals in a particular locality. They found that an influx of low-skilled refugees, who mostly did not speak Danish and filled elementary and manual labour positions, caused unskilled and low-skilled locals to shift towards more complex, higher-skilled, non-manual work, thereby boosting their wages, employment and occupational mobility.[33] Peri and Foged argue that an influx of low-skilled newcomers ought to have a similarly positive impact in other economies with a flexible labour market, such as the US and the UK.

Flexible labour markets can adjust rapidly to even very large inflows of people. After the collapse of the Soviet Union, more than 710,000 Russian Jews emigrated to Israel, increasing its working-age population by over 15 percent in seven years. While they weren't strictly speaking refugees, they were admitted for political reasons – because Jews everywhere have an automatic right to settle in Israel – not economic ones. While many were skilled, they had no experience of a capitalist economy and most spoke no Hebrew. Yet even this very large influx of political migrants – equivalent to fifty million foreigners of working age arriving in the EU, or thirty million in the US – did not harm Israeli workers.[34] Between 1989 and 1997 unemployment among locals fell considerably. The ex-Soviets soon found jobs too: by 1997 their employment rate was comparable to that of locals. While local wages were initially depressed, by 1997 they had recovered to where they would have been without the mass immigration.[35]

Many European countries have inflexible labour markets, however. High wage floors may price unskilled workers out of work. The near-impossibility of firing workers on permanent contracts who underperform may deter employers from taking the risk of employing those whose productivity is uncertain, such as young people and immigrants.[36] It may also create dual labour markets, where some workers enjoy permanent contracts and others are trapped on temporary ones that offer less protection. In inflexible labour markets, there is a higher risk that migrants will end up unemployed.

Low-skilled workers such as Mohammed and Souleymane deliver a sizeable drudgery dividend, providing vital services, doing jobs that locals don't want to do and enabling locals to do better jobs that they prefer. Contrary to fears that they harm locals' job prospects, studies find that they neither displace locals from jobs nor depress their wages.

Perhaps most importantly, remember the point I made in Chapter 6. Narrow studies that look only at the labour market miss out the broader benefits of migration. Some people who start off as poor labourers set up successful businesses. Some parents who go back to work thanks to foreign childminders go on to patent great new ideas. Even in occupations that don't require formal qualifications, having a diversity of experiences and perspectives can improve team performance. Allowing for all that, as the IMF study did, an influx of low-skilled migrants tends to boost local living standards significantly. And young migrants also provide a hefty demographic dividend, as the next chapter explains.

12

DEMOGRAPHIC DIVIDEND

t is time for the exercise class at Shintomi nursing home in Tokyo. The elderly residents, seated in a semi-circle, follow the fitness instructor's movements intently. Left arm forward – and clasp. Right arm forward – and unclasp. Left arm up – and clasp. Right arm up – and wave. A woman gets her moves mixed up and giggles. As the class ends, a man shuffles forward and pats the instructor on the head. The instructor – a humanoid robot called Pepper – beams.

Japan has the world's greyest population. Nearly three in ten people are aged sixty-five or older and some 5.5 million of the country's 127 million people need nursing care.[1] While demand for care is soaring, the working-age population is shrinking fast and fewer young Japanese people want to work in a nursing home. Since Japan has been loath to let in immigrants to look after the elderly, it has a huge and growing shortage of carers. So the government is pumping millions into developing care robots which nursing homes are increasingly deploying to try to fill the gap.

Shintomi is both a showcase and a testing ground for all these newfangled technologies. Twenty different kinds of robot help care for its elderly residents. Some resemble intelligent machines. Resyone, a robotic bed developed by electronics company Panasonic, responds to patients' voice commands and transforms into a wheelchair that resembles a business-class aeroplane seat. Others, such as Pepper, provide more human-like interaction. Like an android version of Alexa, the smart speaker made by Amazon, Pepper can now conduct rudimentary conversations as well as lead exercise classes. Still others offer emotional support. Like a loveable pet, Paro, a furry robotic seal, responds to patients' petting by whimpering, blinking its cute eyes and wriggling its body.

Would you want to be cared for by a robot when you are old and frail? The notion that robots could provide elderly people with human-like care may seem creepy, degrading or even dangerous. Anxious types may fret that the 'hybrid assisted limb' that helps carers lift patients is called HAL – like 'the most reliable computer ever made' that sets about killing the crew in Stanley Kubrick's classic film *2001: A Space Odyssey*. Science fiction these days is full of stories of robots running amok, from the murderous home-assistant 'synths' of the TV series *Humans* to treacherous Ava, the female humanoid in the film *Ex Machina*.

But Shintomi residents mostly seem delighted by their robotic companions. 'These robots are wonderful,' says Kazuko Yamada after an exercise class with Pepper.[2] 'I can talk to them without being too careful about what I say,' says another elderly lady.[3] 'When I first petted it [Paro the seal], it moved in such a cute way. It really seemed like it was alive,' chuckles Saki Sakamoto. 'Once I touched it, I couldn't let go.'

Where Japan leads, other rich, ageing societies are starting to follow. Paro is now in use in more than thirty countries. It seems popular everywhere, including Britain. 'No, I don't feel foolish petting Paro,' says Freda Harris, a resident of Longlands Care Home in Daventry, Northamptonshire. 'When you've got no family, you've got to have somebody, haven't you.'[4] Tellingly, she refers to Paro as somebody, not something. 'He's made me very, very happy,' she says, as researchers take Paro away. 'I shall miss you [*sic*] very very much.'

But whatever your opinion of robot carers, they are unlikely to replace humans any time soon. For a start, they remain very expensive. Paro the seal costs 400,000 yen (£3,100) in Japan and around half as much again in Europe. Pepper the humanoid robot can cost £10,000 or more.[5] Shintomi receives substantial government subsidies to cover their costs. Moreover, there are still many things robots can't do – including basic physical tasks such as helping residents shave, get dressed and brush their teeth, to name but three. Safety and insurance issues are another obstacle.

Perhaps most importantly, robots are primarily complementing human care, not substituting for it. HAL helps carers do heavy lifting. Paro keeps patients with dementia happy while carers focus on other important tasks. Even at Shintomi, robots have not reduced staff costs or their work-ing hours so far.[6] Paro and Pepper are a palliative for Japan's pressing carer shortage, not a panacea. There is another solution, though.

Go, go gaijin

'You look very well,' says a foreign trainee to an elderly resident at the Enzeru no Oka nursing home in Fukaya, a city one hundred kilometres north-west of Tokyo.[7] 'Would you like some tea?' Seven foreign trainees – four Sri Lankan and three Chinese – now work there. 'People living in the home looked perplexed at first,' says Monali Tasheema, who arrived from Sri Lanka six months earlier. 'But I now feel that they are opening up to me.' Like their Japanese counterparts, the foreign trainees help the elderly residents eat, bathe and use the toilet.

Japan has long resisted admitting foreign care workers.[8] But even a country that had prioritised racial homogeneity over economic dynamism has concluded that it cannot rely on robots alone to cope with demo-graphic change. Faced with a projected shortfall of 380,000 care workers by 2025, the government is increasingly trying to attract foreign ones. Prime Minister Shinzo Abe said the shortage of workers was 'an urgent matter' and the country needed 'foreign workers as soon as possible'.[9] Under a new law that came into force in 2019, up to half a million new foreign workers are to be admitted in nursing care and other blue-collar sectors. While Britain, America and many other countries are slamming their doors to immigrants, Japan is opening up.

It is not always easy at first, but contact with foreigners eventually overcomes Japanese reticence. When another home first hired foreign carers in 2012, some elderly residents would summon them by shouting *gaijin* (foreigner), while others avoided contact with them. But Verlian Oktravina, a young Indonesian nurse, says her patients are now more curious than hostile. Yoko Yamashita, the director of Sakura no Mori care home in Kawaguchi, just north of Tokyo, says patients can see that for-eign workers are as good as Japanese ones: 'They accept them.' She herself was initially sceptical about hiring immigrants, but has since changed her mind.[10] Some 8 percent of the home's staff are now foreign.

Ultimately, economic need is decisive. Koichiro Goto, the director of a nursing home company in Kashiwa, a Tokyo suburb, was equally reluctant to hire immigrants. But Mother's Garden, a seventy-room home, had a waiting list of sixty would-be residents, while local job ads almost never attracted applicants. 'If we aren't helped by foreign workers,' he said, 'this business would not survive.'[11]

Young blood

Since every Western society is ageing fast, Japan provides a window on to our demographic future. In the absence of migration, the EU is projected to be as grey in 2040 as Japan was in 2018.[12] As societies age and workforces shrink, rich countries will need more young immigrants to help care for those who can no longer look after themselves. Foreign youngsters also complement older locals in the workforce and help pay for the growing ranks of pensioners – thus providing a hefty demographic dividend.

The US, Canada and Australia have a younger demographic profile than Europe does, but they are also ageing fast. Their population most likely to need care – those aged eighty and older – is, without migration, set to more than double between 2020 and 2040.[13] In the EU, it is set to leap by more than half to 47 million in 2040.[14] In the UK, it is set to rise by two-thirds to 5.6 million. While population projections are always uncertain, short-term ones that exclude migration are much more predictable: all the people in question have already been born and barring a particularly lethal epidemic or catastrophic war their numbers in 2040 are pretty certain. While the coronavirus pandemic is much more dangerous for the elderly than for those of working age, it seems unlikely to make a significant difference to the overall demographic balance. Indeed, future medical breakthroughs may keep many old people alive for longer.

Care workers are already the occupation with the fastest long-term employment growth in rich countries and demand for them is set to continue soaring. In the US, four of the top ten occupations with the most projected job growth between 2018 and 2028 are associated with ageing.[15] Many are low-paid, less-skilled roles such as personal care aides (in first place), home health aides (fourth) and medical assistants (tenth). Others are better-paid, more skilled roles such as registered nurses. In Canada, nurses and nursing aides are the occupations that will see the biggest growth in the years ahead;[16] in Australia, carers and aides are.[17]

Across the EU, substantially increased demand for health professionals, their associates and personal care workers is also foreseen between 2016 and 2030.[18] In Britain, four of the top twelve occupations with the most projected employment growth between 2014 and 2024 are associated with ageing.[19] Care workers and home carers are first, followed by nurses. Nursing assistants are sixth and doctors twelfth.

Like in Japan, care homes in many other countries are desperately short-staffed and cannot find suitable applicants locally.[20] The UK is expected to have a shortfall of 70,000 care workers by 2025.[21] Since immigrants would be happy to do jobs that young locals don't want to do, as Chapter 11 on the drudgery dividend explained, admitting them would benefit older people who need care as well as family members who don't have the time or the means to help, and who might otherwise have to quit their jobs to care for their parents. It would also help stretched elderly care budgets. In the UK immigrants already account for 18 percent and rising of the social-care workforce.[22] In Italy they account for more than half.[23] Elsewhere in the EU, migrants are increasingly important for social-care provision too.[24]

As well as caring for the elderly, young migrants provide an additional demographic dividend: age diversity. Chapter 10 on the diversity dividend explained how diverse workforces where people with different skills, perspectives and experiences complement and learn from each other tend to outperform, and one important form of diversity is age. Healthy economies and most businesses need a workforce with a wide range of skills and ages: older, more experienced types, as well as young, dynamic workers who are physically and mentally at their peak, keen to work hard to get ahead and can help generate new ideas about how to do things better.

Immigrants tend to be young – most arrive in their twenties or early thirties – and their youth is a perfect fit for the ageing workforces of Western societies (and those of other rapidly greying societies, notably China). With the generation born since the turn of the century particularly small, the decline in the working-age population will be concentrated among those aged twenty to forty. Moreover, the average age of the population is rising fast. In Japan the median age is already forty-eight and without migration it will rise to fifty-five by 2040.[25] Without migration, Germany's median age would hit fifty in 2040, while the UK's would be forty-five and the US's forty-three.[26] Even if, as is likely, more people continue working into their late sixties and even their seventies out of choice or necessity, thereby alleviating the demographic decline of the workforce, only the arrival of newcomers can inject youthful dynamism into the workforce, since even an unlikely baby boom would not yield additional local workers until the 2040s.

Local rejuvenation

The Children of Golzow is a famous documentary series in Germany. Starting in 1961 an East German film crew filmed eighteen residents of the town at regular intervals from childhood to adulthood. The series continued even after the Berlin Wall fell and Germany was reunited. But since then the population of Golzow, which lies near the country's eastern border with Poland, has dwindled. 'The big collective farm here closed. People lost their jobs. Younger folks started moving to the cities, and suddenly there were empty houses,' explains Gaby Thomas, the director of the primary school that featured in the series.[27] Eventually, a lack of children threatened the school with closure.

To save the school and revitalise the village, the school director and mayor Frank Schütz came up with a controversial idea: welcome Syrian refugees to the town. 'Madness,' the hairdresser said. 'Impossible,' a farmer added. 'I thought, "This can't work, they have a different religion, our children won't speak proper German any more,"' said Marco Seidelt, whose eleven-year-old son, Davey, suddenly had three Syrians in his class.

Despite this initial scepticism, the arrival, with their parents, of ten Syrian refugee children since 2015 has visibly changed the town of 800 people for the better. Previously vacant properties now hum with life. All six Syrian parents work, one of them in a nursing home that lacked local staff. The newcomers, who have all made an effort to learn German, are always quick to volunteer to spruce up the town. Above all, 'the Syrians saved our school,' says the mayor.[28] Even sceptics have been won over. 'I didn't expect it, but they are really well integrated,' says Marco Seidelt.

The rejuvenation of Golzow is a microcosm of the much broader opportunities for immigrants to reinvigorate declining towns and places that feel 'left behind' by economic and social change and politically neglected.

Dayton, Ohio, is globally renowned as the city where the Dayton Agreement that ended the war in Bosnia and the former Yugoslavia was signed in 1995. But locally it had until recently become synonymous with post-industrial decline. Like many towns in America's Rust Belt, its population and economy had shrivelled as local manufacturing jobs disappeared. Between 1960 and 2010, the local population nearly halved to 140,000.

But then newcomers started to arrive, first from Latin America and Asia and more recently refugees from countries such as Uzbekistan, Rwanda and the Democratic Republic of Congo.[29] Instead of resenting or rejecting the immigrants, local civic leaders decided to welcome them and try to attract more. They did so partly for humanitarian reasons, but also for self-interested ones: to reinvigorate their dying town.

In 2011 the local government adopted a 'Welcome Dayton: Immigrant Friendly City' initiative that has been hugely successful.[30] The town's population, which had fallen by 15 percent between 2000 and 2010, has since stabilised.

The initiative has made a big difference at very little cost.[31] It involves three municipal employees trying to help newcomers in a variety of ways: find jobs, learn to interact with community institutions, establish trust with local police and get used to life in a strange new country. An annual soccer tournament is particularly popular. Above all, it involves a community pitching together to welcome newcomers into their midst.

Welcome Dayton works. The local economy was revitalised.[32] The newcomers started new businesses and provided additional sales for local ones. Their talents attracted new employers to the town. Depressed house prices perked up. Most locals appreciate the newcomers, with a majority saying they would be happy for an immigrant family to move in next door to them.[33]

Dayton is a model for other small towns across the West where the population and the economy are in decline. Far from being a threat, immigrants can help to save them. Indeed, even big cities such as Detroit, Michigan's depressed Motor City, are starting to take a leaf out of Dayton's book.[34]

More broadly, immigrants can provide a shot in the arm for local economies – a demand dividend it could be called.[35] Conversely, businesses in small towns that incur immigration raids tend to suffer afterwards.

Paying for pensioners

The demographic dividend that young newcomers can provide to depressed towns with declining populations highlights their broader benefit to society: helping to support the increasing number of pensioners that shrinking local workforces will struggle to sustain. The IMF estimates that demographic ageing will cause annual government spending on pensions and healthcare to rise by an average of 5 percent of GDP across advanced economies by 2050.[36]

The baby-boom generation born in the two decades after the Second World War was particularly large and the previous, war-depleted generations were particularly small, so baby-boomer taxpayers had relatively few pensioners to support. But subsequent generations are much smaller, while baby boomers are living longer than previous generations. As a result, shrinking working-age populations have increasing numbers of pensioners to support. Migrants offset that; four-fifths of those in OECD countries are of working age.[37]

Without migration, the working-age population would already be falling in both Europe and North America. Without further migration, that decline would accelerate in coming decades. The EU's population aged fifteen to sixty-four would fall by 45 million people between 2020 and 2040 – a 14 percent decline.[38] The UK's would decline by 5.5 percent over the same period, the US's by 4 percent.[39]

While the working-age population is set to shrink, the population aged sixty-five and older is swelling. In the EU, it is set to soar by 36 million people between 2020 and 2040 – a 35 percent rise;[40] in the UK, by nearly 5 million people or 39 percent; in the US, by 24 million or 43 percent.[41]

A rising pensioner population will place a huge strain on a shrinking working population. In the EU, there were 3.3 people of working age per older person in 2018. Without migration, there would be only two in 2040 – and only 1.8 in Germany and 1.6 in Italy. In the UK, the potential support ratio would fall from 3.5 to 2.3 and in the US from 3.9 to 2.6. In Japan, it is already only 1.8.[42]

Those figures underestimate the scale of the demographic challenge. Since many people of working age aren't working – they are studying, looking after children, unemployed, ill, disabled or have taken early retirement – there are actually already far fewer workers supporting each pensioner.

In 2019 Britain had 32.8 million people working and 12.1 million people of pensionable age – only 2.7 workers per pensioner.[43] Without reform, there may be only one worker per pensioner in Germany in 2030 and less than one in Italy.

Admitting young, taxpaying migrant workers is not the only way to mitigate the impact of ageing on dwindling local workforces. Reforms that boost long-term economic growth and living standards would provide greater resources to pay for the pensions, healthcare and social care costs of the elderly. But if societies want pensioners' incomes to keep pace with average earnings, a rising share of workers' pay would still need to be taxed away as the pensioner population rises. Insofar as pensioners provide for themselves through private pensions and their ownership of property and other assets, the redistribution would instead take place through the dividend, interest and rental income accruing to a retired rentier class.[44]

In addition, then, societies need to try to boost the economically active population and shrink the inactive one. Raising the official retirement age and encouraging older people to stay in work, at least part-time, would have the biggest impact. Encouraging more women to work and reducing unemployment more generally would also help – especially in southern European countries where relatively few women work and long-term unemployment is high. But however much countries reform, an influx of foreign workers would make it easier to sustain the growing ranks of pensioners over the next two decades.

While fully offsetting the impact of demographic ageing would require implausibly high inflows, immigration could mitigate it and help smooth the generational adjustment to the post-baby-boomer fertility slump. Migrants who come and work temporarily, as many do, help pay for today's pensioners' pension and healthcare costs without ever claiming a pension themselves. Those who stay and eventually grow old will still have alleviated the burden on today's dwindling workforce.

Take Germany. Without migration, its working-age population is set to fall by nearly ten million people – 18 percent – between 2020 and 2040. If it admitted half a million young migrant workers a year for the next twenty years, the working-age population would remain stable at 54 million. This would make it much easier to support the increase in the retirement-age population from 18 million to 24 million.

Or consider the UK. Without migration, its working-age population is set to fall by 2.3 million by 2040. If it admitted 200,000 young migrant workers a year over the next two decades, the working-age population would edge up by 1.7 million to 41 million. That would make it easier to support the increased retirement-age population of 17.2 million.

Newcomers also tend to have more babies than locals, providing an initial fertility boost too. But over time their fertility rates tend to fall to local rates.[45]

The alternatives to migration are either unpalatable – Hungary passed a so-called 'slave law' that could require workers to do compulsory overtime – or expensive, often ineffective and take a long time to have any impact, such as government bribes to have more babies (which Hungary is also doing). Providing free childcare and promoting a better work-life balance does support fertility in countries such as France and Sweden, but this is still below the replacement rate of 2.1.

In short, immigration is not an antidote to population ageing, but it can allev-iate the symptoms.

Full up?

Attracting more migrants to support the working-age population would provide a demographic dividend. Yet some object that their country is already full up. Far from alleviating demographic pressures, they argue that immigration exacerbates the problems of a rising population, such as higher house prices, more congested roads and urban sprawl. Infamously, Nigel Farage once blamed immigration for traffic on the motorway that delayed his arrival at an event.[46]

For nativists, banging on about population pressures provides a veneer of respectability for their xenophobia, although they object to rising populations only when the extra people come from abroad. For people stuck in traffic or facing a long commute on an overcrowded train because they can't afford to live near the city centre, it is a seductive argument. But is it correct?

Hardly. For a start, no country is running out of space. That is palpably true of places such as Australia, the US and Canada that have vast open spaces. But it is also true of the Netherlands, the most densely populated significantly sized European country. On average each resident enjoys

2,410 square metres each, although in practice most Dutch people congregate in cities, while the rest of the country is mostly farmland.[47]

While the UK has a much lower population density than the Netherlands, England has an equivalent one. As anyone who ventures out of cities can testify, there is still plenty of green and pleasant land. Again, most of the country is used for agriculture; only a tenth of the surface area is lived on and much less of that built on.[48] Housing (and gardens) take up scarcely more than 1 percent of the UK's land mass.[49] Even in cities such as London, there is still plenty of derelict land.

It is true that a rising population – whether from more immigrants or more local babies – raises population density. Some critics of immigration may genuinely prefer to have fewer people around, though if they opt to live in a big city, their personal choices suggest otherwise. But most people prefer to live in more densely populated places. They choose to rub shoulders in diverse cities, rather than spreading out in the countryside.

Unsurprisingly so: there is a bigger choice of jobs, more thrills and a greater mix of people to meet – and as Chapter 10 on the diversity dividend documented, dense, diverse cities are also economically more productive. The London Borough of Islington, where I live, happens to be the most densely populated district in the UK, with more than 16,000 people per square kilometre.[50] It is hardly a hellhole. Indeed, Islington is much less densely populated than it was in 1939. Those who prefer to have more space and fewer people around have a huge choice of suburbs and surrounding countryside. In the event that fewer people choose to live in cities after the coronavirus pandemic, they will have plenty of less densely populated places to move to.

Higher population density need not entail increased congestion. Paris is much more densely populated than even Islington, yet its Metro is less crowded than London's Tube. The Netherlands has more people per square kilometre than Britain, yet its trains are less cramped. The real issue in Britain is decades of underinvestment in infrastructure, in part because the planning system makes it difficult and costly, but also because successive governments have been reluctant to invest. Yet since public infrastructure tends to raise the value of surrounding land, much of it could be self-financing through a tax on land values, as I argued in *European Spring*.[51]

Immigrants are also often blamed for high property prices. Yet often-poorer migrants, who tend to make do with much less space than locals, are scarcely the main cause of inflated property prices in cities such as London, New York, Sydney and Auckland. Moreover, newcomers tend to live in private rented accommodation, whereas a majority of locals are homeowners.[52] Shrinking household sizes, a greater availability of credit at low interest rates and government subsidies and tax breaks for home ownership are bigger factors in boosting demand for housing.

In any case, higher housing demand would not be a problem if the property market worked well: increased demand would lead to increased supply. The real problem is dysfunctional planning laws that choke off the supply of new housing in cities, driving up prices.[53] Britain also bans building on (often ugly) 'green belts' around towns. Far from being 'concreted over', these have more than doubled in size since the 1970s.[54] That, in turn, creates perverse incentives for developers and investors to speculate on further price rises, leading to repeated housing bubbles. There is therefore a strong case not for restricting immigration, but for loosening planning constraints. House prices in the south-east of England would have been around 30 percent lower in 2015 if the region had planning regulations of similar restrictiveness as the north-east of the country.[55] Studies find similar results for other big global cities.

In the US too, immigrants tend to contribute to rising house prices, until supply adjusts.[56] Those who value diversity may also pay more to live in vibrant, mixed neighbourhoods such as Brooklyn or Brixton. But while increased immigration may be a factor in rising house prices at a national level,[57] one UK study finds that at a local level increased immigration lowers house prices a little.[58]

The supply of social housing in the UK has fallen substantially in recent decades and migrants are often blamed for the resulting long waiting lists. Yet recent migrants are less likely to be in social housing than people born in the UK, while overall immigrants and locals are equally likely to be in social housing.[59] Contrary to public perceptions, there is no evidence that immigrants 'jump the queue' for social housing.[60] Indeed, migrants are less likely to be in social housing than people born in Britain who have equivalent demographic, economic and regional characteristics.[61]

In short, increasing population density has benefits as well as costs – and the latter can be mitigated or eliminated through investment and deregulation.

A final argument against migration is environmental. When people move from poor countries to rich ones, they may slightly increase global carbon emissions. But that is an argument for curbing climate emissions in rich countries, not denying poor immigrants the opportunity of a better life.

Also, as Robert Guest points out, migration stimulates scientific research, which will help curb global warming.[62] An Indian in North America is 28,000 times more likely to file a patent than in India. Moreover, people who move from poor countries to rich ones have fewer children than those who don't. For example, ethnic Somali women have an average of 6.2 kids in Somalia but only 2.4 in Norway. Allowing more migration to rich countries would reduce the future global population, and thus future emissions.

Young migrants can deliver a hefty demographic dividend, helping to care and pay for the elderly. More broadly, they can bolster public finances, providing a debt dividend, as the next chapter argues.

13

DEBT DIVIDEND

$26,500,000,000,000 – $26.5 trillion (£20.4 trillion) – and rising. That was what the US national debt amounted to in July 2020.[1] Split among some 330 million US residents, that amounts to $80,300 (£61,800) each. Divided among 123 million taxpayers, that is $215,450 (£165,730) each. Now imagine if you could spread the load of debts incurred for past spending over a wider tax base by welcoming 10 million new taxpayers. The debt per taxpayer would decline to $199,200 (£153,230) each. Newcomers would be providing existing US taxpayers with a debt dividend of $16,250 (£12,500) each.

Similar calculations can be performed in the UK and other countries. The UK's national debt in March 2020 was some £1.95 trillion.[2] That is equivalent to £28,890 per resident and £62,700 per income taxpayer.[3] Add two million new migrant taxpayers and the debt dividend to the 31.1 million existing taxpayers would be £3,800 each.

Most Western governments – Australia and Norway are notable exceptions – have accumulated huge debts. The coronavirus crisis is set to add trillions more. And governments also have vast unfunded liabilities – notably, promises to pay future pensions and commitments to provide future healthcare and social care to growing numbers of retirees that will either be broken or require huge tax rises. By one reckoning, these exceed $127 trillion (£98 trillion) in the US, or $385,000 (£296,000) per resident.[4] Widening the tax base through immigration would reduce the burden on current residents and permit lower taxes or higher public spending than otherwise.

That is true even if welcoming newcomers makes the government incur larger debts, so long as the resulting increase per newcomer is smaller than the existing average debt per local. But the good news is that it typically wouldn't. Newcomers who come to work are typically young, healthy and educated abroad. Most are in work. Many leave before claiming a pension. Overall, migrants tend to pay more in taxes than they take out in welfare benefits and public services – amplifying the debt dividend that arises arithmetically from widening the tax base.

In addition, migrants' work tends to enable locals to earn higher wages, either by becoming more productive in their existing job or by shifting to better-paid ones, as we saw in Chapter 9 on the deftness dividend and Chapter 11 on the drudgery dividend. That too raises more tax revenue and reduces welfare outlays.

It gets better. Since immigration tends to stimulate long-term economic growth and raise local living standards – not least thanks to the boost to innovation and entrepreneurship documented in Chapter 7 on the dynamism dividend and Chapter 10 on the diversity dividend – that gives a further boost to public finances by raising tax receipts and reducing welfare spending. As Chapter 6 noted, a 1 percentage point rise in the immigrant population tends to boost GDP per person by 2 percent longer term, and thus improve public finances too.

Critics who claim that newcomers tend to be a welfare burden have got it all wrong. Immigrants actually tend to subsidise locals, providing a hefty debt dividend. And since migrants more than pay their way, any additional pressures on public services are due to government mismanagement not immigrants themselves.

Welfare magnets?

Perhaps the most pernicious myth about migration is that newcomers move in order to sponge off welfare in rich countries. If welfare benefits in rich countries are higher than wages in poor countries, it may seem logical that they would act as a magnet for free-loading foreigners. And if enough migrants did move to claim welfare, the economic burden on local taxpayers would soon undermine political support for the welfare state. 'A strong magnetic effect, combined with an ineffective border control policy, can literally break the bank,' argues George Borjas, a Cuban-born economist who is a leading critic of immigration in the US.[5] Or as the American free-market economist Milton Friedman once put it, 'It's just obvious that you can't have free immigration and a welfare state.'[6] In fact, they are both mistaken.[7]

For a start, welfare benefits in the US are measly, so most migrants wouldn't be better off incurring the costs and risks of moving in order to try to claim them than staying at home working. The main federal welfare benefit – temporary assistance for needy families – typically provided only $447 (£344) a month for a family of three in 2019.[8] Allowing for the much higher cost of living in the US than in poorer countries, it is scarcely an incentive for people from, for example, Mexico to move. There the minimum daily wage is 102.68 pesos a day, which is around $11 (£8.50) in equivalent purchasing power terms.[9] Working six days a week, that adds up to $285 (£219) a month, or $570 (£438) for a couple working.

In the UK, universal credit is more generous but not princely: in 2019 it started at £251.77 a month for a single person aged under twenty-five, rising to £498.89 a month for a couple aged twenty-five or over.[10] An additional £231.67 a month was available for each child born since April 2017. It would hardly make economic sense for someone from a poor country to risk their life and pay many thousands of pounds to a smuggler to get to Britain in order to claim less than £60 a week in benefits.

While the US, the UK and many other countries have increased welfare benefits during the coronavirus crisis, such measures are only temporary. And even in cases where migrants would be better off on welfare in rich countries than back home – in Sweden, for instance, where the welfare state is very generous – it doesn't necessarily mean that people will move in order to claim benefits.

One reason is that newcomers can be – and often are – denied welfare benefits initially. Most immigrants in the US aren't entitled to welfare benefits for at least five years.[11] The same applies to most non-EU migrants in the UK; asylum seekers are entitled to £37.75 a week, which is scarcely enough to live on.[12]

While the UK was in the EU, EU migrants who were working were entitled to the same benefits as UK citizens; those who were not working could claim some benefits after three months of residence, but only for three months. In Sweden, immigrants who obtain a residence permit are entitled to a host of benefits after a year, while EU citizens who are looking for employment are entitled to many benefits immediately.[13]

But even in cases where migrants would be entitled to benefits, the self-selected minority of foreigners who are enterprising enough to incur the costs and risks of moving to another country would be even better off working – and it is implausible that they would suddenly lose their drive to better themselves once they arrive.

Indeed, if, as Borjas claims, the magnetic effect is 'strong', one would expect to find plenty of evidence of it. Yet even he is forced to concede that it is the 'hardest to corroborate'. In fact, there is no evidence for it.

The eastward enlargement of the EU provided a beautiful natural experiment to test the welfare-magnet hypothesis. When Poland and seven other relatively poor eastern European countries joined the EU in 2004, only three rich existing members gave the newcomers' citizens the right to work there freely immediately: Britain, Ireland and Sweden. Britain and Ireland have relatively meagre welfare benefits and also denied east Europeans access to them for the first year. Sweden has one of the most generous welfare states in the world and immigrants could access support immediately.

Legally, all 75 million people in those eight east European countries could have immediately stampeded to Sweden to claim benefits. Following Friedman's economic logic, nearly all ought to have done so. But in practice most east Europeans stayed put, while of those who did move almost all went to Britain and Ireland to work. The few thousand who moved to Sweden mostly did so to work too.[14] Contrary to public perception, there is no evidence that even Sweden's generous welfare state, let alone the UK's more meagre one, acts as a magnet for 'benefit tourists'. People move to better themselves, not bum off us.

Net contributors

Far from flocking to rich countries to sponge off the state, migrants tend to pay more in taxes than they take out in benefits and services.

Estimating the net impact on public finances of any person – let alone migrants as a whole – is fraught with difficulties. It depends on their characteristics – such as their age, education, employment status, income and number of children – and the tax and welfare system, such as tax rates and migrants' access to welfare benefits and public services. Nor is it a simple matter of totting up how much someone pays in taxes in a year and subtracting what they receive in direct benefits. The calculation depends heavily on which methodology is used, which time frame is considered, which expenditures and revenues are included, how they are allocated and whether individuals or households are considered.

Over a lifetime, people are generally a net burden on the state while they are in state-financed education; net contributors while they are working; and a burden again when they are retired or require very expensive medical services. Immigrants who arrive as young adults, having completed their education abroad and with a full working life ahead of them, are likely to be net contributors over their lifetime if they remain in work – even more so if they leave before claiming a pension. In a progressive tax system, people with higher incomes tend to pay more tax, so highly paid migrants may make a particularly big contribution to public finances.

Families with young children receive more benefits than single people: free public education, as well as child benefits. But this apparent subsidy to children is partly an artefact of a short time horizon and taking a household rather than an individual approach. If one considers children separately from their parents, couples with children do not receive bigger benefits than single people: everyone is subsidised as a child and most pay this back in taxes once they start working.

Any snapshot of the taxes that immigrants pay and the benefits they receive in any year is clearly less representative than a lifetime assessment, but this requires uncertain projections of their tax and benefit profile over future decades. The most comprehensive measure involves an intergenerational approach – estimating the net contribution that immigrants and all their descendants make – but this involves even greater assumptions.

Many studies have estimated the net fiscal impact of immigration. Calculations by the OECD show that in most rich countries migrants made a small positive net contribution to public finances in 2007–09.[15] Educated abroad, migrants are typically young and healthy and are also more likely to be employed than locals, while those who leave again typically don't claim a pension. Over their lifetimes, migrants who arrive before the age of forty are typically net contributors to public finances, even if they stay and claim a pension. This is true even in France, Germany and Nordic countries with very generous welfare states. Building on the OECD's work, Ian Goldin and Citibank find that migrants make large positive direct fiscal contributions in the US, the UK, Australia, France, Germany, Italy and Spain.[16]

A more recent study for the UK government's Migration Advisory Committee found that migrants from the European Economic Area (the EU plus Switzerland, Norway and Iceland, i.e. the EEA) who benefited from free-movement rights – the people about whom Friedman was most worried – made a net contribution to public finances in 2016–17 of £2,310 each.[17] In contrast, non-EEA migrants imposed a net cost of £840 a year each. Contrary to the belief that immigrants are more likely to claim welfare benefits, foreign nationals were less likely to do so, EU citizens especially so.[18]

Over a lifetime, migrants' net contribution really adds up. EEA migrants were estimated to make a total lifetime contribution of £78,000 each, while non-EEA migrants paid in £28,000 more than they took out. In total, the immigrants who were in the UK in 2016 were estimated to make a lifetime net contribution of £26.9 billion to UK public finances. That amounts to an additional debt dividend of £480 for each of the 56.3 million people in the UK in 2016 who were born there. Moreover, this study underestimates the impact of immigration on public finances, because it omits the boost to local earnings and economic growth that migrants provide, not to mention the debt-spreading effect highlighted at the start of the chapter.

The UK's independent Office for Budget Responsibility (OBR) has also estimated the long-term fiscal impact of anticipated future migration flows.[19] It found that if net immigration was high (245,000 people a year), net public debt would be 69 percent of GDP lower in 2067–68 than if net immigration was low (85,000 a year). That is a huge debt dividend.

In the US, the National Academies of Sciences, Engineering and Medicine estimated that if future immigrants resembled recent migrants in 2013 they would make a net lifetime contribution to public finances of $173,000 (£133,000), while if they resembled all migrants in the US their contribution would be $22,000 (£17,000).[20] Again, such calculations underestimate the fiscal contribution of immigrants because they ignore their broader boost to locals' wages and economic growth.

In Germany, foreigners were found to pay €3,300 (£2,800) more in taxes and social security than they received in benefits in 2012. The 6.6

million residents without a German passport boosted public finances by €22 billion (£19 billion) that year.[21] In France, reducing net migration would increase the tax burden of paying for an ageing population.[22] In Sweden, east European migrants make a positive contribution to public coffers.[23] In Australia, the 2014–15 cohort of permanent migrants, temporary skilled migrants and refugees were projected to contribute a net fiscal benefit of A$9.7 billion (£5.1 billion) over fifty years.[24]

Even undocumented immigrants can make a net positive fiscal contribution. The US Social Security Administration estimated that in 2010 earnings by unauthorised immigrants had a net positive impact on the programme's cash flow of roughly $12 billion (£9.2 billion).[25]

In short, migrants tend to be net contributors to public finances and can provide a particularly big fiscal boost by spreading the national debt burden over a wider tax base.

Pressure on public services?

Immigrants are often accused of placing a strain on public services such as healthcare and education. But since migrants typically more than pay their way, any pressures on local public services in places such as Boston, which we visited in Chapter 1, are due to the failings of those services. After all, if a British person moved from Liverpool to Lincolnshire and local services couldn't cope, who would be blamed?

Most mobility typically takes place within countries rather than between them. In Britain, for instance, 3.4 million people moved between local authority areas in the year to June 2018.[26] That dwarfs the fewer than one million people who moved across international borders over that period: 626,000 immigrants plus 351,000 emigrants.[27] Even without international migration, then, public services would need to be able to cope flexibly with a large number of people on the move. And without those immigrants, locals would enjoy less funding for public services or face higher taxes.

Moreover, the perception that public services are under greater strain in areas with more immigrants is often false. Immigrants in the UK don't make greater use of doctors and hospitals than people born in Britain.[28] NHS waiting times are actually lower in areas where there are more migrants.[29] Migrants are typically young and healthy, so make less use of the NHS than the typical Briton, while even older migrants are less likely to see a doctor.

Nor do immigrants tend to harm the quality of public services provided to British people. The presence of non-native English speakers in the classroom was found not to harm the performance of British pupils.[30] Indeed, Polish children actually have a positive effect on local pupils, perhaps because there is a stronger immigrant push to work hard at school. In London, whose multi-ethnic schools have greatly improved in recent years even as migration has increased, ethnic minority pupils typically have greater ambition, aspiration and work harder in school. As a result, local schools record higher than average exam results.[31]

As in universities, exposure to different cultures can broaden children's horizons. In the US, the presence of immigrants in high school increases the likelihood that local children complete school.[32] Similar results are found in the Netherlands.[33]

Last but not least, across rich OECD countries, a large proportion of medical staff are immigrants. More than a third of doctors, pharmacists and dentists in the UK are foreign-born, as are more than a fifth of nurses.[34] In the US, around one in five pharmacists, one in four dentists and nearly three in ten physicians were foreign-born.[35] In Canada, more than a third of doctors are immigrants.[36] As Chapter 9 noted, more than half of doctors in Australia are immigrants.[37] Indeed, many of the healthcare workers who have died while trying to save lives during the coronavirus pandemic were immigrants.[38]

In short, by helping to pay for and provide public services, migrants benefit OECD countries and provide a substantial debt dividend. They are subsidising locals, not scrounging off them. Indeed, so many immigrants work in rich countries that some worry about a medical brain drain from developing countries, an issue discussed in the next chapter on the development dividend.

14

DEVELOPMENT DIVIDEND

F ew people have made a bigger contribution to Africa's development than Mo Ibrahim. He founded one of the continent's most
dynamic mobile phone companies, transforming the lives of tens of
millions of Africans, most of whom previously had no phone at all. He has
set up a foundation to encourage better governance in Africa – including
by awarding a prize to heads of state who govern well and then transfer
power democratically. And he has championed the benefits of immigration and its contribution to development.

The spur for all his achievements as an entrepreneur, philanthropist
and thought leader? His frustration at the bureaucracy of working for British Telecom (BT), the UK's former telecoms monopolist.

Ibrahim was born in northern Sudan in 1946 – 'I'm Nubian,' he says
– and grew up in the Egyptian city of Alexandria. His father worked for a
cotton company: 'We were an average family. We never went hungry, but
we were not rich,' he explains. Fortunately, 'my mother had this obsession
with education as a way to move forward.'[1] Equipped with a degree in
electrical engineering, he returned to Sudan to work for Sudan Telecom
before moving to the UK in 1974 to do a master's degree and a doctorate
in mobile communications.

In 1983, when mobile phones were only just beginning, BT hired him
from academia as technical director of its Cellnet subsidiary, the UK's first
mobile phone provider. In the 1980s, mobile phones were basic, clunky
and eye-wateringly expensive – but unlike BT, Ibrahim realised their huge
potential.

'I never really planned or dreamed to be a businessman,' he explains. 'I went into business out of frustration. I just had to leave [BT]. They totally failed to realise the potential of cellular at that time.'[2] So in 1989 he quit and started his own business from his dining room: MSI, a consultancy that helped the cellular industry across Europe design their networks. 'I never looked back after then. Thanks to BT actually, a wonderful company for me.'

BT's failings were to be Africa's gain too. Leveraging his expertise in designing mobile phone networks, his industry contacts to staff his board, and later the $900 million (£700 million) proceeds from the sale of MSI, in 1998 Ibrahim started an African mobile phone provider that became known as Celtel.

'We saw Africa as a wonderful market potential for us. Because the image of Africa is bad – investors [were] afraid to go to Africa, that's why all the big telecoms companies refrained – and licences were available almost for free. We knew there were issues with Africa. But there was a huge gap between perception and reality… [and that was] a huge business opportunity. That's how we made our fortune.'

By the time Ibrahim sold Celtel for $3.4 billion (£2.6 billion) in 2005 – with the staff sharing $500 million (£380 million) of the proceeds – it had 24 million subscribers across fifteen African countries. 'We were the largest taxpayer in nine or ten African countries,' he recalls.[3]

Ibrahim didn't just make a fortune; he changed many Africans' lives for the better. Hardly any Africans had a phone before Celtel came along – there were fewer landlines in all of sub-Saharan Africa in 2000 than in Manhattan – so mobile phones had a much bigger economic impact in Africa than they did in rich countries. Suddenly, businesses had a means of finding out about market conditions and communicating with distant suppliers and customers. Fishermen could find out the market price of their catch and decide where best to land it. Nomads could work out the best time to bring their animals to market. Farmers could get weather forecasts that boosted crop yields. Taxi drivers could be booked. Unlike in the West at the time, mobile phones were also used to make payments, a boon for the vast majority of people in Africa who lacked a bank account. All of that boosted economic growth and living standards.[4]

As well as contributing to Africa's development as an entrepreneur, Ibrahim has done so as a philanthropist; he has pledged to give more than half his fortune away. The Mo Ibrahim Foundation focuses on improving governance and leadership in Africa, with the view that these lie at the heart of any tangible and shared improvement in Africans' quality of life. Its governance index benchmarks how every African country performs. Its $5 million (£3.8 million) prize rewards African leaders who strengthen development and democracy in their country, most recently Ellen Johnson Sirleaf, the former president of Liberia. Its annual governance weekend and other high-profile forums have immense convening power. And its leadership fellowships help mentor future African leaders.

Mo Ibrahim has made an exceptional contribution to African development. Moving to Britain gave him an education, business know-how, contacts and access to capital, all of which he used to build a groundbreaking business that boosted Africans' opportunities and quality of life. Now he is using his wealth to try to change Africa for the better. His achievements are a powerful example of the development dividend from migration.

While Ibrahim's contribution is exceptional, it is not unique. All migrants contribute to development – first and foremost their own and that of their family. As Bozi Kiekie's life story in Chapter 6 highlighted, migrants from poor countries who move to rich ones vastly increase their opportunities for a better life. Since development is ultimately about people not places – about enhancing people's ability to achieve their goals, as Nobel Laureate Amartya Sen put it[5] – the improvement in migrants' life chances is a very real contribution to development. And contrary to widespread fears about a 'brain drain', their countries of origin tend to benefit too, including through remittances – the money that migrants send home – and returnees.

The power of remittances

Marie lost her home and her livelihood in the devastating earthquake that struck Haiti in 2010. Her house on the outskirts of the capital, Port-au-Prince, was reduced to rubble, as was her busy restaurant in town. 'After the earthquake, we despaired,' she says. 'We didn't think there was a life for us any more.'[6]

Marie's family couldn't afford to rebuild their home, so they scraped together a shelter out of wood and corrugated metal. Her sister Annette and her family, who had moved to Boston, Massachusetts, five years earlier, weren't initially able to help either. As undocumented migrants, they couldn't work legally and so had barely enough to survive themselves.

But in the days after the earthquake, President Obama gave Haitians in the US 'temporary protected status' (TPS) – the right of immigrants from countries devastated by war or natural disaster to live and work in the US on an eighteen-month renewable basis. With Annette's whole family able to work legally, they were able to send money home to Marie and her other relatives.

'They usually call us when they need something,' Annette explains, 'for school or the house, or if they've run out of food.' Thanks to their remittances, Marie has built a small bakery next to her house, which she is also rebuilding.

Remittances, mostly from Haitian migrants in the US, amount to more than a third of the country's meagre GDP.[7] They are a lifeline for a wretchedly poor country where millions live in shacks in slums with no running water or electricity, children go barefoot in rubbish by open sewers and the average income is $350 (£270) a year – and many survive on far less.

Now that the Trump administration has announced the ending of TPS for Haitians, a move that is being challenged in court, the legal status of Annette and her family is in jeopardy – and with it the help they provide to their relatives in Haiti.[8]

The money that migrants send back to their relatives can make a huge difference. Those remittances to poorer countries were an estimated $554 billion in 2019, according to the World Bank – a 60 percent rise since 2010 (although some of that increase may be due to better measurement).[9] Remittances were more than three times official government aid of $163 billion in 2017 – and unlike that aid they end up straight in the pockets of local people, not frittered away on five-star hotels for foreign consultants or siphoned off into Swiss bank accounts.[10] They also dwarf volatile inflows of financial investment – and unlike those portfolio flows they tend to rise when disaster strikes, not flood out. They were also expected to overtake foreign direct investment (FDI) in poorer countries (that is, investment by foreign businesses in factories and operations in those countries).[11]

'In times of economic downturn, natural disaster or political crisis, private capital tends to leave and even official aid is hard to administer,' says Dilip Ratha who heads the migration department at the World Bank. 'Remittances are the first form of help to arrive, and they keep rising.'[12] Unfortunately, the World Bank expects remittances to poorer countries to plunge by 20 percent in 2020 due to the global coronavirus crisis (although remittances to Mexico were actually 10 percent higher in the first half of 2020 than a year earlier).[13] That would be a huge blow. But remittances are forecast to fall much less than foreign direct investment (down more than 35 percent) and financial inflows (down 80 percent), so they remain a relatively stable form of foreign funding.

India ($82 billion, £63 billion), China ($70 billion, £54 billion), Mexico ($39 billion, £30 billion), the Philippines ($35 billion, £27 billion) and Egypt ($26 billion, £20 billion) were the top five recipients of remittances in 2019.[14] But migrants' money makes a proportionally larger impact on smaller economies such as Haiti. Remittances accounted for a whopping 38.5 percent of the economy of the Pacific island of Tonga, whose expatriates mostly live in the US, New Zealand and Australia. They also amounted to 30 percent of the economy of Nepal, primarily from the Gulf states.

Remittances can do a world of good. As the story of Annette and Marie illustrates, they reduce poverty.[15] They help recipients meet their basic needs for food and other essentials. They help build (or rebuild) houses. And they help start new businesses.[16] In poor countries where welfare systems are non-existent, remittances provide social benefits too. They enable children to remain in school rather than being sent out to work.[17] They allow families to spend more on healthcare. And they provide a buffer against hard times.

Moralising foreigners who would think nothing of spending a pay increase on a new flat-screen TV and a luxury foreign holiday tut that remittances are often spent on consumption rather than invested, and that they may lead recipients to work less. But why should poor people not be free to make such choices too? After all, the reason why investment is valuable is that it permits higher future consumption; why, then, is current consumption deemed bad?

In any case, remittances often are invested. Research shows that they are more likely to be invested when they are seen as transitory, when the sender stipulates that they be, when they are sent to women (who may prioritise their children's education) and when there are promising local investment opportunities.[18] Often, remittances are invested in housing and land.[19] That is unsurprising, given the lack of investment opportunities in many poor countries. Property investment provides recipients with security as well as status, even if it is not directly productive unless owners develop it.

Remittances can also boost economic growth.[20] They bolster local spending power. They enable recipients who can't borrow to finance productive investments. They can help stabilise local economies, since unlike inflows of hot money they often remain stable, or even increase, in bad times.[21] And they boost countries' balance of payments and thus their credit ratings, enabling governments, companies and households to borrow more cheaply. Without remittances, the Philippines would have a dangerously high current-account deficit of more than 10 percent of GDP; with them, it recorded a surplus of 2.2 percent of GDP in 2019.

However, their impact on growth depends on local conditions. Sending money home to a family in a failed state may do wonders for their wellbeing, but it is unlikely to spark an economic renaissance unless other improvements happen too. Remittances keep communist Cuba afloat; they don't turn it into an economic speedboat.

Like other capital inflows, remittances may also bid up the exchange rate, stifling exporting industries, especially in small economies where they are large and primarily spent on imports rather than locally. Overall, though, remittances provide a powerful development dividend.

Brain drain?

Against the odds, Oluyinka Olutoye has saved many babies' lives. This brilliant surgeon has mastered a novel procedure for operating on foetuses with breathing problems while they are still attached to the umbilical cord. In 2015 he was one of three Nigerian doctors who successfully separated conjoined twins. A year later he led a team of doctors who saved a twenty-three-week-old foetus from a life-threatening tumour. The baby was removed from the womb to excise the tumour and then returned to the womb to complete its gestation. Newspaper headlines heralded the baby who was born twice.[22] In 2019 he became surgeon-in-chief of the Nationwide Children's Hospital.

Olutoye's achievements have been celebrated by the Nigerian government. Born in Lagos in 1967, his childhood dream was to become a doctor and in 1988 he obtained his medical degree, graduating top of his class at Obafemi Awolowo University. He then moved to the US to complete his studies and has worked there ever since. The babies' lives that he has saved were American, not Nigerian.

Nobody doubts that Olutoye has made an exceptional contribution to the US. His achievements are an excellent example of the deftness dividend from migration (and, indeed, the diploma dividend). But some might argue that by emigrating from Nigeria, a relatively poor country that is desperately short of doctors, to practise in the US, a rich country that already has plenty, he was depriving Nigerians of much-needed talent and care.[23] More broadly, many claim that the emigration of highly skilled workers from poor countries creates a brain drain that is a drag on their development. So they want rich countries to stop 'poaching' talent from poor countries.

The brain-drain argument seems plausible. People in rich countries who want to limit migration from poor ones often use it to give a bogus moral veneer to their anti-immigration views. In *Exodus*, Paul Collier – a development economist who has leveraged his perceived expertise on, and concern for, people in poor countries to write an ill-informed book on immigration – argues for 'ceilings' on the ability of skilled workers from countries like Haiti to emigrate out of 'compassion' for those countries.[24] But although ostensibly well meant, such views are mostly mistaken.

Start with the ethics. If you were born in a remote Welsh village, a run-down town in the Appalachians or a pit stop in the Australian outback and you wanted to become a doctor, should you be obliged to go back and practise there when you qualify? On egalitarian grounds, governments might justifiably want to provide incentives for talented professionals to practise in deprived areas – as the UK does for teachers. Highly paid workers also discharge their duty to society by paying taxes that pay for services for the needy. They may also donate to charity and do pro bono work. But in a free society few would argue that people owe their labour to the place where they were born.

Why, then, should we demand more of people who move between countries than of those who move within them – especially if they come from dangerous places with corrupt or thuggish regimes? Not only would this condemn them to worse lives in almost every respect, it would amount to a punitive tax on the much higher incomes that they could earn in rich countries; doctors in Nigeria typically earn only \$560 (£430) a month.[25] Women are particularly likely to emigrate from countries that deny them rights to those that offer them many more; how is it ethical to deny them those rights?[26]

Next consider the economics. Previous chapters showed that the belief that migrants take local jobs is generally false because there isn't a fixed number of jobs to go around. Economists call this the 'lump-of-labour fallacy'. But the brain-drain argument is in many ways analogous to that fallacy. Just as it is mistaken to claim that every job taken by a migrant is one less for locals, it is incorrect to believe that every doctor who moves to a rich country entails one less for poor countries. There isn't a fixed number of doctors to go around. Michael Clemens, a brilliant economist at the Center for Global Development with a zany sense of humour, calls this the 'lump-of-learning fallacy'.[27]

Far from skilled emigration being a drag on development whose harm needs to be mitigated or limited, it is rarely the cause of the shortages of doctors and other professionals in poor countries. On the contrary, the existence of skilled emigration tends to contribute to their development.

Consider Professor Olutoye again. Brilliant as he is, he would probably not have developed and mastered his innovative paediatric surgery procedures had he remained in Nigeria. He wouldn't have had the superb teaching, team and technological resources that he benefited from in the US. He would doubtless have saved lives in Nigeria, but he wouldn't have performed surgical 'miracles'.

More broadly, the belief that having more skilled workers automatically translates into faster development in poor countries – and thus that their emigration detracts from it – is flawed. Without the right conditions in place – such as investment in health and education, sensible economic policies and good governance – those skilled workers may contribute little to their country's development. Woefully mismanaged countries such as Venezuela and Zimbabwe would scarcely be prospering even if skilled professionals were forced to stay put.

Still, Nigeria would at least have had one more talented paediatrician had Olutoye not been allowed to emigrate, wouldn't it? Not necessarily. Clemens has crunched the data and found that the main determinant of the stock of skilled workers in poor countries is not how many emigrate, but rather a host of other factors. 'By far the most important reason that there are few physicians and scientists in Niger and Laos is that those countries have few physicians and scientists anywhere, not that those people move from one place to the other,' he observes.[28] So stopping skilled emigration wouldn't make a big difference to their healthcare provision, let alone their development.

Most highly skilled migrants from developing countries come from India and China. In each case, they account for a very small proportion of the domestic skilled workforce: less than 2 percent of China's and 3.5 percent of India's in 2015–16.[29] This is much lower than the UK's highly skilled emigration rate of 9 percent.[30]

In some small countries, measured emigration rates may be very high. Among countries with a population exceeding half a million, around ten have a graduate emigration rate of more than 30 percent, with Guyana topping the list at over 70 percent, followed by Trinidad and Tobago, and Mauritius.[31] Only two are in Africa: Liberia (more than half) and Guinea-Bissau (30 percent). In a further twenty countries, 20–30 percent of graduates have emigrated.

That sounds problematic, but since the data doesn't usually distinguish between those who obtained their degree after migrating and those who left after obtaining one, this may be less troubling than it seems. Almost half of African-born doctors in the US were not trained in Africa.[32] Even critics of skilled migration surely aren't troubled by migrants who obtain a degree after leaving their home country.

Moreover, the opportunity to emigrate is a key spur for people in poor countries to invest in acquiring valuable skills in the first place – and some work for a time in their home country before emigrating, while many others never emigrate at all.[33] The possibility of earning higher wages abroad is an added incentive to invest in a medical education; some countries, notably the Philippines, explicitly train nurses in order to export them. Many end up staying; the Philippines still has more nurses per person than the UK.[34]

The knowledge that conflict may force you to emigrate is a further reason to invest in readily transferable skills. Emigrants' success may also spur others to want to invest more in their education. For instance, the possibility of working abroad for the British army as a Gurkha soldier encourages Nepalese people to acquire more education, even though most do not ultimately emigrate.[35] Overall, Clemens finds that emigration has not caused the shortage of doctors in Africa, nor is it associated with worse patient outcomes in their country of origin, which are determined by other factors.[36]

Still, countries could do better. To ensure both developed and developing countries benefit more, Clemens has suggested creating 'global skills partnerships'.[37] The German government is pioneering such partnerships with countries such as Vietnam and Sri Lanka. These involve German employers and taxpayers paying to improve training facilities and programmes in those countries, after which only some of the nurses migrate to Germany, where they are ready to start work as soon as they arrive. There is no brain drain, only shared gains.

Highly skilled emigrants also tend to send more money home than less-skilled ones.[38] Some doctors also return to their country of origin, bringing their skills with them. Olawale Sulaiman, a neurosurgeon in New Orleans, splits his time between the US and Nigeria, spending up to twelve days a month providing healthcare in the country of his birth – sometimes for free.[39]

The emigration of skilled workers also creates diasporas that can boost the development of their country of origin. By moving to the UK, Mo Ibrahim ended up making a much bigger contribution to Africa's development than if he had stayed working at Sudan Telecom. Just imagine if the UK government had heeded Paul Collier's advice and denied Ibrahim entry!

Returnees

Like Mo Ibrahim, many migrants bring back competences, contacts and capital to start and grow new businesses.[40] Faqir Chand Kohli, sometimes dubbed the 'father of the Indian software industry', studied electrical engineering in the US and worked there before returning to India to found Tata Consultancy Services, now the country's largest software consultancy firm. He credits much of his ability to accomplish what he did to his education and social network in North America.[41]

Vivek Paul emigrated to the US after acquiring an engineering degree in India. With his experience working for General Electric (GE), he helped found and then led Wipro GE Medical Systems, a medical equipment maker that became India's largest exporter of high-value electronics goods. He later helped Wipro, an Indian IT outsourcing firm that I profiled in *Open World*, grow into a successful global business.

Tan Hooi Ling studied at Bath University in Britain and also worked for a year before returning to Malaysia to work as a consultant for McKinsey. The US firm, in turn, sponsored her to do an MBA at Harvard, where she met Anthony Tan, a businessman from Singapore. Together they founded Grab, a Singapore-based ride-hailing app which now operates across South East Asia and bought out Uber's local operations. Grab has developed into a 'super-app' that also provides food delivery, digital payments and much else. In 2019 it was valued at $14 billion (£10.8 billion).[42]

More than nine million micro-entrepreneurs – one in 70 people in South East Asia – have earned an income through the Grab platform. More than 20 percent of Grab's drivers did not previously work, and Grab has helped 1.7 million people open their first bank accounts.[43] One beneficiary is Ruri Ruhyaty, who runs a stall called Rice Basket Queen in a suburb of Jakarta, the Indonesian capital. Until recently, Ruri would simply display her fish and vegetable dishes on banana leaves on the counter and wait for passing customers.[44] But now that she has signed up with Grab, online orders are delivered to diners across the city by motorbike. Instead of doing accounts with a pen and paper, she uses an automatically updated digital log. Clients now pay with a smartphone app instead of cash. Her business is booming, so much so that Grab's partner Ovo offered the company a loan of 50 million rupiah (£2,700) – enough to open a new stall. 'I will take the loan when I expand my business next year,' said Ruri, as she cooked a spicy sambal vegetarian dish, one of her top sellers.

Countries such as India and China, and before them South Korea and Taiwan, have also benefited immensely from the return of researchers, engineers and entrepreneurs from the US, and the foreign investment that often follows them.[45] Nearly four in five academics in China have a foreign education, with two-thirds of university and research leaders also having foreign work experience.[46] Robin Li, who studied computer science and then worked in the US, including at Infoseek, a search-engine pioneer, returned to China in 2000 to found Baidu, the country's leading search-engine company. Most of the Chinese companies listed on the NASDAQ, a US stock exchange popular with high-growth technology firms, were founded by returnees.[47] Returnees there are known as 'sea turtles' – the words in Chinese sound the same – while those who fly back and forth are known as 'seagulls'.[48]

The benefits of high-growth technology businesses founded by returnees are particularly large. But many migrants found more modest firms that also enhance their country's development. More than half of Turkish returnees start businesses.[49] So do more than a quarter of Tunisian ones, largely with their own savings.[50] The same is true of Caribbean returnees from the UK.[51] In Egypt small businesses started by returnees contribute 15 percent of the country's job creation and investment.[52]

More broadly, returnees help transfer knowledge to local businesses and universities.[53] Those returning to New Zealand, Tonga and Papua New Guinea to work as scientific researchers are the main source of knowledge transfer between international and local researchers.[54] Two-thirds of Indian entrepreneurs who return home after working in America maintain at least monthly contact with former colleagues, swapping industry gossip and sharing ideas.[55]

Among the good ideas that migrants bring back are political ones. Returnees, especially female ones, from countries where men and women are treated more equally tend to promote gender equality in their country of origin.[56] Poorer countries with more young people studying in democratic countries tend to become more democratic themselves;[57] the highly skilled emigrants tend to later boost the quality of governance in their country of origin.[58] And developing-country leaders with a foreign education tend to govern more democratically.[59] There are exceptions, of course; Syria's Bashar al Assad, who trained as an ophthalmologist in the UK, is a particularly brutal dictator.

Diasporas
Even when migrants don't return home, their country of origin can benefit from its diaspora network. Having citizens abroad tends to boost trade, generate investment and spread ideas back home.

Vinod Khosla studied electrical engineering in India before moving to the US for his postgraduate studies. In 1982 he co-founded Sun Microsystems, a computer company that was eventually bought by Oracle, and then became a venture capitalist. Now a billionaire, his Khosla Ventures invests in clean tech and IT start-ups. He has also established Khosla Labs, a start-up incubator and innovation lab in Bangalore that seeks to solve large-scale problems in India using technology and entrepreneurial zeal.[60] With half of the Indian population unbanked, it is working on mobile solutions to make financial payments possible anytime, anywhere. It is also developing applications that use Aadhaar, the country's digital national identity system, to provide better, lower-cost services. One such initiative is Veri5 Digital, which uses Aadhaar and facial recognition software to help businesses identify their clients.[61]

Indians are the largest group of foreign-born talent in Silicon Valley. They are leading entrepreneurs and top executives, technologists and engineers. While they work in California, they also bolster the Indian economy. They share ideas and technical knowledge with their professional networks in India. Their companies often develop products in cities such as Bangalore, Pune and Chennai, and also import directly from India. Their accomplishments enhance India's reputation and thus its attractiveness as an investment and sourcing location. All that helps spread new technologies faster and stimulates new businesses, better jobs and faster economic growth.

As India's nationalist prime minister Narendra Modi has remarked, 'Brain drain has been considered a loss for the country as Indians went abroad seeking jobs and a better life. But for me and my government, such a movement is not a brain drain but a brain gain as they can help us in the development.'[62] In 2019 he toured the US to mobilise the Indian diaspora, with President Trump appearing with him on stage.

Other countries benefit from their diaspora network too. Ismail Ahmed came to London as a refugee from Somalia. Having received $200,000 (£150,000) from blowing the whistle on alleged corruption while working for the UN, he founded WorldRemit. This helps users send cash cheaply and quickly to more than 140 countries, notably migrants' remittances to countries in Africa, which can otherwise incur hefty fees of as much as 7.5 percent.[63] For Ahmed, overcoming that challenge was personal. 'My family had lost everything,' he said. 'So now I became the one who sent money back.'

Migrants often spread new ideas and technologies to their countries of origin. Mo Ibrahim transferred his knowledge of mobile phone networks in Europe to Africa. Chile started exporting paper products after many Chilean refugees settled in woody Sweden.[64] Patents by ethnic inventors – notably US patents filed by researchers of Indian origin[65] – are disproportionately cited in their country of origin.[66] Inventor diasporas in advanced economies boost patent collaborations involving developing countries.[67]

Developing countries with a big diaspora in the US also tend to receive more investment from US companies, especially when that diaspora is highly skilled[68] and inventive.[69] That, in turn, tends to boost local manufacturing and jobs.[70]

Diaspora networks also foster trust, facilitating trade, as the networks of ethnic Chinese communities in South East Asia have long done. Migrants may also import their preferred products from back home. Highly skilled migrants in particular may boost trade through their knowledge of culture, language and practices in both countries, their business contacts and their information about sales and sourcing opportunities in each country.[71] Highly educated emigrants in business-related occupations help stimulate trade most, particularly among culturally different countries.[72]

Paul Collier claims that many poor countries 'would benefit from emigration controls',[73] yet he presents no evidence that preventing migration boosts development. Cuba's government prevents most Cubans from leaving; that has hardly made the country rich. Stopping people from leaving Haiti wouldn't solve its problems; it would trap people there who could contribute much more from afar.

Granted, if a nasty regime's opponents leave, it might prove harder to topple. But exiled African National Congress (ANC) officials kept up the fight against apartheid in South Africa from afar and then helped end it. Exiles also often have a bigger voice in a free country. They can bring back radical new ideas: think of Mohandas Gandhi in India or Ellen Johnson Sirleaf in Liberia. The knowledge that talented people may leave may also constrain some regimes, although less so if, like Venezuela or Iran, government revenues stem primarily from oil and other natural resources. In any case, it would be immoral to prevent people leaving a country even if it might be in the national interest.

It is time to move beyond the tired debate about the 'brain drain', itself a loaded term. As Clemens rightly observes, 'Calling skilled migration "brain drain" is just as appropriate for unbiased social science as it would be to describe women's participation in the labour market as the "family abandonment rate".

The world is a hugely unequal place. Some countries are rich and relatively free and safe; many more are poor, oppressed and often dangerous. So long as that is the case, people will try to move. In a globalised economy, many people will also continue moving for work. As the previous nine chapters have shown, this movement of people is overwhelmingly positive. Migration provides large dynamism, diploma, deftness, diversity, drudgery, demographic, debt and development dividends. It's good for migrants and their children. It's good for the countries that welcome them. It can be good for the countries they leave. And it's good for the world as a whole.

Those are powerful reasons to be open to migration. But economics isn't everything. What about the social and cultural impacts?

PART FOUR
CULTURAL CHALLENGES

15

CULTURAL CORNUCOPIA

Justin Bieber is not everyone's cup of tea. But for his many millions of young fans, the pop star is an idol. He's also an immigrant: he lives in the US but hails from Canada. Rihanna is a cultural icon as well as a singer, and she too is a migrant: she comes from Barbados. Personally, I prefer house music and Deep Dish, an American house music duo, were among my favourites. Dubfire (Ali Shirazinia) and Sharam (Tayebi) were both born in Iran.

Immigrants enrich our lives culturally as well as economically. They broaden our horizons, form new friendships and relationships, stimulate new art, literature and music and provide a wider choice of ethnic restaurants. Interacting with people from different backgrounds helps us understand our own culture better and discover new ways of thinking and doing things. Newcomers also create novel cultural experiences. In the UK, a third of winners of the Booker Prize for fiction have been migrants; *Midnight's Children* by Salman Rushdie, an Anglo-American writer who was born in India, was deemed the best Booker winner of all time. Many of the recent winners of the Prix Goncourt, a prestigious French literature prize, were immigrants, such as Moroccan-born Leïla Slimani and Afghan-born Atiq Rahimi, or the children of migrants, such as Lydie Salvayre, whose parents were refugees from Spain, and Marie Ndiaye, whose father is Senegalese. Consider too how popular the Notting Hill Carnival, a Caribbean street festival in London, has become with people of all backgrounds. And enjoy the myriad new fusion cuisines that are forever emerging.

American culture is an amalgam of immigrant contributions. Blue jeans were created by two immigrants, Levi Strauss from Germany and Jacob Davis from Latvia. Hamburgers are credited to a Danish immigrant, Louis Lassen, and hot dogs to a German one, Charles Feltman. Doughnuts were introduced by a refugee from Russia, Adolph Levitt. Budweiser beer comes from a German immigrant, Adolphus Busch. Basketball was invented by a Canadian, James Naismith. Even the country's unofficial national anthem, 'God Bless America', was written by an immigrant, Russian-born Irving Berlin.[1]

Immigrants don't just import their own cultural traditions, they help create new hybrid ones. Sephardic Jews from Spain and Portugal introduced battered fried fish to England in the sixteenth century; potatoes chipped and fried in the French manner were added in the nineteenth century. Chicken tikka masala, the most popular dish in British Indian cuisine, adapted Indian food to British palates. Tex-Mex food combines Mexican elements such as tacos with American additions such as cheddar cheese. Fortune cookies, which are often served after a meal in Chinese restaurants in the US but not in China, are a twist on cookies introduced by Japanese immigrants to which Chinese lucky numbers were added.

Immigrants innovate in music as well as food. New York's Broadway musicals help newcomers and their children reimagine what it means to be American. Many of the cast of the hit musical *Hamilton* are the children of immigrants and they inject into their performances their own personal experiences. French rappers such as PNL and MHD fuse their French upbringing with their African heritage through new music styles such as Afro trap.[2] Similarly, in the Belgian city of Liège, the children of immigrants express their hybrid Belgian-African identity through hip hop music whose lyrics express their unique perspective. Soca music, a form of calypso music with Latin influences that originated in Trinidad and Tobago, has been given a new twist by Caribbeans abroad. They have in turn spread it more widely not just in the countries they moved to but also back home.[3]

While some people dislike the idea of diversity in general, many of them will happily cheer foreign-born football players in the country's national shirt, enjoy a curry, a kebab or a Chinese takeaway and listen to jazz or R&B music. Among the performers at Donald and

Melania Trump's wedding in 2005 was Paul Anka, a Canadian-born singer of Syrian and Lebanese descent.[4] In Naples, an Italian city in which the arrival of African migrants has created tensions with some locals, an African restaurant that doubles up as an underground nightclub helps bridge cultural divides. Teranga attracts young Italians as well as young African migrants who dance the night away together to African DJs playing Afrobeats.[5] More than half of Europeans think immigration enriches their country's cultural life, less than three in ten that it undermines it.[6] Even Nigel Farage has a German wife, while Melania Trump is from Slovenia.

Yet many people oppose migration for social and cultural reasons, as well as economic ones. They resent that some people cross borders without permission, whether to claim asylum – which people are legally entitled to do – or to disappear into the shadows as undocumented migrants. Even some people who are well disposed to many immigrants consider this 'jumping the queue'.

A further worry is that the diversity of newcomers threatens the national identity of a country and its citizens. Some think that even foreigners who learn the language change the country for the worse, perhaps because they have a different religion or race. Even many of those who are welcoming towards migrants fear that illiberal ones could undermine the liberalism of society. That desire is explicit among jihadi terrorists and imputed among Muslims in general. Many also worry that newcomers won't try to fit in – won't learn the language, won't behave like locals and may not even respect the law – and that society will end up more segregated and polarised as a result. The following four chapters look at these fears in turn.

16

IRREGULARITY

'I can't find words to describe how bad and shameful the conditions are. The camp is massively overcrowded: its capacity is 2,500 people yet there may be fifteen thousand people there. There were seventeen of us from three different families living in a single tent. You have to queue for four hours to get food. The toilets are filthy. There aren't enough toilets or showers. They cut off the water from eight in the evening to eight in the morning. There is no school for the children. There is one doctor for the whole camp. When children get sick, there are no antibiotics. When pregnant women go into labour, nobody calls an ambulance. There are lots of unaccompanied children and they are preyed on by people smugglers, drug dealers and sexual abusers. Small children have tried to kill themselves with knives. That place is hell.'

Reza Adib can scarcely contain his pain and anger. The beautiful Greek island of Lesbos may seem more like paradise to the many Europeans who holiday there. But a short drive away from the airport of Mitilini where tourists land, amid olive groves and spectacular scenery, lies the hellish Moria refugee camp where Reza and his family ended up in 2018. Around it many others live in tents without electricity or running water. Greek islands such as Lesbos that are only a brief boat ride from Turkey are the main entry point into Europe for foreigners who cannot obtain a visa that would enable them to fly.

While the crisis on Europe's borders is no longer headline news, the human tragedy endures. Desperate people fleeing war and persecution in places such as Syria, Afghanistan and Iran, as well as those escaping from poverty and the effects of climate change, continue to risk their lives crowding onto overladen and often unseaworthy boats to try to reach the promised land: Europe. Thousands die each year trying.[1] Those who make it – 127,600 in 2019, mostly by sea, more than half of them to Greece – are typically detained for months or years in camps such as Moria. Others land in Spain, Italy or Malta. Some are eventually granted asylum or the right to stay. Others disappear into society. Still others are deported.

Reza was a prominent and well-paid TV journalist in Afghanistan. But he was forced to flee with his wife and two young children in late 2015 because he was making a film exposing sexual abuse by members of the Afghan army and police. Reza and his family obtained visas for Iran and initially flew there. But when the country's Revolutionary Guard tried to arrest him for making a documentary exposing sexual abuse of children by Iranian-backed forces in Syria, they fled across the border to Turkey. Within six months, the Turkish government recognised his refugee status and in 2017 UNHCR selected him as a suitable candidate for the US's resettlement programme.

But that potential escape route was soon blocked as President Trump shrivelled the US refugee programme, with Muslims such as Reza hardest hit. When he refused to provide the Turkish authorities with source materials on the sexual abuse in Syria that he had documented, they threatened to deport him back to Afghanistan. So he and his family fled by boat to Lesbos in April 2018.

They were locked up in Moria camp for three months. While the EU struck a deal with the Turkish government in March 2016 to take back migrants who arrive in Greece, in practice many stay. Lesbos is one of the EU's designated 'hotspots' for processing asylum claims pending their relocation across Europe. But the Greek government has neither the resources nor the motivation to process claims speedily, while most other EU countries are loath to receive additional refugees. So many people are left to rot in hell. The cramped, unsanitary conditions in camps such as Moria also leave refugees at much higher risk of contracting coronavirus.

Reza and his family spent three months in Moria before being relocated to Malakasa, a smaller camp on the mainland, forty kilometres north of Athens, the Greek capital. They have lived there since. Now recognised as a refugee, he works as a freelance journalist trying to raise awareness of the plight of other refugees and asylum seekers. His sons, aged eleven and six, are growing up in a refugee camp. *Children of Moria*, his bleak one-minute film on conditions in the camp, is well worth watching on YouTube.[2]

'I want to tell the people who read your book that history is not something you can forget. Imagine how the next generation will think about how Europe has treated us. There is no difference between my two kids and your children. I'm as much a human being as you are. You'd find it impossible to go and live in Moria for even one night. Why in Europe do refugees live in such inhuman conditions?'

European governments like to think of themselves as morally superior to the Trump administration. The EU sees itself as a global paragon of human rights. Yet the consequences of Europeans' neglect, fear and cowardice are almost as callous as those of Trump's wickedness. The treatment of refugees and asylum seekers ought to be a stain on Europeans' conscience. But the people locked up in Moria are largely out of sight and out of mind.

Seeking refuge

People have a right to cross national borders without permission to claim asylum. The 1951 UN Convention on Refugees, and the 1967 Protocol that extends the convention's provisions to non-Europeans, stipulate that those who do so should not be punished.[3] That protocol has been signed by most governments in the world – including the US, Canada, Australia, New Zealand, Japan, the UK and all EU governments. Yet those governments systematically violate international law by locking up asylum seekers, often in terrible conditions.

The Trump administration separates children from their parents and puts them in cages. The Australian government has imprisoned asylum seekers who try to arrive by boat on the Pacific islands of Nauru and Manus in appalling conditions, and refuses to allow even those with legitimate claims to be resettled in the country as refugees. EU governments deport asylum seekers to Libya, where they are sometimes sold into slavery, and bribe African governments to prevent people leaving in the first place. That violates Article 13 of the 1948 UN Declaration of Human Rights, which states that 'Everyone has the right to leave any country, including his own.'[4] In his powerful book *Refuge Beyond Reach*, David Scott FitzGerald documents the various ways, public and secret, that rich democracies seek to repel asylum seekers.[5]

Governments' excuse is that many of the people who try to cross borders without permission are not asylum seekers and therefore have no right to do so. But in that case, governments should process asylum claims promptly and fairly, not treat all newcomers terribly for months and years on end. A further argument is that asylum seekers are trying to jump the queue and each should instead apply to be resettled as a refugee from afar. Yet there were 25.9 million refugees worldwide at the end of 2018 and only 92,400 were resettled that year. At that rate, it would take 280 years to resettle all of them. Many countries hardly resettle any refugees – the UK admits fewer than 6,000 a year, while the US quota for fiscal 2020 has been slashed to 18,000. Even those with more substantial programmes, such as Canada (which admitted 30,000 in 2019)[6] and Australia (18,750 in 2018– 19),[7] still have an obligation to process asylum seekers' claims.

The main reason for governments' appalling and illegal behaviour is that most citizens of rich countries want to control who gets into their country and are particularly wary of asylum seekers, whom they lump together with other irregular migrants and often consider 'illegal' or 'bogus'.

Many kinds of irregular

'Illegal' immigrants are the most demonised of all migrants. The very label 'illegal' immediately condemns them. Yet irregular migrants are a diverse group who don't conform to the negative stereotypes about them.

Pham Thi Tra My was a pretty twenty-six-year-old Vietnamese woman, Nguyen Dinh Luong a fresh-faced twenty-year-old man.[8] Had you seen them in the street or on Instagram, you'd have thought they looked nice. Yet they were – briefly – 'illegal' immigrants to the UK; they were among the thirty-nine people found dead in a refrigerated lorry in Essex on 23 October 2019. On the night before she died, Thi Tra My sent her family a message saying she could not breathe and her 'trip to a foreign land has failed'.

The popular image of an 'illegal' immigrant is of someone smuggled into the US across the desert dodging the Border Patrol, into Europe on a boat in the dead of night or into Britain through the Channel Tunnel in the back of a lorry. Some irregular immigrants are indeed smuggled – or smuggle themselves – across borders.

But most undocumented migrants arrive legally on a tourist or family visa and then stay on. Some cross borders using forged documents. Others are born to parents who are irregular migrants in countries such as the UK and Germany where being born there doesn't automatically give a right to residence or citizenship. Still others – like the Dreamers in the US, whose plight will be discussed later in the chapter – arrived as children and may not even be aware that they do not have a right to remain in the country in which they grew up.

Some become irregular migrants because the law changed and they failed to establish their right to stay; that was the fate of the Windrush scandal victims in the UK and it is the threat hanging over EU migrants who don't obtain settled status to remain after Brexit. Last but not least, some become irregular migrants because borders move and they end up on the wrong side of them, as happened to many people when the Soviet Union broke up in 1991.

However they became irregular migrants, their status is only partly due to their own actions; it also depends on government decisions. Where people can move freely, nobody is an irregular migrant. Moreover, governments can – and sometimes do – decide to regularise migrants' status. President Ronald Reagan, who would have been ashamed of what the Republican party has become under Donald Trump, pushed through a limited amnesty in 1986 that attracted three million applicants. France, Spain, Italy and other European countries also periodically regularise eligible migrants' status.

Even when they remain undocumented, immigrants still contribute to the economy and society and tend to be good people. If there is demand for their labour in rich countries but no legal channel for them to come to work, is it so bad if they are there without permission? Some of the people you interact with and like may be irregular migrants without you being aware of it. Would they suddenly become bad people if you found out their status?

Visa overstayer

Poland was still a communist dictatorship when Gabriela first came to London.[9] She managed to get a two-year visa to study at the Polish

University Abroad in Hammersmith. 'I didn't speak a word of English at the time,' she explains. 'And I planned to go home again after my studies. But then I realised how much better life was in London and I didn't want to go back to Poland. So when my visa expired I stayed.'

Gabriela had worked as a nurse in Poland but that wasn't an option as an undocumented immigrant in Britain. Life was initially very tough. 'I found work in a clothing factory in Finsbury Park. It was owned by a Greek woman and nobody asked me for a National Insurance number. Most people there didn't have one. The pay wasn't much – £70 for a five-day week. It was long hours and very hard work. The factory was cramped with small windows. But it was a job.' She ended up working there for seven years.

Gabriela used to go back to Poland on holiday every summer. 'When I got back to the UK, I got a six-month visa every time. So I was here illegally only part of the time,' she chuckles. Gabriela eventually had a baby boy who was born in a local hospital. 'I was a bit worried. But everyone at the hospital was wonderful. They didn't ask me anything about my immigration status.' Her son's father was English but wanted nothing to do with them. 'I never got a penny off him. One day I ran into him in the street, touched his arm and said, "This is your son." But he replied, "Don't touch me, I'll call the police." He was afraid I was going to ask him for money.

'My mother came over from Poland to look after my son so I could go back to work. I started cleaning offices and homes. It was all cash in hand. One day I was cleaning a house when the burglar alarm went off. The police came and I hid in the bathroom terrified. But after checking the house from the outside for a while, they left again. I took my stuff and ran away. I was lucky. Some of my Polish friends worked as builders and one day the Home Office came to the construction site where they were working and took them away.'

Then in 2004 everything changed. Poland joined the EU and Polish citizens gained the right to live and work legally in the UK. 'I was overjoyed. It changed everything. I no longer had to live in fear. I could walk down the street without worrying about what might happen to me.'

Gabriela has now been in the UK for more than thirty years. Her son is a British citizen. She has a National Insurance number, pays her taxes and has obtained 'settled status' – the right to remain living in Britain permanently after Brexit. 'I work hard. I pay my taxes. This is my home now. My son doesn't know anywhere else.'

Dreamers

'I do not know where I will be when you read this book.

As I write this, a set of creased and folded papers sits on my desk, ten pages in all, issued to me by the Department of Homeland Security. 'Warrant for Arrest of Alien', reads the top right corner of the first page.

These are my first legal American papers, the first time immigration officers acknowledged my presence after arresting, detaining, then releasing me in the summer of 2014. I've been instructed to carry these documents with me wherever I go.'[10]

Thus begins *Dear America: Notes of an Undocumented Citizen*, José Antonio Vargas's powerful memoir of his life as an irregular migrant in the US. He compares the life of the migrant to being homeless and vividly captures 'the unsettled, unmoored psychological state' that it creates. Having to lie to get by. Trying to pass as an ordinary American. Constantly hiding from the government and thus hiding from oneself.

Born in the Philippines, his mother sent him to live in the US with his naturalised American grandparents when he was twelve without obtaining permission for him to stay permanently. He did not realise his status until he applied for a driving licence at the age of sixteen. He then had to lie, pass himself off and hide to get by. But he went on to become a journalist and in 2008 was part of the *Washington Post* team that won a Pulitzer Prize for its coverage of the Virginia Tech shooting.

In 2011, aged thirty, he revealed his undocumented status in an effort to promote debate. He set up Define American, an innovative non-profit that tries to shift the debate about what it means to be American.[11] He also advocates a pathway to citizenship for undocumented residents like him who had arrived in the US as children, through the DREAM Act.[12] While this has garnered widespread political support, it has yet to be approved and President Trump's actions now threaten to lead to the deportation of Dreamers such as Vargas.

America is lucky to have José Antonio Vargas. He is an immensely talented, brave and inspiring individual. Surely he and others like him should be allowed to stay?

Border crosser

'We get these women coming in with like seven children,' President Trump said, putting on a Hispanic accent, according to an anonymous insider account.[13] 'They are saying, "Oh, please help! My husband left me!"' he added, speaking in the Oval Office. 'They are useless. They don't do anything for our country. At least if they came in with a husband we could put him in the fields to pick corn or something.'

Victorina Morales, a poor corn farmer from Guatemala, covertly crossed over from Mexico to the US in 1999 at the age of twenty-six. Starting in 2013 she worked at the Trump National Golf Club in Bedminster, New Jersey – a job she got with false papers. She washed Trump's clothes, made his bed, scrubbed his toilet and dusted his golf trophies.

This tiny woman with only two years of formal education has worked hard to get ahead. She even received a commendation from the White House for her 'outstanding' support during Trump's visits as president. There is no evidence that Trump or Trump Organization executives knew of her immigration status. But at least two supervisors at the club were aware of it, she says, and helped workers avoid detection and keep their jobs.[14]

'I never imagined, as an immigrant from the countryside in Guatemala, that I would see such important people close up,' she said. Even though she could be deported for speaking out, this brave woman felt compelled to speak out. 'We are tired of the abuse, the insults, the way he [Trump] talks about us when he knows that we are here helping him make money,' she said. 'We sweat it out to attend to his every need and have to put up with his humiliation.' After Morales went public to the *New York Times* in late 2018 she lost her job, along with around twenty other undocumented migrants at the club. She now campaigns for immigration reform.

'It was a really hard decision,' she explains. 'I don't think people understand how scary it is for us [undocumented immigrants] to talk about it. We live our lives in hiding, always afraid to come out into the light.' But she is relieved to no longer work for Trump. 'It's incredible how bitter we all became. We were humiliated on a daily basis, and it just got worse. They even called us dogs.'[15]

Victorina, who has two sons, has now applied for asylum. 'Honestly, I'm not scared any more. I have faith in God. And if I have to leave, then I will.'

The US is home to many people like Victorina and José Antonio.[16] Between 10.3 million and 10.7 million unauthorised immigrants were estimated to be in the US in 2017 – around 3 percent of the population.[17]

Europe has fewer: between 3.9 million and 4.8 million unauthorised migrants – less than 1 percent of the population.[18] Unlike in the US, many – around a million – have a pending asylum claim. Half of the unauthorised immigrants were in Germany and the UK, which each had up to 1.2 million. Italy had up to 700,000 and France up to 400,000.[19] Irregular migrants could thus be up to 1.8 percent of the UK population.

Whereas undocumented migrants in the US are mostly from Latin America and the Caribbean, those in Europe come from all the over world. And while most of those in the US have been there for many years, in Europe most are young and arrived in the past five years. The numbers of unauthorised immigrants in Canada and Australia, both of which are geographically remote, are reckoned to be much lower.

Deterrence, deaths, detentions and deportations

Rich-country governments do their best to deter unwanted migrants from arriving. They tighten visa rules. They make passports harder to forge. They use facial recognition software to detect imposters. They build walls, complete with barbed wire, watchtowers, motion detectors and night-vision cameras. They patrol borders and seas. They turn away boats laden with people rescued at sea. They do dirty deals with dodgy governments to prevent people leaving countries, or to take them back. They allow some people to die. They detain those they catch as well as those who claim asylum. They deport many of them. Yet still people come.

President Trump wanted to go much further than he has already, according to a book by *New York Times* journalists Julie Hirschfeld Davies and Michael Shear.[20] He suggested electrifying the border wall and topping it with spikes. He mooted digging a moat and filling it with snakes or alligators. Having publicly suggested that American soldiers shoot migrants who throw rocks at them, he privately suggested shooting them in the legs to slow them down.[21]

Why stop there? East Germany had a shoot-to-kill policy to deter its citizens from trying to cross the heavily militarised Berlin Wall – yet still they did so.[22] They climbed over the wall, dug under it and hid in secret compartments in cars. Some 75,000 people received prison sentences for attempting to flee; 140 died. In 1986, during the apartheid area, South Africa erected an electrified fence on its border with Mozambique and Zimbabwe. Hundreds were electrocuted, while those who tried to bypass the fence by going through a national park got eaten by lions. Even so, migrants managed to get across.[23]

Border enforcement is increasingly costly. Between the creation of the US Department of Homeland Security in 2003 and 2019, the US federal government spent an estimated $324 billion (£249 billion) on immigration enforcement agencies.[24] The annual budget of the US Border Patrol has risen nearly nineteenfold since 1990, to $4.7 billion (£3.6 billion) in fiscal 2019. Spending on Customs and Border Protection (CBP), which also includes operations at border entry points, more than doubled between fiscal 2003 and fiscal 2019, to $17.1 billion (£13.1 billion). The budget for Immigration and Customs Enforcement (ICE), which detains immigrants and conducts raids within the US, also more than doubled over that period, to $7.6 billion (£5.8 billion). In total, the US spent $24.7 billion (£19 billion) on border enforcement in 2019. It employed some 51,000 people to do so, with the number of Border Patrol agents rising nearly fivefold since 1993 and the number of ICE agents soaring too.

In the UK, the government spent just over £400 million on immigration enforcement in 2018–19 and some £650 million on the border force.[25] Within the EU, border enforcement remains largely the responsibility of national governments. The European Commission is also seeking a huge increase in the EU's border security spending to €31 billion (£26.5 billion) in the 2021–27 budget.[26] Both the EU and European governments also bribe neighbouring governments to stop people leaving and take them back. For instance, Italy and the EU promised Libya €285 million (£219 million) in 2017 to beef up its 'coastguard' who are in practice local militias.[27] Australia spent nearly A$4 billion (£2.1 billion) on border enforcement, management, compliance and detention in 2018–19.[28]

The US is not alone in building a border wall. Around the turn of the century Spain erected walls around its North African enclaves of Ceuta and Melilla that border Morocco. Both Greece and Bulgaria have built walls on their border with Turkey. Hungary put up a razor-wire fence with speakers that blare warnings in different languages on its frontiers with Serbia and Croatia in 2015. Slovenia is building one on its border with Croatia too. Many more countries have done so too, or are planning to do so.

The harder that governments make it to cross borders legally, the more criminals can charge to help people do so covertly. People smuggling has become big business; violent criminal gangs and drug cartels have muscled in on what were once peaceful, independent freelance outfits. While data is obviously scant, the International Organisation for Migration reckons people smuggling could be worth $10 billion (£7.7 billion) a year worldwide.[29] Getting smuggled into the US can cost as much as $3,600 (£2,800) from Mexico, $10,300 (£7,900) from Central America and $27,000 (£20,800) from South Asia.[30] Clandestine entry into Europe can cost as little as €700 (£600) from Morocco to Spain, and as much as €15,000 (£12,800) from Turkey to the UK and €22,100 (£18,900) from Afghanistan to Germany. Passage from Indonesia to Australia can cost A$1,650 (£870).

As well as making crossing borders without permission more costly, government actions make it more dangerous. Nearly 2,000 people are known to have died on the border between Mexico and the US between 2014 and 2018.[31] More than 6,600 deaths crossing borders have been recorded within Africa and a further 2,900 in Asia and the Middle East – though data is patchy so the true figures are probably much higher. Nearly 2,000 people have died trying to reach Australia by sea since 2000, although no deaths have been recorded since 2013.[32] But that beautiful playground for tourists, the Mediterranean Sea, is the most murderous barrier of all. Between 2014 and 2019, some 19,000 people died trying to cross it.[33]

Some callous people who have no empathy or personal experience of war, persecution or penury suggest that migrants have only themselves to blame for risking their lives trying to cross a border without permission. Some also argue that rescuing people at sea encourages more people to risk their lives, yet migrant boats are in fact no more likely to set out from

Libya when NGO rescue boats are operating; the weather and the political situation in Libya are the main determinants.[34]

Many more people would rather migrants didn't die and want authorities to do their best to save lives, but don't support allowing people to migrate freely and safely; implicitly, then, they consider those regrettable deaths a price worth paying to control our borders. They are not nasty people, but fearful ones.

Those who escape death but are caught, or claim asylum, at the border are typically detained, often in terrible conditions. Arrests at the US border soared to nearly 860,000 in 2019,[35] their highest since 2007, though still well below the peak of 1.6 million in 2000.[36] Total enforcement actions, which include the deportation of people deemed inadmissible under asylum laws, exceeded 1.1 million people. Contrary to Trump's claims that newcomers are all criminals, the proportion of those apprehended who were convicted criminals was 1.5 percent in fiscal 2019. Including those with warrants for their arrests, the figure was 2 percent.[37]

The crisis on the US-Mexican border has changed considerably since the 2000s. Then, Border Patrol agents played cat and mouse with typically Mexican clandestine migrants and those they caught were returned almost immediately to Mexico, as I described in *Immigrants: Your Country Needs Them*. Now the border crossers are mostly Central American, often claim asylum at the border instead of trying to enter covertly and are then typically locked up.

Nearly half a million people were detained by US Immigration and Customs Enforcement (ICE) in 2019, typically for around a month but sometimes for years. Many had been arrested at the border, others during immigration raids within the US. More than 50,000 are typically detained at any time, a figure that rose by 40 percent between Trump taking office and late 2019.[38] Those detained have not committed a crime, but are nonetheless being held until their hearings to determine their right to stay in the country. ICE's budget for detaining immigrants has soared from $1.8 billion (£1.4 billion) in fiscal 2010 to $3.1 billion (£2.4 billion) in fiscal 2018. It's big business for the private prison contractors that house the immigrants.

The final series of the Netflix prison drama *Orange is the New Black* features the private prison company branching out into housing immigrants on behalf of ICE. But while it provides some insight into the cruelties, injustices, absurdities and perverse incentives of a dysfunctional system, real life is much worse. Although the official policy of separating families was rescinded following a public outcry,[39] children are still torn from their parents, sedated with medication and made to sleep on floors.[40] More than 4,500 complaints have been made over four years of the sexual abuse of children by detention centre staff and minors.[41] People are crammed together in unsanitary conditions without showers, toothbrushes or drinkable water.[42] As of January 2020, thirty adults had died in detention centres since President Trump took office.[43]

In Europe, conditions for asylum seekers are often terrible in EU hotspots such as Moria camp, as we have seen. But across the continent some governments lock up many more migrants than others. While Greece imprisoned 31,100 immigrants in 2018, Spain, the second-biggest Mediterranean point of entry, detained 8,800. France placed more than 46,800 people in detention in 2017, more than half of whom were in its overseas territories.[44]

The UK also mistreats the asylum seekers and migrants whom it detains. Kingsley Newuh came to Britain on a student visa. A campaigner for Movement for Justice, an NGO, he claimed asylum for fear he would be arrested if he returned to Cameroon because of his research critical of the government. He was twice detained at Morton Hall detention centre and claims people died while he was there. 'I felt like a lamb to the slaughter,' he said. 'No one told me how long I was going to be there for – that was the most tormenting aspect of it. It's a prison under a different name. It was unsanitary, very, very dirty and I was locked in my room from 8 a.m. to 8 p.m.'[45]

Nearly 25,000 people were detained in the UK in 2018, roughly the same number as a decade earlier.[46] Only eighty-five were children, a huge decline from 1,119 in 2009. Most remain for only short periods; 1,727 people were in detention in the second quarter of 2019.[47] In mid-2019, the longest anyone had been detained was 818 days. A *Guardian* investigation in 2018 found that more than half of the detainees they interviewed were suicidal, seriously ill or victims of torture.[48] A report by the House of Commons Home Affairs Committee said the Home Office had 'utterly failed' to ensure the safety of people detained.

Australia used to spend £250,000 a year per asylum seeker that it locked up in Manus and Nauru.[49] While the notoriously awful offshore detention centres have now been closed, it still detains people onshore and fresh allegations of abuse have come to light.[50] At the end of September 2019, Australia held 1,347 people in immigration detention centres, of whom 433 had tried to arrive by sea.[51] While the numbers have fallen by nine-tenths since 2013, the average detention period was 502 days and more than one in five had been imprisoned for more than two years.

The final step, for many, is deportation. In the US, ICE deported 256,000 people in fiscal 2018, 161,000 of whom had been arrested by Customs and Border Patrol.[52] Such mass deportations are not new; the Obama administration deported about 2.9 million people between 2009 and 2016, with a peak of 410,000 in fiscal 2012.[53] But unlike before, the Trump administration also now deports asylum seekers to Mexico while their appeal is pending. It has also made it much harder to successfully claim asylum. Some 265,000 people claimed asylum in the US in 2018 – most of whose cases were still pending – while fewer than 39,000 were granted asylum.[54]

European governments also deport many immigrants. More than 170,000 non-EU citizens were removed by EU governments in 2018.[55] Germany deported most (29,000), followed by Poland (25,700) and the UK: some 24,500 people were deported or removed 'voluntarily' from the country in 2018.[56] But many of those ordered to leave by European governments instead disappear, presumably remaining in the country as undocumented migrants.

Safe and legal

Rich countries' border enforcement measures manage to be both cruel and ineffective. Governments are ever nastier to newcomers – including those fleeing war and persecution – to try to deter people from coming, yet people still come and many manage to stay. Moreover, their border controls are counterproductive because they force people who would rather come and go temporarily to settle permanently.

When I worked for the World Trade Organization in Geneva, I was a very temporary migrant: I lived just across the border in France and commuted to Switzerland each day. Had the Swiss government decided to prevent people crossing over from France – as it did during the Second

World War – I would have faced an all-or-nothing choice: either stay in Switzerland permanently or lose my job.

If you live in the suburbs and commute into a big city such as London, a similar logic applies. If London were to become independent, or simply tried to stop outsiders 'stealing' Londoners' jobs, you'd either have to move to the city for good or settle for a worse job in the suburbs.

Internationally, all the evidence shows that most migrants want to move temporarily – and that when they can come and go freely, they do.[57] But if it becomes extremely difficult to come back to a rich country, most migrants stay for good. Perversely, governments that seek to curb border crossing tend to turn temporary migrants into permanent ones.

Until Germany announced the scrapping of its guest worker programme in the 1970s and tried to get foreigners to leave, most came and went. But when it closed it down, many stayed and then managed to bring over their families. When Suriname was a Dutch colony, its citizens had Dutch citizenship and the right to move to the Netherlands. To stop Surinamese coming, the Dutch government precipitated its independence in 1975. This prompted a rush of Surinamese to the Netherlands – some 40 percent of the population moved – before the door shut for good.[58] When Moroccans could move freely to Spain and back, many came to do seasonal work. But in 1991 Spain started requiring visas after it joined the Schengen Agreement that permits passport-free travel among European member countries. Moroccans duly tried to sneak in by boat, while temporary workers became permanent settlers and then brought over their families.

To ensure that temporary migrants leave again, they need to have the possibility to come back. New Zealand's seasonal migration programme for low-skilled workers from Pacific island states has an overstay rate of less than 1 percent because, while migrants can stay only seven months in any season, they can return in subsequent years.[59] In contrast, Britain's seasonal agricultural workers scheme, which was scrapped in 2013 and is set to be reintroduced once the post-Brexit immigration system is in place, had an overstay rate of as much as 10 percent because it was open only to students, who were tempted by other jobs in Britain and could not otherwise return.[60] In contrast, within the EU, where people can move freely, people come and go all the time, and only a minority settle for good.

If governments won't allow people to move freely, they should at least provide safe and legal channels for people to move when their labour is in demand. This would not just be humane, it would also curb irregular migration and all its associated costs. When sufficient renewable visas were provided to Mexicans to come and pick the harvest in the US, there was hardly any irregular migration and few stayed permanently.[61] But when the Bracero scheme was scrapped in 1965, the demand for their labour persisted and Mexicans came irregularly instead. When the US then started to tighten up the border, Mexicans who were already in the US stayed put while many more rushed to move before it became even harder. That is how the US ended up with a large population of undocumented Mexican migrants.

Excessive migration restrictions don't just encourage irregular movement; they spur people to marry to get a visa. This can have the perverse impact of impeding immigrants' intermarriage rates, as they instead marry people from their parents' country of origin, sometimes through arranged marriages. Restrictions on visas for foreign spouses, in turn, violate people's freedom to live with the one they love.

In short, if governments don't want to let people move freely, they could still cut the costs of irregular migration by opening up safe and legal channels for people to come to work temporarily. Those who dislike migration ought to recognise that like the banning of alcohol during the Prohibition era in the US, driving it underground does more damage than making it safe and legal. So that migrants who want to move temporarily have an incentive to leave again, they would need to have the option to return subsequently. Governments should also speed up the processing of asylum claims and not lock up people who have not committed a crime.

Amnesty?

But what to do with the many millions of people who are already in the US and Europe without permission? Hard-liners argue that 'illegals' should all be deported. But to do that, the authorities would first need to find them. While immigration raids do catch some people, most migrants slip through the net. Theresa May's piloting of intimidating vans with the message 'In the UK illegally? Go home or face arrest' was scrapped after only eleven people left the UK as a result of the initiative.[62] Rounding up many more people would require a huge increase in enforcement budgets and police powers. The UK has already gone some way in this direction by requiring employers, landlords and hospitals to act as immigration officials. In countries where the rule of law continued to apply, millions of people would then need to be detained pending determination of their legal claims to remain. All this would be prohibitively expensive and involve creating a police state. In 2005 the UK's National Audit Office (NAO) estimated that forcibly removing a refused asylum seeker cost, on average, £11,000.[63] Even if the figure hasn't risen since then, removing all 1.2 million irregular migrants in the UK would cost at least £13.2 billion.

Even then, the public outcry of companies and communities, colleagues, friends and family would surely be huge. While advocating mass deportation may sound tough, rounding up over a million people, many of whom are long-settled and have children and local connections, is a non-starter practically and politically. Deportations will continue at the margins, so that the undocumented continue to live in the shadows in fear. But they are a distraction, not a solution.

A better way forward would be earned regularisation – an amnesty, if you like. This would recognise that people who have settled in a country for five, ten or however many years are there to stay and that it would be far better for both them and society that they live within the law, with all its protections. Regularising their status would make them less vulnerable to exploitation. It would enable them to secure better-paid jobs. It would ensure they paid taxes. It would mean they could take their children to hospital when they get sick or report a crime to the police without fear of deportation. It would undermine criminal gangs and strengthen communities and the rule of law.

Some object that regularisation would reward illegal behaviour and encourage further migration. But in practice it merely recognises the reality that people are here to stay and seeks to remedy the situation. There is also no evidence that regularisations in other countries have attracted more migrants.[64, 65]

When Boris Johnson was Mayor of London he endorsed the idea of an amnesty for settled undocumented migrants and in 2019 he reiterated his support for such a scheme. A study he commissioned in 2009 concluded that such an amnesty would boost the economy and tax revenues, among other benefits.[66] In practice, visa overstayers who have been in the UK more than twenty years can already apply for limited leave to remain.[67]

To conclude, labels such as 'illegal' make undocumented immigrants sound much more sinister than they are. In real life, they are human beings like you and me with very natural motivations whose actions happen to fall foul of harmful and pernicious laws. Gabriela's life story illustrates this perfectly. She was not a bad person before Poland joined the EU and didn't become a better one after it did. Nor, I would argue, were her actions wicked beforehand and not so afterwards. The law simply changed. Of course, it is generally a good thing to obey the law, but that is not an absolute. Sometimes laws are harmful or ethically dubious – like those that banned women voting and criminalised homosexuality; sometimes it is OK to break them. How else would social change happen?

One likely consequence of Brexit is that after the deadline for regularising their status elapses, some British people will become 'illegal' immigrants in Europe. Either they won't regularise their status, or they will stay on without permission after new rules are introduced. It might be your kids doing a summer job in a bar in Ibiza. It might be them working while in Paris learning French. It might be all sorts of things that British people now take for granted they can do in Europe. Will they suddenly become wicked after Brexit? Or is it Brexit itself that is a terrible mistake?

A big reason for the Brexit vote was the desire to limit immigration, in part because it was deemed to threaten Britons' national identity. But does it?

17

IDENTITY

Nikolaus Schrod arrived in London as a penniless German immigrant with no formal qualifications.[1] It was the 1850s and the Industrial Revolution was in full swing. The economy was booming and Britain's doors were open to newcomers from around the world.

Schrod settled in the German quarter of London by Tottenham Court Road, a deprived area populated by refugees and prostitutes. He made cases for pianos, which were becoming popular among well-to-do Londoners. His wife Bina, whose maiden name was Göring, made money making dresses and doing needlework.

Their only child, Carl, left school at fourteen to become a telegraph messenger. He later changed his name to Charles and wed an English woman, Ellen Abbott. Their daughter Gladys Schrod married a young stockbroker's clerk, Harry Farage, himself descended from Huguenots, Protestant immigrants who fled persecution in France.

Since Nigel Farage – the grandson of Harry and Gladys and the great-great-grandson of Nikolaus and Bina – agrees with the late Conservative politician Enoch Powell that immigration has made the 'indigenous population ... strangers in their own country', is he part of the problem?[2] Indeed, in his own terms, is he really British, let alone English, at all?

Who are 'We'? That crucial and controversial question lies at the heart of the fevered debate about immigration and all the fears about 'Them' – be they newcomers, settled migrants, the children of immigrants, people from an immigrant background, non-white people, people with foreign-sounding names like Legrain, or indeed a whole jumble of people who are lumped together as 'immigrants' in public discourse. Is there only one 'Us'

– the nation – and if so, what defines it? Or do we have many overlapping identities? Perhaps most importantly, can They ever become Us – and if so, how?

In 2017 white supremacists marched through Charlottesville, Virginia, carrying both Confederate flags and Nazi ones, in baseball caps and pointy white hats, chanting slogans like 'You will not replace us' and 'Blood and soil'. Since I became involved in the immigration debate fifteen years ago, I have received hate mail and death threats from people accusing me of wanting to destroy the white race. Never did I imagine that a US president would one day praise vile people like that.

'White nationalists' and the 'alt-right' have an extreme racial, ethnic and religious concept of American identity as white, Anglo and Protestant, though some extend this to white European Christians more broadly. Their notion of American identity excludes the black descendants of African slaves who were brought to the US against their will more than 150 years ago. Nor does it accommodate Jews of European (or Middle Eastern) descent. And it rejects most recent immigrants to the US, who are largely non-European, as well as their descendants. Applied consistently, it would also exclude Americans of Irish descent (Catholic and Celtic), those of Italian descent (Catholic, Latin and of darker complexion) and even those of German descent like Donald Trump (not Anglo). White supremacists tolerate non-white immigrants only insofar as they dominate them, while white separatists want races to live apart.

The American far right's racial concept of national identity has echoes in Europe too. The British National Party (BNP) believed that there was a biologically distinct white-skinned 'British race'[3] and that UK citizens who were not ethnic white Europeans were 'racial foreigners' and should be encouraged to leave (or expelled).[4] The Sweden Democrats originated as a white nationalist neo-Nazi party.[5] Jean-Marie Le Pen, the founder of France's Front National, advocated '*rendre la France aux français*' (returning France to French people), a position now rejected by his more politically flexible daughter, Marine.

In his book *The Great Replacement*, Renaud Camus argues that white 'indigenous French people' (*français de souche*) are being replaced by non-white, non-European and often non-Christian 'colonisers', specifically Arabs and Africans – a process he calls 'genocide by substitution'.[6]

Such far-right views have echoes among more mainstream and supposedly respectable authors. Paul Collier has written that 'the 2011 Census revealed that the indigenous British had become a minority in their own capital.'[7] In fact, it showed that while a majority of London's population were born in Britain, those who identify as 'white British' are no longer a majority. Douglas Murray, author of *The Strange Death of Europe*, used the same figures to argue that London had become a 'foreign country'.[8] As Jonathan Portes observes in his excellent book on immigration, 'the view that you have to be white to be "really" British, and that black or Asian Britons are still somehow alien and threatening, remains prevalent, even if largely hidden, in some elite circles.'[9]

Not all nationalists are as extreme as that, of course. And while an ethnic and racial definition of nationhood cannot accommodate immigrants and minorities, more flexible forms of national identity based on civic values can and do.

Defining a nation

What is a nation, anyway? Broadly speaking, it is a group of people associated with a particular territory – typically a country, a nation-state – who believe that they form a distinct political community. In other words, a nation consists of people who feel they have enough in common with each other to accept being ruled by a government elected by a majority of them. By that definition, Scotland is a nation; even those who want Scotland to remain in the UK accept the legitimacy of the Scottish government. But Northern Ireland isn't: Protestant Unionists and Catholic Nationalists consider themselves so different that they accept only to share power, not to be ruled by a majority of the people of Northern Ireland.

What, though, engenders this common feeling among members of a nation? For a start, they tend to live in the same country, and so vote in the same elections, abide by the same laws, use similar public services and read and watch at least some things in common. In Britain, support for the NHS is akin to a national religion.

Members of a nation typically share a language, although the Swiss have four. Often, they have common customs and culture, or at least elements of them; while people in Massachusetts are very different to those in Mississippi in many ways, Americans do tend to share celebrations such as Thanksgiving and the Fourth of July. They also tend to share an attachment to particular civic values and domestic political institutions. British citizens swear allegiance to the Queen, French ones to the Republican ideals of *liberté, égalité, fraternité* (liberty, equality, fraternity). Americans swear allegiance to the US Constitution, an admirable document drafted in 1787, while Supreme Court judges parse it for guidance on how to deal with modern-day legal and moral issues such as abortion rights – behaviour which seems quaint to most non-Americans. Not all members of a nation share or accept these things, of course, but they share enough of them that they still accept a common government.

Viewed in those loose, civic terms, nations can readily accommodate newcomers. Law-abiding immigrants who have settled in a country for a number of years, learned the local language, gained some appreciation of prevailing cultural norms and customs, declared allegiance to its political institutions and follow the law can become citizens and members of the national political community. The issue of how liberal democracies can cope with people who reject the liberal values on which they are based is considered in the next chapter, while Chapter 19 goes into greater depth on what immigrants need to do to fit into society, and how society ought to adapt to them.

If nations are communities of citizens, membership can be open to anyone who meets the club's entry criteria. If immigrants want to, and We accept them, They can become part of Us. Those entry criteria can be open to immigrants and reflect the existing culture. To become a UK citizen, you now need to pass an English language test. You are also quizzed on your knowledge of British history, political institutions and local norms. The 'Life in Britain' test is a bit of a joke, though; even the prime minister who introduced it, Gordon Brown, couldn't answer many of the questions. Was he therefore not really British?

A largely civic conception of national identity fits easily with the US. After all, its Declaration of Independence is deliberately universalist: 'We hold these truths to be self-evident, that all men are created equal, that they are endowed by their Creator with certain unalienable Rights, that among these are Life, Liberty and the pursuit of Happiness.' The French

Republic has universalist aspirations too. Even countries such as Germany that previously had an exclusively ethnic concept of nationhood have come around to a more civic one.

A civic concept of nationhood that also reflects the prevailing culture tends to work well. Immigrants typically feel a strong attachment to the country that has welcomed them and of which they have chosen to become a citizen.[10] In all OECD countries, more than eight in ten immigrants – rising to 95 percent in France – feel part of their national community; in the UK more immigrants do so than locals.[11] In Australia and New Zealand more than half of immigrants feel 'very close' to their adopted country and a further third 'close'. Most locals accept that law-abiding people with foreign-sounding names and non-white faces who have settled in the country and contribute to the community can become part of the nation. Indeed, in countries such as Canada whose diversity is part of what makes Canadians proud to be Canadian, increased immigration actually strengthens feelings of national identity among both immigrants and locals.[12]

Yet Eric Kaufmann argues that civic nationalism doesn't work because it pursues diametrically opposing goals: universality and particularity.[13] In practice, though, it typically consists of both local particularities and more widely shared liberal values. Many countries have universal social healthcare, yet Brits still love and identify with their own NHS.

Moreover, there are many different ways of being and feeling British; national identity doesn't need to be explicitly delineated for it to be felt more or less strongly by different people. We may not share a common ancestry, but we share a present and a future.

The nationalist delusion

Some people conceive of nations and national identity differently, however. Put simply, some Britons think that being British means being born in Britain to British parents.

More broadly, nationalists – and indeed, some people who haven't thought too deeply about the subject – tend to conceive of nations as ancient, largely unchanging cultural communities that stretch back to the mists of time. They define them in ethnic terms, as if they were an extended family with shared ancestry. They tend to think of nations as uniform, or at least that the differences within them are much smaller than those between nations. Last but not least, they believe that our national identity does – or should – trump all our other affiliations.

In a nationalist world, They can scarcely become Us. Insofar as immigrants are accepted at all, they must remain separate. Indeed, it is almost impossible for immigrants and their descendants to become Japanese citizens and until 2000 nor could they become German ones.

Nationalists are entitled to believe that being American, British, French or whatever uniquely defines who they are – although their basis for doing so, however honestly felt, is factually incorrect. The bigger problem is that nationalists don't just assert their legitimate right to their own collective identity, they also seek to impose it on others. They seek to decide who belongs to a nation and who doesn't, and they demand that all members of a nation give it the same primacy that they do. In other words, they often seek to exclude many or most immigrants from the nation and label fellow members of the nation who disagree with them traitors.

President Trump claims to speak for 'real Americans', implying that not all US citizens are American, whether because of their ethnic heritage or because they disagree with him. Critics such as Congresswoman Alexandria Ocasio-Cortez – one of those whom Trump urged 'to go back and help fix the totally broken and crime-infested places from which they came' – are doubly damned, being both Latina (from Puerto Rico, which has been a US territory since 1898) and a Democrat.

Contrary to the belief that nations are unchanging ancient communities, they are in fact a relatively recent invention. While humans have always lived in groups and distinguished between members of their group and outsiders, the scope, characteristics and membership of those groups have continually evolved.

Humans' concept of Us may initially have consisted only of members of their clan, basically their extended family. Over time, notions of the collective may have broadened to their tribe, a collection of clans with common cultural characteristics. Among those who settled down to farm and then didn't move around much, 'Us' consisted of people from their locality. As a Londoner it is striking how even today if you go into rural areas, people will say 'she's not from round here' of someone from somewhere ten miles away. To be fair, such distinctions still exist within big cities too: note the separate identities of north and south Londoners, or Manhattanites and Brooklynites.

It was only in the nineteenth century and even more so in the twentieth that nations came into their own, as imagined – and coerced – communities that connected citizens to the state. They were primarily forged by the power of modern states keen to control and mobilise their citizens, by increased mobility and the reach of mass communications, and by economic and political upheaval and the collective tragedy of war. Founding myths were created, historical heroes celebrated and newfangled customs presented as venerable traditions.

As the Industrial Revolution gathered pace, millions of people uprooted from the countryside formed new connections in cities, while once-disparate local communities were brought together by the railways, the postal service and other administrative systems. Newspapers and later radio and television created a national conversation.

As state education became compulsory, governments sought to stamp out regional languages and dialects and taught all children a standardised common idiom. The French Republic taught all children a single version of 'French' history that began with '*nos ancêtres les Gaulois*' (our ancestors, the Gauls) – as if everyone in France was a direct descendant of Asterix and Obelix – and enshrined the ideals of the Revolution and *L'Etat laïque* (the secular state). The British government sought to foster a sense of Britishness through the common endeavour of the British Empire, the 'white man's burden', a special calling to greatness (and opportunity to advance oneself) reserved for Britons.

Political changes were crucial too. As rule by often culturally separate aristocratic elites gave way to democracy, and as the franchise was extended in Britain and elsewhere, a sense of national political community developed. Mass conscription, which began with the French Revolution, also required mobilising the masses by fostering a sense of common feeling against a shared enemy, a collective emotion that the terrible experience of war strengthened. Nationalism reached its zenith with the horrors of the First and Second World Wars.

For sure, nation-building did not start with a completely blank slate. Many people in both Britain and France had elements of a common ethnicity and culture, as well as many differences, particularly among regional and religious minorities. But the nationalist notion that, say, people in Cornwall and those in Cumbria have felt part of a single political family for centuries is nonsense, while even today many people in Corsica and some in Brittany don't feel fully French.

Even in cases where the development of national identity partly preceded the state to which the nation attached itself, state efforts did much to foster it. The unification of Germany in 1871 did not occur spontaneously by people conceiving of themselves as German clubbing together in their own state. In the aftermath of the Franco-Prussian war of 1870, Chancellor Otto von Bismarck united Prussians, Bavarians, Saxons and other peoples who considered themselves culturally German but also had many religious, linguistic, social and cultural differences – together with Slavic and other minorities – into the German Empire, with the King of Prussia becoming its first Emperor. Most German nation-building came after unification, not before it.

Nations are not ancient. Nor, as should be obvious from the previous section, are they typically based on common ancestry. That is self-evident in the case of the US, where even the descendants of nineteenth-century immigrants who think of themselves as quintessentially American actually came from all over Europe. But it is also true of Britain, France or Germany. As Chapter 2 highlighted, human beings have moved around a lot and intermarried a lot throughout history.

Nearly all nations are mongrels: mixtures of people who over time have lost sight of, chosen to suppress or been forced to erase their different origins. Like Nigel Farage, they have forgotten their foreign roots. Which is a good thing, in a way, because it means that even nationalists can eventually accept that They can become part of Us.

Neither ancient nor based on ancestry, nations are not set in stone. 'We will decide, and nobody else, who comes to this country,' said John Howard, then Australia's conservative prime minister in 2001. David Goodhart, a British communitarian journalist, echoes that argument, asserting that 'existing citizens have a right, through their politicians, to broadly control the character of their society and therefore who joins in and in what numbers.'[14]

But that is a delusion. However you define the British nation today, it is composed of completely different people than in the Victorian era;

everyone alive then is dead and everyone alive now wasn't born then. While children carry their parents' genes, they are often very different to them.

Moreover, while states can try to control who enters their territory and decide to whom they give citizenship, nations don't otherwise choose their members. Democratic nation-states don't dictate who has children, how many they will have, let alone how they will turn out. Social conservatives hate it, but some people are still born gay – and attitudes towards gay people have changed massively in the blink of an eye.

People also change over time. Even over relatively short periods of time, a nation's supposedly unchanging cultural characteristics are highly mutable. If Englishness is associated with a stiff upper lip, how do you explain daytime TV, or the outpouring of grief when Princess Diana died? Brits may once have been cool, rational and pragmatic people, but in recent years Brexit has made many people on both sides of the debate bonkers.

For centuries after King Henry VIII broke with the Catholic Church in Rome, 'Papists' were viewed with suspicion in England – as being in liege to a foreign power – a view that persists among hard-line Protestants in Northern Ireland. Yet today Roman Catholic and Brexiteer MP Jacob Rees-Mogg is seen as the epitome of Englishness. In the nineteenth century, German immigrants to the US were viewed as an alien threat by established settlers of English heritage; now a president who is the grandson of German immigrants poses as the defender of 'real Americans' like him. While some people still think that non-white Britons such as Chancellor Rishi Sunak and Mayor of London Sadiq Khan are not truly British, most Britons no longer equate Britishness with being white.[15] The notion of a single unchanging national community is a myth.

Diverse nations

Nor have nations ever been as uniform as nationalists think, and they are becoming ever more diverse for many reasons other than immigration.

Social conservatives often hark back to a Golden Era in the mists of time, or more recently the 1950s, when each European nation was supposedly united, uniformly white and everybody knew their place. But that is a myth. Despite governments' efforts and the cohesive impact of collective conflict, nation-building only ever went so far. Even in the heyday of national unity after the Second World War, British society was still fractured along lines of class, ideology, region and religion, while women were second-class citizens and gay people imprisoned. Since then, increasing individualism and social liberalism have enabled many more locals to express their differences, while globalisation has created many more connections that cut across national borders.

Since the 1960s, Westerners have increasingly insisted on the freedom to define and express their own identity, both as individuals and as members of groups, be they women, gays, greens, motorists or nativists. If young people are asked about their identity, they often reply, 'I'm me'; while they also identify with groups, they reject those who want to 'put them in a box'.[16] They clearly don't believe that they are uniquely defined by their national identity and are diverse in all sorts of way unrelated to immigration. At the same time, they want to be different and still belong.

More recently, globalisation – and for Europeans, EU integration – has created new cross-border connections and consciousness. The first Moon landing in 1969 and the photos of our planet that were sent back aroused a common global consciousness and for many an environmental one too. Increasing foreign travel has fostered greater awareness and appreciation of different cultures, as well as foreign friendships.

In our globalised world of easyJet and Erasmus, Facebook, foreign holidays and fusion food, people have an increasingly wide range of international connections. Politics too now cuts across borders, and not just through international institutions such as the EU and the UN. 'Climate strikes' now mobilise schoolchildren across Europe, North America and the world. Black Lives Matter protests have erupted around the globe. Facebook groups bring together people with common passions from all over. People follow on Twitter, and are followed by, people in different countries. Their favourite pop stars and footballers are often foreign.

People increasingly join chosen communities based on common values and interests that cut across national borders. Greens may feel a stronger bond to environmentalists in other countries than to their neighbours. The same is true of international socialists and, ironically, far-right nationalists who now seek to collaborate with their foreign peers.

At the same time, the upheaval of global change and the loosening of the ties of national identity are helping to revive regional and local identities. Scotland is seeking independence from the UK, Catalonia from Spain. Many Londoners feel closer to the capital than to the country, especially after the Brexit vote and the associated anti-London backlash.

The notion that there is a single way of being British or German and that this wholly defines who you are is more absurd than ever, whether your parents were born in Birmingham, Berlin or Bangladesh. It's true that some people have more international connections than others – graduates in cities and young people particularly so. But in *The Road to Somewhere*, David Goodhart goes further, arguing that society is fracturing into 'Anywheres', socially liberal, urban, rootless cosmopolitans who define their identity from their careers and their education, and 'Somewheres', socially conservative, provincial, rooted communitarians who get their identity from a sense of place and the people around them, and who feel a sense of loss due to mass immigration and rapid social change[17] – or as Nigel Farage puts it, 'the metropolitan liberal elites' and 'real people'. 'Somewheres' prize national identity more and feel that immigration threatens both it and them. Leaving aside that some working-class townsfolk are socially liberal internationalists, and some middle-class city-dwellers are bigoted nationalists, does Goodhart have a point?

Multiple identities

If you're looking for a citizen of the world, proud member of the metropolitan liberal 'elite', I fit the bill. I live in London, my parents are both foreign, I speak several languages, have a couple of degrees, detest nationalism, voted to Remain in the EU and earn a living from writing and talking. But does that make me a rootless person from Anywhere? Hardly. I have a very strong sense of identity as a Londoner as well as being British, European and a citizen of the world. Part of what makes me so proud to be a Londoner is the wonderful diversity of people all together in a particular place.

While in many respects I am different from a Brexit Party voter in Stoke-on-Trent, we also have plenty in common. We speak the same language. We both have British passports. We vote in the same elections and referendums and will both suffer the economic consequences of Brexit. We both rely on the NHS to keep us well. We have a common culture, from talking about the weather and commiserating about the football to *Line of*

Duty and Shakespeare. When foreigners see us abroad they may consider us both British (or more likely English).

The small-minded nativists who want to put us all in boxes ignore a deeper truth. Nobody is uniquely and wholly British; 'Somewheres', 'Any-wheres' and immigrants all have multiple, overlapping identities. A Brexit Party voter from Stoke may also identify as a man, a husband, a son, a postman, working class, a Stokie, English, British, European (during golf's Ryder Cup), a human being, a Potter (as Stoke City Football Club support-ers are known), an England fan, a supporter of Team GB, white, straight and much else besides, depending on the context. Indeed, young people increasingly define themselves in very personal ways. Asked to do so in three words, some say things such as 'warm, bright, funny' and 'hopeful, helpful, fortunate' rather than defining themselves through their national identity, job or otherwise.[18] Identity is much more complex and nuanced than anti-immigrant critics claim – and elastic enough to embrace immi-grants and their descendants if we want it to.

Just look at the England football team that the whole nation cheered on as they reached the semi-finals of the 2018 World Cup. Winger Raheem Sterling was born in Jamaica, while the fathers of right back Kyle Walker and midfielder Ashley Young are both Jamaican. Midfielder Ruben Loftus-Cheek is of Guyanese descent. Dele Alli's father is Nigerian. Striker Marcus Rashford is of St Kitts descent. Jesse Lingard's grandparents came from St Vincent and the Grenadines. In all its glorious diversity, did the England team not bring the country together in a moment of national pride?

Post-nationalism?

It is quite possible, even plausible, that the pull of the nation and the political power of the nation-state will decrease over time. City states and empires have come and gone; nation-states are Johnny-come-latelies that may eventually do so too. Even today, with the resurgence of nationalism, national identity is typically felt less strongly than in, say, 1945. Only 27 percent of Britons and a mere 15 percent of Dutch people would be willing to fight for their country.[19]

Internationalism, for all its weaknesses, still has its appeal. Even Hungary's Viktor Orbán does not want to pull his country out of the EU. In *Sapiens*, Yuval Noah Harari argues that global identity will ultimately win

– and I hope he is right.[20] But much can go wrong between here and there. For now, nation-states are still the main players politically and national identity still matters to most people to some extent. The good news is that when defined in civic terms with a cultural component, nations can be open to immigrants who want to fit in. But what if they don't want to?

18

ILLIBERALISM

Salman Ramadan Abedi had an unfortunate birthday: New Year's Eve. But that didn't stop him enjoying a good time with his mates in his native Manchester. He was a 'fun guy' who drank, smoked dope and rarely went to the mosque. Yet on 22 May 2017 he blew himself up as people left a concert by Ariana Grande at the Manchester Arena, killing twenty-two innocent people and injuring over five hundred. It was the deadliest terrorist atrocity in Britain since the 7/7 London bombings in 2005.

Abedi was the son of Libyan refugees who fled to the UK to escape the regime of Muammar Gaddafi. In 2011, when he was sixteen, his parents went home to Libya after Colonel Gaddafi's overthrow, but he stayed in Britain. He later enrolled at the University of Salford, where he studied business management, but then dropped out to work in a bakery. Police believe he used student loans to travel to ISIS-controlled territory in Syria where he learned how to make bombs.

How, when and why the fun-loving young Mancunian signed up for an Islamist death cult remains unclear. Many young people struggle with their identity, those from an immigrant background particularly so. Many feel alienated from their parents and society. Some get involved in gangs and crime. But becoming a suicide bomber is still an extreme step.

Islamist terrorists and the white nationalist ones who featured at the beginning of this book are evil twins. Both hate modern, diverse Western societies. Both want to impose their vile views on others through violence, and to a certain extent they feed off each other. And both are unrepresentative of the people they claim to represent. Almost all Muslims in the West abhor jihadi terrorism, just as almost all whites loathe white nationalist terrorism.

There is no excuse for what Abedi did. The jihadist attacks, mostly by French and Belgian citizens, that killed 130 people in Paris in 2015 are equally loathsome. The murder of eighty-six people in Nice in 2016 by a Tunisian-born immigrant and the killing of thirty-two people in Brussels later that year were vile. That a tiny minority of Muslims in the West kill others in the name of Islamist ideology is tragic.

Governments need to be vigilant and tough in combating terrorism of all kinds. But it would be wrong to tar all Muslims with the same brush and seek to halt immigration by Muslims. Indeed, the UK didn't stop Irish people coming to the country without even showing their passports during the long bombing campaign by the Irish Republican Army (IRA).

In any case, the most murderous act of Islamist terrorism in the West – the 9/11 attacks in the US in 2001 that killed nearly three thousand people – was perpetrated by foreign visitors, not immigrants. Two of the four fatal Islamist attacks in Canada since 2014 (and indeed ever) – which together killed two people – were perpetrated by converts to Islam.[1] So keeping out Muslim immigrants would be ineffective at stopping terrorism as well as unfair. Indeed, in the US around one in eight Muslims are converts.[2]

Between 9/11 and September 2019, jihadists killed 104 people in the US.[3] In the EU, they killed 620, starting with the 193 killed in Madrid in 2004 up to the end of 2018.[4] In Australia, Islamist terrorists, all immigrants or their children, have killed four people since 2014 (and indeed ever).[5] Many more plots are foiled. In 2018, 511 people were arrested on suspicion of offences related to jihadist terrorism; just over half were born outside the EU.[6]

Muslim threat?

Awful as it is, terrorism remains mercifully rare. But the bigger question is whether illiberal immigrants and their descendants threaten Westerners' way of life. Some even claim that Islam is incompatible with liberal democracy.

It's regrettable if some people are deeply illiberal, but it's not a threat to society as a whole if they are not numerous enough to undermine liberal democracy. Even if Muslims were all deeply illiberal – which they're not – their numbers are not that large.

Locals tend to vastly overestimate the Muslim population in the West. Americans think one in seven people in the US are Muslim; only one in a hundred are.[7] Britons estimate that more than a sixth of the UK population is Muslim; less than one in twenty are. Canadians think 22 percent are; the true figure is only 3 percent. Australians believe one in six are Muslim when only one in forty are. In France, people think 28 percent of the population is Muslim; in fact, 9 percent is, the highest share among Western countries. That is a significant proportion, but much less than people think.

While Muslims are often perceived as a homogeneous threat, they are a diverse group, just as Christians are. They originate from different countries, practise different versions of the faith to varying intensities and are individuals as well as believers. In the UK nearly two-thirds describe themselves as highly religious; in France only a third do.

Most Muslims are well integrated into society. Even though one in five locals say they would not want Muslims as neighbours, some 96 percent of Muslims in France and Germany and 89 percent in the UK feel closely connected to their country.[8] Three-quarters of Muslims in France, Britain, Austria, Germany and Switzerland regularly spend their free time with non-Muslims.

In Britain, around half of Muslims say they would like full integration with non-Muslims in all aspects of life, younger Muslims and those born in the UK especially so.[9] Five in six agree that 'it is possible to fully belong to Britain and maintain a separate cultural or religious identity'; two-thirds of Britons in general agree with them. More than seven in ten Muslims reject the idea that Western liberal society is incompatible with Islam.

It's true that Muslims tend to be more socially conservative than other Britons, although ironically some of their views are often shared by Muslim-hating people on the far right. Close to half of Muslim men and a third of Muslim women in Britain agree that 'wives should always obey their husbands'. A majority think that homosexuality shouldn't be legal, although attitudes among young Muslims are somewhat more liberal. That said, in the 2017 parliamentary vote in Germany on legalising gay marriage, all Muslim MPs backed the move (and many Christian ones didn't). Most Muslim MPs in the UK backed equivalent legislation in 2013.

Being socially liberal myself, I regret such reactionary views. I hope they evolve over time and we should certainly try to change minds. But such views also exist among the rest of the population; indeed, they were a majority view a few decades ago. While they are more prevalent among the Muslim minority than the non-Muslim majority, non-Muslims are much more numerous, so most social conservatives are non-Muslims. How, then, can we all get along?

Learning to live together

Undeniably, getting along with others can be tough. People have different values, competing interests, peculiar habits and different ways of seeing, interpreting and expressing things. Disagreements and misunderstandings are all too common. Just ask any family at Christmas.

So the question of how different people in society can find a way to live together freely, peacefully and productively is crucial. But it's not new and it doesn't arise solely because of immigration: it applies to each individual and group who must find a place for themselves in society.

Throughout history European societies have wrestled with how diverse individuals and groups can coexist. Wars of religion between Catholics and Protestants were fought. Minorities such as the Jews were in turn persecuted and exiled. An independent thinker such as Galileo – who, contrary to seventeenth-century Catholic dogma, rightly thought the Earth rotated around the Sun – was convicted of heresy and spent the rest of his life under house arrest. Civil wars and revolutions erupted over clashing concepts of how a country should be governed.

The good news is that a *modus vivendi* was eventually achieved, one so successful and enduring that most people now take it for granted. Imperfectly but still importantly, in modern, liberal democracies differences are tolerated within the framework of the rule of law that applies equally to all, while robust democratic institutions help settle disagreements through political negotiation and compromise.

Even in the absence of immigration, people aren't all alike – and they don't need to be in order to live together. If modern societies are broad enough to include both nuns and atheists, Marxists and libertarians, radical environmentalists and oil company bosses, surely they can embrace many different kinds of immigrant too, including Muslims?

We just need to respect the basic principles on which our liberal democracies are based. Laws are made by people, not God. The people who make those laws are elected. And their ability to make laws is constrained by certain fundamental principles such as freedom within the law, equality before the law and tolerance of differences.

These are sometimes described as 'British', 'European', 'American' or 'Western' values, to which immigrants are expected to conform. Others call them universal values. But they are neither. They are liberal values – values that are shared by many non-Westerners and rejected by some locals, notably far-right bigots. While people cannot be forced to believe in liberal values, they can be required to obey the law: even those who believe that women are not equal to men must treat them as such. Likewise, people can dream of a communist or Islamist revolution and argue for it peacefully, but not act violently to achieve it.

Of course, all societies fall short of the lofty ideals of liberal democracy – discrimination is rife and tolerance limited – but they are still the standards we aspire to and the basis of our peaceful coexistence.

Regrettably, governments sometimes act illiberally, ostensibly in defence of liberal values. Many countries have banned burqas, the outer garments that cover the body and face which some Muslim women wear; France even passed a law banning religious symbols (including headscarves) from public institutions. But people should be free to wear what they please. A problem arises only if men are forcing women to wear outfits they don't want, or indeed abusing them in other ways. Such abuse needs tackling, not women's choice of clothing.

Liberals must always be vigilant to defend our societies' liberal institutions, but immigration need not threaten them. More than nine in ten Muslims agree that 'Muslims in Britain should always obey British laws'.[10] Only a tiny percentage express support or sympathy for terrorism, indeed less so than among the general population. In the US, support for terrorism is likewise very low, lower than among Americans as a whole.[11]

Criminal migrants?

President Trump also often accuses immigrants of being criminals. The kernel of truth to that sweeping generalisation is that organised crime is often based on ethnic networks – be they Russian mobsters, Italian mafiosi or Albanian gangsters – as well as local ones. Some Mexican migrants are drug dealers, as are some Americans. But overall, migrants are typically less likely to commit crimes than locals.

In the US, immigrants tend to commit far fewer crimes than locals and are less likely to be in prison too.[12] Among young less-educated males, locals are four times more likely to be in prison.[13] Nor are irregular migrants criminal: they too have lower incarceration rates than people born in the US.[14] A higher population of undocumented immigrants does not raise violent crime rates[15] and is associated with much lower drug arrests.[16] Despite possessing characteristics normally associated with higher crime rates, irregular migrants are a third less likely to be imprisoned than similar US-born people.[17]

In England and Wales, increased east European migration was associated with a fall in local property crime, while higher numbers of asylum seekers were associated with a slight rise in property crime. Neither group had a significant impact on violent crime. Since asylum seekers account for only 0.1 percent of the UK population, their impact on crime levels was minuscule. Crime would doubtless be lower if asylum seekers were allowed to work.

It's true that a gang of British men of Pakistani origin sexually abused hundreds of young girls in Yorkshire. It was a vile set of crimes and local police were wrong to turn a blind eye to this; at the same time, there are white British paedophiles too. Looking at the UK prison population as a whole, foreigners account for around 12 percent, similar to their share of the adult population. Indeed, crime has fallen sharply in Britain over the past twenty years while the immigrant population has grown quickly.[18]

In Australia too, immigrants are much less likely to be in prison.[19] In Germany, there is no evidence that immigrants increase crime.[20] This despite the fact that a study across European countries showed that immigrants were more likely to be sent to prison than locals for equivalent convictions.[21] Not for the first time, Donald Trump is wrong to slander immigrants as criminals.

Dysfunctional cultures?

Even so, Paul Collier argues that people from poor countries bring the dysfunctional culture of their home country with them, threatening the good institutions and rule of law in rich countries. If, say, enough Zimbabweans moved, they would make the UK more like Zimbabwe. But not enough people do move for that to be a realistic concern. The few that do tend to be those that value everything that life in the West brings – including the rule of law. Even those for whom that is not important tend to change when they arrive, and their children who are born in the West even more so.

As Robert Guest points out, 'America's population has risen sixty-fold since 1800. It has absorbed migrants from Tsarist Russia, Hitler's Germany, Ho Chi Minh's Vietnam and nearly every other dictatorship of the past 200 years, without losing its democratic soul. On the contrary, migrants head to America because they prefer its institutions to the ones back home.'[22]

We need to defend liberal values and the laws and institutions based on them. Islamist terrorists are evil and their sympathisers are misguided. Opposition to the war in Iraq, for instance, doesn't justify blowing up innocent civilians in Europe or the US. At the same time, the biggest threat to our liberal democracies comes not from a tiny minority of Islamist extremists, but from the likes of Donald Trump and Viktor Orbán.

The bare minimum necessary for peaceful coexistence is respect for liberal laws and institutions. But what more should immigrants do to fit in? And how should the rest of society adapt?

19

INTEGRATION

Hillcroft Avenue looks like a typically American suburban street. Eight lanes of traffic filled with vehicles ranging from large to huge are lined by strip malls fronted by ample parking lots. Signs advertising local businesses jostle for the attention of passing drivers; nobody walks. But look more closely at those advertising hoardings. 'Patel Brothers, Indian and Pakistani Grocers' stands above 'Bombay Sweets, Vegetarian Restaurant' and 'Maharaja Jewelers'. This is the Mahatma Gandhi district of Houston, Texas, also known as Little India.

Hillcroft is much more than just an Indian enclave, though. Next to Masala Munchies lies the Consultorio Medico Hispano, a Latino clinic. A few doors down, squeezed between yet more Indian eateries, sits Crystal Nite Club, which attracts mainly a gay Latino crowd. A bit up the road, you can find Jerusalem Halal Meats, a Middle Eastern butcher and deli, next to Quan Pham, a Vietnamese-run insurance broker, and Restaurant Guatemala. Refugees from Iraq, Afghanistan and Eritrea shop at a market where the traders mainly speak Spanish.

'I love Houston because we're able to be in a place where I don't have to be afraid of people that don't look like me,' said Nicole Walters, a Houston-born African-American woman married to a Jamaican, who was out shopping for a sari to wear to a Bollywood event.[1]

Houston wasn't always like that. Founded in 1836, the city was named after General Sam Houston, a president of what was then the Republic of Texas. In the twentieth century, it grew to become the state's largest city as the oil industry expanded along with Houston's international port, America's biggest. But a city of oil men and dockworkers has since also attracted a world-beating cluster of healthcare companies and medical research institutions, as well as NASA's Johnson Space Center.

Now the fourth-largest US city, Houston's booming local economy, plentiful employment opportunities, affordable property prices and low taxes have enticed people from around the country and around the world. Refugees from Vietnam and elsewhere have also been welcomed. What was once a segregated Southern city with a hefty white majority and sizeable black minority has become the most ethnically and racially diverse metropolis in the US.

Three in ten Houstonians were born abroad, more than twice the proportion in the US as a whole. In Harris County, which encompasses the broader Houston area, 42 percent self-identified as Latino, 31 percent as Anglo, 19 percent as black and 8 percent as Asian or other in 2016.[2] As such, Houston provides a window on to a more diverse future America – one where, as many whites fear, white people, as currently defined, are no longer a majority. So, is Houston still recognisably American? Do all these different people get along? Or has society collapsed?

Growing together

Margaret Long Wisdom High School in Southwest Houston used to be named after Robert E. Lee, the commander of the Confederate Army in the American Civil War. Now, nearly half of the student population are recent immigrants. They speak more than forty different languages and many need help learning English. Teenage girls wearing hijabs and jeans chat to a boy from El Salvador with bleached blond hair. 'It's really surprising to see a place like this in the South, where you consider it to be racist and xenophobic,' said Michael Negussie, a student who was born in Ethiopia. 'Stereotypes of Texas don't apply here.'[3]

All this diversity angers some local residents. 'Having bilingual teachers and specific programmes just to address those folks I think is overwhelmingly tilted in the wrong direction,' said Sam Herrera of Stop the Magnet, a pressure group that supports deporting 'illegal' immigrants. 'Folks need to come here, they need to assimilate and they need to learn the language.'[4]

All the children at the school are learning English; its previously poor academic record has much improved; and on the soccer field, its football team is hard to beat. The boys play in a white strip with yellow numbers, but sport a plethora of outrageously multicoloured boots, just like their football idols do. '*Búscalo, búscalo*,' shouts the coach in Spanish, spurring the boys to sprint for the ball. '*Umusitari!*' – run down the line – calls out a voice from the Democratic Republic of Congo.[5] The players speak a mixture of Spanish, Swahili and, yes, often English. Beware Liverpool FC, they are all becoming fluent in football too.

US-born Anglos are mostly happy with the increasingly diverse direction Houston has taken. Seven in ten believe the city's increasing ethnic diversity will become a source of great strength for the region.[6] Nearly four in five think the US should admit as many, or more, immigrants over the next ten years as in the previous decade, as do three in four US-born blacks there and eight in nine US-born Latinos. In a city thought to be home to the third-largest population of undocumented migrants in the US, the proportion of US-born white Anglos who favour granting law-abiding, English-speaking irregulars a pathway to citizenship has risen to 71 percent. It is a far cry from the racial hatred of the El Paso shooter.

Undeniably, the complexion and culture of Houston are changing. But the newcomers are absorbing Texan culture too. 'Hey y'all. Swing by! Saddle up,' urges Whiskey River, a local dance hall and saloon. Mixed-race couples do, bringing their children kitted out in cowboy hats and boots. While a former marine celebrates his birthday with a big cake, others feast on barbecue. Patrons try to master a mechanical bucking bull, while the mixed crowd spills outside to dance to country and western bands. Houston may be exceptionally diverse, but it's still Texas.

Better still, all these diverse people are increasingly mixing with – and marrying – each other. Most Houstonians have a close friend from a different race or ethnicity.[7] Younger people are mixing much more than older ones. To them diversity is familiar, and so feels normal.

Immigrants' children are also more integrated than their parents. While three in five foreign-born Latinos have a close Anglo friend, four in five US-born ones do. Nearly three in five US-born Latinos had been in a romantic relationship with a non-Latino. The proportions for Asians are pretty similar. Marriage statistics confirm this. Nearly three in ten marriages of US-born Latinos in Harris County are with a non-Latino. The proportion is similar for Asians. Black intermarriages have soared from 5 percent in 1980 to 18 percent in 2017.

Of course, Houston isn't perfect. There are big disparities between rich and poor. The legacy of racial segregation endures, although immigrants are increasingly spreading out. But the future is looking good. 'The world of the 2000s and 2010s, when the younger generations were coming of age, is a place of thriving interethnic friendships and increasing rates of inter-marriage,' observes Stephen Klineberg of the Kinder Institute for Urban Research. 'This is a decidedly different era compared to the more rigidly segregated world of the 1960s and 1970s when today's older Americans were moving into adulthood.'

Where Houston leads, the rest of America is following, albeit at different speeds. Ethnic and racial diversity has increased in 98 percent of big cities, 97 percent of smaller ones and nine out of ten rural counties since 1980.[8] If Houston – a hard-nosed place, not an idealistic one – is anything to go by, there is every chance that they will all eventually get along fine.

Participating in society

To live together without coming to blows, we all need to abide by laws based on liberal values, as Chapter 18 argued. But what more do immigrants need to do to fit in? What do locals need to do to adjust? And what role is there for governments?

Some locals object to the presence of immigrants no matter what. Others expect them to adopt the local culture wholesale (while still providing ethnic restaurants). Still others see adaptation as a two-way street, albeit one where immigrants have to adapt more. Everyone agrees that newcomers need to learn the local language.

Although in principle different people in society could live separate lives and not tread on each other's toes, it would be better if people interacted more. To make the most of the economic and cultural benefits of diversity, people need to mix productively. Most people also think that it is good for society that different people interact at school, at work, in the street and socially. They may do so naturally, or they may be unable or reluctant to do so and need a helping hand – or a push.

Again, this issue is not new and is not posed solely by recent immigration. Would it be better if Dutch-speaking Flemish people and

French-speaking Walloons in Belgium interacted more, and what should be done to encourage – or force – them to do so? Should long-established religious communities such as the Amish in Pennsylvania or the ultra-orthodox Hasidic Jews in London's Stamford Hill be left to their own devices, or should their children be exposed to outsiders with different views at school and elsewhere? Would it be better if neighbourhoods and schools had a mix of rich and poor – or whites and blacks – and how should one achieve this? Is it OK for gay people to cluster together – whether out of choice, fear or both? Are religious schools a good idea – and does your answer depend on whether they are Christian, Jewish, Muslim or indeed Scientologist?

There is no universally applicable answer to such questions. All societies seek to balance the freedom of individuals and groups to be left alone to live their lives as they see fit with their duties and responsibilities as members of society, but different societies reach different conclusions at different times and on different issues. In the American West in the late nineteenth century, society tended towards the libertarian. Japan is much more conformist and collectivist. Most European countries are liberal in many respects, less so in others.

As regards immigrants, governments have tended to take one of three broad approaches. The first, which could be called indifference, is to expect nothing of newcomers except their labour and their respect for the law – and to do nothing for them beyond perhaps job-specific training – in the expectation that they will leave again, or in the belief that foreigners can never become full members of society, or both. That is the bargain that the Gulf states explicitly offer their foreign workers. It is the basis on which highly skilled temporary workers tend to move (although some end up settling). And it is how Germany treated those it considered guest workers – even after many had settled and had children there. Unsurprisingly, this led to resentment among both immigrants and locals. Fortunately, Germany has since changed course, and since 2000 those who are not of German ethnicity can apply for citizenship. But even today Austria and Switzerland make it almost impossible for immigrants and their children to become citizens; they remain citizens of countries they have long left or never lived in.

At the other extreme, France makes it easy for newcomers and their children to become French citizens but expects them to assimilate: to give up their foreign language and culture and become fully French. Everyone is taught that their ancestors are the Gauls. That may sound intolerant – and it is illiberal – but in principle it isn't discriminatory: it is in keeping with the egalitarian principles of the French Republic. All citizens are meant to be equal; all French people are just French, not hyphenated French, unlike say Hispanic Americans. The French state professes to be blind to people's ethnic and cultural background and doesn't even collect data on citizens' ethnicity and race, although it does now collect data on their country of birth.

In practice, though, non-white African and Asian migrants and their children have been treated differently. Many were housed and became trapped in deprived suburban housing estates with few job opportunities, *banlieues* that periodically erupt into riots. Employers discriminate against job applicants with non-European names. They may be citizens, but they aren't treated as fully French, so they don't feel like it either.

Australia and Canada, and to a lesser extent the UK and the US, also make it relatively easy for most newcomers to become citizens. But unlike France, they have pursued a third approach known as multiculturalism, an often misused and misunderstood term, which can take different forms.

Multiculturalism and the backlash against it

Multiculturalism seeks to enable immigrants to participate fully in society as equals without having to give up their language, culture or religion. In the US, this traditionally involved a live-and-let-live approach: cultural diversity was accepted but not promoted, and it was expected that newcomers would organically become American as they and their children settled in. But since the 1960s, affirmative-action policies designed to give a leg up to the descendants of slaves and 'native' Americans have encouraged newcomers to continue identifying as 'Hispanic' or 'Asian' for economic reasons to benefit from preferential hiring and promotion. That, in turn, has sparked a backlash among non-beneficiaries.

While affirmative-action policies may be necessary for short periods to right entrenched injustices, they become pernicious if sustained over time, since they encourage people to club together in rival groups to compete for privileges. The size of the Mexican influx and the misperception that people of Mexican descent don't learn English has also sparked a backlash against Spanish speaking, and thus greater pressure to learn English.

Britain too has traditionally taken a live-and-let-live approach. As in France, this partly reflects history: when the British state was nation-building in the nineteenth century it accepted differences between English, Scottish, Welsh and Irish people, and Protestants and Catholics, so long as everyone was loyal to the Crown.[9] There was much to be said for such a liberal approach. So long as newcomers didn't break the law, they could more or less do as they pleased. It was assumed that people would learn English – and they did. But the downside was that tolerance masked neglect of festering social problems. Later, under the guise of promoting good 'race relations', the UK has also pursued more Canadian-style multiculturalist policies.

In Canada, Australia and some other countries, multiculturalism involves government recognition of, and support for, minority ethnic communities. Canada's 1971 Multiculturalism Act not only talked of respecting diversity, but also a duty to 'promote the understanding that multiculturalism is a fundamental characteristic of the Canadian heritage and identity and that it provides an invaluable resource in the shaping of Canada's future' and to 'advance multiculturalism throughout Canada'.

At its most benign and banal, this involves government funding for the likes of Diwali festivals, the five-day festival of lights celebrated by Hindus, Sikhs and Jains, or indeed celebrations of St Patrick's Day, the Irish national day. More controversially, it involves support for immigrants' languages, such as translation services, and for ethnic community groups, which some locals resent. More perniciously, it can put immigrants into different boxes, ostensibly to protect them, but often trapping them there. For instance, respecting Muslim women's right to wear the veil is a good thing; turning a blind eye to some Muslim men's mistreatment of their wives and daughters out of 'cultural sensitivity' is not. Pushed to its extreme, multiculturalism can lead society to fragment into myriad competing mini-nationalisms.

In *Whiteshift*, Eric Kaufmann criticises what he calls 'asymmetrical multiculturalism' whereby minority identities are lauded while white majority ones are denigrated.[10] But his solution is not to try to limit the excesses of identity politics but rather to extend it to whites, who 'should feel free to express a group self-interest'. Responding to claims that this would be racist, he argues that 'majority ethnic groups' attachment to their in-group is not racist unless it leads to unequal treatment of out-groups or a quest for racial purity. Social psychologists tell us that attachment to in-groups is not correlated with dislike of out-groups ... Identifying as white, or with a white tradition of nationhood, is no more racist than identifying as black.'

Yet Kaufmann's solution would entail a communitarian hell based on accommodation between ethnic groups instead of the interaction of free and equal individual citizens with complex overlapping identities. Worse, he wants to limit immigration on the basis of perceived cultural affinity. 'Excluding particular people, such as Muslim ethnic groups, is racist,' he writes, 'but trying to protect established groups is not.' Yet he wants to limit immigration by groups, such as Muslims, who are perceived to be culturally difficult to integrate.

The backlash against multiculturalism, along with France's realisation of the flaws of its assimilation policies, have led many governments to converge on hybrid 'integration' policies. These are more prescriptive than multiculturalist policies but more accepting of difference than assimilationist ones. Governments have imposed on immigrants a battery of language tests, citizenship tests and 'integration contracts' that, among other things, involve signing up to 'Western' – that is, liberal – values.

Integration?

In public discourse, 'integration' means different things to different people. For some, it is code for assimilation: 'immigrants must become like us'. For others, it means 'immigrants must have access to jobs'. For still others, it means 'communities should have things in common'. The notion of integration often plays into a false notion of 'Them' and 'Us'; each Western society is not a monolithic whole, and neither are immigrants. Very often, I suspect, people who use the word 'integration' don't have a clear idea of what they mean by it.

Everyone in a country should be able to communicate with each other (although it is natural that immigrants will take time to learn the local language and right that they should continue speaking other languages if they wish). It is also desirable for different people to mix (although it is natural that newcomers will initially want to stick together as they adjust to a foreign land). It is likewise positive that people should have an idea of prevailing norms, how government functions and the values on which liberal democracy is based. Indeed, civics should be taught in schools to all pupils, not just to immigrants. Remember that then Prime Minister Gordon Brown couldn't answer his own citizenship test questions.

Beyond that, requiring immigrants to 'behave like us' begs the question: behave like whom? Should they model themselves on Barack Obama or Donald Trump? Is their role model trans woman Chelsea Manning – a whistle-blower for some, a traitor who betrayed official secrets to others – or Jerry Falwell Jr. – a conservative evangelical icon for some, a hypocrite accused of an improper relationship with a male pool attendant (a relationship he denies), to others? In the UK, should they emulate environmentalist David Attenborough or petrol-head Jeremy Clarkson? Should they be Brexiteers or Remainers? Is it OK for nuns to cover their hair but not Muslim women? Is it acceptable to cover one's face to limit coronavirus transmission, but not otherwise? Modern societies are inescapably diverse in all sorts of ways, so there are – or ought to be – many different ways of behaving and fitting in.

The bigger issue is that for immigrants to fit into society, they – and their children – need to be accepted into it. However 'integration' is defined, it needs to be a two-way street. And for immigrants and their children to participate fully in society, they need to have the same opportunities as everyone else and be made to feel welcome.

Many politicians lambaste multiculturalism for enabling or even encouraging immigrants to lead 'parallel lives' – which typically isn't true – yet French-style assimilation policies have scarcely eradicated the problems of the segregated *banlieue* underclass. If immigrants and their children get trapped in deprived ghettoes, they suffer and feel excluded, while locals accuse them of not fitting in.

That is not an argument for affirmative action, though newly arrived refugees need specific help.[11] It is an argument for vigorously pursuing policies that advance equal opportunities, non-discrimination policies and social mobility for everyone in society – not just immigrants – as well as providing a pathway to citizenship for newcomers who choose to settle.

Indeed, in some countries access to political rights precedes the acquisition of citizenship: New Zealand allows migrants to vote after a year in the country, while the UK has long allowed Commonwealth (but not EU) citizens to vote in national elections.

Globally, immigrants are most accepted in countries such as New Zealand, Canada and Australia.[12] In the US and the UK immigrants also tend to fit in easily, thanks to the countries' job-rich, flexible labour markets. Through work newcomers become self-reliant, learn English, develop local contacts and become acquainted with local customs. Over time they and their children tend to better themselves through school and hard work, and move to more prosperous, mixed areas – with little state support in the UK and scarcely any in the US.

Pockets of entrenched exclusion exist – notably in former industrial towns in the North of England – but the problems there are largely socio-economic, not cultural. When white Britons rot away in depressed former mining villages, their plight is correctly seen as a consequence of post-industrial neglect. When the same is true of both whites and people of Pakistani origin in Oldham, a former mill town that has not recovered from the death of the local textile industry, this is interpreted as a failure by immigrants to integrate. Undeniably, deprivation can cause tensions, even riots, such as those in 2001, but these are not typically 'race riots' as commonly described, rather symptoms of deprivation and despair. In the super diverse but poor London borough of Hackney, in contrast, living with all sorts of different people is the norm. People mix and typically get along fine.[13]

In Canada and Australia, which have flexible labour markets while also providing more government support for immigrants, newcomers also tend to fare well. In contrast immigrants often fare less well in Sweden, despite the abundant help with training and language and generous welfare that the government provides, because immigrants are often excluded from the labour market, and therefore from society. France's rigid labour market likewise excludes immigrants (and young people). Problems such as a failure to recognise foreign qualifications, a lack of local job experience, excessive regulatory requirements and inadequate language training impede both economic and social integration.

Adapting to a new life

Nazek Ramadan arrived in London in 1986 speaking no English and knowing nothing of British culture. She had been forced to leave Lebanon when the civil war threatened her life and that of her children.

'We stayed in Lebanon as long as we could,' she explained. 'When my son was born, we had to flee the hospital and seek refuge in an underground shelter for two weeks, but we still stayed after that. Then one day, when my son was three and my daughter was four, they were at a school that didn't have an underground shelter and the shelling started. So I threw myself in a taxi, picked them up and drove to the airport. We got one of the last flights out before it closed. I never thought I would leave Lebanon. But I wanted to survive and have a normal life. We had to leave or we would die.'

The family initially stayed by London's Edgware Road, a Middle Eastern enclave. But soon they had to move to Abbey Wood in the eastern suburbs for financial reasons. There, Nazek experienced poverty, abuse and discrimination.

'At the beginning life was a nightmare. I didn't speak the language or know the culture. I felt so fragile and vulnerable. Even when I didn't understand what people were saying, I could tell they were swearing at me.' One day a neighbour put lit cigarettes through her letterbox, burning the carpet. 'I could hear them laughing next door. I thought, why do they hate us so much when they don't even know us? They made my life hell.' She started putting a bucket of water under the letterbox just in case.

'One old woman used to abuse me and call me "dirty Arab" in the local shop. I did my best to ignore her. Then one day before Christmas she came up to me and hugged me and said, "Please forgive me." Sometimes people do change.'

Eventually, Nazek moved to a nicer suburb. She learned English, got a degree in politics from Kingston University and started working for a charity that helps migrants. In 2010 she set up a group called Migrant Voice that we will hear more about in Chapter 20. And over time, London and Britain have become her home.

'You want to feel you belong here. When I go to Lebanon now I feel like a foreigner. It doesn't feel like home any more. Here in London I'm part of the local community. My job is here and so are my friends. But

some politicians make you feel like you don't fully belong to the country
– like when Theresa May sent out those vans saying "go home".'

Nazek's kids have grown up in Britain and learned from their peers.
'My son doesn't feel Lebanese. He sees my culture as alien. He speaks fluent Arabic but people in Lebanon can tell he's not Lebanese. He is a mix
of two different cultures. My daughter has married a British man. Their
children speak only a few words of Arabic.' That is how immigrants tend to
fit into society over time – through work, friendships and education. Later
generations tend to feel like locals – if locals treat them as such.

How, then, are countries doing in practice? Start with socio-economic
indicators such as employment, incomes and social mobility. Across
OECD countries, immigrants are as likely to be employed as locals.[14] In
the US and Italy, migrants – including low-skilled ones – are likelier to be
in work than locals. In Australia, Canada and the UK they are almost as
likely; EU-born migrants in the UK are more likely. But in many European
countries, non-EU migrants in particular are much less likely to have a job.
Labour-force participation rates are typically higher among men but lower
among women.[15] Immigrant women in many European countries such as
Sweden are much less likely to be economically active.

Migrants tend to be as healthy as locals, or more so. But on average
they tend to earn 10 percent less – except in Spain where they tend to earn
more – and poverty rates among immigrants tend to be higher. They may
work in jobs in which they don't use all their skills. And they are also likelier to live in substandard or overcrowded housing.

But none of this is necessarily a failure of integration. Migrants are still
better off than before moving; the crucial question is whether they and their
children progress over time. In the US, the children of poor, uneducated,
less-skilled, low-paid migrants tend to do much better than their parents,
although they do not always catch up with the children of locals.[16] Across
OECD countries, immigrants' children tend to lag a bit behind those of
locals at school, but they do as well as locals' children in Britain, better
than them in Canada and much better in Australia. But in some countries,
such as France, Germany, Sweden and Switzerland, they do considerably
worse; apps such as Century Tech's could help, as Chapter 9 explained.
Positively, among the children of immigrants from a very disadvantaged
socio-economic background, the share of top academic performers has

soared; in many countries they now outperform the equivalent children of locals.

On average across the OECD, the children of immigrants are less likely to be economically inactive, that is not in education, employment or training (NEET). Both in absolute and relative terms, they do particularly well in Canada and Australia, and better than locals' children in the US. In the UK they do as well as locals' children, but they do much less well in France, Belgium, Austria and the Netherlands. Among the low educated, NEET rates tend to be considerably higher among locals' children.

Turning to political integration, around two-thirds of settled migrants in OECD countries have become citizens. Four in five in Australia have, as have nine in ten in Canada, but in the US only three in five have. Similarly, three in five immigrants from non-EU countries who have been in the EU at least ten years have become citizens, while fewer than half of EU migrants have done so. In the UK three-quarters of settled non-EU migrants have become citizens, whereas only a third of EU-born ones have. This discrepancy is understandable: since EU migrants already enjoy equivalent rights to locals in most areas, there is much less incentive for them to acquire local citizenship. Now that Britain has left the EU, many more EU citizens are applying for citizenship.

Finally, consider cultural indicators, such as language and mixing. Contrary to popular fears, most immigrants do learn the local language. In the UK, 89 percent speak English as a mother tongue, proficiently or moderately well.[17] The proportion who speak the local language is similar in France and Italy and slightly lower in Germany. Language skills tend to improve over time. Across the EU, the proportion of non-EU migrants who speak the local language only at a basic level declines from 24 percent among those in the country less than five years to 8 percent among those there ten years or more.[18]

In the US, more than half of immigrants were proficient in English in 2017.[19] While more than a third of Hispanic immigrants spoke English at least 'very well', nine in ten Hispanics born in the US did.[20] A National Academies study found that immigrants' children are acquiring English and losing their ancestors' language at roughly the same rates as previous immigrant waves; the transition to speaking solely English usually occurs within three generations. Although Spanish-speaking immigrants appear to be acquiring English and losing Spanish more slowly than other immigrants, only 6 percent of the children of Hispanic immigrants speak mostly Spanish. Even in Southern California, only 4 percent of the grandchildren of Hispanic immigrants still speak primarily Spanish at home.[21]

Speaking the same language is a prerequisite for mixing. Living nearby also helps. In the US, cities and counties have long been segregated by race, a regrettable situation that has nothing to do with voluntary migration. But since 1990, more than 90 percent of US urban areas – including Houston – have seen a decline in racial stratification.[22] As Hispanics and Asians get richer and more established, they tend to move to richer, more mixed suburbs. Over time most immigrants and their descendants tend to gradually mix with white locals and disperse across regions, cities, communities and neighbourhoods.[23]

Contrary to public perception, segregation is generally not increasing in European cities.[24] In the UK, contrary to what some claim, it is decreasing. In 2005 Trevor Phillips, then the head of the Commission for Racial Equality, claimed the UK was 'sleepwalking to segregation'.[25] In 2016 the Casey Review commissioned by the UK government said some, mostly Muslim, communities were living 'isolated, separate lives'.[26] But as Jonathan Portes points out, 'the evidence for this is weak'.[27] Some places are more integrated than others;[28] by one measure, Boston in Lincolnshire is the least integrated place in Britain. While ethnic groups do sometimes congregate in particular areas, such as Sikhs in Southall, Pakistanis in Bradford and Koreans in New Malden, residential segregation has decreased over time.[29] Even immigrants who live in areas with many other immigrants are not typically segregated because those immigrants are increasingly diverse. Inner-city suburbs such as Newham in London are often 'arrival cities', with high concentrations of immigrants who then move on.[30]

Across EU countries, 44 percent of locals report interacting with non-EU migrants at least once a week in their neighbourhoods, while 28 percent do so at work; the average in the UK is a bit higher.[31] More than six in ten locals in Ireland mix with immigrants in their neighbourhoods, while fewer than four in ten do so in France. At work, the proportion is highest in Sweden – nearly half – but less than three-tenths in France.

To the extent that different people do live apart, it is important to know why. While mixing is preferable and should be encouraged, it shouldn't be compulsory. In a free society, people have a right to live where they choose. Indeed, society is often segmented not just by ethnicity, but also by class, age and increasingly by values too.[32] Nobody prevents rich whites clustering in parts of Cheshire or Connecticut, so why should poor immigrants be criticised for living together? There is a problem, however, if people – immigrants or locals – become trapped in deprived areas for economic reasons or because of discrimination.

Surprisingly few immigrants say they suffer discrimination. Around one in seven immigrants across OECD countries report being discriminated against on the basis of ethnicity, nationality or race. Self-reported discrimination is only 7 percent in the US, but rises to more than a fifth among non-EU migrants in France and Denmark, nearly a quarter in Belgium and the Netherlands and nearly a third in Greece. Troublingly, one in five migrants who have become Dutch citizens or been there ten or more years say they are discriminated against.

While racism and xenophobia are still prevalent, they are typically less bad than a generation ago. Few Brits would be unhappy if someone from a different background moved next door (10 percent), was their boss at work (7 percent) or married their son or daughter (16 percent).[33] The proportion of white Brits saying all their close friends were white fell from half in 2005 to 37 percent in 2015.[34] In the UK, the presence of immigrants has a small, positive effect on locals' subjective wellbeing in local authority areas.[35] Nor is there any evidence that this is because people who do not like immigration move away from high-immigration areas. Across Europe, the findings are similar.[36]

Opposition to mixed-race relationships has slumped. In the US, the proportion of people not of that race or ethnicity saying they would object to a close relative marrying a black person has plunged to 14 percent; only 9 percent would object to them marrying a Hispanic or Asian.[37] In the UK, the proportion of whites who say they would mind at least a little if a close relative married someone black or Asian fell from more than half in 1989 to about a quarter in 2013.[38] Far fewer blacks would object to a relative marrying a white person, but as many as 35 percent of those who identify as Pakistani British would.[39]

Opposition to mixed religion relationships has also fallen. In the UK in 2018, 82 percent said they would definitely or probably accept a person from a different religion marrying a relative, up from 74 percent a decade earlier.[40] While 23 percent of white British people would object a lot and 21 percent a little to a close relative marrying a Muslim, this falls to 11 percent and 16 percent respectively among young people.[41]

The surest way in which 'They' become 'Us' is through intermarriage – and the good news is that it is on the rise. It was only in 1967 – in a case about a couple aptly named Richard and Mildred Loving – that the US Supreme Court ruled that American states could not ban interracial marriage, thereby striking down laws banning mixed-race marriages in sixteen states. Back then, only 3 percent of newlyweds had a spouse of a different race or ethnicity; by 2015, 17 percent did. Among Asians the proportion was 29 percent and Hispanics 27 percent. Increasingly, mixed-race people don't fit into the boxes of census forms. American golfer Tiger Woods, who is half African-American, a quarter Thai, an eighth Dutch and an eighth Chinese, labels himself 'Cablinasian'.

Whereas the legacy of slavery and racial segregation has been a barrier to interracial unions in the US, black people are much more likely to marry white people in Canada, the UK and other European countries.[42] In Canada, the number of interracial relationships more than doubled between 1991 and 2011. Some 5 percent of all unions were between people of different ethnic origins, religions, languages and birthplaces in 2011, rising to 8 percent in Toronto and 10 percent in Vancouver.[43]

European countries tend not to collect census data on ethnicity, but surveys show that as many as 70 percent of people of Caribbean origin in the Netherlands marry whites. The biggest cleavage is often between Muslim and non-Muslim, though it is hard to disentangle social exclusion from cultural segregation.[44] Even so, whereas one in sixteen Muslim immigrants in Europe marry white locals, more than one in ten European-born Muslims do.[45] In France, nearly half of – typically North African – Muslims marry white locals.

While Prince Harry's marriage to Meghan Markle, an American of mixed race, was exceptional by royal standards, interracial marriages are increasingly common in Britain too. In England and Wales, 2.3 million people were in an interethnic relationship in 2011, accounting for 9 percent of people living as a couple, up from 7 percent in 2001.[46] The share of white Britons living in mixed ethnicity households doubled to 12 percent over that period. While immigrants are much more likely to marry people from the same country of origin, their children are typically much less so.[47] By far the fastest-growing ethnic group in the UK is 'mixed race'. The mixed-race population doubled to 1.2 million in the decade to 2011: witness sports stars such as Jessica Ennis-Hill and Lewis Hamilton, and former MPs such as Adam Afriyie and Chuka Umunna. More than one in twenty of those aged five to nine in 2011 were mixed race.

Across the OECD, 5 percent of young people have a mixed background – that is, one foreign-born parent and one local one – a share that has risen fast over the past decade.[48] The figure is 9 percent in Canada, 11 percent in New Zealand and 13 percent in Australia. In Europe, 10 percent of French youth are of a mixed background, while only 3 percent of German youth are.

Overall, then, the picture is broadly positive in English-speaking countries and more mixed in some EU countries. Indeed, while immigrants are as satisfied with their lives as locals are in North America and Australasia, they are less so in many EU countries.

Social cohesion

Despite all the evidence that immigrants are fitting into society, many still argue that immigration undermines social cohesion. Research by the American political scientist Robert Putnam suggests that in the US increased diversity correlates with diminished feelings of trust within a community.[49] But America's history of slavery and racial segregation is very different to other countries' immigration experience, and Putnam's findings do not generalise. Indeed, trust is arguably based more on a sense that society's rules are fair and applied impartially and that economic rewards are deserved.[50]

Contrary to Putnam's findings, younger Canadians with racial and ethnic diversity in their social networks show higher levels of generalised trust.[51] Nor have Putnam's findings been replicated in Europe. A comprehensive study of twenty-one countries concludes that 'in Europe it was not confirmed that rising ethnic diversity or even the rate of influx of foreign citizens had any significant detrimental effects on social cohesion.'[52] A survey of the literature likewise suggests that diversity does not reduce social cohesion in Britain – and increases it in London.[53] That should not be surprising: a sense of community does not need to be based on ethnic homogeneity. Indeed, London's diversity is part of its appeal to most Londoners and enhances a feeling of belonging to the city.

A related worry among some on the Left is that increasing diversity will reduce support for the welfare state. Yet a study of seventeen rich countries fails to find any evidence that it does.[54] Globally, there is no obvious correlation between ethnic homogeneity and the size of the welfare state. America is diverse and has a threadbare welfare state, while Belgium is split between Flemish and French speakers, but has a developed one. Sweden was ethnically homogeneous with a big welfare state, while South Korea and Japan are still ethnically homogeneous, but do not have European-style welfare states. Support for the welfare state is much higher in diverse cities such as London and New York than in more homogeneous Surrey or Wyoming. And even though immigrants now account for a larger share of Sweden's population than they do of the US's, Sweden's welfare state has hardly collapsed.

Moreover, support for the welfare state isn't just based on solidarity, it's also about social insurance for risks such as ill health that are hard to properly insure privately. If immigration ever did undermine public support for the welfare state, reforms could shore it up. If new arrivals are seen as a drain on the public purse, they can be denied social benefits initially. If some people – wherever they were born – are perceived as lazy or undeserving of assistance, welfare rules can be tightened. Welfare systems can also be reformed to increase incentives to work and tie some benefits more closely to previous contributions.

Overall, then, the picture tends to be mixed but improving. Immigrants and even more so their children tend to fit into society and are accepted by many locals. As the global Black Lives Matter protests have highlighted, racism is still far too prevalent; at the same time, it is not as bad as a few decades ago. Economically, the children of immigrants typically do much better than their parents. But of course societies can do much better. A good place to start is by persuading more sceptics of the merits of immigration and diversity.

PART FIVE
SEEKING SOLUTIONS

20

PERSUADING SCEPTICS

'It was the run-up to the 2010 [UK general] election and the debate about immigration was toxic. I was doing media work for an NGO [non-governmental organisation] that helps migrants and it was taking up my life. We were often working until eleven or twelve at night.

'One day we had a meeting with all the charities and organisations that help migrants and I was the only migrant in the room. They all agreed that "we need to keep a low profile during the election campaign." And I thought: you're taking that decision. What about us? We're the ones who are going to be bashed by the media. Our kids are the ones who aren't safe. You're not affected. And I realised it was time for us to come forward and speak for ourselves. So I set up Migrant Voice.'

Nazek Ramadan (whom we met in the previous chapter) is small and soft-spoken, but she certainly packs a punch. With very little funding but lots of passion and grit, she has helped give migrants a voice in the media and public debate. Her organisation's Twitter account, @MigrantVoiceUK, has more than 30,000 followers. 'Before they were always talking about us, but never to us,' she explains. 'Our stories were never told.' Now they are. She has also helped set up a pan-European network of similar organisations led by migrants and refugees called RISE.[1]

Migrant Voice seeks to change sceptics' minds. 'Maybe people can change,' she says. 'Maybe they don't know. Maybe it's for us to tell them. That's why we have to speak up and engage people. For me it's not just a job, it's a passion to bring about a change in attitudes towards migrants. We do so through telling stories, and now we're also doing campaigns with students as well as lobbying.'

Changing attitudes

Contrary to many people's perceptions, immigration is overwhelmingly a good thing. As this book has documented, it boosts the economy, society and culture, making migrants as well as locals better off. But many people remain unconvinced. How, then, can one change sceptics' attitudes?

Some people are irredeemably racist and xenophobic. In many countries they now feel freer to express their vile views because mainstream politicians and pundits have normalised them. Boris Johnson (who is partly of Turkish descent) and the Leave campaign whipped up fears about Turkish immigrants and refugees during the EU referendum campaign, and won. Trump slurred Mexicans and Muslims and still became president. When taboos are broken, it can be very difficult to restore them. Racists and xenophobes who cannot be persuaded must be confronted.

Many more people fear change, or tend to experience it as loss, and often focus that fear on its most visible – and vulnerable – forms: poorer people with different-looking faces and foreign-sounding names, some of whom are newly arrived immigrants, others long-established ones and many more of whom were born in the country. This change-fearing group is growing as societies age and many older people become nostalgic about a less diverse past – their youth – and fear the future: their death. Their impact is amplified because they are much likelier to vote than younger, more open-minded people and immigrants who have become citizens.

Some of those who focus their fears on immigrants live in areas that have only recently started receiving significant numbers of them, notably rural areas where the proportion of migrants has gone from zero to low. Others live in places that still have very few immigrants, but fear that their neighbourhoods will eventually become as diverse as the big cities that they barely know and so find alienating. People in those big, diverse cities – and especially young people who grew up there – tend to be much more positive about diversity, and find it normal rather than threatening.

Some people's fears are focused on economics, others on cultural change, many on both. Analysts disagree as to which matters most.[2] In the UK, around a third of voters think the economic impact of immigration on locals is positive, a third think it is negative and a third is in two minds.[3] When asked if they are OK with the way the population is changing, the three-way split is similar.

In practice, economics and culture are often interrelated and are not easily disentangled. In some cases, people whose real objection is cultural use economic arguments so as not to seem racist or xenophobic. In other cases, opposition to immigration that is ostensibly based on race, religion and identity issues is also tied to economic and social deprivation, loss of status or the fear of such loss. When people lose status as individuals – when they lose a good job, for instance – they often prize their group identity more. And in times of economic decline, people are often more nostalgic for the past. People who feel economically vulnerable tend to find all change more threatening.[4] Economic pain brings distributional conflicts to the fore and migrants may be a convenient scapegoat. Witness how the difficult decade since the financial crisis has seen more distributional conflicts over access to public services, for which migrants are blamed, and over housing, where older locals are also blamed. Better economic conditions[5] and tackling economic problems can thus alleviate some – but not all – cultural anxieties.

The task is not to try to win over all critics, sceptics and bigots, still less pander to their views. It is to mobilise enough people to get out and vote for pro-immigrant parties. It is to convince mainstream politicians not to echo the far right or emulate their policies, let alone ally with them. And it is to win over reasonable people in the middle who may be in two minds about immigration: who may have nothing against particular individuals they know but fear the amorphous whole.

This chapter sets out some suggestions for pro-immigrant voices on how to do that, in the hope that others will come up with their own ideas – and act on them. Please share them with me too. Let's consider changes in communication, behaviour, policy and politics in turn.

Facts are not enough

Nazek is right: migrants and locals who empathise with them should not keep quiet and concede the debate to anti-immigrant voices. Politics is a clash between competing ideas and interests; if only one side is vocal, the 'centre ground' shifts towards them. Politicians need to have an incentive to chase pro-migrant votes, and to fear losing them if they adopt anti-immigrant stances. Campaigners need to mobilise pro-immigrant voices, notably young people, and make their voices heard. Migrants who are citizens ought to register to vote and then do so. Young people should try to persuade sceptical parents and grandparents. Everyone needs to speak to their neighbours and colleagues. People also ought to go on marches (coronavirus permitting), write to newspapers and to their elected representatives, phone in to radio programmes, tweet and engage on Facebook and Instagram.

Regrettably, many progressives and liberals who don't have a direct stake in the issue sometimes conclude that it is best to keep their heads down. They may care more about other priorities such as social justice or free trade. Openness and welcoming migrants matter to them, but they're willing to trade them off to secure other goals. But that is short-sighted: witness the huge cost everyone in Britain is paying because misperceptions about migration contributed to the catastrophic decision to leave the EU.

To some extent, some progressives and liberals may also have internalised anti-immigrant arguments. And they may take public opinion as given, instead of trying to change it. This pessimism is unwarranted: witness how views about interracial marriage – and indeed same-sex marriage – have evolved relatively quickly through a combination of campaigning and societal change. Observe how much more positive views about immigration in Britain have become in recent years.[6] Notice how little headway anti-immigrant voices have made in countries such as Canada and Ireland. There is nothing inevitable or fixed about many sceptics' concerns about immigration.

To help dispel misperceptions, it's important to present the facts about immigration. Ignorance, misinformation and misinterpretations are rife, as Chapter 1 highlighted. Instead of validating misperceptions and lies about immigrants, we need politicians, campaigners, opinion-formers and indeed all of us to put a positive, evidence-based case for immigration. We need to dispel ignorance with information, misinformation with truth, misinterpretation with explanation and confront prejudice head on. Hopefully the evidence and arguments in this book will help.

Facts and arguments *do* make a difference; just over half of the people in the UK who have become more positive about immigration in recent years say this is because discussions have highlighted how much immigrants contribute.[7] The coronavirus crisis may produce a lasting shift in perceptions of migrants previously dismissed as 'low-skilled' who in fact do essential work.

Being specific helps. Many people for whom immigration in general has negative connotations are in favour of admitting specific types of immigrants, whose contribution they can readily identify. In the UK, nearly three in five people would like immigrant inflows reduced.[8] But when asked about specific types of migrant, they favour admitting as many, or more, of every occupation they were asked about, and likewise foreign spouses and partners. They were keenest about nurses and doctors, followed by care workers. But they were also positive about construction labourers; foreign bankers were least popular. So pro-immigrant voices shouldn't just make the case for immigration in general, they should also talk about specific people.

But even specific facts are not enough to persuade everyone. Many people have lost faith in experts, notably since the financial crisis. People who wrongly claim to be experts also put forward 'alternative facts'. And many people dismiss or ignore facts and arguments that challenge their views. Indeed, presenting facts alone can sometimes even be counterproductive if it brings to the fore critics' negative associations of immigrants that might otherwise have remained at the back of their minds.

Campaigners therefore need to deploy stories as well as statistics. Bogus and untypical second-hand anecdotes feed anti-immigrant myths. If, say, newspapers splash on a story about a refugee with eight children living off the public purse, it's important to point out that, even if that particular story is true (and it often isn't), refugees actually tend to become net contributors to public finances sooner than locals.[9]

At the same time, campaigners need to highlight positive personal stories of immigrants, as Nazek and Migrant Voice do, and as Define American, the organisation founded by Dreamer José Antonio Vargas, whom we met in Chapter 16, does. Prime Minister Boris Johnson had a global impact when he paid special tribute to Jenny McGee, from Invercargill, New Zealand, and Luis Pitarma, from Aveiro, Portugal, two of the nurses who cared for him when he almost died from coronavirus, leading to glowing coverage even in publications that are often hostile to immigrants.[10]

Inspiring role models can help too. Fans of Liverpool Football Club chant 'Mo Sa-la-la-la-lah, Mo Sa-la-la-la-lah, if he's good enough for you,

he's good enough for me, if he scores another few, then I'll be Muslim too'
to celebrate their star Egyptian striker, Mohamed Salah. While hate crimes
against Muslims have generally been rising, they have dropped nearly a
fifth in Liverpool since Salah signed for the club in June 2017. A survey
of Liverpool fans suggested Salah was familiarising his fans with Islam,
through his observation of the faith, while his image as a bubbly father,
friend and fantastic footballer was breaking down stereotypes of 'threatening Muslims'.[11]

Sometimes the most compelling stories are visual. The image of Alan
Kurdi, the Syrian toddler who washed up dead on a Turkish beach in 2015,
produced an outpouring of empathy for refugees that for a while trumped
xenophobia. So did the heartbreaking photo of a father and his daughter
– Óscar Alberto Martinez Ramírez and his two-year-old daughter Angie
Valeria, from El Salvador – lying dead on the bank of the Rio Grande,
entwined in an embrace, after drowning in their attempt to swim across
the border from Mexico to the US in 2019.[12]

A crucial part of good story-telling is crafting compelling narratives.
People tend to understand a complex world through simplifying stories, so
ideas that are encapsulated in persuasive narratives are much more effective. I've found that comparing immigrants' impact on the labour market
to that of women entering the workforce in the past helps convey the fact
that there isn't a fixed number of jobs to go around. One six-country study
found that while correcting people's misperceptions about immigrant
numbers and origins didn't make locals more likely to favour redistribution towards migrants, an anecdote about a 'hard-working immigrant' was
more effective.[13]

Accentuating the positive can make a big difference too. Opponents of
immigration aren't the only ones who tend to be negative about the subject; so too are many pro-immigrant voices. While they are right to point
out that immigrants are often poor and discriminated against, that is only
part of the story. Overwhelmingly, newcomers are dynamic people who
are trying to better themselves against the odds. If pro-immigrant voices
focus only on the negative aspects of immigrants' lives, critics will tend to
respond along the lines of, 'Why do immigrants come/stay here if they are
so miserable?' Talking only about immigrants' suffering also raises many
locals' hackles by making them feel like bad people.

Consider how refugees tend to be talked about. Critics portray them as a burden to be avoided, while even sympathisers tend to refer to them as a burden – one that we have a duty to share. They also tend to talk about refugees as victims. While most refugees have suffered immensely, as I know from my own family, they also tend to be exceptionally resilient and resourceful people. They typically don't want to be seen, or treated, as victims or charity cases. So accentuating the positive, while acknowledging the negative, is both accurate and often more persuasive.

Language matters too. Our words shape how we perceive the world. To many people, the labels 'immigrant' and 'migrant' have acquired negative associations. Using more neutral terms such as 'newcomers' can help. The negative association can also be subverted by juxtaposing it with a positive word: talking about 'refugee entrepreneurs' immediately shifts perceptions; it's hard to be against them. Ultimately, we need to reclaim the word 'immigrant' as positive, just as gay people reclaimed 'queer', but that takes time.

Eliciting empathy can also be effective. One reason why Irish people are much more positive about immigration is that Ireland has long been a country of emigration, most recently during and after the 2010–12 crisis in the eurozone, so everyone knows someone who has migrated and locals can understand their motivations.

Britain has long been a country of emigration too, yet Brits abroad tend to think of themselves as – and be considered – expats, not migrants. I was once on a BBC television programme about Brits who had emigrated to Cyprus because they thought there were too many foreigners in London. As if going abroad to escape from foreigners wasn't absurd enough, they then ranted and raved about how immigrants in London didn't bother to learn the language, behaved differently and didn't want to fit in. This from Brits in Cyprus who didn't speak a word of Greek, only socialised among fellow Brits, read the *Sun* newspaper and ate fish and chips in English cafés. Even when the presenter pointed out the irony of the situation to them, they couldn't – or wouldn't – accept it. In effect, they perceived themselves as the salt of the earth, whereas immigrants in London were not.

Even so, encouraging locals to put themselves in newcomers' shoes may persuade some sceptics. The UK has more of its citizens living abroad than any other rich country. That story – of Brits in the US, Australia, Singapore, Dubai, Spain and Germany – needs to be told so that, hopefully, there is more understanding of the migrant experience. Brexit may have an impact too, since some Brits will come back to the UK and others who want to leave may struggle to do so.

#EUsupergirl

If your mental image of the EU is of a faceless Brussels bureaucrat, a grey, grizzled old politician like former European Commission president Jean-Claude Juncker or a dull but worthy matriarch like German chancellor Angela Merkel, Madeleina Kay is a shock to the system. With her bleached blonde bob with a blue fringe, luminescent blue shades and supergirl outfit, this self-styled #EUsupergirl certainly makes a visual impression. Born in 1994, the Young European of the Year 2018 brings a breath of fresh air to often-stale pro-European campaigning. She sings. She plays the guitar. She writes illustrated books. And she unabashedly speaks up not just for the EU but for immigrants in general. *Go Back to Where You Came From!*, her children's storybook on the refugee crisis, helped raise money for a refugee charity in her native Sheffield.

A silver lining of the Brexit disaster is that it has spurred many young people who were previously disengaged from electoral politics to come out and campaign in creative ways for an open, liberal and progressive European future. Like many other young Brits, Madeleina had previously benefited from her EU free-movement rights. Before going to university she worked in a children's activity centre in Brittany and as an au pair with a family in the south of France. 'I'm a musician and I believe that music and creativity know no borders,' she says. 'They thrive on the free exchange and the free flow of ideas, people and imagination. It's not the big-name artists who will suffer, it's the smaller people who will get hurt. And there will be less diversity.'

She has a positive message for other young Britons who feel disenfranchised. 'What I'm trying to do with my campaigning is empower others. My message is be yourself, communicate in whatever way suits you best, express yourself. Your voice matters. Speak out. Everyone's contribution counts. Everyone's vote matters. Get active. Get involved. Communicate to your friends and peers. Do whatever you feel you can to speak out. Go to a march with a handmade placard. Go out stickering in your local area. Tweet.'

Madeleina Kay won't persuade everyone. But her efforts on behalf of immigrants will reach many people whom traditional politicians and campaigners leave cold.

Emphasise what connects us

As well as speaking up for migrants through facts, arguments, stories and innovative campaigning, it's important to speak up for society as whole. Celebrating diversity can seem threatening and excluding to people who aren't migrants. It may make them feel like they aren't valued or that others' interests are prioritised. Throughout this book, I've emphasised that diversity includes everyone: migrants from all countries as well as locals of all backgrounds, women and men, young and old, rich and poor. Making the most of diversity is not about privileging some people at the expense of others. While migrants are often exceptional people with a lot to contribute, diverse societies in which everyone works together both amplify and add to those individual strengths.

It is also crucial to emphasise what connects us. Newcomers are different in many respects; and those differences tend to complement our own. Over time, though, they – and even more so their children and grandchildren – become more like everyone else in society. Some of the benefits of their diversity thus dilute over generations – although people (including locals) who speak several languages and have connections with several cultures have something special to contribute. At the same time, newcomers become – or ought to become – full members of society: your neighbours, colleagues, friends, relatives, partners and fellow citizens. We may come from different places, but we have a shared present and a common future.

Whether you were born in the country of which you are a citizen or chose to adopt it, there are many different ways to be American, British, French or whatever. At the same time, everyone in a country is part of the same national community, as well as having other connections – just as everyone in a neighbourhood is part of the local community too. Diversity is great; so is what people in a particular place have in common. As Jonathan Haidt explains in his excellent book *The Righteous Mind*, you can make people care less about race and group identities 'by drowning them in a sea of similarities, shared goals and mutual interdependencies'.[14]

Part of that involves reclaiming patriotism. Reactionary and xenophobic nationalists such as Donald Trump, Marine Le Pen and Nigel Farage cast themselves as the only true patriots and argue that excluding immigrants is patriotic. Since liberals and progressives often feel uncomfortable talking about patriotism, they tend to surrender this political ground. But that's a mistake. Because the way to win over people for whom patriotism matters is not to ignore, let alone dismiss, their feelings but rather to persuade them that supporting open societies makes their country great.

If patriotism means wanting the best for your country, going it alone and pulling up the drawbridge is not defending the national interest, it is betraying it. Patriotism does not have to consist of harking back to an idealised past; it can also involve imagining how much better a country can become and overcoming the barriers to progress. Welcoming refugees was thus a point of national pride for many Germans. Admitting newcomers is also true to Britain's long tradition of openness. As Jack Graham puts it: 'You don't have to see yourself as a "citizen of the world" to understand that countries can benefit from cooperating with others and being open to outsiders, and that defining national identity in opposition to others is dangerous.'[15]

Likewise, immigration ought to be presented as a sign of a society's success. That is one reason why Irish people tend to see it positively, according to Brian Killoran, the head of the Immigrant Council of Ireland. The same ought to be true of Britain: when it was in economic decline, more people used to leave Britain than arrive, but that turned around in recent decades as its economy outperformed (until the Brexit vote). The decline in EU migration to the UK because of a weaker pound and a flagging economy is a sign of failure, not a success. Is national decline really what Brexiteers want?

Crucially, pro-immigrant voices also need to reach out to those with different values and speak their language, rather than ignoring or abusing them. That doesn't mean accepting racism and xenophobia, but it does mean accepting some people value order more than freedom, tradition more than change, and family ties more than equal rights. Some people also have a different concept of justice than others. You don't have to agree with someone in order to try to win them over.

Jonathan Haidt argues that liberal Westerners suffer from a rationalist delusion that reasoning can cause good behaviour and is our pathway to moral truth. Yet according to him, most of our conscious reasoning is after-the-fact justification for our moral intuitions, which shape our emotions and unconsciously govern our behaviour. 'The mind is divided, like a rider on an elephant, and the rider's job is to serve the elephant. Therefore if you want to change someone's mind about a moral or political issue, talk to the elephant first. If you ask someone to believe something that violates their intuitions, they will devote their efforts to finding an escape hatch – a reason to doubt your argument or conclusion. They will almost always succeed.'[16]

So it is important to make the case for immigration in ways that appeal to people with different values too, and to use different arguments with different people. To social conservatives, point out that immigrants are fewer than they think, and so the changes newcomers bring about are smaller and less threatening than they might have realised. Emphasise how newcomers are fitting in and adopting local ways. Mention how many children of immigrants marry locals. Highlight those who protect their adopted country by serving in the army or the police, as well as those who save lives as doctors and nurses. Talk about how Latino immigrants in the US share their family values, or indeed how Muslims in Europe are often socially conservative. Emphasise that an amnesty for irregular immigrants would help restore law and order.

To nationalists worried about their country's decline, emphasise that a growing population would enhance its power and influence and that newcomers can become like locals over time. To greens concerned about population pressures, point out that migration doesn't add to the global population, it shifts people around and tends to lead to lower birth rates among those who have moved to a richer country. To free-traders, explain how immigration is a form of trade. To those who believe in international solidarity, argue that the surest way to help the poor is to allow them to come work here.

All these things are true, even if they don't matter to pro-immigrant liberals and progressives or may even seem like negatives to them. Pro-immigrant voices need to do more than just preach to the converted, and shouldn't use only arguments that appeal to cosmopolitan liberals and progressives.

Engaging won't always work. While liberals and progressives need to listen and talk to moderate sceptics to try to persuade them, some opponents of immigration aren't interested in dialogue. But you won't find out until you try.

Mix

Communicating more effectively is crucial; so too is changing people's behaviour. Personal contact tends to overcome fear, prejudice and conflict. The evidence on this is overwhelmingly powerful. When different people mix, 'not only do attitudes toward the immediate participants usually become more favourable, but so do attitudes toward the entire out-group, out-group members in other situations, and even out-groups not involved in the contact.'[17] Just knowing that other members of your community have positive contact with other groups can be helpful. Contact reduces fear of outsiders and enables people to see the world from each other's perspective. Importantly, improved attitudes towards a particular group can also change people's attitudes towards other out-groups. According to a comprehensive report by the US National Academies of Science, 'even individuals experiencing no direct, face-to-face intergroup contact can benefit from living in mixed settings where fellow in-group members do engage in such contact.'[18] Global Gallup polls confirm that the more locals interact with migrants, the more accepting of them they tend to be.[19]

The Welcome Dayton initiative mentioned in Chapter 12 is a good example. One city-wide event called 'Voices of the Immigrant' involves newcomers sitting on a panel to share their stories and experiences. The audience then breaks into small groups, so they can share their own stories and get to know each other.

That inspired Elizabeth Koproski to hold a similar event among parents at her kids' Montessori school. 'It was at one of these first events that I met two of my dear friends,' she says. 'They are from Iraq and came to the United States for safety reasons because one of them worked as a translator for the US Army. Never in a million years would I have thought that an American Christian family and an Iraqi Muslim family would sit down around a dinner table (sometimes at their house and sometimes at ours) and build a friendship. That is exactly what happened as we shared deep matters of the heart. We laughed together, we cried together but all the while we were becoming friends. As we did so, I saw the walls of fear and suspicion on both sides crumble.'[20]

One reason why homophobia has decreased is that most people now know an openly gay person. If you're a migrant, get out there and meet people, as I'm sure you do. If you're a sympathetic local, engage with people outside your comfort zone. Get to know people of different persuasions, listen, try to find points of agreement. Citizens' assemblies – which bring together a representative sample of people who are provided with information on a contested issue and then debate and try to reach conclusions – tend to find reasonable compromises on even the most controversial issues. So organising events that bring people together may help, as the charity More in Common does in Britain.

Government policies

Persuading people about the merits of migration is not just about narrative, framing and behaviour. It also requires a change in government policies. It's little good telling people migration is good for the economy if they themselves are suffering – and wrongly blame migrants for this. Pointing out that migrants aren't to blame for depressed wages, stretched public services or a lack of affordable housing is important and true, but it isn't much comfort to those suffering from those problems. Campaigners also need to lobby for, and governments need to put in place, policies and investment to remedy those problems.

Governments can make a difference in all sorts of ways. They can redistribute incomes and wealth, help retrain workers and help regenerate depressed areas. They can reform labour markets and change welfare rules. They can raise the minimum wage and adapt pensions systems. They can relax planning restrictions and build more social housing. And they can expand access to university, which as well as boosting opportunity and social mobility tends to make graduates more socially liberal and favourable to immigration. As the coronavirus crisis has highlighted, governments can make decisive changes quickly – for good or ill – when the need seems pressing enough.

While economic fears are easier to address, there is also plenty that government can do to alleviate cultural anxieties. They can encourage people to mix in neighbourhoods, at school, at work and elsewhere. Providing funding for local events, sports and social activities is a great way to do this. Requiring schools to admit people from all backgrounds is another, as is vigorously enforcing anti-discrimination laws. Providing language classes, networking opportunities, mentoring and other support to help people fit in, together with social enterprises and NGOs, would also make a big difference.

Governments can also do more to ensure that immigration is seen to benefit everyone. The evidence shows that it typically does, but policy can make this clearer. Sweden's pension system, for instance, ties the generosity of pension payments to the size of the workforce, so the elderly can see directly that they are better off when more immigrants are allowed in to work. Indeed, this gives them a direct incentive to allow in more young foreign taxpayers. Counting changes in the local population quickly and accurately and ensuring public funds flow to where people are is also crucial.

Governments should also experiment. Policymakers often take decisions on gut instinct in a fog of uncertainty, as I know from personal experience as a policy adviser. A better approach is to use randomised controlled trials – scientific methods normally used for things such as testing the safety of new drugs – to test the effectiveness of policy innovations, as Nobel Laureates Esther Duflo and Abhijit Banerjee do.

Their work – highlighted in *Good Economics for Hard Times* – happens to show that many fears about migration are misplaced.[21] Their methods should also be employed by policymakers, who should pilot and rigorously test new ideas for tackling issues associated with migration and persuading people. Ratna Omidvar, an independent Canadian senator, thinks one of the reasons why Canada has been so successful in immigration, both in outcomes and public acceptance, is because of a willingness to try out new policy ideas.

As well as experimenting, governments should emulate what works well in other countries. Freedom of movement works well within the EU, as well as between Australia and New Zealand. Sweden's flexible and non-discriminatory work-visa system is a model for countries that are not ready to embrace freedom of movement. Like Canada, other governments ought to have an independent immigration ministry with its own budget, instead of including it in a home affairs or interior ministry charged primarily with domestic security.

Canada's asylum system – including community sponsorship of refugees – is particularly effective. Canada is also a role model with the generosity of its post-study work visas. New Zealand's temporary-work scheme works well. Australia's regional-visa system would allow places such as London and Scotland that are keener on migration to be more open than the rest of the UK. The US's diversity lottery is a small step towards offsetting the lottery of life and the underrepresentation of migrants from certain countries.

Politics

Politicians also have a role to play. They shouldn't ignore the far right. Dismissing far-right views or treating them as beyond the pale doesn't make them disappear. On the contrary, it plays into anti-immigrant populists' narrative that they are the only ones speaking up for ordinary people against the immigrant-loving liberal establishment. Instead, far-right politicians' views need to be challenged, their lies and hypocrisies exposed. Demolishing their arguments, or better still ridiculing them, can help.

The far right needs to be isolated, not ignored. Mainstream politicians often swing from dismissing far-right views to pandering to them. Centre-right politicians worry about being outflanked on the right and losing socially conservative voters. Centre-left ones fret about losing socially disaffected and conservative working-class voters. Both then try to win back those voters by emulating the far right. In effect, they say, 'Populists are right. Don't vote for them.' Unsurprisingly, this doesn't work.[22] Worse, it legitimises their arguments. People tend to be less supportive of anti-immigration statements when told they come from far-right parties – so other politicians shouldn't echo them and normalise them.[23]

Eric Kaufmann attributes the lack of an anti-immigrant party in Canada to the enforcement of strong anti-racist taboos, aided by the fact it lacks a right-wing tabloid press. Witness how Don Cherry, a hockey commentator once seen as a national hero for his past achievements as a player and coach, was forced to quit his prime-time job after a public outcry at his saying 'you people that come here … whatever it is, you love our milk and honey, at least you could pay a couple of bucks for a [Remembrance Day] poppy.' But once anti-racist taboos are broken, it's hard to put the genie back in the bottle.

Some argue that in politics perceptions are everything, and that even well-meaning politicians and campaigners must accept many voters' incorrect perceptions about migration as a given. But it is neither right nor effective for politicians to pander to people's misperceptions and prejudices. If people wrongly believe that their long wait to see a doctor is due to immigrants, even though migrants are in fact net contributors to public finances and disproportionately medical-care providers, it is neither fair to migrants nor helpful to voters to validate their mistaken view.

The claim that such pandering is nonetheless necessary to ward off the far right is wrong-headed. Anti-immigrant prejudice isn't acceptable simply because it comes from a 'mainstream' politician. Centre-left or centre-right politicians who echo the lines of the far right don't defeat it, they become it. In contrast, Emmanuel Macron defeated Marine Le Pen to become president of France in 2017 by refusing to pander to anti-immigrant views, showing that openness could go hand in hand with security and appealing to moderate sceptics' values, notably by arguing that being open was patriotic.

Worse, some mainstream parties don't only echo nativists' lines; they also get into bed with them. Witness Austria, whose prime minister Sebastian Kurz was fêted among many European conservatives for having halted the rise of the far right. His strategy: copy many of the Freedom Party's policies and much of its rhetoric and bring it into his coalition government. Who, then, was co-opting whom? That a scandal has since undermined support for the Freedom Party doesn't mean Kurz was right.

Through both their policies and their pronouncements, politicians should emphasise the win-win aspects of immigration, instead of allowing opponents to portray it as zero sum. The point is not that migrants deserve special favours, but that their hard work and enterprise make both themselves and the rest of society better off.

In short, pro-immigrant voices need to tell emotionally compelling stories that resonate with different voters, reclaim some of the language and values that the enemies of open societies have seized as their own and put forward policies to address the very real problems of angry and anxious voters who incorrectly blame their plight on immigrants. And we all need to get out and mix more.

21

CONCLUSION

Open Future(s)

mmigrants are extraordinary people. They are a tiny minority of the world's population, yet they have an outsized impact. While others stand still, they are on the move and on the up. While many stay put, they shake things up. Whether by choice or out of necessity, out of aspiration or desperation, their moving can make all the difference. They are adventurers, explorers, inventors, entrepreneurs, traders, battlers and grafters. Whether they are refugees, regular migrants or irregular ones, they tend to be remarkably resilient, risk-taking and resolute. They are the salt of the earth and the likes of Donald Trump, who hate them, are its scum.

Against all the odds, without the advantages of birth or belonging, they survive and often thrive. They spin the wheel on the lottery of life and better their lives – and ours. They broaden our horizons and we broaden theirs. They care for us and we care for them – or at least ought to.

Even in an economy as vast and advanced as America's, the dynamism dividend that those who end up starting businesses generate is so huge that it is reason enough to admit the 'huddled masses yearning to breathe free'. Nearly half of the start-ups in Silicon Valley, of Britain's fastest-growing firms and of new German businesses were co-founded by immigrants. The likes of Jan Koum, Saeid Esmaeilzadeh and Sukhpal Singh Ahluwalia were not – and could not have been – selected; they started from nothing and seized the opportunities of the society that happened to admit them.

The deftness dividend that talented outsiders such as Rúben Canhoto create and the diploma dividend that international students such as Yusra

Uzair contribute may be easier to discern but is no less exceptional. More than half of Switzerland's scientists, Australia's doctors and America's computer-science PhDs were born abroad. Much less predictable is the diversity dividend sparked by people of different backgrounds – migrant and local, female and male, Mo Salah and Jordan Henderson – the new moves, big and small, that enable teams to achieve their goals and change everyone's lives for the better. Diverse teams patent much more and are more productive.

All this is made possible by the toilers who take on the tasks that locals spurn, jobs that may be poorly rewarded but are nonetheless essential: construction workers such as Souleymane, cleaners such as Gabriela and carers such as Monali. Without the drudgery and demographic dividends of young, industrious hands, the more glamorous and gainful industries would grind to a halt. And don't forget our debts that they take on – a dividend indeed.

Overall, thanks to the diversity of skills and ideas they bring, and their youth, immigrants make people in both Britain and America some 30 percent better off. These disparate diasporas also deliver a hefty development dividend, doling out cash to the poor, disseminating ideas to new places and deepening trade and investment ties. And to think some ignorant fools would have wanted the likes of Mo Ibrahim to have stayed working for Sudan Telecom!

While the dividends their differences generate are huge, so too are the divisions. No matter what immigrants do, how much they contribute, how much they try to fit in, they are in the firing line because they are the focus for much broader concerns. Immigration is now the frontline of an almighty culture clash between open-minded social liberals and progressives and closed-minded social conservatives and reactionaries. It is delusional to think that changes in immigration or integration policy alone could satisfy critics who are dissatisfied with the state of the world, the state of society and their place in it, and who fear a future that they cannot control. Nor would it be right to throw immigrants under the bus to appease them; should we also start discriminating against gay people again because social conservatives disapprove of them?

Open or closed?

Western countries – the focus of this book – are at a dangerous juncture. In Britain, America and elsewhere, populist nationalists have assembled vote-winning coalitions to seize power and push though anti-immigrant legislation; in Italy, France and perhaps even Sweden they threaten to do so too. While earlier delusions about the inevitability of ever-greater openness, diversity and social liberalism have been shattered, there is still a dangerous complacency in the US among many liberals and progressives that the 'normal' order of things will soon – or at least eventually – be restored. In Europe, conversely, there is often fatalism that closed minds about immigration are shut forever.

In fact, the future is uncertain: there are powerful trends favouring greater openness longer term, and mighty headwinds pushing towards greater closure right now. The negative framing is that we shouldn't take openness for granted; the positive one is that there is still all to play for. The future is ours to fight for and shape.

The trends favouring greater long-term openness are many. Foreign talent is in ever greater demand. Ageing populations need care, prompting even Japan to open up. Younger people who grew up in diverse societies consider it normal; they have friends from all different backgrounds and often don't even think of them as different. Ever more people go to university, which tends to make graduates less susceptible to populism and more open to outsiders.[1] Low-paid service workers such as bar staff, carers and call-centre workers who now outnumber the traditional working classes also tend to be more positive about immigrants, perhaps because they have more social contact with them.[2] Ever more voters are from an immigrant background, and most support continued openness. Mixed marriages and relationships are multiplying and mixed-race children proliferating. Attitudes towards immigration have also improved as countries have slowly recovered from the 2008 financial crisis. With luck, the coronavirus crisis will durably make locals appreciate more the often-low-paid immigrants who provide essential services.

In every Western country surveyed by Pew except Italy and Greece, a majority of young people favour more diversity – in the UK nearly four in five do – and in every country that proportion is higher than among older people.[3] Younger, more educated locals are much, much keener on admitting more migrants from poorer non-European countries than older, less educated locals.[4]

Sadly, the trends pushing towards closing borders and stamping on difference are powerful too. Governments around the world have shut borders to limit coronavirus transmission, and greater restrictions may remain once the pandemic passes. Economies may not bounce back quickly from their coronavirus collapse and high unemployment may endure. Public finances and public services are often strained. Housing in desirable cities remains unaffordable for most. Small towns are sometimes left behind by economic progress.

Cultural fears compound economic concerns. Whites are a declining share of the population locally as well as globally. Those who are struggling economically feel they are losing status not just within society but also more broadly, as China rises and the West declines. Muslims in general and Islamist terrorists in particular loom large. Foreigners are seen as vectors of disease. Opportunistic politicians play on people's fears and polarise politics, aided and abetted by the likes of Vladimir Putin's Russia, shady billionaires and hate-filled pundits. Barriers are going up, borders are closing and minds with them. In the face of rapid and seemingly threatening change, technological and social, many people want to 'take back control' – even if it makes them poorer, and however illusory that control may prove to be. People who feel they have lost control of their own lives are much keener for society to try to reassert control by repelling outsiders.[5]

Things could get worse – much worse – before they get better, notably in Brexit Britain. There, and in many other countries, the culture clash between younger, more educated and more socially liberal voters and older, less educated and more socially conservative ones remains bitter.

History does not progress in a straight line. Countries take wrong turns and go down blind alleys; witness Brexit and Trump. On the plus side, that may deter other countries from making similar mistakes. But that is little comfort to the UK and the US, where disastrous decisions can create vicious circles, rather than lead people to realise that they've made mistakes and correct them.

But looking to the future, there are grounds for cautious optimism. Time is on our side. Older, often more reactionary people will die. Younger, often more open-minded people will start voting.[6] Most people will get used to, and adapt to, greater diversity: they will get to know neighbours, meet colleagues, make friends and find the love of their life – who may happen to come from somewhere else. What was once frighteningly foreign will become reassuringly familiar.

Ron Inglehart and Pippa Norris argue that we are experiencing turbulence on the road to a more liberal-cosmopolitan West that is comfortable with higher diversity.[7] Eric Kaufmann counters that people tend to become more conservative as they age.[8] Yet the baby boomers have remained socially liberal, so why should young people who have grown up in a diverse society suddenly find it threatening as they go grey?[9]

Interestingly, Kaufmann, a Canadian communitarian conservative, thinks that Western societies will ultimately become less diverse – not necessarily because of lower immigration, but rather because of high intermarriage rates. Indeed, he thinks that mixed-race people will ultimately – in the next century – become a majority in the West, although they may choose to identify as white or white European. America is already going 'beige', as Michael Lind puts it.[10]

Alternatively, and preferably, we may achieve Martin Luther King's vision of a society where people are judged 'not by the colour of their skin, but by the content of their character'.

With luck, we will eventually end up in a world where people can move freely – as the rich and talented can increasingly do globally, and as everyone can do within the EU. Discrimination on the basis of characteristics we don't control – such as race, gender and sexuality – is no longer accepted; why is it still deemed acceptable to discriminate against people on the basis of where they happen to have been born? Especially when the accident of birth – whether you came into the world in America inheriting millions or were born in Africa to peasant farmers – determines so much.

Contrary to fears that everyone in poor countries would move if they were allowed to, the evidence within the EU, where the richest regions are more than four times more prosperous than the poorest ones, is that few do. As Abhijit Banerjee and Esther Duflo point out in *Good Economics for Hard Times*, most people who would benefit from moving stay put because they value the familiar, overestimate the risks of moving and do not know anyone or have anywhere to stay in the place they could go to. Even within Europe, the self-selected minority who up sticks are exceptional.

All of Us

To secure an open future, we need to frame the debate as broadly as possible. The debate about 'Them' is largely a debate about Us. What kind of society do we want to live in? Those who favour open, liberal and progressive societies that offer opportunities to people of all backgrounds, wherever they were born, also need to engage with those who have different ideas of a good society. Those who value order more than freedom, national identity more than individuality and global citizenship, and traditional communities rather than chosen ones need reassurance that the future has space for them too.

And it does. The future is already here, if you look for it.

People who prefer to live surrounded by people of the same race or ethnicity can choose to do so. Diverse cities can coexist with mono-ethnic commuter towns, suburbs and countryside. Mixing would be preferable, in my view, but it isn't mandatory. People who hate London don't have to live there. Even global cities can have different political characters: Sydney tends to have a more conservative government and Melbourne a more progressive one.

Countrywide, immigrants are twice as prevalent in Australia as they are in America, yet society has not collapsed, nor social conservatives been marginalised; its federal government is led by one. Canada – which has the highest immigration rate of any major economy and whose citizens are the most enthusiastic about it[11] – often has robustly conservative governments; Justin Trudeau's Conservative predecessor, Stephen Harper, was prime minister for just under a decade. For all the fears among some white Americans about whites, as currently defined, becoming a minority of the US population in future – which may not happen if people intermarry and 'whiteness' comes to encompass people with Spanish names as it already does those with Italian ones – Houston provides a glimpse of America's more mixed future, where different ethnicities and races coexist more harmoniously than previously and traditional Texan culture endures.

National identity is looser than it once was, but it's still alive and kicking, not least in sport. All but the most inveterate racists can rally around a diverse-looking national team. Witness how Germans celebrated their 'multi culti' football team – where half of the squad was an immigrant or the son of one – when they won the 2014 World Cup in Brazil. National identity can be defined in civic as well as ethnic terms: a British Dream defined by Mo Farah's feats, not Nigel Farage's fears. And people can all feel British, American, French or German for different reasons and in different ways.

Far from it being a vision of super-diverse hell, most people in London, conservative and liberal, tend to get along. The likes of David Goodhart hate it, and yet he still chooses to live there. A majority of people in Toronto are foreign-born, yet it is eminently likeable and liveable. Our diversity – of locals and migrants – can be a source of strength, not of weakness, a reason to belong not an excuse to exclude. We should embrace it rather than seek to deny it, just as we also celebrate what we have in common.

At the same time, we also need to robustly defend liberal values such as the equality of men and women, the rule of law and our democratic institutions, against both Islamist and nationalist extremists. We can also do much more to make the most of migration: mix more, communicate better, open up opportunities to all in society whatever their backgrounds.

The future is open. Let's make the best of it, together.

NOTES

Introduction

1　Julia Carrie Wong, 'Trump referred to immigrant "invasion" in 2,000 Facebook ads, analysis reveals', *Guardian*, 5 August 2019. https://www.theguardian.com/us-news/2019/aug/05/trump-internet-facebook-ads-racism-immigrant-invasion

2　Vivian Ho, 'Family of El Paso baby doesn't want Trump photo politicized: "It's time to grieve"', *Guardian*, 9 August 2019. https://www.theguardian.com/us-news/2019/aug/09/el-paso-shooting-baby-trump-photo

3　Simon Romero and Rick Rojas, 'Trump comes to console. El Paso says no thanks', *New York Times*, 7 August 2019. https://www.nytimes.com/2019/08/07/us/el-paso-trump-escobar.html

4　Tobias Buck and Guy Chazan, 'Gunman suspected of far-right links kills 10 in Germany', *Financial Times*, 20 February 2020. https://www.ft.com/content/e088cfbc-53b1-11ea-8841-482eed0038b1

5　Philip Oltermann, 'German politicians' support for refugees prompts death threats', *Guardian*, 20 June 2019. https://www.theguardian.com/world/2019/jun/20/german-politicians-support-for-refugees-prompts-death-threats

6　*New America*, 'Terrorism in America after 9/11. Part IV. What is the Threat to the United States Today?' Accessed on 22 January 2020 at https://www.newamerica.org/in-depth/terrorism-in-america/what-threat-united-states-today/

7　'America grapples with a lethal mix of terrorism and lax gun laws', *The Economist*, 8 August 2019. https://www.economist.com/united-states/2019/08/08/america-grapples-with-a-lethal-mix-of-terrorism-and-lax-gun-laws

8　Vikram Dodd and Jamie Grierson, 'Fastest-growing UK terrorist threat is from far right, say police', *Guardian*, 19 September 2019. https://www.theguardian.com/uk-news/2019/sep/19/fastest-growing-uk-terrorist-threat-is-from-far-right-say-police

9　Alexandra Brzozowski, 'Far-right terrorism has more than tripled over last four years, report warns', *EURACTIV*, 20 November 2019. https://www.euractiv.com/section/justice-home-affairs/news/far-right-terrorism-has-more-than-tripled-over-last-four-years-report-warns/

10　*Institute for Economics & Peace*, 'Global Terrorism Index 2019: Measuring the Impact of Terrorism', November 2019. http://visionofhumanity.org/app/uploads/2019/11/GTI-2019web.pdf

11　Marnie Banger and Daniel McCulloch, 'PM fans fears about rapists and murderers', *Newcastle Herald*, 6 February 2019. https://www.newcastleherald.com.au/story/5889562/pm-fans-fears-about-rapists-and-murderers/?cs=7

12　Ciar Byrne, 'No PCC probe into "swan eating" story', *Guardian*, 10 December 2003. https://www.theguardian.com/media/2003/dec/10/sun.pressandpublishing

13　Jeremy W. Peters, Michael M. Grynbaum, Keith Collins, Rich Harris and Rumsey Taylor, 'How the El Paso Killer Echoed the Incendiary Words of Conservative Media Stars', *New York Times*, 11 August 2019. https://www.nytimes.com/interactive/2019/08/11/business/media/el-paso-killer-conservative-media.html

14　Hate crimes have soared in the US, Australia, the UK and some other European countries. Ben Quinn, 'Hate crimes double in five years in England and Wales', *Guardian*, 15 October 2019.

https://www.theguardian.com/society/2019/oct/15/hate-crimes-double-england-wales; Adeel Hassan, 'Hate-Crime Violence Hits 16-Year High, FBI Reports', *New York Times*, 12 November 2019. https://www.nytimes.com/2019/11/12/us/hate-crimes-fbi-report.html; Hagar Cohen, 'From bias to brutality: How Australia is failing minority groups', *ABC*, 5 May 2019. https://www.abc.net.au/radionational/programs/backgroundbriefing/hate-crimes-rising-minority-groups-say/11059378; Organisation for Security and Co-operation in Europe, 'Xenophobia, Radicalism and Hate Crime in Europe. Annual Report', 2018. https://www.osce.org/odihr/395336?download=true

15   'Far-right Sweden Democrats top opinion poll in historic shift', *The Local*, 15 November 2019. https://www.thelocal.se/20191115/sweden-democrats-now-swedens-biggest-party-historic-poll

16   John Sides, 'Race, Religion, and Immigration in 2016', *Democracy Fund Voter Study Group*, June 2017. https://www.voterstudygroup.org/publication/race-religion-immigration-2016

17   'How Viktor Orban hollowed out Hungary's democracy', *The Economist*, 29 August 2019. https://www.economist.com/briefing/2019/08/29/how-viktor-orban-hollowed-out-hungarys-democracy

18   May Bulman, 'Boris Johnson faces backlash and claims of racism after saying migrants should not "treat UK as their own"', *Independent*, 9 December 2019. https://www.independent.co.uk/news/uk/home-news/boris-johnson-eu-migrants-immigration-britain-general-election-a9238941.html

19   'Trump's Executive Order Limiting Immigration: What You Need to Know', *Boundless*, 23 April 2020. https://www.boundless.com/blog/donald-trump-suspends-us-immigration/

20   Nicola Bartlett, 'Theresa May boasted as home secretary that she would "deport first and hear appeals later"', *Mirror*, 20 April 2018. https://www.mirror.co.uk/news/politics/theresa-boasted-home-secretary-would-12398544

21   https://twitter.com/realDonaldTrump/status/1150381394234941448?s=20

22   The seven countries are Iran, Iraq, Libya, Somalia, Sudan, Syria and Yemen. 'Protecting the Nation From Foreign Terrorist Entry Into the United States. Executive Order 13769', *Federal Register*, 27 January 2017. https://www.federalregister.gov/documents/2017/02/01/2017-02281/protecting-the-nation-from-foreign-terrorist-entry-into-the-united-states

23   Zachary Wolf, 'Yes, Obama deported more people than Trump but context is everything', *CNN*, 13 July 2019. https://edition.cnn.com/2019/07/13/politics/obama-trump-deportations-illegal-immigration/index.html

24   Henry Samuel, 'Nicolas Sarkozy says immigrants must accept "your ancestors are the Gauls"', *Telegraph*, 20 September 2016. https://www.telegraph.co.uk/news/2016/09/20/nicolas-sarkozy-says-immigrants-should-live-like-the-french/

25   Matthias Galante, 'Presidential hopeful Fillon says France needs immigration quotas', *Reuters*, 11 January 2017. https://www.reuters.com/article/us-france-election-fillon-immigration-idUSKBN14V0TN

26   Yonette Joseph, 'In Their Own Words: Marine Le Pen and Emmanuel Macron', *New York Times*, 5 May 2017. https://www.nytimes.com/2017/05/05/world/europe/emmanuel-macron-marine-le-pen-quotes.html

27   William Booth, Karla Adam and Christine Spolar, 'Boris Johnson praises immigrant nurses who saved his life, as Britain's NHS becomes a rallying cry', *Washington Post*, 13 April 2020. https://www.washingtonpost.com/world/europe/boris-johnson-nurses-nhs/2020/04/13/51498d34-7bfa-11ea-a311-adb1344719a9_story.html

28   Philippe Legrain, *Immigrants: Your Country Needs Them*, Abacus, 2007.

29   Open Political Economy Network's website is http://www.opennetwork.net and on Twitter it is @open2progress.

30   Robert Guest, 'Why people should leave the countryside', *The Economist*, 14 November 2019. https://www.economist.com/special-report/2019/11/14why-people-should-leave-the-countryside

1 Why is Immigration So Unpopular?

1   Anoosh Chakelian, 'A view from Brexitland: Boston, the town that voted strongest to leave the EU', *New Statesman*, 1 July 2016. https://www.newstatesman.com/politics/uk/2016/07/view-brexitland-boston-town-voted-strongest-leave-eu

2   Paul Gallagher, 'Boston: How a Lincolnshire town became "the most divided place in England"', *Independent*, 28 January 2016. https://www.independent.co.uk/news/uk/home-news/boston-how-a-lincolnshire-town-became-the-most-divided-place-in-england-a6838041.html

3   *Office for National Statistics (ONS)*, 'Population of the UK by country of birth and nationality. July 2018 to June 2019'. Accessed on 22 January 2020 at https://www.ons.gov.uk/peoplepopulationandcommunity/populationandmigration/internationalmigration/datasets/populationoftheunitedkingdombycountryofbirthandnationality

4   Sarah Young, 'Migrants remain political bystanders in England's "Little Poland"', *Reuters*, 31 March 2015. https://uk.reuters.com/article/uk-britain-election-boston-insight/insight-migrants-remain-political-bystanders-in-englands-little-poland-idUKKBN0MR1YN20150331

5   Median wages are those paid to those who earn more than the bottom half of workers in Britain and less than the top half. *ONS*, 'Employee earnings in the UK: 2019'. Accessed on 22 January 2020 at https://www.ons.gov.uk/employmentandlabourmarket/peopleinwork/earningsandworkinghours/bulletins/annualsurveyofhoursandearnings/2019

6   Charles Hymas, 'Only 112 of 50,000 UK applicants for fruit pickers take jobs amid farmers' fears over skills and application', *Telegraph*, 27 April 2020. https://www.telegraph.co.uk/news/2020/04/27/112-50000-uk-applicants-fruit-pickers-take-jobs-amid-farmers/

7   Kimiko de Freytas-Tamura, 'As More Immigrants Arrive, Some Britons Want to Show Them and EU the Door', *New York Times*, 14 March 2016. https://www.nytimes.com/2016/03/15/world/europe/boston-england-immigrants-brexit.html

8   *Ipsos*, 'Global Views on Immigration and the Refugee Crisis', September 2017. https://www.ipsos.com/ipsos-mori/en-uk/new-global-study-reveals-unease-about-immigration-around-world

9   *Pew Research Center*, 'Spring 2018 Global Attitudes Survey'. https://www.pewresearch.org/global/2019/03/14/around-the-world-more-say-immigrants-are-a-strength-than-a-burden/

10 The proportion of people in the UK who thought immigration had a positive impact on their country rose from 19 percent in 2011 to 35 percent in 2016; in the US it increased from 18 percent to 35 percent over the same period. The proportion who thought there were too many immigrants in the country fell from 71 percent to 49 percent in the UK over the period and from 59 percent to 51 percent in the US.

11 This section draws on Philippe Legrain, 'Even when they're wrong, they're right', *Open Democracy*, 27 October 2017. https://www.opendemocracy.net/en/even-when-they-re-wrong-they-re-right/

12 For instance, an Ipsos Mori poll in June 2016 found that while 42 percent of respondents thought that EU migration had been bad for Britain as a whole, only 19 percent said it had been bad for them personally. 'Just one in five Britons say EU immigration has had a negative effect on them personally', *Ipsos Mori*, 20 June 2016. https://www.ipsos-mori.com/researchpublications/researcharchive/3749/Just-one-in-five-Britons-say-EU-immigration-has-had-a-negative-effect-on-them-personally.aspx

13 Roy Greenslade, 'Newspapers publish anti-immigration stories – but what is to be done?', *Guardian*, 5 September 2016. https://www.theguardian.com/media/greenslade/2016/sep/05/newspapers-publish-anti-immigration-stories-but-what-is-to-be-done

14 *Ipsos*, 'Global Views on Immigration and the Refugee Crisis', September 2017 https://www.ipsos.com/ipsos-mori/en-uk/new-global-study-reveals-unease-about-immigration-around-world

15 Alberto Alesina, Armando Miano and Stefanie Stantcheva, 'Immigration and Redistribution',

NBER Working Paper 24733, updated 2019. https://scholar.harvard.edu/stantcheva/publications/immigration-and-support-redistribution

16　*Ipsos Mori*, 'European Union: The Perils of Perception Survey', June 2016. https://www.ipsos-mori.com/researchpublications/researcharchive/3742/The-Perils-of-Perception-and-the-EU.aspx

17　Stock of foreign-born population from Organisation for Economic Co-operation and Development (OECD), International Migration Database, 2018.

18　*International Organisation for Migration (IOM)*, 'Europe – Mixed Migration Flows To Europe, Yearly Overview (2018)', 8 February 2019. https://migration.iom.int/datasets/europe-mixed-migration-flows-europe-yearly-overview-2018

19　*ONS*, 'Population of the UK by country of birth and nationality. July 2018 to June 2019'. https://www.ons.gov.uk/peoplepopulationandcommunity/populationandmigration/internationalmigration/datasets/populationoftheunitedkingdombycountryofbirthandnationality

20　*ONS*, 'Migration Statistics Quarterly Report: November 2019'. Accessed on 22 January 2020 at https://www.ons.gov.uk/peoplepopulationandcommunity/populationandmigration/internationalmigration/bulletins/migrationstatisticsquarterlyreport/november2019

21　Net overseas migration to Australia in 2018 was 248,446. This was 1 percent of Australia's population of 25 million. *Statista*, 'Number of net overseas migration from Australia between 2011 and 2018'. Accessed on 22 January 2020 at https://www.statista.com/statistics/608052/australia-net-overseas-migration/

22　According to Lord Ashcroft's polls, 80 percent of those who thought immigration was a force for ill voted Leave, as did 80 percent of those who thought social liberalism was a force for ill. http://lordashcroftpolls.com/wp-content/uploads/2016/06/Ill-vs-Good.jpg; Eric Kaufmann, 'It's NOT the economy, stupid: Brexit as a story of personal values', *London School of Economics and Political Science*, British Politics and Policy blog, July 2016. http://blogs.lse.ac.uk/politicsandpolicy/personal-values-brexit-vote/

23　*Ipsos*, 'Global Views on Immigration and the Refugee Crisis', September 2017. https://www.ipsos.com/ipsos-mori/en-uk/new-global-study-reveals-unease-about-immigration-around-world

24　Eric Kaufmann, *Whiteshift: Populism, Immigration and the Future of White Majorities*, Penguin, 2018.

2　A Very Brief History of Migration

1　*Department for Digital, Culture, Media & Sport*, 'Community Life Survey 2016–17', 25 July 2017. https://www.gov.uk/government/statistics/community-life-survey-2016-17

2　*ONS*, Population of the UK by country of birth and nationality. July 2018 to June 2019'. https://www.ons.gov.uk/peoplepopulationandcommunity/populationandmigration/international-migration/datasets/populationoftheunitedkingdombycountryofbirthandnationality

3　19 Princelet Street. https://www.19princeletstreet.org.uk/about.html

4　Migration Museum. https://www.migrationmuseum.org/workshop/

5　To shed light on Britain's history of immigration, I highly recommend Robert Winder, *Bloody Foreigners: The Story of Immigration to Britain*, Little, Brown, 2004.

6　Selina Brace et al, 'Population Replacement in Early Neolithic Britain', *bioRxiv*, 18 February 2018. https://doi.org/10.1101/267443; That it is possible to determine the skin colour of Cheddar Man is disputed, see Colin Barras, 'Ancient "dark-skinned" Briton Cheddar Man find may not be true', *New Scientist*, 21 February 2018. https://www.newscientist.com/article/2161867-ancient-dark-skinned-briton-cheddar-man-find-may-not-be-true/

7　'French immigrants founded first British farms', *New Scientist*, 2 December 2009. https://www.newscientist.com/article/mg20427374-200-french-immigrants-founded-first-british-farms/

8　Germany aims to eventually open a migration museum in Cologne. https://domid.org/news/presse/bund-bewilligt-mittel-fur-haus-der-einwanderungsgesellschaft/

9   *Wikimedia*, 'US immigration records'. https://upload.wikimedia.org/wikipedia/commons/
    9/93/U.S._Immigration_records_mentioning_Friedr_Trumpf.jpg

10 Donald Trump with Tony Schwartz, *Trump: The Art of the Deal*, Random House, 1987.

11 As far back as 1751, in his *Observations Concerning the Increase of Mankind*, Benjamin Franklin
    abhorred the arrival of Germans ('Palatine boors'), whom he contrasted with English descen-
    dants not just in custom but also in 'complexion'. Janan Ganesh, 'The US should not give in
    to the pessimism of white nationalism', *Financial Times*, 7 August 2019. https://www.ft.com/
    content/a6f54234-b8e9-11e9-96bd-8e884d3ea203

12 Jeffrey Williamson, 'Global Migration', *Finance and Development*, 43:3, September 2006.
    https://www.imf.org/external/pubs/ft/fandd/2006/09/williams.htm

13 Eric Hobsbawm, *The Age of Empire*, Abacus, 1987, table 3, p. 344.

14 In 1910, 14.7 percent of the US population were foreign-born. The US Census Bureau calculates
    that 13.7 percent of the US population were foreign-born in 2017. Williamson, 'Global Migra-
    tion'. https://www.imf.org/external/pubs/ft/fandd/2006/09/williams.htm

15 Amy J. Lloyd, 'Emigration, Immigration and Migration in Nineteenth-Century Brit-
    ain', *British Library Newspapers, Gale*, 2007. https://www.gale.com/binaries/content/
    assets/gale-us-en/primary-sources/intl-gps/intl-gps-essays/full-ghn-contextual-essays/
    ghn_essay_bln_lloyd1_website.pdf

16 https://en.wikipedia.org/wiki/Demography_of_the_United_Kingdom

17 Kevin H. O'Rourke and Jeffrey G. Williamson, *Globalization and History: The Evolution of a
    Nineteenth-Century Atlantic Economy*, MIT, 1999.

18 Adam McKeown, 'Global Migration, 1846–1940', *Journal of World History*, 15:2, 2004,
    pp. 155–89.

19 Oriana Bandiera, Imran Rasul and Martina Viarengo, 'The Making of Modern America: Migra-
    tory Flows in the Age of Mass Migration', *Journal of Development Economics*, 102, 2013, pp.
    23–47.

20 Quoted in John Torpey, *The Invention of the Passport: Surveillance, Citizenship and the State*,
    Cambridge, 2000.

3 Post-1945 Migration

1   Richard Cavendish, 'Arrival of SS Empire Windrush', *History Today*, 48:6, June 1998. https://
    www.historytoday.com/archive/months-past/arrival-ss-empire-windrush

2   David Olusoga, 'The Windrush story was not a rosy one even before the ship arrived', *Guardian*,
    22 April 2018. https://www.theguardian.com/commentisfree/2018/apr/22/windrush-story-
    not-a-rosy-one-even-before-ship-arrived

3   Marc Wadsworth, 'Sam King obituary', *Guardian*, 30 June 2016. https://www.theguardian.
    com/society/2016/jun/30/sam-king-obituary

4   Rachel Sylvester, 'Both sides now: inside the rise of Sajid Javid', *Prospect*, 27 January 2019.
    https://www.prospectmagazine.co.uk/magazine/both-sides-now-inside-the-rise-of-
    sajid-javid

5   Dave Hill, 'Zac Versus Sadiq: The Fight to Become London Mayor', *Double Q*, 2016.

6   Henry McDonald, 'Leo Varadkar, gay son of Indian immigrant, to be next Irish PM', *Guardian*,
    2 June 2017. https://www.theguardian.com/world/2017/jun/02/leo-varadkar-becomes-
    irelands-prime-minister-elect

7   *ONS*, 'Population of the UK by country of birth and nationality. March 2000 to February
    2001'. https://www.ons.gov.uk/peoplepopulationandcommunity/populationandmigration/
    internationalmigration/datasets/populationoftheunitedkingdombycountryofbirthandnationality

8   *ONS*, 'Population of the UK by country of birth and nationality. July 2015 to June 2016'.
    https://www.ons.gov.uk/peoplepopulationandcommunity/populationandmigration/
    internationalmigration/datasets/populationoftheunitedkingdombycountryofbirthandnationality

9   ONS, 'Population of the UK by country of birth and nationality. July 2018 to June 2019'. https://www.ons.gov.uk/peoplepopulationandcommunity/populationandmigration/internationalmigration/datasets/populationoftheunitedkingdombycountryofbirthandnationality

10 Eurostat, 'Migration and migrant population statistics. Statistics explained', 3 September 2019. https://ec.europa.eu/eurostat/statistics-explained/pdfscache/1275.pdf

11 https://twitter.com/CSOIreland/status/1166290134993657856/photo/1

12 Elena Vaccarino and Zsolt Darvas, '"Social dumping" and posted workers: a new clash within the EU', Bruegel, 7 March 2016. https://bruegel.org/2016/03/social-dumping-and-posted-workers-a-new-clash-within-the-eu/

13 'Eastern Europe berates Wilders over anti-east website', DW, 14 February 2012. https://www.dw.com/en/eastern-europe-berates-wilders-over-anti-east-website/a-15742494

14 The photo of Alan Kurdi can be seen at http://100photos.time.com/photos/nilufer-demir-alan-kurdi

15 Eurostat, 'Asylum statistics'. Accessed on 1 July 2020. https://ec.europa.eu/eurostat/statistics-explained/index.php?title=Asylum_statistics

16 UNHCR, 'Global Trends: Forced Displacement in 2019', 2020. https://www.unhcr.org/globaltrends2019

17 Ibid.

18 Lebanon hosts 916,000, Germany 1,146,000.

19 Eurostat, 'First time asylum applicants'. Code: migr_asyappctza

20 Frank Shyong, 'Sriracha hot sauce purveyor turns up the heat', Los Angeles Times, 12 April 2013. https://www.latimes.com/business/la-xpm-2013-apr-12-la-fi-himi-tran-20130414-story.html

21 Vietnamese refugees had higher employment rates than US-born people in 2009–11, while their median household income was also slightly higher. Randy Capps and Kathleen Newland et al, 'The Integration Outcomes of U.S. Refugees: Successes and Challenges', Migration Policy Institute, 2015, pp. 16, 21.

22 Alana Abramson, '"I Believe in My Work." How Rep. Ilhan Omar Rose From Refugee to Trump's Top Target', Time, 18 July 2019. https://time.com/5628844/ilhan-omar-profile/

23 Benjamin Wallace-Wells, 'Ilhan Omar's Embattled First Months in Office', New Yorker, 27 March 2019. https://www.newyorker.com/news/the-political-scene/ilhan-omars-embattled-first-months-in-office

24 US Department of Homeland Security, 'Table 1. Persons Obtaining Lawful Permanent Resident Status: Fiscal Years 1820 to 2018'. Accessed on 22 January 2020 at https://www.dhs.gov/immigration-statistics/yearbook/2018/table1#

25 Jeffrey S. Passel and D'Vera Cohn, 'Mexicans decline to less than half the US unauthorized immigrant population for the first time', Pew Research Center, 12 June 2019. https://www.pewresearch.org/fact-tank/2019/06/12/us-unauthorized-immigrant-population-2017/

26 Ibid.

27 Jie Zong, Jeanne Batalova, and Micayla Burrows, 'Frequently Requested Statistics on Immigrants and Immigration in the United States', Migration Policy Institute, 14 March 2019. https://www.migrationpolicy.org/article/frequently-requested-statistics-immigrants-and-immigration-united-states

28 'The other African-Americans', The Economist, 19 October 2019. https://www.economist.com/united-states/2019/10/19/the-other-african-americans

29 Refugee Processing Center, 'Admissions & Arrivals'. Accessed on 22 January 2020 at https://www.wrapsnet.org/admissions-and-arrivals

30 Catherine Porter, 'In Canada, an Immigration Minister Who Himself Is a Refugee', New York Times, 6 September 2017. https://www.nytimes.com/2017/09/06/world/canada/ahmed-hussen-canada-immigration-minister.html

31 Hugo O'Doherty, 'Canada Immigration Levels Plan: 2019–2021', *Moving2Canada*, 31 October 2018. https://moving2canada.com/canada-immigration-levels-plan-2019-2021/

32 *Australian Bureau of Statistics (ABS)*, '3101.0 - Australian Demographic Statistics, Jun 2019', 19 December 2019. https://www.abs.gov.au/ausstats/abs@.nsf/Latestproducts/3101.0Main%20 Features2Jun%202019?opendocument&tabname=Summary&prodno=3101.0&issue= Jun%202019&num=&view=

4 The Current Picture

1 *Migration Data Portal*, 'Total number of international migrants at mid-year 2019'. Accessed on 23 January 2020 at https://migrationdataportal.org/data?i=stock_abs_&t=2019

2 *Ibid*. 'International migrant stock as a percentage of the total population at mid-year 2019'. https://migrationdataportal.org/data?i=stock_perc_&t=2019

3 Rich countries are those the United Nations classifies as high-income countries. Poorer countries are all the rest.

4 *Migration Data Portal*, 'Total number of international migrants at mid-year 2019. United States'. https://migrationdataportal.org/data?i=stock_abs_&t=2019&cm49=840 and US Census Bureau, 'Current Population Survey. Annual Social and Economic Supplement 2018'. https://www.census.gov/cps/data/cpstablecreator.html?#

5 *IOM*, 'World Migration Report 2020', 2019. https://publications.iom.int/system/files/pdf/wmr_2020.pdf

6 *United Nations Department of Economic and Social Affairs (UN-DESA)*, 'International migrant stock 2019: Graphs'. Accessed on 23 January 2020 at https://www.un.org/en/development/desa/population/migration/data/estimates2/estimatesgraphs.asp?3g3

7 *UN-DESA*, 'International Migration Report 2017', 2017, Figure I.6. https://www.un.org/en/development/desa/population/migration/publications/migrationreport/docs/Migration-Report2017.pdf

8 *UN-DESA*, 'International migrant stock 2019'. Accessed on 23 January 2020 at https://www.un.org/en/development/desa/population/migration/data/estimates2/estimates19.asp

9 Some 52 percent of migrants are male and 48 percent female. IOM, 'World Migration Report 2020', 2019. https://publications.iom.int/system/files/pdf/wmr_2020.pdf

10 Working-age migrants are those aged twenty to sixty-four. https://publications.iom.int/system/files/pdf/wmr_2020.pdf

11 *OECD*, 'International Migration Outlook 2019', 2019. http://www.oecd.org/migration/international-migration-outlook-1999124x.htm

12 The migrant share of the population was 13.7 percent in the US in 2017 and 14.2 percent in the UK in 2018. *ONS*, 'Population of the UK by country of birth and nationality. July 2018 to June 2019.' Accessed on 23 January 2020 at https://www.ons.gov.uk/peoplepopulationandcommunity/populationandmigration/internationalmigration/datasets/populationoftheunitedkingdom bycountryofbirthandnationality

13 In Singapore 37 percent of the population was foreign-born in 2019.

14 New Zealand figure is from the 2013 census.

15 The migrant share of the population in 2018 was as follows: Germany 16.6 percent, Ireland 16.8 percent, Austria 19.2 percent, Spain 13.3 percent, Netherlands 12.9 percent, France 12.2 percent, Denmark 11.9 percent, Greece 11.9 percent, Italy 10.2 percent, Portugal 8.8 percent. *Eurostat*, 'Population on 1 January by age, sex and broad group of country of birth'. Code: migr_pop4ctb; the share for Sweden in 2018 was 19.1 percent according to Statistics Sweden.

16 'Foreign Resident Population in Japan Rises Above 2%', nippon.com, 24 July 2019. https://www.nippon.com/en/japan-data/h00498/foreign-resident-population-in-japan-rises-above-2.html

17 Hatsuki Sato, 'Foreign workers in Japan double in 5 years, hitting record', *Nikkei Asian Review*,

25 January 2019. https://asia.nikkei.com/Spotlight/Japan-immigration/Foreign-workers-in-Japan-double-in-5-years-hitting-record

18 *IOM*, 'World Migration Report 2020', Figure 4. https://publications.iom.int/system/files/pdf/wmr_2020.pdf

19 *UN-DESA*, 'World Population Prospects 2019. Volume I: Comprehensive Tables', 2019, Table A.22. Total fertility, 2015–20. https://population.un.org/wpp/Publications/Files/WPP2019_Volume-I_Comprehensive-Tables.pdf

20 The total fertility rate was 1.52 in Canada, 1.75 in the UK, 1.78 in the US, 1.83 in Australia, 1.90 in New Zealand, 1.29 in Portugal, 1.30 in Greece, 1.33 in both Italy and Spain, and 1.11 in South Korea.

21 *OECD*, 'International Migration Outlook 2019'. US: http://dx.doi.org/10.1787/888933990938; UK: http://dx.doi.org/10.1787/888933990919; Australia: http://dx.doi.org/10.1787/888933990216; Canada: http://dx.doi.org/10.1787/888933990292

22 *Ibid*. In Germany net migration accounts for 154 percent of population growth. http://dx.doi.org/10.1787/888933990444; in Italy, the net migration rate is 0.14 percent while the natural increase is -0.32 percent. http://dx.doi.org/10.1787/888933990539; in Japan the net migration rate is 0.15 percent while the rate of natural increase is -0.31 percent. http://dx.doi.org/10.1787/888933990558

23 *OECD*, 'The new immigrants. Global trends in migration towards OECD countries between 2000/01 and 2015/16', Migration Data Brief 4, June 2019. http://www.oecd.org/els/mig/Migration-data-brief-4-EN.pdf

24 *Migration Policy Institute*, 'Largest US Immigrant Groups over Time, 1960–Present'. Accessed on 23 January 2020 at https://www.migrationpolicy.org/programs/data-hub/charts/largest-immigrant-groups-over-time

25 *Statistics Canada*, 'Place of birth for the immigrant population by period of immigration, 2006 counts and percentage distribution, for Canada, provinces and territories – 20% sample'. Accessed on 23 January 2020 at datahttps://www12.statcan.gc.ca/census-recensement/2006/dp-pd/hlt/97-557/T404-eng.cfm?Lang=E&T=404&GH=4&GF=1&SC=1&S=1&O=D

26 *Statistics Canada*, 'Immigrant population by place of birth, period of immigration, 2016 counts, both sexes, age (total), Canada, 2016 Census – 25% Sample data'. Accessed on 23 January 2020 at https://www12.statcan.gc.ca/census-recensement/2016/dp-pd/hlt-fst/imm/Table.cfm?Lang=E&T=21&Geo=01&SO=4D

27 *ABS*, '3412.0 - Migration, Australia, 2017-18', 3 April 2019. https://www.abs.gov.au/AUSSTATS/abs@.nsf/Latestproducts/3412.0Main%20Features22017-18?opendocument&tabname=Summary&prodno=3412.0&issue=2017-18&num=&view=

28 In New Zealand, Britain was still by far immigrants' top country of origin in the 2013 census, but as of 2018 two-thirds of net migration was from Asia and hardly any from the UK. Stats NZ, 'International migration: June 2019', 8 August 2019. https://www.stats.govt.nz/information-releases/international-migration-june-2019

29 *ONS*, 'Population of the UK by country of birth and nationality. July 2018 to June 2019'. https://www.ons.gov.uk/peoplepopulationandcommunity/populationandmigration/internationalmigration/datasets/populationoftheunitedkingdombycountryofbirthandnationality

30 *OECD*, 'International Migration Outlook 2019'. http://dx.doi.org/10.1787/888933990919

31 https://ec.europa.eu/eurostat/statistics-explained/pdfscache/1275.pdf

32 *OECD*, 'International Migration Outlook 2008', 2008.

33 Christian Dustmann and Joseph-Simon Görlach, 'The Economics of Temporary Migrations', *Journal of Economic Literature*, 54:1, 2016, pp. 98–136.

34 *OECD*, 'International Migration Outlook 2019'.

35 Personal calculations from Tables 1 and 4 of ONS, 'Provisional long-term international migration estimates', 28 November 2019. https://www.ons.gov.uk/peoplepopulationandcommunity/

populationandmigration/internationalmigration/datasets/migrationstatisticsquarterlyre
portprovisionallongterminternationalmigrationltimestimates

36   Erhan Artuç and Çaglar Özden, 'Transit Migration: All Roads Lead to the United States', *World Bank Policy Research Working Paper 7880*, revised 27 April 2018. https://papers.ssrn.com/sol3/papers.cfm?abstract_id=2867661#

5 Future Flows

1   *UN-DESA*, 'World Population Prospects 2019', 2019, medium variant. https://population.un.org/wpp/

2   Michael Clemens, 'Does Development Reduce Migration?', *Center for Global Development Working Paper 359*, March 2014. https://www.cgdev.org/sites/default/files/does-development-reduce-migration_final_0.pdf

3   Gordon Hanson, Chen Liu and Craig McIntosh, 'The Rise and Fall of US Low-Skilled Immigration', *NBER Working Paper 23753*, August 2017. https://www.nber.org/papers/w23753

4   Gordon Hanson and Craig McIntosh, 'Is the Mediterranean the New Rio Grande? US and EU Immigration Pressures in the Long Run', *NBER Working Paper 22622*, September 2016. https://www.nber.org/papers/w22622

5   Carl Benedikt Frey and Michael A. Osborne, 'The Future of Employment: How Susceptible are Jobs to Computerisation?', 17 September 2013. https://www.oxfordmartin.ox.ac.uk/downloads/academic/The_Future_of_Employment.pdf

6   'Will a robot really take your job?', *The Economist*, 27 June 2019. https://www.economist.com/business/2019/06/27/will-a-robot-really-take-your-job

7   Melanie Arntz, Terry Gregory and Ulrich Zierahn, 'The risk of automation for jobs in OECD countries: A comparative analysis', *OECD Social, Employment and Migration Working Paper 189*, May 2016. https://doi.org/10.1787/5jlz9h56dvq7-en

8   For instance, consultants at McKinsey estimate that AI will both displace and create around 300,000 jobs a year in the 2020s in Europe's 'digital front-runners'. https://www.mckinsey.com/~/media/mckinsey/featured%20insights/europe/shaping%20the%20future%20of%20work%20in%20europes%20nine%20digital%20front%20runner%20countries/shaping-the-future-of-work-in-europes-digital-front-runners.ashx

9   Richard Baldwin, *The Great Convergence: Information Technology and the New Globalization*, Harvard, 2016.

10   See kwiziq.com

11   Richard Baldwin, *The Great Convergence*.

12   *UNHCR*, 'Global Trends 2019'. https://www.unhcr.org/globaltrends2019/

13   Cristina Cattaneo and Giovanni Peri, 'The Migration Response to Increasing Temperatures', *NBER Working Paper 21622*, October 2015. https://www.nber.org/papers/w21622.pdf

14   Jonathan Blitzer, 'How Climate Change is Fuelling the US Border Crisis', *New Yorker*, 3 April 2019. https://www.newyorker.com/news/dispatch/how-climate-change-is-fuelling-the-us-border-crisis

15   *UK Government Office for Science*, 'Foresight: Migration and Global Environmental Change', 2011. https://assets.publishing.service.gov.uk/government/uploads/system/uploads/attachment_data/file/287722/11-1115-migration-and-global-environmental-change-summary.pdf

16   Guy J. Abel, Michael Brottrager, Jesus Crespo Cuaresma and Raya Muttarak, 'Climate, conflict and forced migration', *Global Environmental Change*, 54, January 2019, pp. 239–49. https://www.sciencedirect.com/science/article/pii/S0959378018301596

17   The Global Compact commits to developing 'tailored migration schemes of various duration … to facilitate migration as an adaptation strategy to slow-onset environmental degradation.'

18   Rebekah Smith, 'Two cheers for the Global Compact', *OPEN*, 6 March 2018. http://www.opennetwork.net/two-cheers-global-compact/

6 The Lottery of Life

1   Bozi Kiekie, 'Bozi Kiekie: Central Illinois home to immigrant from Africa', *State Journal-Register*, 20 January 2013. https://www.sj-r.com/x1665864190/Central-Illinois-home-to-immigrant-from-Africa

2   *US Department of State*, 'Visa Bulletin For August 2019', 5 July 2019. https://travel.state.gov/content/travel/en/legal/visa-law0/visa-bulletin/2019/visa-bulletin-for-august-2019.html

3   'He Won the Lottery: One Congolese Man's Incredible Diversity Visa Story', *New American Economy*, 21 December 2016. https://www.newamericaneconomy.org/feature/this-congolese-winner-of-the-diversity-visa-lottery-earned-a-college-degree-worked-his-way-into-the-middle-class-and-became-an-american-citizen/

4   See, for instance, Branko Milanović, 'Global Inequality of Opportunity: How Much of Our Income is Determined by Where We Live?', *Review of Economics and Statistics*, 97: 2, May 2015, pp. 452–60. https://www.mitpressjournals.org/doi/abs/10.1162/REST_a_00432

5   Michael Clemens, 'Economics and Emigration: Trillion-Dollar Bills on the Sidewalk?', *Journal of Economic Perspectives*, 25: 3, Summer 2011, pp. 83–106. https://pubs.aeaweb.org/doi/pdf-plus/10.1257/jep.25.3.83

6   Gross domestic product at current prices. *International Monetary Fund (IMF)*, 'World Economic Outlook database', October 2019.

7   *McKinsey Global Institute*, 'Global migration's impact and opportunity', November 2016. https://www.mckinsey.com/featured-insights/employment-and-growth/global-migrations-impact-and-opportunity

8   Bryan Caplan, 'Open Borders Are a Trillion-Dollar Idea', *Foreign Policy*, 1 November 2019. https://foreignpolicy.com/2019/11/01/immigration-wall-open-borders-trillion-dollar-idea/

9   Michael Clemens, 'Measuring the Spatial Misallocation of Labor: The Returns to India-Gulf Guest Work in a Natural Experiment', *Center for Global Development Working Paper 501*, January 2019. https://www.cgdev.org/publication/measuring-spatial-misallocation-labor-returns-india-gulf-guest-work-natural-experiment

10 John Gibson, David McKenzie, Halahingao Rohorua and Steven Stillman, 'International migration's long-term impact: Evidence from a lottery', *VoxDev*, 5 February 2018. https://voxdev.org/topic/labour-markets-migration/international-migrations-long-term-impact-evidence-lottery

11 Michael Clemens, 'Why Do Programmers Earn More in Houston Than Hyderabad? Evidence from Randomized Processing of US Visas', *American Economic Association Review*, 103:3, May 2013, pp. 198–202. https://www.aeaweb.org/articles?id=10.1257/aer.103.3.198

12 Michael Clemens, Claudio Montenegro and Lant Pritchett, 'Bounding the Price Equivalent of Migration Barriers', *Center for Global Development Working Paper 428*, June 2016. https://www.cgdev.org/sites/default/files/Clemens-Montenegro-Pritchett-Price-Equivalent-Migration-Barriers_CGDWP428.pdf

13 See also Francesc Ortega and Giovanni Peri, 'Openness and income: The roles of trade and migration', *Journal of International Economics*, 92, 2014, pp. 231–51. https://www.sciencedirect.com/science/article/abs/pii/S0022199613001268; Alberto Alesina, Johann Harnoss and Hillel Rapoport, 'Birthplace Diversity and Economic Prosperity', *Journal of Economic Growth*, 21:2, 2016, pp. 101–38. https://link.springer.com/article/10.1007/s10887-016-9127-6

14 Florence Jaumotte, Ksenia Koloskova and Sweta Chaman Saxena, 'Impact of Migration on Income Levels in Advanced Economies', *IMF Spillover Notes No. 16/08*, 24 October 2016. https://www.imf.org/en/Publications/Spillover-Notes/Issues/2016/12/31/Impact-of-Migration-on-Income-Levels-in-Advanced-Economies-44343

15 Migration increases the average income per person of both the bottom 90 percent and the top 10 percent of earners, even though high-skill migration benefits top earners more. Moreover, there is no evidence that immigration exacerbates inequality within the bottom 90 percent of earners.

7 Dynamism Dividend

1   43.9 percent of start-ups in Silicon Valley were founded by foreign-born entrepreneurs in 2006–12. 'America's New Immigrant Entrepreneurs: Then and Now', *Kauffman Foundation*, 2 October 2012. https://www.kauffman.org/what-we-do/research/immigration-and-the-american-economy/americas-new-immigrant-entrepreneurs-then-and-now

2   Immigrants co-founded 51 percent of US unicorns. Stuart Anderson, 'Immigrants and Billion Dollar Startups', *National Foundation for American Policy Brief*, March 2016. http://nfap.com/wp-content/uploads/2016/03/Immigrants-and-Billion-Dollar-Startups.NFAP-Policy-Brief.March-2016.pdf

3   Dave Lee, 'Tony Xu, the steady hand steering DoorDash's delivery empire', *Financial Times*, 28 February 2020. https://www.ft.com/content/53e32708-59ea-11ea-a528-dd0f971febbc

4   William Kerr, *The Gift of Global Talent: How Migration Shapes Business, Economy & Society*, Stanford, 2018, Figure 3.3. https://www.sup.org/books/title/?id=29770

5   Rani Molla, 'More than half of the most valuable US tech companies were founded by first- or second-generation immigrants', *Vox*, 30 May 2018. https://www.vox.com/2018/5/30/17385226/kleiner-perkins-mary-meeker-immigration-tech-founders-jobs-slides-code-conference

6   'New American Fortune 500 in 2019: Top American Companies and Their Immigrant Roots', *New American Economy*, 22 July 2019. https://data.newamericaneconomy.org/en/fortune500-2019/

7   The rate of new entrepreneurs was 0.53 percent for immigrants in 2018, which means they are twice as likely to start businesses as the US-born (0.27 percent). Kauffman Indicators of Entrepreneurship, '2018 National Report on Early-Stage Entrepreneurship', *Kauffman Foundation*, September 2019. https://indicators.kauffman.org/wp-content/uploads/sites/2/2019/09/National_Report_Sept_2019.pdf

8   *Ibid.*

9   David Dyssegaard Kallick, 'Bringing Vitality to Main Street: How Immigrant Small Businesses Help Local Economies Grow', *Fiscal Policy Institute and Americas Society/Council of the Americas*, 2015. https://www.as-coa.org/articles/bringing-vitality-main-street-how-immigrant-small-businesses-help-local-economies-grow

10   'Entrepreneurship', *New American Economy*. Accessed on 23 January 2020 at https://www.newamericaneconomy.org/issues/entrepreneurship/

11   James Warrington, 'TransferWise revenue soars as business customers help fuel growth', *City AM*, 18 September 2019. https://www.cityam.com/transferwise-revenue-soars-as-business-customers-help-fuel-growth/

12   *The Entrepreneurs Network*, 'Job Creators'. Accessed on 23 January 2020 at https://www.tenentrepreneurs.org/immigrantfounders

13   Sam Dumitriu, 'The vital role of immigrants in start-up Britain', *CapX*, 11 July 2019. https://capx.co/the-vital-role-of-immigrants-in-start-up-britain/

14   A young firm is one less than three and a half years old.

15   Mark Hart, Karen Bonner, Jonathan Levie and Laura Heery, 'Global Entrepreneurship Monitor. United Kingdom 2017 Monitoring Report'. https://www.gemconsortium.org/economy-profiles/united-kingdom

16   Philip Salter, 'Half of UK's Fastest-Growing Businesses Have A Foreign-Born Founder', *Forbes*, 11 July 2019. https://www.forbes.com/sites/philipsalter/2019/07/11/half-of-uks-fastest-growing-businesses-have-a-foreign-born-founder/

17   Jack Torrance, '5 Refugee Entrepreneurs who have thrived in Britain', *Real Business*, 16 June 2014. http://realbusiness.co.uk/article/26957-5-refugee-entrepreneurs-who-have-thrived-in-britain

18   'Australia's 50 Richest. #2 Harry Triguboff', *Forbes*. Accessed on 23 January 2020 at https://www.forbes.com/profile/harry-triguboff/?list=australia-billionaires#3141b3399785

19 'Australia's 50 Richest. #39 Maha Sinnathamby', *Forbes*. Accessed on 23 January 2020 at https://www.forbes.com/profile/maha-sinnathamby/?list=australia-billionaires#c29c9fc3caaf

20 'Australia's 50 Richest. #25 David Teoh & family', *Forbes*. Accessed on 23 January 2020 at https://www.forbes.com/profile/david-teoh/?list=australia-billionaires#1723ba6ace0f

21 'Australia's 50 Richest. #4 Frank Lowy', *Forbes*. Accessed on 23 January 2020 at https://www.forbes.com/profile/frank-lowy/?list=australia-billionaires#56e427ee3f74

22 https://www.ey.com/en_gl/weoy/past-winners/manny-stul

23 https://apo.org.au/sites/default/files/resource-files/2018/01/apo-nid128756-1240451.pdf

24 *Australian Bureau of Statistics*, '3418.0 – Personal Income of Migrants, Australia, 2013–14', 27 July 2017. Tables 4 and 11 http://www.abs.gov.au/AUSSTATS/abs@.nsf/DetailsPage/3418.02013-14?OpenDocument

25 Philippe Legrain and Andrew Burridge, 'Seven Steps to Success: Enabling refugee entrepreneurs to flourish', *Centre for Policy Development and Open Political Economy Network*, April 2019. https://cpd.org.au/2019/04/seven-steps-to-success-report/

26 Ashley Robinson, 'Beyond the businessman: Murad Al-Katib', *Regina Leader-Post*, 10 February 2017. https://leaderpost.com/life/qc/beyond-the-businessman-murad-al-katib

27 'Murad Al-Katib. 2017 award winner', *EY*. https://www.ey.com/en_gl/weoy/past-winners/murad-al-katib

28 *Statistics Canada*, 'Immigrant Entrepreneurs', 28 August 2018. https://www.statscan.gc.ca/eng/blog/cs/immigrant-entrepreneurs

29 Garnett Picot and Anne-Marie Rollin, 'Immigrant Entrepreneurs as Job Creators: The Case of Canadian Private Incorporated Companies', *Statistics Canada Analytical Studies Branch Research Paper Series 11F0019M No. 423*, 24 April 2019. https://www150.statcan.gc.ca/n1/pub/11f0019m/11f0019m2019011-eng.htm

30 Bessma Momani, 'New Canadian Entrepreneurs', *6 Degrees-CIGI*, 2016. https://www.cigionline.org/sites/default/files/6degrees_working_paper_web.pdf

31 *World Bank*, 'Doing Business'. Accessed on 23 January 2020 at https://www.doingbusiness.org/en/rankings

32 René Leicht and Stefan Berwing, 'Start-up potential among people with foreign roots. Trends, drivers, obstacles', 30 November 2017. https://www.researchgate.net/publication/321533016_Start-up_potential_among_people_with_foreign_roots_Trends_drivers_obstacles

33 Charmaine Li, 'Sizing up Navabi, the German startup tapping into plus-size fashion', *TechEU*, 19 June 2015. https://tech.eu/features/5091/navabi-profile/

34 Annalisa Merelli, 'The most common surnames of new entrepreneurs in Italy are Hu, Chen, and Singh', *Quartz*, 30 August 2015. https://qz.com/490867/the-most-common-surnames-of-new-entrepreneurs-in-italy-are-hu-chen-and-singh/

35 'Migrant Entrepreneurship', *IFS*. Accessed on 23 January 2020 at https://www.ifs.a.se/migrant-entrepreurship/?sp=Engelska

36 'Mohed Altrad', *EY*. https://www.ey.com/en_gl/weoy/past-winners/mohed-altrad

37 'Hamdi Ulukaya', *EY*. https://www.ey.com/en_gl/weoy/past-winners/hamdi-ulukaya

38 *GEM*, 'GEM 2012 Global Report'. https://www.gemconsortium.org/report

39 Peter Vandor and Nikolaus Franke, 'See Paris and … found a business? The impact of cross-cultural experience on opportunity recognition capabilities', *Journal of Business Venturing*, 31:4, July 2016, pp. 388–407. https://www.sciencedirect.com/science/article/pii/S0883902616300052

40 Peter Vandor and Nikolaus Franke, 'Why Are Immigrants More Entrepreneurial?', *Harvard Business Review*, 27 October 2016. https://hbr.org/2016/10/why-are-immigrants-more-entrepreneurial

41 Will Somerville and Madeleine Sumption, 'Immigration and the Labour Market: Theory, Evidence and Policy?', *Equality and Human Rights Commission*, 2009. https://www.migrationpolicy.org/pubs/Immigration-and-the-Labour-Market.pdf

42   George Borjas, 'Does immigration grease the wheels of the labor market?', *Brookings Papers on Economic Activity*, 32:1, 2001, pp. 69–134. https://www.brookings.edu/bpea-articles/does-immigration-grease-the-wheels-of-the-labor-market/

43   Madeline Zavodny and Tamar Jacoby, 'Filling the gap: Less-skilled immigration in a changing economy', *American Enterprise Institute*, June 2013.

44   Sari Pekkala Kerr, William Kerr, Çağlar Özden and Christopher Parsons, 'High-Skilled Migration & Agglomeration', *Annual Review of Economics*, 9:1, 2017, pp. 201–34. https://www.annualreviews.org/doi/abs/10.1146/annurev-economics-063016-103705

45   *Australian Government Department of Home Affairs*, 'Business Innovation and Investment (Provisional) visa (subclass 188). Entrepreneur stream'. Accessed on 23 January 2020 at https://immi.homeaffairs.gov.au/visas/getting-a-visa/visa-listing/business-innovation-and-investment-188/entrepreneur-stream#Overviewhttps://immi.homeaffairs.gov.au/visas/getting-a-visa/visa-listing/business-talent-permanent-132/venture-capital-entrepreneur-stream

46   UK Government, 'Start-up visa'. Accessed on 23 January 2020 at https://www.gov.uk/start-up-visa

8 Diploma Dividend

1   The university with the highest proportion of foreign students was the American University of Sharjah, United Arab Emirates. 'International student table 2018: top 200 universities', *Times Higher Education*, 16 May 2018. https://www.timeshighereducation.com/student/best-universities/international-student-table-2018-top-200-universities#survey-answer

2   'Yusra Uzair', LinkedIn. Accessed on 23 January 2020 at https://www.linkedin.com/in/yusra-uzair/

3   *OECD*, 'Enrolment of international students by origin, 2017'. Accessed on 23 January 2020 at https://stats.oecd.org/viewhtml.aspx?datasetcode=EDU_ENRL_MOBILE&lang=en

4   *OECD*, 'Share of international, foreign and all students enrolled by field of education, 2017'. Accessed on 23 January 2020 at https://stats.oecd.org/viewhtml.aspx?datasetcode=EAG_ENRL_MOBILES_FIELDS&lang=en

5   *OECD*, 'Enrolment of international students by origin, 2017'. Accessed on 23 January 2020 at https://stats.oecd.org/viewhtml.aspx?datasetcode=EDU_ENRL_MOBILE&lang=en

6   'Erasmus: What could happen to scheme after Brexit?', BBC, 9 January 2020. https://www.bbc.co.uk/news/education-47293927

7   Sally Weale, 'Chinese students' applications to UK universities up by 30%', *Guardian*, 11 July 2019. https://www.theguardian.com/education/2019/jul/11/chinese-students-applications-to-uk-universities-up-by-30

8   Natasha Robinson, 'Australian universities risk catastrophe due to over-reliance on Chinese students, expert warns', ABC, 20 August 2019. https://www.abc.net.au/news/2019-08-21/australian-universities-too-dependent-on-chinese-students-report/11427272

9   https://www.universityworldnews.com/post.php?story=20190619103340651

10   'The costs and benefits of international students by parliamentary constituency', *Report for the Higher Education Policy Institute and Kaplan International Pathways*, January 2018. https://www.hepi.ac.uk/wp-content/uploads/2018/01/Economic-benefits-of-international-students-by-constituency-Final-11-01-2018.pdf

11   'NAFSA International Student Economic Value Tool', *NAFSA*. Accessed on 23 January 2020 at https://www.nafsa.org/policy-and-advocacy/policy-resources/nafsa-international-student-economic-value-tool-v2

12   Chris Isidore, 'These are the top US exports', CNN, 7 March 2018. https://money.cnn.com/2018/03/07/news/economy/top-us-exports/index.html

13   Email from Stephen Jenner, MSc Programmes Administrator, *European Institute*.

14   'Student Academic Experience Survey 2018', *AdvanceHE and HEPI*, June 2018. https://

www.hepi.ac.uk/wp-content/uploads/2018/06/STRICTLY-EMBARGOED-UNTIL-THURSDAY-7-JUNE-2018-Student-Academic-Experience-Survey-report-2018.pdf

15 'Fee Levels for 2019/20', *London School of Economics and Political Science*. https://info.lse.ac.uk/staff/divisions/Planning-Division/Assets/Documents/2019-20-Fees-Table.pdf

16 Kevin Shih, 'Do International Students Crowd-Out or Cross-Subsidize Americans in Higher Education?', *Journal of Public Economics*, 156, 2017, pp. 170–84. http://kevinyshih.weebly.com/uploads/5/5/8/7/5587146/shih_crowdcross_2017.pdf

17 Australian students pay A\$9,527 (£5,000). 'Bachelor of Advanced Computing', *University of Sydney*. Accessed on 23 January 2020 at https://sydney.edu.au/courses/courses/uc/bachelor-of-advanced-computing.html

18 *British Council*, 'Visas and Student Recruitment', 2016. https://www.britishcouncil.org/organisation/facts/key-issues/visas

19 Paula Stephan, Giuseppe Scellato and Chiara Franzoni, 'International Competition for PhDs and Postdoctoral Scholars: What Does (and Does Not) Matter', *Innovation Policy and the Economy*, 15:1, 2015, pp. 73–113. https://www.journals.uchicago.edu/doi/abs/10.1086/680060

20 Keith Maskus, Ahmed Mushfiq Mobarak and Eric Stuen, 'Skilled Immigration and Innovation: Evidence from Enrollment Fluctuations in US Doctoral Programs', *CEPR Discussion Paper No. DP7709*, February 2010. https://ssrn.com/abstract=1559665

21 A 10 percent increase in the number of foreign graduate students raises patent applications by 4.7 percent, university patent grants by 5.3 percent and non-university patent grants by 6.7 percent. Gnanaraj Chellaraj, Keith Maskus and Aaditya Mattoo, 'The Contribution of Skilled Immigration and International Graduate Students to US Innovation', *World Bank Policy Research Working Paper 3588*, June 2005. https://papers.ssrn.com/sol3/papers.cfm?abstract_id=74462

22 Giuseppe Scellato, Chiara Franzoni and Paula Stephan, 'Mobile Scientists and International Networks, *NBER Working Paper 18613*, December 2012. https://www.nber.org/papers/w18613.pdf

23 Patrick Gaulé and Mario Piacentini, 'Chinese Graduate Students and US Scientific Productivity', *Review of Economics and Statistics*, 2010. https://www.researchgate.net/publication/254926283_Chinese_Graduate_Students_and_US_Scientific_Productivity

24 Jeffrey Grogger and Gordon H. Hanson, 'Attracting Talent: Location Choices of Foreign-Born PhDs in the United States', *Journal of Labor Economics*, 33: S1, Pt. 2, July 2015, pp. S5–S38. https://www.journals.uchicago.edu/doi/abs/10.1086/679062

25 *Australian Government Department of Home Affairs*, 'Temporary Graduate visa (subclass 485) Post-Study Work stream'. Accessed on 23 January 2020 at https://immi.homeaffairs.gov.au/visas/getting-a-visa/visa-listing/temporary-graduate-485/post-study-work#Overview

26 'Streamlining Legal Immigration', Obama White House archives. Accessed on 23 January 2020 at https://obamawhitehouse.archives.gov/issues/immigration/streamlining-immigration

27 Takao Kato and Chad Sparber, 'Quotas and Quality: The Effect of H-1B Visa Restrictions on the Pool of Prospective Undergraduate Students from Abroad', *Review of Economics and Statistics*, 95:1, 2013, pp. 109–26. https://www.mitpressjournals.org/doi/abs/10.1162/REST_a_00245

28 *Migration Advisory Committee (MAC)*, 'Impact of international students in the UK', September 2018. https://assets.publishing.service.gov.uk/government/uploads/system/uploads/attachment_data/file/739089/Impact_intl_students_report_published_v1.1.pdf

29 *UK Government*, 'Horizon 2020 funding if there's no Brexit deal', updated 28 June 2019. https://www.gov.uk/government/publications/horizon-2020-funding-if-theres-no-brexit-deal/horizon-2020-funding-if-theres-no-brexit-deal--2

30 London First submission to MAC, 'Impact of international students in the UK', September 2018. https://assets.publishing.service.gov.uk/government/uploads/system/uploads/attachment_data/file/739089/Impact_intl_students_report_published_v1.1.pdf

31   Nick Hillman and Tom Huxley, 'The soft-power benefits of educating the world's leaders', *HEPI Policy Note 16*, September 2019. https://www.hepi.ac.uk/wp-content/uploads/2019/09/Policy-Note-16-_-The-soft-power-benefits-of-educating-the-world's-leaders-05_09_19-Screen.pdf

9 Deftness Dividend

1   'Watch Solver Priya Lakhani Pitch CENTURY Tech', YouTube, 28 November 2018. https://www.youtube.com/watch?v=xH8dD2vrI2M

2   Chiara Franzoni, Giuseppe Scellato and Paula Stephan, 'Foreign Born Scientists: Mobility Patterns for Sixteen Countries', *NBER Working Paper 18067*, May 2012. https://www.nber.org/papers/w18067.pdf

3   Joel Negin, Aneuryn Rozea, Ben Cloyd and Alexandra LC Martiniuk, 'Foreign-born health workers in Australia: an analysis of census data', *Human Resources for Health*, 11:69, 2013. https://www.ncbi.nlm.nih.gov/pmc/articles/PMC3882294/

4   'NHS staff from overseas: statistics', House of Commons Library, 8 July 2019. https://research-briefings.parliament.uk/ResearchBriefing/Summary/CBP-7783

5   *US Census Bureau*, 'American Community Survey 2017'. https://datausa.io/visualize?groups=0-1kzwvK&groups=1-1vG6TK-24&measure=1qWfo

6   Mark Sweney, 'Fears for Sunderland workers as Nissan plans to shed 10,000 jobs worldwide', *Guardian*, 24 July 2019. https://www.theguardian.com/business/2019/jul/24/nissan-plans-to-shed-10000-jobs-worldwide-reports-claim

7   Maurice Kugler and Hillel Rapoport, 'Migration, FDI and the margins of trade', *CID Working Paper 222*, Harvard, June 2011. https://www.hks.harvard.edu/sites/default/files/centers/cid/files/publications/faculty-working-papers/222.pdf

8   Andreas Hatzigeorgiou and Magnus Lodefalk, 'Migrants' Influence on Firm-level Exports', *Journal of Industry, Competition & Trade*, 16:4, 2016, pp. 477–97. https://ideas.repec.org/a/kap/jincot/v16y2016i4d10.1007_s10842-015-0215-7.html

9   Indians also lead top UK firms. Rakesh Kapoor, the chief executive of Reckitt Benckiser, was born and educated in India, as was NMC Health boss Prasanth Manghat.

10   Many others are Americans by birth who were born abroad. 'List of foreign-born United States politicians', Wikipedia. Accessed on 23 January 2020 at https://en.m.wikipedia.org/wiki/List_of_foreign-born_United_States_politicians

11   Jarni Blakkarly, 'Australia's new parliament is no more multicultural than the last one', SBS News, 21 May 2019. https://www.sbs.com.au/news/australia-s-new-parliament-is-no-more-multicultural-than-the-last-one

12   Proportion of STEM workers with bachelor's degree or higher who are foreign-born, 2017. 'Silicon Valley Competitiveness and Innovation Project – 2019 Update', *SVCIP*, 2019. https://www.svcip.com/files/SVCIP_2019.pdf#page=13

13   William Kerr, *The Gift of Global Talent: How Migration Shapes Business, Economy & Society*, Stanford, 2018. https://www.sup.org/books/title/?id=29770

14   'Facing Facts: The impact of migrants on London, its workforce and its economy', *PWC and London First*, March 2017. https://www.londonfirst.co.uk/sites/default/files/documents/2018-04/Facing-Facts.pdf

15   Paul McQueen, 'The Famous Fashion Designers Behind Paris's Biggest Fashion Houses', Culture Trip, 1 July 2019. https://theculturetrip.com/europe/france/paris/articles/the-leading-creatives-behind-paris-most-famous-fashion-houses/

16   'List of highest-grossing films', Wikipedia. Accessed on 23 January 2020 at https://en.wikipedia.org/wiki/List_of_highest-grossing_films

17   In 2010, 5.31 percent of highly educated residents aged twenty-five and older had emigrated, compared with 1.29 percent of those with medium skills and 1.4 percent of those with low skills. 'The IAB brain-drain data', *IAB*. Accessed on 23 January 2020 at http://www.iab.de/en/daten/iab-brain-drain-data.aspx

18   Carsten Fink and Ernest Miguelez, 'Measuring the International Mobility of Inventors: A New Database', *WIPO Economic Research Working Paper 8*, 2013. https://www.wipo.int/edocs/pubdocs/en/wipo_pub_econstat_wp_8.pdf

19   'List of Nobel laureates', Wikipedia. Accessed on 23 January 2020 at https://en.wikipedia.org/wiki/List_of_Nobel_laureates

20   *OECD*, 'The new immigrants. Global trends in migration towards OECD countries between 2000/01 and 2015/16', Migration Data Brief 4, June 2019. http://www.oecd.org/els/mig/Migration-data-brief-4-EN.pdf

21   Educational attainment of twenty-five to sixty-four-year-olds. *OECD*, 'Education at a Glance 2019', 2019, Table A1.1, p. 49. https://read.oecd-ilibrary.org/education/education-at-a-glance-2019_f8d7880d-en#page51

22   In the US, 31 percent of immigrants aged twenty-five and older in 2017 had a bachelor's degree or higher, as did 32 percent of US-born adults. Jie Zong, Jeanne Batalova, and Micayla Burrows, 'Frequently Requested Statistics on Immigrants and Immigration in the United States', *Migration Policy Institute*, 14 March 2019. https://www.migrationpolicy.org/article/frequently-requested-statistics-immigrants-and-immigration-united-states

23   *Ibid*. 47 percent of immigrants aged twenty-five and older in 2017 who arrived in the US between 2012 and 2017 had a bachelor's degree.

24   48 percent of immigrants aged twenty-five to fifty-four in 2018 had a university degree, while a further 27 percent had a post-secondary certificate or diploma. *Statistics Canada*, 'Labour force characteristics of immigrants by educational attainment, annual, Table: 14-10-0087-01'. https://doi.org/10.25318/1410008701-eng

25   *ABS*, '6250.0 - Characteristics of Recent Migrants, Australia, November 2016', 14 June 2017. https://www.abs.gov.au/ausstats/abs@.nsf/Latestproducts/6250.0Main%20Features1November%202016?opendocument&tabname=Summary&prodno=6250.0&issue=November%202016&num=&view=

26   52.2 percent did in 2018. *Eurostat*, 'Population by educational attainment level, sex, age and country of birth'. Code: edat_lfs_9912

27   Cansin Arslan et al, 'A New Profile of Migrants in the Aftermath of the Recent Economic Crisis', *OECD Social, Employment and Migration Working Papers 160*, 2014, Table A3. http://www.oecd.org/els/mig/WP160.pdf

28   Sari Pekkala Kerr, William Kerr, Çaglar Ozden and Christopher Parsons, 'Global Talent Flows', *World Bank Policy Research Working Paper 7852*, October 2016. https://papers.ssrn.com/sol3/papers.cfm?abstract_id=2849156

29   Carsten Fink and Ernest Miguelez, 'Measuring the International Mobility of Inventors: A New Database', *WIPO Economic Research Working Paper 8*, 2013. https://www.wipo.int/edocs/pubdocs/en/wipo_pub_econstat_wp_8.pdf

30   William Kerr, *The Gift of Global Talent*, 2018.

31   The UK offered 2,000 Tier 1 visas for people with exceptional talent or promise in the 2019–20 financial year. https://www.gov.uk/tier-1-exceptional-talent The US issued 17,000 O-1 visas for people with extraordinary ability in the sciences, art, education, business or athletics in fiscal year 2018. *US Department of State*, 'Report of the Visa Office 2018', Table XVI(B). https://travel.state.gov/content/dam/visas/Statistics/AnnualReports/FY2018AnnualReport/FY18AnnualReport%20-%20TableXVIB.pdf

32   *UN-DESA*, 'International Migration Policies: Data Booklet', 2017. https://www.un.org/en/development/desa/population/publications/pdf/policy/international_migration_policies_data_booklet.pdf

33   The US offers 65,000 H-1B three-year once-renewable temporary work visas a year plus 20,000 for those with a postgraduate degree from a US university. Including renewals 180,000 were issued in fiscal 2018. *US State Department*, 'Worldwide NIV Workload by Visa Category FY

2018'. https://travel.state.gov/content/dam/visas/Statistics/Non-Immigrant-Statistics/NIV-Workload/FY2018NIVWorkloadbyVisaCategory.pdf

34   TN visas were created as part of the North American Free Trade Agreement (NAFTA). The figure is for fiscal 2018. E3 visas are for Australian professionals.

35   *US Department of State*, 'Report of the Visa Office 2018', Table XVI(B). https://travel.state.gov/content/dam/visas/Statistics/AnnualReports/FY2018AnnualReport/FY18AnnualReport%20-%20TableXVIB.pdf

36   The US offers 124,365 EB-1, EB-2 and EB-3 permanent work visas a year.

37   Jessica Kwong, 'H-1B Visa Program and Trump: How High-Skilled Immigrants are being Threatened by President's Administration', *Newsweek*, 1 March 2018. http://www.newsweek.com/h-1b-visa-program-trump-administration-824688

38   'Presidential Executive Order on Buy American and Hire American', 18 April 2017. https://www.whitehouse.gov/presidential-actions/presidential-executive-order-buy-american-hire-american/

39   William Kerr, *The Gift of Global Talent*, 2018

40   Demetri Sevastopulo and Yuan Yang, 'Ex-Google chief warns of need for AI co-operation with China', *Financial Times*, 5 November 2019. https://www.ft.com/content/6a1de5b6-ff5f-11e9-b7bc-f3fa4e77dd47

41   'Relations between China and America are infected with coronavirus', *The Economist*, 26 March 2020. https://www.economist.com/united-states/2020/03/26/relations-between-china-and-america-are-infected-with-coronavirus

42   Michael Savage, 'NHS winter crisis fears grow after thousands of EU staff quit', *Guardian*, 24 November 2019. https://www.theguardian.com/society/2019/nov/24/nhs-winter-crisis-thousands-eu-staff-quit

43   Alan Travis, 'UK hits visa cap on skilled workers for third month in row', *Guardian*, 18 February 2018. https://www.theguardian.com/uk-news/2018/feb/18/uk-hits-skilled-worker-visa-cap-third-month-home-office-refuses-applications

44   Jack Graham, 'The New Global Talent Race', *OPEN*, 13 June 2018. http://www.opennetwork.net/the-new-global-talent-race/

45   Hugo O'Doherty, 'Canada Immigration Levels Plan: 2019–2021', *Moving2Canada*, 31 October 2018. https://moving2canada.com/canada-immigration-levels-plan-2019-2021/

46   *Government of Canada*, 'Hire a top foreign talent through the Global Talent Stream'. Accessed on 23 January 2020 at https://www.canada.ca/en/employment-social-development/services/foreign-workers/global-talent.html

47   Andrew Edgecliffe-Johnson, 'Corporate America's visa loss is Canada's brain gain', *Financial Times*, 28 December 2018. https://www.ft.com/content/b99c0090-0a01-11e9-9fe8-acdb36967cfc

48   Robert Guest, 'How migration makes the world brainier', *The Economist*, 14 November 2019. https://www.economist.com/special-report/2019/11/14/how-migration-makes-the-world-brainier

49   *CBRE*, 'Top-ranked and momentum tech talent markets. Tech Talent Analyzer 2018.' https://mapping.cbre.com/maps/Scoring-Tech-Talent-2018/Analyzer/

50   Andrew Edgecliffe-Johnson, 'Toronto tech: why Canada is attracting the 'best' people', *Financial Times*, 26 February 2019. https://www.ft.com/content/de63f33c-34e6-11e9-bd3a-8b2a211d90d5

51   Rosemary Bolger, 'Skilled visas to be processed within a week to fill temporary shortages', SBS News, 8 March 2019. https://www.sbs.com.au/news/skilled-visas-to-be-processed-within-a-week-to-fill-temporary-shortages

52   An influx of foreign STEM workers that boosted local employment by one percentage point tended to boost the wages of local graduates by 7–8 percentage points and those of non-graduates by 3–4 percentage points. Giovanni Peri, Kevin Shih and Chad Sparber, 'STEM Workers, H-1B

Visas, and Productivity in US Cities', *Journal of Labor Economics*, 33:S1 Part 2, July 2015, pp. S225–255. http://giovanniperi.ucdavis.edu/uploads/5/6/8/2/56826033/stem-workers.pdf

53   Giovanni Peri and Chad Sparber, 'Highly Educated Immigrants and Native Occupational Choice', *Industrial Relations*, 50:3, 2011, pp. 385–411. https://papers.ssrn.com/sol3/papers.cfm?abstract_id=1874552#

54   Gordon Hanson and Chen Liu, 'High-Skilled Immigration and the Comparative Advantage of Foreign Born Workers across US Occupations', October 2016. https://gps.ucsd.edu/_files/faculty/hanson/hanson_publication_immigration_foreign-workers.pdf

55   *Committee for Economic Development of Australia*, 'Effects of Temporary Migration', July 2019. https://www.ceda.com.au/Research-and-policy/All-CEDA-research/Research-catalogue/Effects-of-temporary-migration

56   Giovanni Peri, Kevin Shih and Chad Sparber, 'STEM Workers, H-1B Visas, and Productivity in US Cities', *Journal of Labor Economics*, 33:S1 Part 2, July 2015, pp. S225–255. http://giovanniperi.ucdavis.edu/uploads/5/6/8/2/56826033/stem-workers.pdf

57   Francesc Ortega and Giovanni Peri, 'The Effects of Brain Gain on Growth, Investment, and Employment: Evidence from the OECD countries, 1980–2005', in Tito Boeri, Herbert Brücker, Frédéric Docquier and Hillel Rapoport (eds), *Brain Drain and Brain Gain*, 2012.

58   Anirban Ghosh, Anna Maria Mayda and Francesc Ortega, 'The Impact of Skilled Foreign Workers on Firms: An Investigation of Publicly Traded US Firms', *IZA Discussion Paper 8684*, November 2014. http://ftp.iza.org/dp8684.pdf

59   William R. Kerr and William F. Lincoln, 'The Supply Side of Innovation: H-1B Visa Reforms and US Ethnic Invention', *Journal of Labor Economics*, 28:3, 2010, pp. 473–508. https://ideas.repec.org/a/ucp/jlabec/v28y2010i3p473-508.html

60   Gaurav Khanna and Munseob Lee, 'High-Skill Immigration, Innovation, and Creative Destruction', *SSRN*, 6 June 2018. http://dx.doi.org/10.2139/ssrn.3207942

61   Sari Pekkala Kerr, William Kerr and William Lincoln, 'Skilled Immigration and the Employment Structures of US Firms', *Journal of Labor Economics*, 33:S1, 2015, pp. S147–86. https://ideas.repec.org/a/ucp/jlabec/doi10.1086-678986.html

62   Robert Guest, 'How Migration Makes the World Brainier', *The Economist*, 14 November 2019. https://www.economist.com/special-report/2019/11/14/how-migration-makes-the-world-brainier

63   Anna Maria Mayda, Francesc Ortega, Giovanni Peri, Kevin Shih and Chad Sparber, 'The Effect of the H-1B Quota on Employment and Selection of Foreign-Born Labor', *NBER Working Paper 23902*, October 2017. https://www.nber.org/papers/w23902.pdf

64   Britta Glennon, 'How Do Restrictions on High-Skilled Immigration Affect Offshoring? Evidence from the H-1B Program', May 2019. https://www.dropbox.com/s/tp4okwocw2pajw5/BGlennon_JMP%20Draft.pdf?dl=0

65   23 percent of the UK-born have some higher education, as do 43 percent of EU migrants and 45 percent of all migrants. Jonathan Wadsworth, Swati Dhingra, Gianmarco Ottaviano and John Van Reenen, 'Brexit and the Impact of Immigration on the UK', *Centre for Economic Performance Brexit Analysis 5*, LSE, 2016 http://cep.lse.ac.uk/pubs/download/brexit05.pdf

66   *Home Office*, 'The UK's points-based immigration system: policy statement', 19 February 2020. https://www.gov.uk/government/publications/the-uks-points-based-immigration-system-policy-statement/the-uks-points-based-immigration-system-policy-statement

67   Philippe Legrain, 'Boris Johnson's New Immigration Rules Will Harm Britain's Economy'. *Foreign Policy*, 21 February 2020. https://foreignpolicy.com/2020/02/21/boris-johnsons-new-immigration-rules-will-harm-britains-economy/

68   Subclass 189

69   *Australian Government Department of Home Affairs*, 'Points table for Skilled Independent visa (subclass 189)'. Accessed on 23 January 2020 at https://immi.homeaffairs.gov.au/visas/getting-a-visa/visa-listing/skilled-independent-189/points-table

70 *Australian Government Department of Home Affairs*, 'SkillSelect. Occupation Ceilings'. Accessed on 23 January 2020 at https://immi.homeaffairs.gov.au/visas/working-in-australia/skillselect/occupation-ceilings

71 Business Innovation and Investment (Provisional) visa (subclass 188), Skilled Independent visa (subclass 189), Skilled Nominated visa (subclass 190), Skilled Regional (Provisional) visa (subclass 489), Skilled Work Regional (Provisional) visa (subclass 491).

72 Mathias Czaika and Christopher R. Parsons, 'The Gravity of High-Skilled Migration Policies', *Demography* 54: 2, April 2017, pp. 603–63. https://doi.org/10.1007/s13524-017-0559-1

73 Job mobility is reduced by around 20 percent by US H-1B visas, according to one study. Jennifer Hunt and Bin Xie, 'How Restricted is the Job Mobility of Skilled Temporary Work Visa Holders?', *Journal of Policy Analysis and Management*, 38:1, 2019, pp. 41–64. https://doi.org/10.1002/pam.22110

74 Philippe Legrain, 'Boris Johnson's New Immigration Rules Will Harm Britain's Economy'. *Foreign Policy*, 21 February 2020. https://foreignpolicy.com/2020/02/21/boris-johnsons-new-immigration-rules-will-harm-britains-economy/

75 Frey Lindsay, 'Why Sweden Is Deporting High-Skilled Labor Migrants', *Forbes*, 13 February 2019. https://www.forbes.com/sites/freylindsay/2019/02/13/why-sweden-is-deporting-high-skilled-labor-migrants/

76 'How do OECD countries compare in their attractiveness for talented migrants?', Migration Policy Debates 19, *OECD*, May 2019. https://www.oecd.org/migration/mig/migration-policy-debates-19.pdf

77 The top ten countries in terms of their attractiveness to highly educated workers, before factoring in visa rules, are the US, Australia, New Zealand, Canada, Sweden, Ireland, Switzerland, Norway, the Netherlands and the UK.

78 The top ten most attractive OECD countries to highly educated workers are Australia, Sweden, Switzerland, New Zealand, Canada, Ireland, the US, the Netherlands, Slovenia and Norway.

10 Diversity Dividend

1 Chris Bascombe, 'Jurgen Klopp delights in diverse personalities of Liverpool's record-hunting defensive bedrock', *Telegraph*, 4 April 2019. https://www.telegraph.co.uk/football/2019/04/04/jurgen-klopp-delights-diverse-personalities-liverpools-record/

2 Leslie Pray, 'Discovery of DNA structure and function: Watson and Crick', *Nature Education*, 1:1, 2008. https://www.nature.com/scitable/topicpage/discovery-of-dna-structure-and-function-watson-397/

3 David Rowan, 'DeepMind: inside Google's super-brain', *Wired*, 22 June 2015. https://www.wired.co.uk/article/deepmind

4 Ernest Miguelez, Julio Raffo, Christian Chacua, Massimiliano Coda-Zabetta, Deyun Yin, Francesco Lissoni, Gianluca Tarasconi, 'Tied in: The Global Network of Local Innovation', *WIPO Economic Research Working Paper 58*, November 2019. https://www.wipo.int/publications/en/details.jsp?id=4472&plang=EN

5 Quoted in Daniel Finkelstein, 'How to bring brains together – at top speed', *The Times*, 11 September 2013. http://www.thetimes.co.uk/tto/opinion/columnists/danielfinkelstein/article3865753.ece

6 Jane Jacobs, *The Death and Life of Great American Cities*, Random House, 1961.

7 Edward Glaeser, *Triumph of the City: How Our Greatest Invention Makes Us Richer, Smarter, Greener, Healthier and Happier*, Macmillan, 2011.

8 Richard Florida, *The Rise of The Creative Class: And How It's Transforming Work, Leisure, Community And Everyday Life*, Basic Books, 2002.

9 'Mayors and mammon', *The Economist*, 13 July 2013. http://www.economist.com/news/business/21581695-city-leaders-are-increasingly-adopting-business-methods-and-promoting-business-mayors-and-mammon

10   Frans Johansson, *The Medici Effect: Breakthrough Insights at the Intersection of Ideas, Concepts, and Cultures*, Harvard Business School, 2004.

11   Donald Campbell, 'Blind Variation and Selective Retention in Creative Thought as in Other Knowledge Processes', *Psychological Review*, 67:6, 1960, pp. 380–400.

12   Dean Simonton, *Origins of Genius*, Oxford, 1999.

13   Scott Page, *The Difference: How the Power of Diversity Creates Better Groups, Firms, Schools, and Societies*, Princeton, 2007.

14   *Ibid.*

15   Chiara Franzoni, Giuseppe Scellato and Paula Stephan, 'The mover's advantage: The superior performance of migrant scientists', *Economics Letters*, 122:1, January 2014, pp. 89–93. http://www.sciencedirect.com/science/article/pii/S0165176513004874

16   Jennifer Hunt and Marjolaine Gauthier-Loiselle, 'How Much Does Immigration Boost Innovation?', *American Economic Journal: Macroeconomics*, 2:2, 2010, pp. 31–56. https://www.aeaweb.org/articles?id=10.1257/mac.2.2.31

17   Richard B. Freeman and Wei Huang, 'Collaborating with People Like Me: Ethnic co-authorship within the US', *NBER Working Paper 19905*, February 2014. http://www.nber.org/papers/w19905

18   'Patent Pending: How Immigrants Are Reinventing The American Economy', *New American Economy*, 26 June 2012. http://www.renewoureconomy.org/research/patent-pending-how-immigrants-are-reinventing-the-american-economy-2/

19   *US Patent and Trademark Office*, 'US Patent Statistics Chart, Calendar years 1963–2018. Accessed on 23 January 2020 at https://www.uspto.gov/web/offices/ac/ido/oeip/taf/us_stat.htm

20   Shai Bernstein, Rebecca Diamond, Timothy James McQuade and Beatriz Pousada, 'The Contribution of High-Skilled Immigrants to Innovation in the United States', *Stanford Graduate School of Business Working Paper 3748*, 6 November 2018. https://www.gsb.stanford.edu/faculty-research/working-papers/contribution-high-skilled-immigrants-innovation-united-states

21   Frédéric Docquier, Riccardo Turati, Jérôme Valette and Chrysovalantis Vasilakis, 'Birthplace Diversity and Economic Growth: Evidence from the US States in the Post-World War II Period', *IZA Discussion Paper 11802*, September 2018. https://perso.uclouvain.be/frederic.docquier/filePDF/DTVV_Birthplace.pdf

22   Jamie Partridge and William Hartley Furtan, 'Increasing Canada's international competitiveness: is there a link between skilled immigrants & innovation?', paper presented at the American Agricultural Economics Association Annual Meeting, Orlando, FL, 27–29 July 2018. https://ideas.repec.org/p/ags/aaea08/6504.html

23   Alberto Alesina, Arnaud Devleeschauwer, William Easterly, Sergio Kurlat and Romain Wacziarg, 'Fractionalization', *Journal of Economic Growth*, 8:2, 2003, pp. 155–94.

24   Alberto Alesina, Johann Harnoss and Hillel Rapoport, 'Birthplace diversity and economic prosperity', *NBER Working Paper 18699*, January 2013. http://www.nber.org/papers/w18699

25   Ceren Ozgen, Peter Nijkamp and Jacques Poot, 'Immigration and innovation in European regions', *Tinbergen Institute Discussion Paper 11-112/3*, 11 August 2011. https://papers.ssrn.com/sol3/papers.cfm?abstract_id=1908138

26   Luisa Gagliardi, 'Does Skilled Migration Foster Innovative Performance? Evidence from British Local Areas' *Papers in Regional Science*, 94:4, 2014. https://www.researchgate.net/publication/241753837_Does_Skilled_Migration_Foster_Innovative_Performance_Evidence_from_British_Local_Areas

27   Valentina Bosetti, Cristina Cattaneo and Elena Verdolini, 'Migration, Cultural Diversity and Innovation: A European Perspective', *FEEM Working Paper 69*, 2012. https://papers.ssrn.com/sol3/papers.cfm?abstract_id=2162836

28   Annekatrin Niebuhr, 'Migration and innovation: does cultural diversity matter for regional

R&D activity?', *Papers in Regional Science*, 89:3, 2010, pp. 563–85. https://rsaiconnect.onlinelibrary.wiley.com/doi/abs/10.1111/j.1435-5957.2009.00271.x

29 Max Nathan, 'Same Difference? Minority ethnic inventors, diversity and innovation in the UK', *Journal of Economic Geography*, 15: 1, January 2015, pp. 129–68. https://doi.org/10.1093/jeg/lbu006

30 Alessandra Venturini, Fabio Montobbio and Claudio Fassio, 'Are migrants spurring innovation', *MPC Research Report 2012/11*, 2012. http://www.migrationpolicycentre.eu/docs/MPC%202012%20EN%2011.pdf

31 Katharina Candel-Haug, Alexander Cuntz and Oliver Falck, 'Polish immigrants stimulate innovation in Germany', *LSE Business Review*, 10 May 2018. https://blogs.lse.ac.uk/business-review/2018/05/10/polish-immigrants-stimulate-innovation-in-germany/

32 Pierpaolo Parrotta, Dario Pozzoli and Mariola Pytlikova, 'The nexus between labor diversity and firm's innovation', *Journal of Population Economics*, 27, April 2014, pp. 303–64. https://link.springer.com/article/10.1007/s00148-013-0491-7

33 Ceren Ozgen, Peter Nijkamp and Jacques Poot, 'Measuring Cultural Diversity and its Impact on Innovation: Longitudinal Evidence from Dutch Firms', *IZA Discussion Paper 7129*, January 2013. http://ftp.iza.org/dp7129.pdf

34 Michaela Trax, Stephan Brunow and Jens Suedekum, 'Cultural Diversity and Plant-Level Productivity', *IZA Discussion Paper 6845*, September 2012. http://ftp.iza.org/dp6845.pdf

35 Jens Suedekum, Katja Wolf and Uwe Blien, 'Cultural Diversity and Local Labour Markets', *Regional Studies*, 48:1, January 2014, pp. 173–91. https://ideas.repec.org/a/taf/regstd/v48y2014i1p173-191.html

36 'Fostering Innovation Through a Diverse Workforce', *Forbes Insights*. https://images.forbes.com/forbesinsights/StudyPDFs/Innovation_Through_Diversity.pdf

37 Adam Galinsky et al, 'Maximizing the Gains and Minimizing the Pains of Diversity: A Policy Perspective', *Perspectives on Psychological Science*, 10:6, 2015, pp. 742–48. https://journals.sagepub.com/doi/pdf/10.1177/1745691615598513

38 Samuel R. Sommers, 'On racial diversity and group decision making: Identifying multiple effects of racial composition on jury deliberations', *Journal of Personality and Social Psychology*, 90, 2016, pp. 597–612.

39 Juliet Bourke, 'Which two heads are better than one? How diverse teams create breakthrough ideas and make smarter decisions', *Australian Institute of Company Directors*, 2016. https://www2.deloitte.com/au/en/pages/human-capital/articles/creating-high-performing-leadership-teams.html

40 *Ibid.*

41 Denise Lewin Lloyd., Cynthia S. Wang, Katherine W. Phillips, and Robert B. Lount, Jr, 'Social category diversity promotes pre-meeting elaboration: The role of relationship focus', *Organization Science*, 24:3, 2013, pp. 757–72. https://www8.gsb.columbia.edu/researcharchive/articles/6392

42 Juliet Bourke, 'Which two heads are better than one?', 2016.

43 Scott Page, *The Difference*, 2007.

44 *McKinsey*, 'Why diversity matters', 2015. https://www.mckinsey.com/business-functions/organization/our-insights/why-diversity-matters

45 *McKinsey*, 'Delivering through diversity', January 2018. https://www.mckinsey.com/business-functions/organization/our-insights/delivering-through-diversity

46 Max Nathan and Neil Lee, 'Cultural Diversity, Innovation, and Entrepreneurship: Firm-level Evidence from London', *Economic Geography*, 89, 2013, pp. 367–94. http://onlinelibrary.wiley.com/doi/10.1111/ecge.12016/abstract

47 Max Nathan, 'All in the mix? Top team demographics and business performance in UK firms, 2008–9', *LLAKES Research Paper 42*, 2013. https://www.llakes.ac.uk/sites/default/files/42.%20Nathan.pdf

48 Rocío Lorenzo, Nicole Voigt, Miki Tsusaka, Matt Krentz and Katie Abouzahr, 'How Diverse Leadership Teams Boost Innovation', *Boston Consulting Group*, 23 January 2018. https://www.bcg.com/en-us/publications/2018/how-diverse-leadership-teams-boost-innovation.aspx

49 Cedric Herring, 'Does diversity pay? Race, gender, and the business case for diversity', *American Sociological Review*, 74, 2009, pp. 208–24. http://www.uww.edu/Documents/diversity/does%20diversity%20pay.pdf

50 Sylvia Ann Hewlett, Melinda Marshall and Laura Sherbin, 'How Diversity Can Drive Innovation', *Harvard Business Review*, December 2013. https://hbr.org/2013/12/how-diversity-can-drive-innovation

51 Roger C. Mayer, Richard S. Warr and Jing Zhao, 'Do Pro-Diversity Policies Improve Corporate Innovation?', *Financial Management*, 47: 3, Fall 2018, pp. 617–50. https://onlinelibrary.wiley.com/doi/full/10.1111/fima.12205

11 Drudgery Dividend

1 Hermann Boko, 'Malte, un eldorado pour les migrants africains?', France24, 21 July 2019. https://www.france24.com/fr/20190721-malte-eldorado-migrants-africains-italie-union-europenne

2 *European Commission*, 'Economic forecast for Malta'. Accessed on 24 January 2020 at https://ec.europa.eu/info/business-economy-euro/economic-performance-and-forecasts/economic-performance-country/malta/economic-forecast-malta_en

3 *Eurostat*, 'population change – demographic balance and crude rates at national level'. Code: demo_gind

4 *National Statistics Office Malta*, 'News Release. World Population Day: 2019', 10 July 2019. https://nso.gov.mt/en/News_Releases/View_by_Unit/Unit_C5/Population_and_Migration_Statistics/Documents/2019/News2019_108.pdf

5 Vanessa Macdonald, 'The economy cannot do without foreign workers', *Times of Malta*, 20 January 2019. https://timesofmalta.com/articles/view/the-economy-cannot-do-without-foreign-workers.699661

6 Leanne Tory-Murphy, 'Migrants Malta Does Not Want Are Powering Its Economy', *Refugees Deeply*, 6 August 2018. https://www.newsdeeply.com/refugees/articles/2018/08/06/migrants-malta-does-not-want-are-powering-its-economy

7 *Jobs Europe*, 'What is the average salary on Malta?', 29 June 2018. https://jobseurope.net/average-salaries-malta/

8 *Central Bank of Malta*, 'Assessing the Impact of Foreign Workers in Malta', *Quarterly Review*, 2016:1, 2016, pp. 39–44. https://www.centralbankmalta.org/quarterly-review

9 OECD, 'The new immigrants. Global trends in migration towards OECD countries between 2000/01 and 2015/16', *Migration Data Brief 4*, June 2019. http://www.oecd.org/els/mig/Migration-data-brief-4-EN.pdf

10 *US Bureau of Labor Statistics*, 'Occupations with the most job growth'. Accessed on 7 July 2020 at https://www.bls.gov/emp/tables/occupations-most-job-growth.htm

11 *UK Commission for Employment and Skills*, 'Working Futures 2014-2024', May 2016, Annexes, Table C.2. https://assets.publishing.service.gov.uk/government/uploads/system/uploads/attachment_data/file/523332/Working_Futures_Annexes_1424.pdf

12 *Cedefop*, 'Skills forecast: trends and challenges to 2030', 2018, Table A7. https://www.cedefop.europa.eu/files/3077_en.pdf

13 According to the US Bureau of Labor Statistics, 38.8 percent of immigrants in the US work in the two lowest-wage categories – service occupations and production, transport and material-moving occupations – compared with just 27.3 percent of locals.

14 More than two-fifths of farm labourers and supervisors in the US are migrants.

15 *Australian Government Department of Immigration and Border Protection*, 'The place of migrants in contemporary Australia: A summary report', July 2014.

16   Sally Kohn, 'Nothing Donald Trump Says on Immigration Holds Up', *Time*, 29 June 2016. https://time.com/4386240/donald-trump-immigration-arguments/

17   Deborah Summers, 'Brown stands by British jobs for British workers remark', *Guardian*, 30 January 2009. https://www.theguardian.com/politics/2009/jan/30/brown-british-jobs-workers

18   'Theresa May's conference speech in full', *Telegraph*, 5 October 2016. https://www.telegraph.co.uk/news/2016/10/05/theresa-mays-conference-speech-in-full/

19   Guglielmo Barone and Sauro Mocetti, 'With a little help from abroad: The effect of low-skilled immigration on the female labour supply', *Labour Economics*, 18:5, 2011, pp. 664–75. https://www.sciencedirect.com/science/article/abs/pii/S0927537111000273; Delia Furtado and Heinrich Hock, 'Low Skilled Immigration & Work-Fertility Tradeoffs among High Skilled Us Natives', *American Economic Review*, 100(2), 2010, pp. 224–28 https://www.ncbi.nlm.nih.gov/pmc/articles/PMC4160832/

20   Philippe Legrain, 'Free to Move', *Institute of Economic Affairs*, 17 November 2016. https://iea.org.uk/publications/free-to-move/

21   See, for example, George J. Borjas, 'The Labor Demand Curve Is Downward Sloping: Reexamining the Impact of Immigration on the Labor Market', *Quarterly Journal of Economics*, 118:4, November 2003, pp. 1335–74. https://sites.hks.harvard.edu/fs/gborjas/publications/journal/QJE2003.pdf

22   Michael Clemens, 'The Effect of Foreign Labor on Native Employment: A Job-Specific Approach and Application to North Carolina Farms', *Center for Global Development Working Paper 326*, May 2013. https://www.cgdev.org/publication/effect-foreign-labor-native-employment-job-specific-approach-and-application-north

23   Charles Hymas, 'Only 112 of 50,000 UK applicants for fruit pickers take jobs amid farmers' fears over skills and application', *Telegraph*, 27 April 2020. https://www.telegraph.co.uk/news/2020/04/27/112-50000-uk-applicants-fruit-pickers-take-jobs-amid-farmers/

24   *ONS*, 'Employee earnings in the UK: 2019'. Accessed on 24 January 2020 at https://ons.gov.uk/employmentandlabourmarket/peopleinwork/earningsandworkinghours/bulletins/annualsurveyofhoursandearnings/2019

25   Giovanni Peri, 'Did immigration contribute to wage stagnation of unskilled workers?', *Research in Economics*, 72:2, 2018, pp. 356–65. https://ideas.repec.org/a/eee/reecon/v72y2018i2p356-365.html

26   *Ibid.*

27   One UK study, using data from 1997–2005, found that an increase in the number of migrants equivalent to 1 percent of the UK-born working-age population boosted average wages by 0.2–0.3 percent. Increased migration boosted the median wage by 0.7 percent, while reducing the wages of the lowest-paid 5 percent of workers by 0.6 percent. In practice, this meant hourly wages for the lowest-paid 10 percent rose by 18 pence per year instead of 18.7 pence. Christian Dustmann, Tommaso Frattini and Ian Preston, 'The Effect of Immigration along the Distribution of Wages', *Review of Economic Studies*, 80:1, 2013, pp. 145–73.

28   One study found no statistically significant relationship between changes in the share of EU migrants in the local population between 2008 and 2015 and the wages of people born in the UK. Jonathan Wadsworth, Swati Dhingra, Gianmarco Ottaviano and John Van Reenen, 'Brexit and the Impact of Immigration on the UK', *CEP Brexit Analysis 5*, 2016. http://cep.lse.ac.uk/pubs/download/brexit05.pdf. Another study found that net EU migration between 2000 and 2015 had a tiny impact on local workers' pay. At most, EU migration depressed natives' hourly wages by four pence a year in skilled trades. Stephen Clarke, 'A brave new world: How reduced migration could affect earnings, employment and the labour market', *Resolution Foundation*, 2016. https://www.resolutionfoundation.org/publications/a-brave-new-world-how-reduced-migration-could-affect-earnings-employment-and-the-labour-market/

29 *MAC, EEA migration in the UK'*, 18 September 2018. https://www.gov.uk/government/ publications/migration-advisory-committee-mac-report-eea-migration

30 *Ibid.*

31 *Ibid.*

32 *National Academies of Sciences, Engineering and Medicine*, 'The Economic and Fiscal Consequences of Immigration', 2016. https://d279m997dpfwgl.cloudfront.net/wp/ 2016/09/0922_immigrant-economics-full-report.pdf

33 Mette Foged and Giovanni Peri, 'Immigrants and Native Workers: New Analysis on Longitudinal Data', *NBER Working Paper 19315*, revised March 2015. http://www.nber.org/papers/ w19315. Foged and Peri analyse inflows of low-skilled migrants from the eight main refugee source countries during that period: Bosnia and Herzegovina, Afghanistan, Somalia, Iraq, Iran, Vietnam, Sri Lanka and Lebanon. Since low-skilled migration to Denmark from those countries is almost impossible, the migrants are almost all refugees.

34 Sarit Cohen Goldner and Chang-Tai Hsieh, 'Macroeconomic and Labor Market Impact of Russian Immigration in Israel', May 2000. https://www.researchgate.net/publication/ 228885737_Macroeconomic_and_Labor_Market_Impact_of_Russian_Immigration_ in_Israel

35 The finding that post-Soviet migrants did not harm Israelis' labour-market outcomes is confirmed by Rachel Friedberg, 'The Impact of Mass Migration on the Israeli Labor Market', *Quarterly Journal of Economics*, CXVI:4, 2001, pp. 1373–408. https://www. brown.edu/Departments/Economics/Faculty/Rachel_Friedberg/Links/Friedberg%20QJE. pdf

36 Olivier Blanchard, Florence Jaumotte and Prakash Loungani, 'Labor Market Policies and IMF Advice in Advanced Economies during the Great Recession', *IMF Staff Discussion Note 13/02*, 2013. https://www.imf.org/external/pubs/ft/sdn/2013/sdn1302.pdf

12 Demographic Dividend

1 Japan's elderly accounted for 28.4 percent of its population in 2018, a proportion that is expected to reach 30 percent by 2025. 'World's most aged society just got older – Japan sets new records', *South China Morning Post*, 15 September 2019. https://www.scmp.com/news/ asia/east-asia/article/3027329/worlds-most-aged-society-just-got-older-japan-sets-new- records

2 'Robots may have role in future of elder care in rapidly ageing Japan', *Straits Times*, 28 March 2018. https://www.straitstimes.com/asia/east-asia/robots-may-have-role-in-future-of-elder- care-in-rapidly-ageing-japan

3 TRT World, 'Robots help the elderly in Japan's nursing homes', YouTube, 29 March 2018. https://www.youtube.com/watch?v=2xUkVrJUB20

4 FT Content Solutions, 'Undiscovered Japan: Using robots to care for the elderly', YouTube, 16 December 2016. https://www.youtube.com/watch?v=yYFLVFni1to

5 Jane Wakefield, 'Robot 'talks' to MPs about future of AI in the classroom', BBC, 16 October 2018. https://www.bbc.co.uk/news/technology-45879961

6 'Robots may have role in future of elder care in rapidly ageing Japan', *Straits Times*, 28 March 2018. https://www.straitstimes.com/asia/east-asia/robots-may-have-role-in-future-of-elder- care-in-rapidly-ageing-japan

7 'Japanese firms seek to retain foreign workers amid labor shortage', *Japan News*, 29 March 2019. https://www.sfgate.com/news/article/Japanese-firms-seek-to-retain-foreign-workers- 13726861.php%20target=

8 As recently as 2015, Prime Minister Shinzo Abe said 'there are many things that we should do before accepting immigrants.' 'Abe says Japan must solve its own problems before accepting any Syria refugees', *Reuters*, 30 September 2015. https://www.reuters.com/article/

us-un-assembly-japan-syria/abe-says-japan-must-solve-its-own-problems-before-accepting-any-syria-refugees-idUSKCN0RT2WK20150929

9   Motoko Rich, 'Bucking a Global Trend, Japan Seeks More Immigrants. Ambivalently', *New York Times*, 7 December 2018. https://www.nytimes.com/2018/12/07/world/asia/japan-parliament-foreign-workers.html

10 'Japan is Finally Starting to Admit More Foreign Workers', *The Economist*, 5 July 2018. https://www.economist.com/asia/2018/07/05/japan-is-finally-starting-to-admit-more-foreign-workers

11 Motoko Rich, 'Bucking a Global Trend, Japan Seeks More Immigrants. Ambivalently', *New York Times*, 7 December 2018. https://www.nytimes.com/2018/12/07/world/asia/japan-parliament-foreign-workers.html

12 In 2040, 28.7 percent of the EU population are forecast to be aged sixty-five and older. *Eurostat*, 'Population Projections 2018-based'. Code: proj_18np

13 *UN-DESA*, 'World Population Prospects 2019. Zero-migration variant'. https://population.un.org/wpp/

14 Personal calculations from Eurostat, 'Population Projections 2018-based'. Code: proj_18np

15 *US Bureau of Labor Statistics*, 'Employment Projections. Occupations with the most job growth 2018 and projected 2028'. Accessed on 24 January 2020 at https://www.bls.gov/emp/tables/occupations-most-job-growth.htm

16 *Government of Canada*, 'Canadian Occupational Projection System (COPS) – 2017 to 2026 projections'. Accessed on 24 January 2020 at https://open.canada.ca/data/en/dataset/e80851b8-de68-43bd-a85c-c72e1b3a3890

17 *Australian Government Labour Market Information Portal*, '2019 Employment Projections – for the five years to May 2024'. Accessed on 24 January 2020 at http://lmip.gov.au/default.aspx?LMIP/GainInsights/EmploymentProjections

18 *Cedefop*, 'Skills forecast: trends and challenges to 2030', 2018, Table A7. https://www.cedefop.europa.eu/files/3077_en.pdf

19 *UK Commission for Employment and Skills*, 'Working Futures 2014–2024', May 2016, Annexes, Table C.2. https://assets.publishing.service.gov.uk/government/uploads/system/uploads/attachment_data/file/523332/Working_Futures_Annexes_1424.pdf

20 'Relentless staff shortage leaves home care sector struggling', *The King's Fund*, 11 December 2018. https://www.kingsfund.org.uk/press/press-releases/relentless-staff-shortage-leaves-home-care-sector-struggling

21 Mark Dayan, 'The end state & the NHS', Nuffield Trust comment, 2018. https://www.nuffieldtrust.org.uk/news-item/theend-state-&-the-nhs

22 *MAC*, EEA migration in the UK: Final report', 18 September 2018, Para 5.24. https://www.gov.uk/government/publications/migration-advisory-committee-mac-report-eea-migration

23 *OECD*, 'Help wanted? Providing and paying for long-term care', 2011. https://www.oecd.org/health/health-systems/help-wanted-9789264097759-en.htm

24 Barbara Da Roit and Bernhard Weicht, 'Migrant Care Work & Care, Migration & Employment Regimes: A Fuzzy-Set Analysis', *Journal of European Social Policy*, 23:5, 2013, pp. 469–86 https://journals.sagepub.com/doi/abs/10.1177/0958928713499175?journalCode=espa

25 *UN-DESA*, 'World Population Prospects 2019. Zero-migration variant'. https://population.un.org/wpp/

26 Canada's median age would hit forty-eight in 2040 and Australia's forty-five.

27 Matthew Bell, 'Worried about its future, this former East German city recruited Syrian refugees, *PRI*, 10 January 2017. https://www.pri.org/stories/2017-01-10/worried-about-its-future-former-east-german-city-recruited-syrian-refugees

28 Katrin Bennhold, 'Syrian Children Saved a German Village. And a Village Saved Itself', *New York Times*, 19 September 2019. https://www.nytimes.com/2019/09/19/world/europe/germany-golzow-syria-refugees.html

29 Miranda Cady Hallett, 'The benefits that places like Dayton, Ohio, reap by welcoming immigrants', *The Conversation*, 29 April 2019. https://theconversation.com/the-benefits-that-places-like-dayton-ohio-reap-by-welcoming-immigrants-107949

30 Theo Majka and Jamie Longazel, 'Becoming Welcoming: Organizational Collaboration and Immigrant Integration in Dayton, Ohio', *Public Integrity*, 19:2, 2017, pp. 151–63. https://www.tandfonline.com/doi/abs/10.1080/10999922.2016.1256697?journalCode=mpin20

31 Miranda Cady Hallett, 'The benefits that places like Dayton, Ohio, reap by welcoming immigrants', *The Conversation*, 29 April 2019. https://theconversation.com/the-benefits-that-places-like-dayton-ohio-reap-by-welcoming-immigrants-107949

32 'Welcome to Dayton', *Partnership for a New American Economy*, July 2015. http://research.newamericaneconomy.org/wp-content/uploads/2015/07/Dayton-Research-Brief-FINAL-July-7-12pm.pdf

33 Cornelius Frolik, 'What we know about Dayton's immigrant population', *Dayton Daily News*, 16 March 2018. https://www.daytondailynews.com/news/local/what-know-about-dayton-immigrant-population/Jang0N3cHhp4C3H1ioleyH/

34 Jason Margolis, 'Detroit welcomes immigrants to spur the city's revival', *PRI*, 18 September 2018. https://www.pri.org/stories/2018-09-18/detroit-welcomes-immigrants-spur-city-s-revival

35 Gihoon Hong and John McLaren, 'Are Immigrants a Shot in the Arm for the Local Economy?' *NBER Working Paper 21123*, April 2015. http://www.nber.org/papers/w21123

36 Benedict Clements, Kamil Dybczak, Vitor Gaspar, Sanjeev Gupta and Mauricio Soto, 'The Fiscal Consequences of Shrinking Populations', *IMF Staff Discussion Note SDN/15/21*, October 2015. https://www.imf.org/external/pubs/ft/sdn/2015/sdn1521.pdf

37 *OECD*, 'Settling in 2018. Main indicators of Immigrant Integration', 2018. https://www.oecd.org/els/mig/Main-Indicators-of-Immigrant-Integration.pdf

38 Personal calculations from Eurostat, 'Population Projections 2018-based'. Code: proj_18np

39 *United Nations Population Division*, 'World Population Prospects 2019'. https://population.un.org/wpp/DataQuery/

40 Personal calculations from Eurostat, 'Population Projections 2018-based'. Code: proj_18np

41 *United Nations Population Division*, 'World Population Prospects 2019'. https://population.un.org/wpp/DataQuery/

42 *UN-DESA*, 'World Population Prospects 2019: Highlights', 17 June 2019. https://www.un.org/development/desa/publications/world-population-prospects-2019-highlights.html

43 Employment figures from ONS, 'Number of People in Employment (aged 16 and over, seasonally adjusted)'. Accessed on 24 January 2020 at https://www.ons.gov.uk/employmentandlabourmarket/peopleinwork/employmentandemployeetypes/timeseries/mgrz/lms; Pension-age population from 'Table 1: Projected number of people in the UK of State Pension age (SPa) or older', *Pensions Policy Institute*. Accessed on 24 January 2020 at https://www.pensionspolicyinstitute.org.uk/research/pension-facts/table-1/

44 To the extent that pensioners own foreign assets, the redistribution occurs from foreigners.

45 In the US, there were 90 births per 1,000 foreign-born women aged fifteen to forty-four, compared with just 59 per thousand local women in 2010. Similarly, in the UK, there were 88 births per 1,000 foreign-born women and 60 per thousand native women in 2011. *Pew Research Center; Office for National Statistics*.

46 Matthew Holehouse, 'Nigel Farage blames immigration after missing Ukip reception', *Telegraph*, 7 December 2014. http://www.telegraph.co.uk/news/politics/nigel-farage/11278440/Nigel-Farage-blames-immigration-after-missing-Ukip-reception.html

47 Personal calculations from 'List of countries and dependencies by population density', Wikipedia. Accessed on 24 January 2020 at https://en.wikipedia.org/wiki/List_of_countries_and_dependencies_by_population_density

48 Alan W. Evans and Oliver Marc Hartwich, 'The best laid plans: How planning prevents economic growth', *Policy Exchange*, 2007. https://www.policyexchange.org.uk/wp-content/uploads/2016/09/the-best-laid-plans-jan-07.pdf

49 Liam Halligan, 'How to fix Britain's housebuilding problem', *Financial Times*, 14 February 2020. https://www.ft.com/content/a63013ea-4da1-11ea-95a0-43d18ec715f5

50 'List of English districts by population density', Wikipedia. Accessed on 24 January 2020 at https://en.wikipedia.org/wiki/List_of_English_districts_by_population_density

51 Philippe Legrain, *European Spring: Why Our Economies and Politics are in a Mess – and How to Put Them Right*, CB Books, 2014.

52 In the UK, migrants were much more likely to be in private rented accommodation (39 percent) than people born in Britain (14 percent) and much less likely to be homeowners (43 percent) than the UK-born (68 percent), *Office for National Statistics*, 'Labour Force Survey, 2015, Q1'.

53 See, for instance, Christian Hilber, 'UK Housing and Planning Policies', *CEP Election Analysis* 3, 2015. http://cep.lse.ac.uk/pubs/download/EA033.pdf

54 Liam Halligan, 'How to fix Britain's housebuilding problem', *Financial Times*, 14 February 2020. https://www.ft.com/content/a63013ea-4da1-11ea-95a0-43d18ec715f5

55 Christian Hilber and Wouter Vermeulen, 'The extraordinarily rigid planning system is the main reason homes in England are unaffordable', *LSE British Politics and Policy*, 12 March 2016. https://blogs.lse.ac.uk/politicsandpolicy/three-reasons-homes-in-england-are-unaffordable/

56 Gianmarco Ottaviano and Giovanni Peri, 'Rethinking the effect of immigration on wages' *Journal of the European Economic Association*, 10:1, 2012, pp. 152–97. https://academic.oup.com/jeea/article-abstract/10/1/152/2182016?redirectedFrom=fulltext

57 Matthew P. Larkin, Zohid Askarov, Chris Doucouliagos, Chris Dubelaar, Maria Klona, Joshua Newton, T.D. Stanley and Andrea Vocino, 'Do House Prices Sink or Ride the Wave of Immigration?', *IZA Discussion Paper 11497*, April 2018. http://ftp.iza.org/dp11497.pdf

58 A 1 percent increase in the migrant share of the population in a local area is associated with a fall in house prices of almost 2 percent. Filipa Sa, 'Immigration and House Prices in the UK', *Economic Journal*, 125, September 2015, pp. 1393–424. https://www.onlinelibrary.wiley.com/doi/abs/10.1111/ecoj.12158

59 13 percent of migrants who had been in the UK less than five years were in social housing in 2015, as were 18 percent overall. This compares with 17 percent of the UK-born. *Office for National Statistics*, 'Labour Force Survey, 2015, Q1'.

60 See, for instance, David Robinson, 'New Immigrants and Migrants in Social Housing in Britain: Discursive Themes and Lived Realities', *Policy and Politics*, 38:1, January 2010. https://www.researchgate.net/publication/229053845_New_immigrants_and_migrants_in_social_housing_in_Britain_Discursive_themes_and_lived_realities; Jill Rutter and Maria Latorre, 'Social Housing Allocation and Immigrant Communities', *Equality and Human Rights Commission*, 2009. https://www.equalityhumanrights.com/en/publication-download/research-report-4-social-housing-allocation-and-immigrant-communities

61 Diego Battiston, Richard Dickens, Alan Manning and Jonathan Wadsworth, 'Immigration and the Access to Social Housing in the UK', *CEP Discussion Paper 1264*, April 2014. http://cep.lse.ac.uk/pubs/download/dp1264.pdf

62 Robert Guest, 'Why the Arguments Against Immigration are So Popular', *The Economist*, 14 November 2019. https://www.economist.com/special-report/2019/11/14/why-the-arguments-against-immigration-are-so-popular

13 Debt Dividend

1 'US Debt Clock'. Accessed on 3 July 2020 at https://www.usdebtclock.org/#

2 'What is the UK National Debt', *Economics Help*. Accessed on 3 July 2020 at https://www.economicshelp.org/blog/334/uk-economy/uk-national-debt/

3 *HM Revenue & Customs*, 'Table 2.2 Number of income taxpayers by country'. Accessed on 24 January 2020 at https://www.gov.uk/government/statistics/number-of-individual-income-taxpayers-by-marginal-rate-gender-and-age-by-country

4 'US Debt Clock'. Accessed on 24 January 2020 at https://www.usdebtclock.org/#

5 George Borjas, *Heaven's Door: Immigration Policy and the American Economy*, Princeton, 1999, p. 114.

6 Quoted in *Forbes*, 'Milton Friedman at 85', 29 December 1997.

7 Philippe Legrain, '*Is Free Migration Compatible with a European-Style Welfare State?*', Expert report no. 11 to Sweden's Globalisation Council, 2008. https://www.regeringen.se/contentassets/880ac1658a944d31906ec26f9607c080/is-free-migration-compatible-with-a-european-style-welfare-state

8 Kimberley Amadeo, 'US Welfare Programs, the Myths Versus the Facts', *The Balance*, updated 14 January 2020. https://www.thebalance.com/welfare-programs-definition-and-list-3305759

9 Purchasing power parities from https://data.oecd.org/conversion/purchasing-power-parities-ppp.htm

10 *UK Government*, 'Universal Credit. What You'll Get'. Accessed on 24 January 2020 at https://www.gov.uk/universal-credit/what-youll-get

11 'Policy Basics: An Introduction to TANF', *Center on Budget and Policy Priorities*, updated 15 August 2018. https://www.cbpp.org/research/family-income-support/policy-basics-an-introduction-to-tanf

12 *UK Government*, 'Asylum Support. What You'll Get'. Accessed on 24 January 2020 at https://www.gov.uk/asylum-support/what-youll-get

13 *European Commission*, 'Your social security rights in Sweden'. Accessed on 24 January 2020 at https://ec.europa.eu/social/BlobServlet?docId=13776&langId=en

14 Joakim Ruist, 'Free immigration and welfare access: the Swedish experience', April 2012. https://www.gu.se/digitalAssets/1368/1368294_free-immigration-welfare-120419.pdf

15 *OECD*, 'International Migration Outlook 2013, 2013, Chapter 3: The fiscal impact of immigration in OECD countries, Table 3.7. https://www.oecd-ilibrary.org/social-issues-migration-health/international-migration-outlook-2013/the-fiscal-impact-of-immigration-in-oecd-countries_migr_outlook-2013-6-en

16 Ian Goldin et al, 'Migration and the Economy: Economic Realities, Social Impacts and Political Choices', *Citi GPS*, September 2018. https://www.oxfordmartin.ox.ac.uk/downloads/reports/2018_OMS_Citi_Migration_GPS.pdf

17 *Oxford Economics*, 'The Fiscal Impact of Immigration on the UK', June 2018. https://assets.publishing.service.gov.uk/government/uploads/system/uploads/attachment_data/file/759376/The_Fiscal_Impact_of_Immigration_on_the_UK.pdf

18 *MAC*, 'EEA migration in the UK: Final report', September 2018, Para 4.27. https://assets.publishing.service.gov.uk/government/uploads/system/uploads/attachment_data/file/741926/Final_EEA_report.PDF

19 *Office for Budget Responsibility*, '2018 Fiscal Sustainability Report', 2018, Para 3.129. https://cdn.obr.uk/FSR-July-2018-1.pdf

20 Those figures assume that public finances develop in line with the Congressional Budget Office's long-term budget outlook. If, on the other hand, the US government continued to run huge budget deficits, the net contribution would fall to $92,000 (£71,000) if future immigrants resembled recent ones and be slightly negative if they resembled all migrants. Clearly, if Trump-style profligacy persists, with government spending far outpacing tax revenues, most locals as well as most migrants would be net beneficiaries of public largesse if one ignores the ultimate need for higher taxes to restore public finances. *National Academies of Sciences, Engineering and Medicine*, 'The Economic and Fiscal Consequences of Immigration', 2016, Table 8–12. https://d279m997dpfwgl.cloudfront.net/wp/2016/09/0922_immigrant-economics-full-report.pdf

21 Ulrich Kober and Orkan Kösemen, 'Welfare state profits from migration', *Bertelsmann Stiftung*, 2 November 2015. https://www.bertelsmann-stiftung.de/en/topics/latest-news/2014/november/welfare-state-profits-from-migration/

22   Xavier Chojnicki and Lionel Ragot, 'Impacts of Immigration on an Ageing Welfare State: An Applied General Equilibrium Model for France', *Fiscal Studies*, 37:2, 2016, pp. 258–84. https://www.ifs.org.uk/publications/8311

23   Joakim Ruist, 'Free immigration and welfare access: the Swedish experience', April 2012. https://www.gu.se/digitalAssets/1368/1368294_free-immigration-welfare-120419.pdf; Joakim Ruist, 'The fiscal consequences of unrestricted immigration from Romania and Bulgaria', *Vox*, 18 January 2014. https://voxeu.org/article/immigration-romania-and-bulgaria-fiscal-impact

24   *Australian Government*, 'Shaping a Nation: Population growth and immigration over time', 2018. https://cdn.tspace.gov.au/uploads/sites/107/2018/04/Shaping-a-Nation.pdf

25   Stephen Goss et al, 'Effects of unauthorized immigration on the actuarial status of the Social Security Trust Funds', *Social Security Administration Actuarial Note 151*, April 2013. https://www.ssa.gov/oact/NOTES/pdf_notes/note151.pdf

26   ONS, 'Internal migration: by local authority and region, age and sex. Year ending June 2018'. Accessed on 24 January 2020 at https://www.ons.gov.uk/peoplepopulationandcommunity/populationandmigration/migrationwithintheuk/datasets/internalmigrationlaandregionmovesandbysexandsingleyearofagetotals

27   ONS, 'Population estimates for the UK, England and Wales, Scotland and Northern Ireland: mid-2018'. Accessed on 24 January 2020 at https://www.ons.gov.uk/peoplepopulationandcommunity/populationandmigration/populationestimates/bulletins/annualmidyearpopulationestimates/mid2018#local-population-change

28   Jonathan Wadsworth, 'Mustn't Grumble: Immigration, Health and Health Service Use in the UK and Germany', *Fiscal Studies*, 34:1, 2013, pp. 55–82. https://www.ifs.org.uk/publications/6628

29   Carlos Vargas-Silva, Osea Giuntella and Catia Nicodemo, 'The effects of immigration on NHS waiting times', *Journal of Health Economics*, 58, March 2018, pp. 123–43. https://doi.org/10.1016/j.jhealeco.2018.02.001

30   Charlotte Geay, Sandra McNally and Shqiponja Telhaj, 'Non-Native Speakers of English in the Classroom: What are the Effects on Pupil Performance', *Centre for the Economics of Education discussion paper 137*, 2012. http://cee.lse.ac.uk/ceedps/ceedp137.pdf

31   Simon Burgess, 'Understanding the success of London's schools', *CMPO Working Paper 14/333*, October 2014. http://www.bristol.ac.uk/media-library/sites/cmpo/migrated/documents/wp333.pdf

32   Jennifer Hunt, 'The Impact of Immigration on the Educational Attainment of Natives', *Journal of Human Resources*, 52:4, Fall 2017, pp. 1060–118. http://jhr.uwpress.org/content/52/4/1060.short

33   Asako Ohinata and Jan C. van Ours, 'Spillover Effects of Studying with Immigrant Students: A Quantile Regression Approach', *IZA Discussion Paper 7720*, November 2013. http://ftp.iza.org/dp7720.pdf

34   In 2012, 37 percent of pharmacists, 35 percent of medical practitioners, 35 percent of dental practitioners and 22 percent of nurses in the UK were foreign-born, according to ONS data reported in World Health Organisation, 'Migration of Health Workers', 2014. http://www.who.int/hrh/migration/14075_MigrationofHealth_Workers.pdf#page=173

35   Marie Mccullough, 'Nearly 1 in 3 US physicians were born abroad', *Medical Xpress*, 5 December 2018. https://medicalxpress.com/news/2018-12-physicians-born.html

36   *World Health Organisation*, 'Migration of Health Workers', 2014. https://www.who.int/hrh/migration/14075_MigrationofHealth_Workers.pdf?ua=1

37   Joel Negin, Aneuryn Rozea, Ben Cloyd and Alexandra LC Martiniuk, 'Foreign-born health workers in Australia: an analysis of census data', *Human Resources for Health*, 11:69, 2013. https://www.ncbi.nlm.nih.gov/pmc/articles/PMC3882294/

38   Tim Cook, Emira Kursumovic and Simon Lennane, 'Exclusive: deaths of NHS staff from covid-19 analysed', *HSJ*, 22 April 2020. https://www.hsj.co.uk/exclusive-deaths-of-nhs-staff-from-covid-19-analysed/7027471.article

14 Development Dividend

1   'HBO History Makers Series with Mo Ibrahim', *Council on Foreign Relations*, 9 October 2013. https://www.cfr.org/event/hbo-history-makers-series-mo-ibrahim

2   *London Business School*, 'Profile: Mo Ibrahim, Chairman and Founder, Mo Ibrahim Foundation & Celtel International', YouTube, 24 June 2011. https://www.youtube.com/watch?v=HFcX0oWivLE

3   'HBO History Makers Series with Mo Ibrahim', *Council on Foreign Relations*, 9 October 2013. https://www.cfr.org/event/hbo-history-makers-series-mo-ibrahim

4   *International Telecoms Union*, 'Africa: The Impact of Mobile Phones', Vodafone Paper Series 3, March 2005. https://www.itu.int/osg/spu/dtis/documents/Papers/vodafonepapers.pdf

5   Amartya Sen, *Development as Freedom*, Oxford, 1999.

6   Amy Bracken, 'A family split between the US and Haiti dreads looming loss of legal status', *PRI*, 10 April 2019. https://www.pri.org/stories/2019-04-10/family-split-between-us-and-haiti-dreads-looming-loss-legal-status

7   Dilip Ratha et al, 'Data release: Remittances to low- and middle-income countries on track to reach $551 billion in 2019 and $597 billion by 2021', World Bank Blogs, 16 October 2019. https://blogs.worldbank.org/peoplemove/data-release-remittances-low-and-middle-income-countries-track-reach-551-billion-2019

8   D'Vera Cohn, Jeffrey S. Passel and Kristen Bialik, 'Many immigrants with Temporary Protected Status face uncertain future in US', *Pew Research Center*, 27 November 2019. https://www.pewresearch.org/fact-tank/2019/11/27/immigrants-temporary-protected-status-in-us/

9   'Migration and Remittances Data', *World Bank*. Accessed on 14 May 2020 at https://www.worldbank.org/en/topic/migrationremittancesdiasporaissues/brief/migration-remittances-data

10 'Net official development assistance and official aid received (current US$)', *World Bank*. Accessed on 24 January 2020 at https://data.worldbank.org/indicator/DT.ODA.ALLD.CD

11 Dilip Ratha et al, 'Data release: Remittances to low- and middle-income countries on track to reach $551 billion in 2019 and $597 billion by 2021', World Bank Blogs, 16 October 2019. https://blogs.worldbank.org/peoplemove/data-release-remittances-low-and-middle-income-countries-track-reach-551-billion-2019

12 Federica Cocco, Jonathan Wheatley, Jane Pong, David Blood and Andrew Rininsland, 'Remittances: the hidden engine of globalisation', *Financial Times*, 28 August 2019. https://ig.ft.com/remittances-capital-flow-emerging-markets/

13 'Remittances/demographics: an expensive exodus', *Financial Times*, 9 August 2020. https://www.ft.com/content/13637e53-9a5e-4f18-b62d-5543743cd30e

14 Dilip Ratha et al, 'Data release: Remittances to low- and middle-income countries on track to reach $551 billion in 2019 and $597 billion by 2021', World Bank Blogs, 16 October 2019. https://blogs.worldbank.org/peoplemove/data-release-remittances-low-and-middle-income-countries-track-reach-551-billion-2019

15 Jessica Hagen-Zanker, 'Effects of remittances and migration on migrant sending countries, communities and households', *EPS-Peaks*, January 2015. https://assets.publishing.service.gov.uk/media/57a08999ed915d3cfd000326/Effects_of_remittances_and_migration_56.pdf

16 Dean Yang and Claudia Martinez, 'Remittances and Poverty in Migrants' Home Areas: Evidence from the Philippines', April 2005. https://www.cbd.int/financial/charity/philippines-remittance.pdf

17 Dean Yang, 'International Migration, Remittances and Household Investment: Evidence from Philippine Migrants Exchange Rate Shocks', *Economic Journal*, 118:528, 2008, pp. 591–630. https://papers.ssrn.com/sol3/papers.cfm?abstract_id=1111799

18 *World Bank*, 'Global Economics Prospects: Economic Implications of Remittances and Migration', 2006. http://documents.worldbank.org/curated/en/507301468142196936/Global-economic-prospects-2006-economic-implications-of-remittances-and-migration

19 Sanket Mohapatra and Dilip Ratha, 'Remittance Markets in Africa', *World Bank*, 2011. http://documents.worldbank.org/curated/en/248331468193493657/Remittance-markets-in-Africa

20 Paola Giuliano and Marta Ruiz-Arranz, 'Remittances, Financial Development, and Growth', *IMF Working Paper WP/05/234*, 2005. https://www.imf.org/external/pubs/ft/wp/2005/wp05234.pdf

21 *World Bank*, 'Global Economics Prospects: Economic Implications of Remittances and Migration', 2006. http://documents.worldbank.org/curated/en/507301468142196936/Global-economic-prospects-2006-economic-implications-of-remittances-and-migration.

22 'Prof. Oluyinka Olutoye – The Surgeon With A Difference', *Pharmanews*, 4 April 2017. https://www.pharmanewsonline.com/prof-oluyinka-olutoye-the-surgeon-with-a-difference/

23 Nigeria has one doctor for every 5,000 people. Mercy Abang, 'Nigeria's medical brain drain: Healthcare woes as doctors flee', Al Jazeera, 8 April 2019. https://www.aljazeera.com/indepth/features/nigeria-medical-brain-drain-healthcare-woes-doctors-flee-190407210251424.html

24 Paul Collier, *Exodus: How Migration is Changing Our World*, Oxford, 2013, pp. 218, 257.

25 Mercy Abang, 'Nigeria's medical brain drain: Healthcare woes as doctors flee', Al Jazeera, 8 April 2019. https://www.aljazeera.com/indepth/features/nigeria-medical-brain-drain-health-care-woes-doctors-flee-190407210251424.html

26 Maryam Naghsh Nejad and Andrew Young, 'Female Brain Drains and Women's Rights Gaps: A Gravity Model Analysis of Bilateral Migration Flows', *IZA Discussion Paper 8067*, 2014. https://www.iza.org/publications/dp/8067

27 Michael A. Clemens, 'Losing Our Minds? New Research Directions on Skilled Migration and Development', *Center for Global Development Working Paper 415*, September 2015. https://www.cgdev.org/sites/default/files/clemens-losing-our-minds-CGD-working-paper-415.pdf

28 *Ibid.*

29 *OECD*, 'The new immigrants. Global trends in migration towards OECD countries between 2000/01 and 2015/16', Migration Data Brief 4, June 2019. http://www.oecd.org/els/mig/Migration-data-brief-4-EN.pdf

30 *OECD*, 'G20 International Migration Trends Report 2018', September 2018. http://www.oecd.org/els/mig/G20-international-migration-and-displacement-trends-report-2018.pdf

31 The other countries with a high skilled emigration rate exceeding 30 percent are Liberia, Jamaica, Haiti, Fiji, Albania, Bosnia and Herzegovina, Cuba and Guinea-Bissau.

32 Çaglar Özden and David Phillips, 'What really is Brain Drain? Location of Birth, Education, and Migration Dynamics of African Doctors', *KNOMAD Working Paper 4*, February 2015. https://www.knomad.org/sites/default/files/2017-05/Knomad%20Working%20Paper%204%20Brain%20Drain%20African%20Doctors.pdf

33 Çaglar Özden and David Phillips, 'What really is Brain Drain? Location of Birth, Education, and Migration Dynamics of African Doctors', *KNOMAD Working Paper 4*, February 2015. https://www.knomad.org/sites/default/files/2017-05/Knomad%20Working%20Paper%204%20Brain%20Drain%20African%20Doctors.pdf

34 Ian Goldin, Geoffrey Cameron, and Meera Balarajan, *Exceptional people: How migration shaped our world and will define our future*, Princeton, 2012.

35 Slesh Shrestha, 'No Man Left Behind: Effects of Emigration Prospects on Educational and Labor Outcomes of Non-migrants', *Economic Journal*, 127: 600, March 2017, pp. 495–521. https://doi.org/10.1111/ecoj.12306

36 Michael Clemens, 'Do visas kill? Health effects of African health professional emigration', *Center for Global Development Working Paper 114*, March 2007. https://www.cgdev.org/sites/default/files/13123_file_Clemens_Do_visas_kill_3_.pdf

37 Michael Clemens, Cindy Huang, Jimmy Graham and Kate Gough, 'Migration Is What You Make It: Seven Policy Decisions that Turned Challenges into Opportunities', *Center for Global*

Development, May 2018. https://www.cgdev.org/publication/migration-what-you-make-it-seven-policy-decisions-turned-challenges-opportunities#ftnref8

38　Albert Bollard, David McKenzie, Melanie Morten and Hillel Rapoport, 'Remittances and the brain drain revisited: The microdata show that more educated migrants remit more', *World Bank Economic Review*, 25:1, 2011, pp. 132–56. https://doi.org/10.1093/wber/lhr013

39　Aisha Salaudeen, 'Nigerian neurosurgeon takes pay cut to perform free operations', CNN, 4 October 2019. https://edition.cnn.com/2019/10/03/africa/dr-sulaiman-free-surgeries-intl/index.html

40　For an overview, see Priyanka Debnath, 'Leveraging Return Migration for Development: The Role of Countries of Origin – A Literature Review', *KNOMAD*, November 2016. https://www.knomad.org/publication/leveraging-return-migration-development-role-countries-origin-literature-review

41　F.C. Kohli, *The IT Revolution in India: Selected Speeches and Writings*, Rupa, 2005.

42　*Forbes*, '2019 Malaysia's 50 Richest Net Worth. #38 Anthony Tan'. Accessed on 24 January 2020 at https://www.forbes.com/profile/anthony-tan/#6d35624a485c

43　Anthony Tan, 'Tech groups must address the digital divide in south-east Asia', *Financial Times*, 9 January 2020. https://www.ft.com/content/f5818706-3093-11ea-a329-0bcf87a328f2

44　Mercedes Ruehl and James Kynge, 'Fintech: the rise of the Asian 'super app'', *Financial Times*, 12 December 2019. https://www.ft.com/content/0788d906-1a7b-11ea-97df-cc63de1d73f4

45　Jinyoung Kim and Jungsoo Park, 'Foreign Direct Investment and Country-Specific Human Capital', *Economic Inquiry*, 51:1, 2013, pp. 198–210. https://ideas.repec.org/a/bla/ecinqu/v51y2013i1p198-210.html

46　Huiyao Yang, 'China's Return Migration and its Impact on Home Development', *UN Chronicle*, L:3, September 2013. http://unchronicle.un.org/article/chinas-return-migration-and-its-impact-homedevelopment

47　'What happens when Chinese students abroad return home', *The Economist*, 17 May 2018. https://www.economist.com/special-report/2018/05/17/what-happens-when-chinese-students-abroad-return-home?frsc=dg%7Ce

48　Robert Guest, *Borderless Economics: Chinese Sea Turtles, Indian Fridges and the New Fruits of Global Capitalism*, Palgrave Macmillan, 2011.

49　Christian Dustmann and Oliver Kirchkamp, 'The Optimal Migration Duration and Activity Choice after Re-migration', *Journal of Development Economics*, 67:2, 2002, pp. 351–72. https://www.ucl.ac.uk/~uctpb21/Cpapers/optimalmigrationduration.pdf

50　Alice Mesnard, 'Temporary Migration and Capital Market Imperfections', *Oxford Economic Papers*, 56:2, 2004, pp. 242–62. https://econpapers.repec.org/article/oupoxecpp/v_3a56_3ay_3a2004_3ai_3a2_3ap_3a242-262.htm

51　Harry Goulborne, 'Exodus? Some Social and Policy Implications of Return Migration from the UK to the Commonwealth Caribbean in the 1990s', *Policy Studies*, 20:3, 1999, pp. 157–72. https://www.tandfonline.com/doi/abs/10.1080/01442879908423775

52　Barry Mccormick and Jackline Wahba, 'Return Migration and Entrepreneurship in Egypt', *Middle East Development Journal*, 2011. https://www.researchgate.net/publication/266568390_Return_Migration_and_Entrepreneurship_in_Egypt

53　Dan Wang, 'Activating Cross-border Brokerage: Interorganizational Knowledge Transfer through Skilled Return Migration', *Administrative Science Quarterly*, 60:1, 2015, pp. 133–76. https://doi.org/10.1177%2F0001839214551943

54　John Gibson and David McKenzie, 'Scientific mobility and knowledge networks in high emigration countries: evidence from the Pacific', *Research Policy*, 43:9, November 2014, pp. 1486–95. https://www.sciencedirect.com/science/article/abs/pii/S0048733314000663

55　Robert Guest, 'How Migration Makes the World Brainier', *The Economist*, 14 November 2019. https://www.economist.com/special-report/2019/11/14/how-migration-makes-the-world-brainier

56 Gaëlle Ferrant and Michele Tuccio, 'South–South Migration and Discrimination Against Women in Social Institutions: A Two-way Relationship', *World Development*, 72:C, 2015, pp. 240–54. https://ideas.repec.org/a/eee/wdevel/v72y2015icp240-254.html

57 Alberto Spilimbergo, 'Democracy and Foreign Education', *American Economic Review*, 99:1, 2009, pp. 528–43. https://www.aeaweb.org/articles?id=10.1257/aer.99.1.528

58 Michel Beine and Khalid Sekkat, 'Skilled migration and the transfer of institutional norms', *IZA Journal of Development and Migration*, 2:1, 2013, pp. 1–19. https://izajodm.springeropen.com/articles/10.1186/2193-9039-2-9

59 Marion Mercier, 'The Return of the Prodigy Son: Do Return Migrants Make Better Leaders?', *IZA Discussion Paper 7780*, November 2013. https://www.iza.org/en/publications/dp/7780/the-return-of-the-prodigy-son-do-return-migrants-make-better-leaders

60 'Khosla Labs'. http://khoslalabs.com/

61 'Veri5 Digital'. https://www.veri5digital.com/

62 'PM Narendra Modi Asks Diaspora To First Develop India', NDTV, 8 January 2017. https://www.ndtv.com/india-news/pm-modi-asks-diaspora-to-first-develop-india-1646376

63 Leigh Cuen, 'Refugee-Turned-Fintech Entrepreneur Is Shaking Up The Remittance Market', *International Business Times*, 5 September 2017. https://www.ibtimes.com/refugee-turned-fintech-entrepreneur-shaking-remittance-market-2536644

64 Dany Bahar and Hillel Rapoport, 'Migration, knowledge diffusion and the comparative advantage of nations', *Economic Journal*, 128:612, July 2018, pp. F273–305. https://onlinelibrary.wiley.com/doi/abs/10.1111/ecoj.12450

65 William R Kerr, 'Ethnic scientific communities and international technology diffusion', *Review of Economics and Statistics*, 90 (3), 2008, pp. 518–37. https://www.mitpressjournals.org/doi/abs/10.1162/rest.90.3.518?mobileUi=0&

66 Stefano Breschi, Francesco Lissoni and Ernest Miguelez, 'Foreign inventors in the USA: Testing for Diaspora and Brain Gain Effects', *Journal of Economic Geography*, 17:5, September 2017, pp. 1009–38. https://academic.oup.com/joeg/article-abstract/17/5/1009/2888532

67 Ernest Miguelez, 'Inventor Diasporas and the Internationalization of Technology', *World Bank Policy Research Working Paper 7619*, April 2016. http://documents.worldbank.org/curated/en/952541467993510170/pdf/WPS7619.pdf

68 Beata Javorcik, Çaglar Özden, Mariana Spatareanu and Cristina Neagu, 'Migrant networks and foreign direct investment', *Journal of Development Economics*, 2011, 94 (2), pp. 231–41. https://www.sciencedirect.com/science/article/abs/pii/S0304387810000222?via%3Dihub

69 C. Fritz Foley and William Kerr, 'Ethnic Innovation and U.S. Multinational Firm Activity', *Management Science*, 59:7, July 2013, pp. 1529–44. https://pubsonline.informs.org/doi/abs/10.1287/mnsc.1120.1684?journalCode=mnsc

70 William Kerr, 'Ethnic Scientific Communities and International Technology Diffusion', *Review of Economics and Statistics*, 90:3, 2008, pp. 518–37. https://ssrn.com/abstract=983573

71 Gabriel Felbermayr and Farid Toubal, 'Revisiting the trade-migration nexus: Evidence from new OECD data', *World Development*, 40:5, 2012, pp. 928–37. https://ideas.repec.org/a/eee/wdevel/v40y2012i5p928-937.html

72 Mariya Aleksynska and Giovanni Peri, 'Isolating the network effect of immigrants on trade', *The World Economy*, 37:3, 2014, pp. 434–55. https://onlinelibrary.wiley.com/doi/abs/10.1111/twec.12079

73 Paul Collier, *Exodus*, 2013, p. 200.

15 Cultural Cornucopia

1 Alison Caporimo, '15 Iconic American Things That Wouldn't Exist Without Immigrants', BuzzFeed, 2 February 2017. https://www.buzzfeed.com/alisoncaporimo/inventions-made-by-famous-immigrants-america

2   Michael Oliver, '"You're not welcome": rap's racial divide in France', *Guardian*, 22 April 2020. https://www.theguardian.com/music/2020/apr/22/rap-music-racial-divide-france

3   Philip Kasinitz and Marco Martiniello, 'Music, migration and the city', *Ethnic and Racial Studies*, 42:6, 2019, pp. 857–64. https://www.tandfonline.com/doi/full/10.1080/01419870.2019.1567930

4   Emma Bleznak, 'Inside Melania and Donald Trump's Extravagant Wedding (Plus, the Real Reason Melania Had 2 Wedding Dresses)', *Showbiz Cheatsheet*, 27 April 2018. https://www.cheatsheet.com/health-fitness/inside-melania-and-donald-trumps-extravagant-wedding-plus-the-real-reason-melania-had-2-wedding-dresses.html/

5   'The Afrobeats nightclub uniting Naples – Ternanga', *Guardian*, 7 February 2020. https://www.theguardian.com/news/ng-interactive/2020/feb/07/teranga-the-migrant-run-afrobeat-nightclub-uniting-naples-video

6   'Attitudes towards Immigration and their Antecedents: Topline Results from Round 7 of the European Social Survey', *ESS Topline Results Series 7*, November 2016. http://www.european-socialsurvey.org/docs/findings/ESS7_toplines_issue_7_immigration.pdf

16 Irregularity

1   *IOM*, 'Flow Monitoring Europe'. Accessed on 24 January 2020 at https://migration.iom.int/europe?type=arrivals

2   Caravan, 'Children of Moria (Said Reza Adib & Mohammad Javad Mousavi)', YouTube, 20 September 2019. https://www.youtube.com/watch?v=1M5u__o0waQ

3   Convention and Protocol relating to the Status of Refugees, 1967, Article 31. http://www.unhcr.org/3b66c2aa10.html

4   Universal Declaration of Human Rights https://www.un.org/en/universal-declaration-human-rights/

5   David Scott FitzGerald, *Refuge Beyond Reach: How Rich Democracies Repel Asylum Seekers*, Oxford, 2019

6   *Government of Canada*, 'Canada welcomes more privately sponsored refugees in 2019'. Accessed on 24 January 2020 at https://www.canada.ca/en/immigration-refugees-citizenship/corporate/mandate/policies-operational-instructions-agreements/timely-protection-privately-sponsored-refugees.html

7   *Australian Government Department of Home Affairs*, 'Refugee and humanitarian program. About the program'. Accessed on 24 January 2020 at https://immi.homeaffairs.gov.au/what-we-do/refugee-and-humanitarian-program/about-the-program/about-the-program

8   'Essex lorry deaths: Police name 39 Vietnamese victims,' BBC, 8 November 2019. You can see their pictures here: https://www.bbc.co.uk/news/uk-england-essex-50350481

9   Her name has been changed to protect her identity.

10   José Antonio Vargas, *Dear America: Notes of an Undocumented Citizen*, Dey Street Books, 2018. https://www.harpercollins.com/9780062851345/dear-america/

11   Define American https://defineamerican.com/about/

12   'DREAM Act', Wikipedia. Accessed on 24 January 2020 at https://en.wikipedia.org/wiki/DREAM_Act

13   Anonymous, *A Warning*, Twelve, 2019.

14   Miriam Jordan, 'Making President Trump's Bed: A Housekeeper Without Papers', *New York Times*, 6 December 2018. https://www.nytimes.com/2018/12/06/us/trump-bedminster-golf-undocumented-workers.html

15   Alexia Fernández Campbell, "I found my voice': undocumented worker from Trump golf club will attend the State of the Union', *Vox*, 5 February 2019. https://www.vox.com/2019/2/4/18207096/victorina-morales-undocumented-immigrant-trump

16   For an explanation of how undocumented-migrant numbers are estimated, see Janes Manuel Krogstad, 'Q&A: How Pew Research Center estimated the number of

unauthorized immigrants in Europe', *Pew Research Center*, 15 November 2019. https://www.pewresearch.org/fact-tank/2019/11/15/qa-how-pew-research-center-estimated-the-number-of-unauthorized-immigrants-in-europe/

17   Phillip Connor, Jeffrey S. Passell and Jens Manuel Krogstad, 'How European and U.S. unauthorized immigrant populations compare', *Pew Research Center*, 13 November 2019. https://www.pewresearch.org/fact-tank/2019/11/13/how-european-and-u-s-unauthorized-immigrant-populations-compare/

18   Unauthorised immigrants accounted for less than 1 percent of the 525 million population of the EU, Switzerland, Norway, Iceland and Liechtenstein. Phillip Connor and Jeffrey S. Passell, '5 facts about unauthorized immigration in Europe', *Pew Research Center*, 14 November 2019. https://www.pewresearch.org/fact-tank/2019/11/14/5-facts-about-unauthorized-immigration-in-europe/

19   Germany had 1 million to 1.2 million, the UK between 800,000 and 1.2 million, Italy 500,000 to 700,000 and France 300,000 to 400,000.

20   Julie Hirschfeld Davies and Michael Shear, *Border Wars: Inside Trump's Assault on Immigration*, Simon & Schuster, 2019.

21   Michael Shear and Julie Hirschfeld Davies, 'Shoot Migrants' Legs, Build Alligator Moat: Behind Trump's Ideas for Border', *New York Times*, 1 October 2019. https://www.nytimes.com/2019/10/01/us/politics/trump-border-wars.html

22   'Berlin Wall guards had 'shoot to kill' orders', *Mail Online*, 12 August 2007. https://www.dailymail.co.uk/news/article-474885/Berlin-Wall-guards-shoot-kill-orders.html

23   Victoria Vernon and Klaus F. Zimmermann, 'Walls and Fences: A Journey Through History and Economics', *GLO Discussion Paper 330*, 2019. https://www.econstor.eu/bitstream/10419/193640/1/GLO-DP-0330.pdf

24   'The Cost of Immigration Enforcement and Border Security', *American Immigration Council*, 14 October 2019. https://www.americanimmigrationcouncil.org/research/the-cost-of-immigration-enforcement-and-border-security

25   'Main Estimates Memorandum (2019/20) for the Home Office'. https://www.parliament.uk/documents/commons-committees/home-affairs/Estimates-Memoranda-17-19/Home-Office-2019-20-Main-Estimate-Memorandum.pdf

26   Jorge Valero, 'EU will spend more on border and migration control than on Africa', *EURACTIV*, 6 August 2018. https://www.euractiv.com/section/africa/news/for-tomorrow-eu-will-spend-more-on-border-and-migration-control-than-on-africa/

27   Nicolaj Nielsen, 'EU and Italy put aside €285m to boost Libyan coast guard', *EUobserver*, 29 November 2017. https://euobserver.com/migration/140067

28   Jorge Valero, 'EU will spend more on border and migration control than on Africa', *EURACTIV*, 6 August 2018, Table 2.1.1. https://www.euractiv.com/section/africa/news/for-tomorrow-eu-will-spend-more-on-border-and-migration-control-than-on-africa/

29   'Smuggling of migrants', *Migration Data Portal*. Accessed on 24 January 2020 at https://migrationdataportal.org/themen/menschenschmuggel

30   'Migrant Smuggling in the World: A Global Story'. https://res.cloudinary.com/cognitives/image/upload/v1496814536/oetzd46s0s2ogfgephtz.png

31   *IOM*, '30,000 Irregular Migration Deaths, Disappearances Between 2014-2018: IOM Report', 1 November 2019. https://www.iom.int/news/30000-irregular-migration-deaths-disappearances-between-2014-2018-iom-report

32   Australian Border Deaths Database, 'Annual report on border-related deaths, 2018', *Border Crossing Research Brief 14*, March 2019. https://www.monash.edu/__data/assets/pdf_file/0008/1703636/BOb-Annual-Report-2018.pdf

33   *UNHCR*, 'Operational Portal. Mediterranean Situation'. Accessed on 24 January 2020 at https://data2.unhcr.org/en/situations/mediterranean

34 Patrick Wintour, 'Migrants from Libya not driven by hope of being rescued at sea – study', *Guardian*, 18 November 2019. https://www.theguardian.com/world/2019/nov/18/migrants-from-libya-not-driven-by-hope-of-being-rescued-at-sea-study

35 *US Customs and Border Protection*, 'CBP Enforcement Statistics Fiscal Year 2020'. Accessed on 24 January 2020 at https://www.cbp.gov/newsroom/stats/cbp-enforcement-statistics

36 Ian Kullgren, 'CBP: Border arrests doubled in 2019', *Politico*, 19 October 2019. https://www.politico.com/news/2019/10/29/us-mexico-border-2019-arrests-061168

37 Alex Nowrasteh, 'Crime Along the Border Is Historically Low', *Cato Institute*, 20 June 2019. https://www.cato.org/blog/crime-along-border-historically-low

38 Emily Kassie, 'Detained: How the US built the world's largest immigrant detention system', *Guardian*, 24 September 2019. https://www.theguardian.com/us-news/2019/sep/24/detained-us-largest-immigrant-detention-trump

39 Randy Capps, Doris Meissner, Ariel G. Ruiz Soto, Jessica Bolter and Sarah Pierce, 'From Control to Crisis: Changing Trends and Policies Reshaping US-Mexico Border', *Migration Policy Institute*, August 2019. https://www.migrationpolicy.org/research/changing-trends-policies-reshaping-us-mexico-border-enforcement

40 Jamiles Lartey, 'No more psychotropic drugs to migrant children without consent, US judge rules', *Guardian*, 1 August 2018. https://www.theguardian.com/us-news/2018/aug/01/judge-california-psychotropic-medication-border

41 Matthew Haag, 'Thousands of Immigrant Children Said They Were Sexually Abused in US Detention Centers, Report Says', *New York Times*, 27 February 2019. https://www.nytimes.com/2019/02/27/us/immigrant-children-sexual-abuse.html

42 Associated Press, 'Video shows final hours of sick teen who died in US border patrol custody', *Guardian*, 5 December 2019. https://www.theguardian.com/us-news/2019/dec/05/video-border-patrol-teen-death-us-immigration

43 *American Immigration Lawyers Association*, 'Deaths at Adult Detention Centers', AILA Doc. 16050900', 1 January 2020. https://www.aila.org/infonet/deaths-at-adult-detention-centers

44 *Global Detention Project*, 'Europe'. Accessed on 24 January 2020 at https://www.global detentionproject.org/regions-subregions/europe

45 Shamaan Freeman-Powell, 'Home Office 'utterly failing' over immigration detention centres', BBC, 21 March 2019. https://www.bbc.co.uk/news/uk-47645883

46 *UK Government*, 'Detention data tables – Immigration Statistics, year ending June 2019'. https://www.gov.uk/government/statistical-data-sets/immigration-statistics-data-tables-year-ending-june-2019#detention

47 *Ibid.*

48 Diane Taylor and Niamh McIntyre, 'Revealed: sick, tortured immigrants locked up for months in Britain', *Guardian*, 10 October 2018. https://www.theguardian.com/uk-news/2018/oct/10/revealed-sick-tortured-immigrants-locked-up-for-months-in-britain

49 *National Commission of Audit*, 'Towards Responsible Government', February 2014, Appendix to Volume 2, Section 10.14 Illegal Maritime Arrival costs. https://www.ncoa.gov.au/sites/default/files/appendix_volume_2.pdf

50 Helen Davidson, 'Secret recordings allege excessive force by guards in Australia's detention centres', *Guardian*, 24 March 2019. https://www.theguardian.com/australia-news/2019/mar/25/secret-recordings-allege-excessive-force-by-guards-in-australias-detention-centres

51 *Australian Government Department of Home Affairs*, 'Immigration Detention and Community Statistics Summary', 30 June 2019. https://www.homeaffairs.gov.au/research-and-stats/files/immigration-detention-statistics-30-june-2019.pdf

52 *US Immigration and Customs Enforcement*, 'Fiscal Year 2018 ICE Enforcement and Removal Operations Report'. https://www.ice.gov/doclib/about/offices/ero/pdf/eroFY2018Report.pdf

53 Stef W. Kight and Alayna Treene, 'Trump isn't matching Obama deportation numbers',

Axios, 21 June 2019. https://www.axios.com/immigration-ice-deportation-trump-obama-a72a0a44-540d-46bc-a671-cd65cf72f4b1.html

54   *US Department of Homeland Security*, 'Annual Flow Report. Refugees and Asylees: 2018', October 2019. https://www.dhs.gov/sites/default/files/images/OIS/2018/refugees_asylees_2018.pdf

55   *Eurostat*, 'Third-country nationals returned following an order to leave – annual data (rounded)'. Code: migr_eirtn

56   Peter William Walsh, 'Deportation and Voluntary Departure from the UK', *Migration Observatory*, 11 July 2019. https://migrationobservatory.ox.ac.uk/resources/briefings/deportation-and-voluntary-departure-from-the-uk/

57   *OECD*, 'International Migration Outlook 2008', 2008, Part III, Return Migration: A New Perspective. http://www.oecd.org/migration/mig/43999382.pdf

58   Hein de Haas, Stephen Castles, Mark J Miller, *The Age of Migration: International Population Movements in the Modern World*, 6th edition, Red Globe, 2019.

59   Michael Clemens, Cindy Huang, Jimmy Graham and Kate Gough, 'Migration Is What You Make It: Seven Policy Decisions that Turned Challenges into Opportunities', *Center for Global Development*, May 2018. https://www.cgdev.org/publication/migration-what-you-make-it-seven-policy-decisions-turned-challenges-opportunities#ftn2

60   The UK scheme was the Seasonal Agricultural Workers Scheme.

61   Between 1942 and 1964, Mexicans were allowed to work in the US for up to six months under the Bracero programme. Most returned home at the end of their seasonal jobs. Philip Martin, Manolo Abella and Christiane Kuptsch, *Managing Labor Migration in the Twenty-first Century*, Yale, 2006.

62   Jessica Elgot, 'May was not opposed to 'go home' vans, official accounts suggest', *Guardian*, 19 April 2018. https://www.theguardian.com/uk-news/2018/apr/19/theresa-may-was-not-opposed-to-go-home-vans-official-accounts-suggest

63   National Audit Office, 'Returning failed asylum applicants', 2005. https://www.nao.org.uk/wp-content/uploads/2005/07/050676.pdf

64   ICMPD, 'REGINE Regularisations in Europe. A study on practices in the area of regularisation of illegally staying third-country nationals in the Member States of the European Union', *ICMPD Policy Brief*, 2009. http://research.icmpd.org/projects/migration-governance/regine/

65   Tom K. Wong and Hillary Kosnac, 'Does The Legalization of Undocumented Immigrants in the US Encourage Unauthorized Immigration from Mexico? An Empirical Analysis of the Moral Hazard of Legalization', *International Migration*, 55:2, April 2017, pp. 159–73. https://onlinelibrary.wiley.com/doi/abs/10.1111/imig.12319

66   *GLA Economics*, 'Economic impact on the London and UK economy of an earned regularisation of irregular migrants to the UK', May 2009. https://www.london.gov.uk/sites/default/files/gla_migrate_files_destination/irregular-migrants-report.pdf

67   'What are the 10 and 20 year rules on long residence?', Freemovement. Accessed on 24 January 2020 at https://www.freemovement.org.uk/what-are-10-20-year-rules-on-long-residence-immigration-rules-paragraph-276-continuous-lawful-residence/

17   Identity

1   Christopher Wilson, 'Revealed: Penniless German immigrant was great-great-grandfather of Nigel Farage! He has a famously no-nonsense stance in migrants – but Ukip chief had no idea about ancestor', *Mail on Sunday*, updated 29 August 2014. https://www.dailymail.co.uk/news/article-2726735/REVEALED-Penniless-German-immigrant-great-great-grandfather-Nigel-Farage-He-famously-no-nonsense-stance-migrants-Ukip-chief-no-idea-ancestor.html

2   Rowena Mason, 'Nigel Farage backs 'basic principle' of Enoch Powell's immigration warning',

Guardian, 5 January 2014. https://www.theguardian.com/politics/2014/jan/05/nigel-farage-enoch-powell-immigration

3   Nigel Copsey, *Contemporary British Fascism: The British National Party and the Quest for Legitimacy* (second ed.), Routledge, 2008.

4   John E. Richardson, 'Race and Racial Difference: The Surface and Depth of BNP Ideology', in Nigel Copsey and Graham Macklin (eds.), *British National Party: Contemporary Perspectives*, Routledge, 2011, pp. 38–61.

5   Erica Treijs, 'Nazist arbetade för SS – var med och grundade SD', *Svenska Dagbladet*, 30 April 2017. https://www.svd.se/nazist-arbetade-for-ss--var-med-och-grundade-sd

6   'Great Replacement', Wikipedia. Accessed on 25 January 2020 at https://en.wikipedia.org/wiki/Great_Replacement

7   Paul Collier, *Exodus*, 2013.

8   Douglas Murray, *The Strange Death of Europe: Immigration, Identity, Islam*, Bloomsbury, 2017.

9   Jonathan Portes, *What Do We Know and What Should We Do About Immigration?*, SAGE Publications, 2019.

10   NatCen, ''Britishness' and diversity', *Understanding Society*, September 2013. https://www.understandingsociety.ac.uk/sites/default/files/downloads/legacy/Britishness_and_diversity_briefing.pdf?1380013386

11   *OECD*, 'Settling In: Indicators of Immigrant Integration 2018', 2018. http://dx.doi.org/10.1787/888933843496

12   Jack Citrin, Richard Johnston and Matthew Wright, 'Do Patriotism and Multiculturalism Collide? Competing Perspectives from Canada and the United States', *Canadian Journal of Political Science*, 45:3, September 2012, pp. 531–52. https://www.cambridge.org/core/journals/canadian-journal-of-political-science-revue-canadienne-de-science-politique/article/do-patriotism-and-multiculturalism-collide-competing-perspectives-from-canada-and-the-united-states/729B1F99D80B1B344CAC0550A7CE4963

13   Eric Kaufmann, *Whiteshift*, 2018.

14   David Goodhart, *The Road to Somewhere: The New Tribes Shaping British Politics*, Penguin, 2017.

15   Just over 10 percent of people in England in 2019 believe that ethnicity is an important determining factor in being English, down from 20 percent in a 2012 study. Inigo Alexander, 'Now 90% of England agrees: being English is not about colour', *Guardian*, 30 June 2019. https://www.theguardian.com/society/2019/jun/30/being-english-not-about-colour-say-majority

16   Simon Fanshawe and Dhananjayan Sriskandarajah, 'You Can't Put Me In A Box', *IPPR*, January 2010. https://www.ippr.org/files/images/media/files/publication/2011/05/you_cant_put_me_in_a_box_1749.pdf

17   David Goodhart, *The Road to Somewhere*, 2017.

18   Simon Fanshawe and Dhananjayan Sriskandarajah, 'You Can't Put Me In A Box', 2010. https://www.ippr.org/files/images/media/files/publication/2011/05/you_cant_put_me_in_a_box_1749.pdf

19   'Percentage of Europeans Who Are Willing To Fight A War For Their Country', *Brilliant Maps*, 27 January 2017. https://brilliantmaps.com/europe-fight-war/

20   Yuval Noah Hariri, *Sapiens: A Brief History of Humankind*, Harvill Secker, 2014.

18 Illiberalism

1   'Terrorism in Canada', Wikipedia. Accessed on 14 May 2020 at https://en.wikipedia.org/wiki/Terrorism_in_Canada

2   Besheer Mohamed and Jeff Diamant, 'Black Muslims account for a fifth of all US Muslims, and about half are converts to Islam', *Pew Research Center*, 17 January 2019. https://www.pewresearch.org/fact-tank/2019/01/17/black-muslims-account-for-a-fifth-of-all-u-s-muslims-and-about-half-are-converts-to-islam/

3   *New America*, 'Terrorism in America After 9/11. Part IV. What is the Threat to the United States Today?'. Accessed on 22 January 2020 at https://www.newamerica.org/in-depth/terrorism-in-america/what-threat-united-states-today/

4   *Europol*, 'Terrorism Situation and Trend Report 2019', 27 June 2019. https://www.europol.europa.eu/activities-services/main-reports/terrorism-situation-and-trend-report-2019-te-sat

5   'List of terrorist incidents in Australia', Wikipedia. Accessed on 25 January 2020 at https://en.wikipedia.org/wiki/List_of_terrorist_incidents_in_Australia

6   https://www.europol.europa.eu/activities-services/main-reports/terrorism-situation-and-trend-report-2019-te-sat

7   *Ipsos*, 'Perils of Perception 2018', 2018. https://perils.ipsos.com/slides/index.html

8   Bertelsmann Stiftung, 'Muslims in Europe: Integrated not Accepted?', *Religion Monitor*, August 2017. https://www.bertelsmann-stiftung.de/fileadmin/files/BSt/Publikationen/GrauePublikationen/Study_LW_Religion-Monitor-2017_Muslims-in-Europe_Results-and-Country-Profiles.pdf

9   *Ipsos Mori*, 'A review of survey research on Muslims in Britain', February 2018. https://www.ipsos.com/sites/default/files/ct/publication/documents/2018-03/a-review-of-survey-research-on-muslims-in-great-britain-ipsos-mori_0.pdf

10 *Ibid.*

11 'US Muslims Concerned About Their Place in Society, but Continue to Believe in the American Dream', *Pew Research Center*, 26 July 2017. https://www.pewforum.org/2017/07/26/findings-from-pew-research-centers-2017-survey-of-us-muslims/

12 Walter Ewing, Daniel E Martínez and Rubén G. Rumbaut, 'The Criminalization of Immigration in the United States', *American Immigration Council*, 13 July 2015. https://www.americanimmigrationcouncil.org/research/criminalization-immigration-united-states

13 Young men are those aged eighteen to thirty-nine.

14 Michelangelo Landgrave and Alex Nowrasteh, 'Criminal Immigrants: Their Numbers, Demographics, and Countries of Origin', *Cato Institute Immigration Research and Policy Brief 1*, 15 March 2017. https://www.cato.org/publications/immigration-reform-bulletin/criminal-immigrants-their-numbers-demographics-countries

15 Michael T. Light and Ty Miller, 'Does Undocumented Immigration Increase Violent Crime?', *Criminology*, 56:2, May 2018, pp. 370–401. https://onlinelibrary.wiley.com/doi/abs/10.1111/1745-9125.12175

16 Michael T. Light, Ty Miller and BC Kelly, 'Undocumented Immigration, Drug Problems, and Driving Under the Influence in the United States, 1990–2014', *American Journal of Public Health*, 107:9, September 2017, pp. 1448–54. https://www.ncbi.nlm.nih.gov/pubmed/28727520

17 Christian Gunadi, 'On the association between undocumented immigration and crime in the United States', *Oxford Economic Papers*, 2019. https://academic.oup.com/oep/advance-article-abstract/doi/10.1093/oep/gpz057/5572162

18 Jonathan Portes, *What Do We Know and What Should We Do About Immigration?*, 2019.

19 In Australia, where 27.7 percent of the population is foreign-born versus just 19.7 percent of prisoners. 'World Prison Brief'. https://www.prisonstudies.org/

20 Friedrich Heinemann, 'Do Immigrants Affect Crime? Evidence from Panel Data for Germany', 26 September 2019. https://www.zew.de/en/veranstaltungen-und-weiterbildung/detail/do-immigrants-affect-crime-evidence-from-panel-data-for-germany/2904/?cHash=595b99992fd9d0ab30d9a6b9ad99ef30

21 Ludovica Gazzè, Francesco Fasani, Paolo Pinotti and Marco Tonello, 'Immigration Policy and Crime', *Report for the XV European Conference*, Fondazione Rodolfo DeBenedetti, June 2013. http://www.frdb.org/page/publications/categoria/reports/topic/immigration/scheda/immigration-policy-and-crime/doc_pk/11176

22 Robert Guest, 'Why the Arguments against Immigration are so Popular', *The Economist*,

14 November 2019. https://www.economist.com/special-report/2019/11/14/why-the-arguments-against-immigration-are-so-popular

19 Integration

1   Brittny Mejia, 'How Houston has become the most diverse place in America', *Los Angeles Times*, 9 May 2017. https://www.latimes.com/nation/la-na-houston-diversity-2017-htmlstory.html

2   Stephen L. Klineberg, 'The 2019 Kinder Houston Area Survey', *Kinder Institute for Urban Research*, 2019. https://kinder.rice.edu/sites/g/files/bxs1676/f/documents/KI%202019%20Houston%20Area%20Survey%20Report.pdf

3   Brittny Mejia, 'How Houston has become the most diverse place in America', *Los Angeles Times*, 9 May 2017. https://www.latimes.com/nation/la-na-houston-diversity-2017-htmlstory.html

4   *Ibid.*

5   *Ibid.*

6   Stephen L. Klineberg, 'The 2019 Kinder Houston Area Survey', *Kinder Institute for Urban Research*, 2019. https://kinder.rice.edu/sites/g/files/bxs1676/f/documents/KI%202019%20Houston%20Area%20Survey%20Report.pdf

7   *Ibid.* The proportion of Anglos who said they had a close friend who was African-American rose from 69 percent in 2002 to 80 percent in 2019. The share of blacks who had a close friend who was Asian leapt from 32 to 54 percent. The numbers of Asians with a close friend who was Hispanic increased from 53 to 83 percent.

8   Jennifer Van Hook and Barrett Lee, 'Diversity is on the Rise in Urban and Rural Communities, and It's Here to Stay', *Kinder Institute for Urban Research*, 23 February 2017. https://kinder.rice.edu/2017/02/23/diversity-is-on-the-rise-in-urban-and-rural-communities-and-its-here-to-stay

9   Hein de Haas, Stephen Castles, Mark J Miller, *The Age of Migration*, 6th edition, 2019.

10 Eric Kaufmann, *Whiteshift*, 2018.

11 Philippe Legrain, *Refugees Work: A humanitarian investment that yields economic dividends*, Tent Foundation and Open Political Economy Network, May 2016. http://www.opennetwork.net/refugeeswork/

12 Environics Institute for Survey Research, 'Focus Canada – Winter 2018', 22 March 2018. https://www.environicsinstitute.org/docs/default-source/project-documents/focus-canada-winter-2018---immigration-and-minority-groups/focus-canada-winter-2018-survey-on-immigration-and-minority-groups---final-report.pdf?sfvrsn=ede94c5f_2

13 Susanne Wessendorf, 'Commonplace Diversity: Social Interactions in a Super-diverse Context', *MMG Working Paper 10–11*, 2010. https://www.mmg.mpg.de/59151/WP_10-11_Wessendorf_Commonplace-Diversity.pdf

14 *OECD*, 'Settling in 2018: Main Indicators of Immigrant Integration', 2018. https://www.oecd.org/els/mig/Main-Indicators-of-Immigrant-Integration.pdf

15 Ian Goldin et al, 'Migration and the Economy: Economic Realities, Social Impacts and Political Choices', *Citi GPS*, September 2018, Figures 89 and 90. https://www.oxfordmartin.ox.ac.uk/downloads/reports/2018_OMS_Citi_Migration_GPS.pdf

16 *The National Academies of Sciences, Engineering and Medicine*, 'The Integration of Immigrants into American Society', 2015. https://www.nap.edu/read/21746/chapter/2#3

17 *Eurostat*, 'Skills in host country language by migration status and citizenship', 2014. Code: lfso_14blang

18 *Eurostat*, 'Migrant integration. 2017 edition', 2017, Figure 2.30. https://ec.europa.eu/eurostat/documents/3217494/8787947/KS-05-17-100-EN-N.pdf/f6c45af2-6c4f-4ca0-b547-d25e6ef9c359

19 *Pew Research Center*, 'English proficiency among US immigrants, 1980–2017', 3 June 2019. https://www.pewresearch.org/hispanic/chart/immigrant-statistical-portrait-english-proficiency-among-u-s-immigrants/

20 *Pew Research Center*, 'English proficiency of Hispanic population in the US, 2017', 16 September 2019. https://www.pewresearch.org/hispanic/chart/u-s-hispanics-english-proficiency/

21 *The National Academies of Sciences, Engineering and Medicine*, 'The Integration of Immigrants into American Society. Issue Brief: Language Integration', 2015. https://www.nap.edu/resource/21746/issue_brief_language_integration.pdf

22 Aaron Williams and Armand Emamdjomeh, 'America is more diverse than ever — but still segregated', *Washington Post*, 10 May 2018. https://www.washingtonpost.com/graphics/2018/national/segregation-us-cities/

23 *The National Academies of Sciences, Engineering and Medicine*, 'The Integration of Immigrants into American Society', 2015. https://www.nap.edu/read/21746/chapter/2#5

24 Sako Musterd and Ronald van Kempen, 'Segregation and Housing of Minority Ethnic Groups in Western European Cities, *Journal of Economic and Social Geography*, 100:4, September 2009, pp. 559–66. https://onlinelibrary.wiley.com/doi/abs/10.1111/j.1467-9663.2009.00558.x

25 'Sleepwalking to segregation', *The Times*, 23 September 2005. https://www.thetimes.co.uk/article/sleepwalking-to-segregation-jhz9ktlwlzg

26 Louise Casey, 'The Casey Review', December 2016. https://assets.publishing.service.gov.uk/government/uploads/system/uploads/attachment_data/file/575973/The_Casey_Review_Report.pdf

27 Jonathan Portes, *What Do We Know and What Should We Do About Immigration*, 2019.

28 *Policy Exchange*, 'Integration Hub. Index of Integration'. Accessed on 25 January 2020 at http://www.integrationhub.net/module/index-of-integration/

29 Gemma Catney, 'Has neighbourhood ethnic segregation decreased?', *ESRC Centre on Dynamics of Ethnicity (CoDE)*, February 2013. http://hummedia.manchester.ac.uk/institutes/code/briefingsupdated/has-neighbourhood-ethnic-segregation-decreased.pdf

30 Doug Saunders, *Arrival City: How the Largest Migration in History is Reshaping Our World*, Pantheon, 2011.

31 *OECD*, 'Settling in 2018: Main Indicators of Immigrant Integration', 2018. https://www.oecd-ilibrary.org/docserver/9789264307216-en.pdf

32 *Social Integration Commission*, 'How integrated is modern Britain?', 2015. https://the-challenge.org/impact/reports/social-integration-commission/

33 Peter Kellner, 'Why we like migrants but not immigration', YouGov, 2 March 2015. https://yougov.co.uk/topics/politics/articles-reports/2015/03/02/why-we-like-migrants-not-immigration

34 'YouGov/*The Times* survey results', fieldwork 24–25 February 2015. http://cdn.yougov.com/cumulus_uploads/document/f4rr9eo24l/YG-Archive-Pol-Times-results-2502015-W.pdf

35 Corrado Giulietti and Zizhong Yan, 'The Impact of Immigration on the Well-being of UK Natives', *Report prepared for the Migration Advisory Committee*, May 2018. https://assets.publishing.service.gov.uk/government/uploads/system/uploads/attachment_data/file/740985/Giulietti_2018.pdf

36 William Betz and Nicole B Simpson, 'The effects of international migration on the well-being of native populations in Europe', *IZA Journal of Migration*, 2:12, 2013. https://izajodm.springeropen.com/articles/10.1186/2193-9039-2-12

37 Gretchen Livingston and Anna Brown, 'Intermarriage in the US 50 Years After Loving v. Virginia', *Pew Research Center*, 18 May 2017. https://www.pewsocialtrends.org/2017/05/18/intermarriage-in-the-u-s-50-years-after-loving-v-virginia/

38 Robert Ford, 'A close inspection of the British Social Attitudes Survey shows that racial prejudice is in long-term decline', *Democratic Audit*, 27 August 2014. http://www.democraticaudit.com/2014/08/27/a-close-inspection-of-the-british-social-attitudes-survey-shows-that-racial-prejudice-is-in-long-term-decline/

39 David Goodhart and Richard Norrie, 'Accentuating the negative on race', *Policy Exchange*, 2 October 2017. https://policyexchange.org.uk/accentuating-the-negative-on-race/

40 John Curtice, Elizabeth Clery, Jane Perry, Miranda Phillips and Nilufer Rahim (eds.), 'British Social Attitudes: The 36th Report', *National Centre for Social Research*, 2019, Table 11. https://www.bsa.natcen.ac.uk/media/39363/bsa_36.pdf

41 Young people are those aged seventeen to thirty-four. David Goodhart and Richard Norrie, 'Accentuating the negative on race', *Policy Exchange*, 2 October 2017. https://policyexchange.org.uk/accentuating-the-negative-on-race/

42 Richard Alba and Nancy Foner, 'How successful is immigrant group integration in the United States and Western Europe? A comparative review and analysis', *Geografie*, 122:4, 2017, pp. 409–28. https://www.researchgate.net/publication/326834184_How_successful_is_immigrant_group_integration_in_the_United_States_and_Western_Europe_A_comparative_review_and_analysis

43 Zosia Bielski, 'Where is the love: How tolerant is Canada of its interracial couples?', *Globe and Mail*, updated 17 May 2018. https://www.theglobeandmail.com/life/relationships/where-is-the-love-how-tolerant-is-canada-of-its-interracial-couples/article32206930/

44 Richard Alba and Nancy Foner, 'Mixed unions reveal progress in integration but also enduring societal social cleavages, which revolve around race in the US and religion in Europe', LSE blogs, 15 December 2015. https://blogs.lse.ac.uk/usappblog/2015/12/15/mixed-unions-reveal-progress-in-integration-but-also-enduring-societal-social-cleavages-which-revolve-around-race-in-the-us-and-religion-in-europe/

45 Leo Lucassen and Charlotte Laarman, 'Immigration, intermarriage and the changing face of Europe in the post war period', *History of the Family*, 14:1, 2009, pp. 52–68. https://openaccess.leidenuniv.nl/bitstream/handle/1887/15000/HISFAM307.pdf

46 ONS, '2011 Census analysis: What does the 2011 Census tell us about Inter-ethnic Relationships?', 3 July 2014. https://www.ons.gov.uk/peoplepopulationandcommunity/birthsdeathsandmarriages/marriagecohabitationandcivilpartnerships/articles/whatdoesthe2011censustellusaboutinterethnicrelationships/2014-07-03

47 Hill Kulu and Tina Hannemann, 'Mixed marriage among immigrants and their descendants in the United Kingdom: Analysis of longitudinal data with missing information', *Population Studies*, 73:2, 2019, pp. 179–96. https://www.tandfonline.com/doi/full/10.1080/00324728.2018.1493136

48 Young people are those aged fifteen to thirty-four. OECD, 'Settling in 2018: Main Indicators of Immigrant Integration', 2018. https://www.oecd.org/els/mig/Main-Indicators-of-Immigrant-Integration.pdf

49 Robert Putnam, *Bowling Alone: The Collapse and Revival of American Community*, Simon & Schuster, 2000.

50 Jong-sung You, 'Social Trust: Fairness Matters More than Homogeneity', *Political Psychology*, 33;5, 2012, pp. 701–21. https://www.jstor.org/stable/23324182?seq=1

51 Dietlind Stolle and Allison Harell, 'Social Capital and Ethno-racial Diversity: Learning to Trust in an Immigrant Society', *Political Studies*, 61: 1, 2013. https://journals.sagepub.com/doi/10.1111/j.1467-9248.2012.00969.x

52 Marc Hooge, Tim Reeskens, Dietlind Stolle and Ann Trappers, 'Ethnic Diversity, Trust and Ethnocentrism and Europe: A Multilevel Analysis of 21 European Countries', paper presented at the 102nd Annual Meeting of the American Political Science Association, Philadelphia, 31 August–3 September 2006.

53 James Dobson, 'The Ties that Bind: An analysis of the relationship between social cohesion, diversity, and immigration', *Adam Smith Institute*, 2015. http://static1.squarespace.com/static/56eddde762cd9413e151ac92/56fa8e425bd3306c4a738644/56fa8fa45bd3306c4a73c9be/1459261348843/The-Ties-that-Bind.pdf

54 David Brady and Ryan Finnigan, 'Does Immigration Undermine Public Support for Social Policy?', *American Sociological Review*, 79:1, 2014. https://journals.sagepub.com/doi/full/10.1177/0003122413513022

20 Persuading Sceptics

1 RISE. https://risenetwork.eu/

2 Some believe economics matters more. Luigi Guiso, Helios Herrera, Massimo Morelli and Tommaso Sonno, 'Populism: Demand and Supply', *CEPR Discussion Papers 11871*, 2017. https://ideas.repec.org/p/cpr/ceprdp/11871.html Others think cultural issues do. David Card, Christian Dustmann and Ian Preston, 'Immigration, Wages, and Compositional Amenities', *Norface Migration Discussion Paper 2012–13*, February 2012. http://davidcard.berkeley.edu/papers/immigration-wages-compositional-amenities.pdf

3 *Ipsos*, 'Attitudes towards immigration. Survey conducted on behalf of IMiX,' 2019. https://www.ipsos.com/sites/default/files/ct/news/documents/2019-03/public-attitudes-towards-immigration-survey-for-imix.pdf

4 Marco Van Setten, Peer Scheepers & Marcel Lubbers, 'Support For Restrictive Immigration Policies In The European Union 2002–2013: The Impact Of Economic Strain And Ethnic Threat For Vulnerable Economic Groups', *European Societies*, 19:4, 2017, pp. 440–65. https://www.tandfonline.com/doi/full/10.1080/14616696.2016.1268705

5 Joakim Ruist, 'How The Macroeconomic Context Impacts On Attitudes To Immigration: Evidence From Within-Country Variation', *Social Science Research*, 60, 2016, pp. 125–34. https://www.sciencedirect.com/science/article/abs/pii/S0049089X15301800

6 In 2019, 45 percent of Britons thought immigration had a positive impact, 31 percent negative and 17 percent are indecisive, a positive shift that began before the EU referendum in 2016. *Ipsos*, 'Attitudes towards immigration. Survey conducted on behalf of IMiX,' 2019. https://www.ipsos.com/sites/default/files/ct/news/documents/2019-03/public-attitudes-towards-immigration-survey-for-imix.pdf

7 *Ibid.*

8 *Ibid.*

9 Philippe Legrain, 'Refugees Work: A humanitarian investment that yields economic dividends', *Tent Foundation* and *Open Political Economy Network*, May 2016. http://www.opennetwork.net/refugeeswork/

10 Jessica Carpani, 'Nurses who saved Boris Johnson's life speak out for the first time', *Telegraph*, 23 April 2020. https://www.telegraph.co.uk/news/2020/04/23/boris-johnson-absolutely-needed-intensive-care-says-nurse-looked/

11 Ala' Alrababa'h, William Marble, Salma Mousa and Alexandra Siegel, 'Can Exposure to Celebrities Reduce Prejudice? The Effect of Mohamed Salah on Islamophobic Behaviors and Attitudes', *Immigration Policy Lab*, 2019. https://immigrationlab.org/working-paper-series/can-exposure-celebrities-reduce-prejudice-effect-mohamed-salah-islamophobic-behaviors-attitudes-2/

12 Kate Whiting, 'How Mo Salah may have reduced Islamophobia in Liverpool', *World Economic Forum*, June 2019. https://www.weforum.org/agenda/2019/06/how-mo-salah-might-have-reduced-islamophobia-in-liverpool/

13 The six countries are France, Germany, Italy, Sweden, the UK and the US. Alberto Alesina, Armando Miano, Stefanie Stantcheva, 'Immigration and Redistribution', *NBER Working Paper 24733*, revised September 2019. https://www.nber.org/papers/w24733

14 Jonathan Haidt, *The Righteous Mind: Why Good People are Divided by Politics and Religion*, Penguin, 2012.

15 Jack Graham, 'There's nothing more patriotic than wanting your country to be better', *OPEN*, 13 October 2017. http://www.opennetwork.net/theres-nothing-patriotic-wanting-country-better/

16 Jonathan Haidt, *The Righteous Mind*, 2012.

17 Thomas Fraser Pettigrew and Linda Tropp, 'Does Intergroup Contact Reduce Prejudice? Recent Meta-Analytic Findings', January 2000. https://www.researchgate.net/publication/281453353_Does_Intergroup_Contact_Reduce_Prejudice_Recent_Meta-Analytic_Findings

18 Oliver Christ, Katharina Schmid, Simon Lolliot, Hermann Swart, Dietlind Stolle, Nicole Tausch, Ananthi Al Ramiah, Ulrich Wagner, Steven Vertovec, and Miles Hewstone, 'Contextual effect of positive intergroup contact on outgroup prejudice', *Proceedings of the National Academies of Science of the United States of America (PNAS)*, 111:11, March 2014, pp. 3996–4000. https://www.pnas.org/content/111/11/3996.short

19 Neli Esipova, Anita Pugliese and Julie Ray, 'Acceptance of Migrants Increases With Social Interaction', *Gallup*, 29 August 2017. https://news.gallup.com/poll/217250/acceptance-migrants-increases-social-interaction.aspx

20 Elizabeth Koproski, 'What I learned about the world from my neighbors', *Dayton Daily News*, 7 June 2017. https://www.daytondailynews.com/news/opinion/perspective-what-learned-about-the-world-from-neighbors/idTsAD3n2tLJcxavnEayDK/

21 Esther Duflo and Abhijit Banerjee, *Good Economics for Hard Times: Better Answers to Our Biggest Problems*, Public Affairs, 2019.

22 Cas Mudde, 'Why copying the populist right isn't going to save the left', *Guardian*, 14 May 2019. https://www.theguardian.com/news/2019/may/14/why-copying-the-populist-right-isnt-going-to-save-the-left

23 Scott Blinder, Robert Ford and Elisabeth Ivarsflaten, 'The Better Angels of Our Nature: How the Antiprejudice Norm Affects Policy and Party Preferences in Great Britain and Germany', *American Journal of Political Science*, 57:4, 2013, pp. 841–57. https://www.compas.ox.ac.uk/2013/blinder-ford-ivarsflaten_ajps_2015/

21 Conclusion

1 Jacob Poushter and Janell Fetterolf, 'A Changing World: Global Views on Diversity, Gender Equality, Family Life and the Importance of Religion', *Pew Research Center*, 22 April 2019. https://www.pewresearch.org/global/2019/04/22/a-changing-world-global-views-on-diversity-gender-equality-family-life-and-the-importance-of-religion/

2 See for instance, Jeremy Cliffe, 'Britain's cosmopolitan future', *Policy Network*, 2015. https://policynetwork.org/publications/papers/britains-cosmopolitan-future/

3 Young people are those aged eighteen to twenty-nine; older people are those aged fifty and older. Jacob Poushter and Janell Fetterolf, 'A Changing World: Global Views on Diversity, Gender Equality, Family Life and the Importance of Religion', *Pew Research Center*, 22 April 2019. https://www.pewresearch.org/global/2019/04/22/a-changing-world-global-views-on-diversity-gender-equality-family-life-and-the-importance-of-religion/

4 Attitudes towards Immigration and their Antecedents: Topline Results from Round 7 of the European Social Survey', *ESS Topline Results Series 7*, November 2016. http://www.europeansocialsurvey.org/docs/findings/ESS7_toplines_issue_7_immigration.pdf

5 Allison Harell, Stuart Soroka & Shanto Iyengar, 'Locus of Control and Anti-Immigrant Sentiment in Canada, the United States, and the United Kingdom', *Political Psychology*, 38:2, April 2017, pp. 245–60. https://onlinelibrary.wiley.com/doi/abs/10.1111/pops.12338

6 Across OECD countries, young people are much more positive about immigration than older ones. *OECD*, 'Settling In 2018: Indicators of Immigrant Integration', Figure 5.6. https://www.oecd-ilibrary.org/docserver/9789264307216-en.pdf

7 Ron Inglehart & Pippa Norris, 'Trump and the Populist Authoritarian Parties: The Silent Revolution in Reverse. Perspectives on Politics', 15(2), 2017, pp. 443–54. https://www.cambridge.org/core/journals/perspectives-on-politics/article/trump-and-the-populist-authoritarian-parties-the-silent-revolution-in-reverse/FE06E514F88A13C8DBFD41984D12D88D

8 Eric Kaufmann, *Whiteshift*, 2018.

9 Lauren McLaren, Anja Neundorf and Ian Paterson, 'Diversity and Perceptions of Immigration: How the Past Influences the Present', *Nottingham Interdisciplinary Centre for Economic and Political Research Working Paper 2019-01*, 2019. https://nicep.nottingham.ac.uk/wp-content/uploads/2019/07/2019-01-Mclaren-Neundorf-Paterson.pdf

10   Michael Lind, 'The future of whiteness', *Salon*, 29 May 2012. https://www.salon.com/2012/05/29/the_future_of_whiteness/

11   Michael Adams, Keith Neuman, 'Canadian exceptionalism in attitudes towards immigration', *Policy Options*, 2 April 2018. https://policyoptions.irpp.org/magazines/april-2018/canadian-exceptionalism-attitudes-toward-immigration/

INDEX